Ludwig Feuerbach is traditionally regarded as a significant but transitional figure in the development of nineteenth-century German thought. Readings of Feuerbach's *The Essence of Christianity* tend to focus on those features which made it seem liberating to the Young Hegelians; namely, its criticism of reification as abstraction, and its interpretation of religion as alienation. In short, Feuerbach is seen primarily as a precursor to the true "masters of suspicion" in religious studies: Nietzsche, Marx, and Freud. In this long-awaited book, the first of an important new series, Van A. Harvey claims that this is a limited and inadequate view of Feuerbach's work, especially of his critique of religion. The author argues that Feuerbach's philosophical development led him to a much more complex and interesting theory of religion, which he expounded in works that have been virtually ignored hitherto. By exploring these works, Harvey gives them a significant contemporary restatement, and brings Feuerbach into conversation with a number of modern theorists of religion.

CAMBRIDGE STUDIES IN RELIGION AND
CRITICAL THOUGHT I

CAMBRIDGE STUDIES IN RELIGION AND
CRITICAL THOUGHT

Edited by Wayne Proudfoot (Columbia University), Jeffrey L. Stout
(Princeton University), and Nicholas Wolterstorff (Yale University)

Since the Enlightenment, there has been debate, at times heated, over the
implications of critical thought for our understanding of religious ideas and
institutions. Disciplinary boundaries have always mattered less to the debate
than certain acknowledged exemplars of critical thinking. Locke, Hume,
Kant, Marx, Feuerbach, Nietzsche, Freud, and Durkheim long ago became
canonical figures, but the list of model critics has never been stable, and
continues to proliferate. Struggles against sexism, racism, and imperialism
have all produced prominent critics of their own. Now, complicating matters
further, the idea of critical thought is itself under attack. At the same time,
many scholars are returning to religious traditions in search of resources for
their critique of contemporary society and culture. Cambridge Studies in
Religion and Critical Thought is a series of books intended to address the
various interactions of critical thinking and religious tradition in this rapidly
changing context. The series will take up the following questions, either by
reflecting on them philosophically or by pursuing their ramifications in
studies of specific figures and movements: Is a coherent critical perspective
on religion desirable or even possible? If so, what would it look like, and how
might it answer charges of reductionism, relativism, and nihilism? Should it
aspire to take the form of a systematic theory? What sort of relationship to
religious tradition ought a critic to have? One of detachment? Of active
opposition? Of empathy? Of identification? What, if anything, is worth
saving from the Enlightenment legacy or from critics of religion like Hume
and Feuerbach? Where else should we look for guidance in critically
appraising religious traditions? To premodern philosophers? To postmodern
texts? To the religious traditions themselves? When we turn to specific
religious traditions, what resources for criticizing modern society and culture
do we find? The answers offered will be varied, but will uniformly constitute
distinguished, philosophically informed, critical analyses of particular
religious topics.

FEUERBACH AND THE INTERPRETATION OF RELIGION

VAN A. HARVEY

George Edwin Burnell Professor of Religious Studies, Stanford University

CAMBRIDGE
UNIVERSITY PRESS

Published by the Press Syndicate of the University of Cambridge
The Pitt Building, Trumpington Street, Cambridge CB2 1RP
40 West 20th Street, New York, NY 10011–4211, USA
10 Stamford Road, Oakleigh, Melbourne 3166, Australia

First published 1995

Printed in Great Britain at the University Press, Cambridge

A catalogue record for this book is available from the British Library

Library of Congress cataloguing in publication data

Harvey, Van Austin.
Feuerbach and the interpretation of religion / by Van A. Harvey.
p.   cm. – (Cambridge studies in religion and critical thought: 1)
ISBN 0 521 47049 8 (hardback)
1. Feuerbach, Ludwig, 1804–1872.   2. Atheism – History – 19th century.
I. Title.   II. Series.
B2973.R4H37   1995
200′.92 – dc20   94–42936   CIP

ISBN 0 521 47049 8 hardback

Contents

Acknowledgments

I first encountered Feuerbach in a graduate seminar led by H. Richard Niebuhr in Yale Divinity School in the early fifties, when I was preparing to become a Christian theologian. Niebuhr had assigned me to present a report on *The Essence of Christianity*. While writing my report, I cannot claim to have experienced a disturbing premonition about Feuerbach's atheism rather like that which the young Anglican John Henry Newman confessed to having about Roman Catholicism – that it would be proved to be correct after all. Nevertheless, I can remember being strangely disturbed by the nineteenth-century atheist; and in the succeeding years, I have found myself returning to him again and again. So in this sense, my first expression of indebtedness for this book must go to H. Richard Niebuhr and to the members of that remarkably stimulating seminar which included James Gustafson, Gordon Kaufman, Art McGill, and Richard R. Niebuhr.

I also wish to thank the National Endowment for the Humanities as well as Clare Hall, Cambridge, for making possible the idyllic year in which this book was begun. A few years later, the Stanford Humanities Center also provided the support that enabled me to continue the project.

Then there are those selfless colleagues who were kind enough to read and comment on initial drafts of the typescript: Karen Carr, Arnold Eisen, Joseph Frank, P. J. Ivanhoe, Marie-Luise and Ernst Keller, Wayne Proudfoot, Richard Schacht, Jeffrey Stout, Irving Yalom, and Charles A. Wilson. The last named gave me an especially detailed and useful response. I should also include among these colleagues my research assistant, Elizabeth Ewing, who gave indispensable and excellent assistance in the final stages of the preparation of the typescript. And without diminishing the contribution of any of those mentioned, I should like to single out my friend and colleague James J. Sheehan, who not only gave me many helpful suggestions along the way but came to my aid as a friend at one of those black moments many authors have when the project itself seems to founder and sink.

And finally – but not "of course" – I should like to acknowledge my wife Margaret, who has had to live with this project for over fourteen years but has never failed to listen to passages read aloud, to make suggestions, and, above all, to accept gracefully those sacrifices of family life such projects as these sometimes entail.

Note on the text and abbreviations

The reader should consult the Select Bibliography for the full details concerning the works cited. For Feuerbach's works, I have used the critical edition, *Gesammelte Werke* (19 volumes), edited under the supervision of Werner Schuffenhauer and published by Akademie-Verlag in Berlin. In the footnotes, my practice is to list the full bibliographic data at the first mention of a text. Thereafter, all subsequent references to it will be to a shortened title. In the case of the most often used of Feuerbach's works, I have used the abbreviations listed below.

German texts

GW	(plus volume and page number) *Gesammelte Werke*
Christentums	*Das Wesen des Christentums* (*GW* v)
Religion	*Das Wesen der Religion*, in *Kleinere Schriften III (1846–1850)* (*GW* x)
Luther	*Das Wesen des Glaubens im Sinne Luthers*, in *Kleinere Schriften II (1839–1846)* (*GW* ix)
Gedanken	*Gedanken über Tod und Unsterblichkeit*, in *Frühe Schriften, Kritiken und Reflexionen (1828–1834)* (*GW* i)
Gründsätze	*Grundsätze der Philosophie der Zukunft*, in *Kleinere Schriften II (1839–1846)* (*GW* ix)
Vorlesungen	*Vorlesungen über das Wesen der Religion* (*GW* vi)

English translations

Christianity	*The Essence of Christianity*
Luther	*The Essence of Faith According to Luther*
Lectures	*Lectures on the Essence of Religion*
Principles	*Principles of the Philosophy of the Future*
Thoughts	*Thoughts on Death and Immortality*

Introduction

FEUERBACH AND THE SUSPICIOUS INTERPRETATION OF RELIGION

In the initial pages of his book on Freud, Paul Ricoeur made a now familiar distinction between two types of interpretation of religion to which he then attached the formidable labels "the hermeneutics of recollection," on the one hand, and "the hermeneutics of suspicion," on the other.[1] The former type is basically sympathetic to religion because it assumes that the religious consciousness is in touch with something real and contains, therefore, a message that can be retrieved or "recollected." The hermeneutics of suspicion, by contrast, assumes that there is no religious object and that the religious consciousness is bewitched by an illusion. Consequently, the aim of interpretation is not to retrieve but to explain; not to "recollect" but to demystify.

Ricoeur claimed that the charitable mode of interpretation is now most systematically practiced by phenomenologists of religion who argue that it is only possible to understand religion by bracketing one's own assumptions and attempting to "get inside" the religious consciousness and to apprehend what it apprehends albeit "in a neutralized mode."[2] The interpreter of religion must take the religious consciousness and its object, the sacred, with the utmost seriousness; so much so, that he/she must be willing to accept the possibility not only that there is a message imbedded in the symbolic utterances of religion but that this message may even have relevance for the interpreter himself/herself. To use the language of Protestant theology, the religious interpreter must be capable of living in the

[1] Paul Ricoeur, *Freud and Philosophy: An Essay on Interpretation*, trans. Denis Savage (New Haven: Yale University Press, 1970), pp. 28–36.
[2] Ricoeur, *Freud and Philosophy*, p. 29.

"expectancy of a new Word."[3] One might even say that the "hermeneutics of recollection" aims at achieving a type of faith, a "second naïveté" which has passed through the fires of criticism.

The practitioners of suspicion, by contrast, are basically skeptical about religion. They regard the religious consciousness as a false consciousness; therefore, they do not regard the aim of interpretation to be the retrieval of a message but the discovery of a latent and hidden meaning lying behind the conscious expressions. Their aim is to explain and to demystify. And in order to do this, the most influential practitioners of suspicion have developed what Ricoeur has called "a mediate science of meaning," which is to say, they have devised various sorts of psychological and sociological theories that explain the way in which the manifest or expressed meaning is a function of an unconscious, hidden meaning. They have approached religious symbolic systems as if they were codes that require deciphering, and the theories they have devised provide the keys to breaking these codes.

There have been many suspicious interpreters of religion in the history of the West, but Ricoeur elevated three of them to the rank of "masters of suspicion": Marx, Nietzsche, and Freud. Each of them believed that the religious consciousness should not be taken at face value because it has been influenced or determined by powerful forces of which the believers themselves are unaware. And each of them developed a conceptually elaborate "mediate science" or theory that provided the key to deciphering the religious code by systematically connecting the symbols of religion with these powerful, unconscious forces. And although Ricoeur himself did not make much of the fact, at the core of these three suspicious theories of religion is the notion that religion is a "projection," which is to say that the gods are regarded as "objectifications" or "externalizations" or "reifications" – the language varies – of some internal or subjective trait or attribute that has then been (mistakenly) taken to be real. The gods, as it were, are internally generated superhuman "others," and religion is the attempt to cajole, appease, mollify, and worship these "others."

To understand this concept of projection – its meaning and uses – is to understand why the interpreter of religion must practice suspicion. It dictates that religious expressions cannot be taken at face value because they have been generated by unconscious causes of some

---

[3] Ricoeur, *Freud and Philosophy*, p. 31.

kind. To be sure, each of the three masters of suspicion conceived of projection in his own way, but the concept itself was crucial as an explanatory and interpretative tool. As an explanatory tool, projection accounted for the way in which the gods came into existence as both superhuman yet anthropomorphically conceived powers. As an hermeneutical device, projection provided the bridge that could link the consciously entertained symbols with the unconscious psychological or sociological forces determining them. For Marx, the gods were created by the deepest longings of a human being deprived of his/her own authentic powers by a repressive economic order. They were, in his language, expressions of the *"inverted consciousness of the world . . . the fantastic realization* of the human essence."[4] For Nietzsche, the gods were generated by what he called "the psychology of error," the inveterate tendency of the human mind to see conscious agency behind everything in nature and then to reify the results of this tendency.[5] And for Freud, the gods were seen as the objectified unconscious drives and wishes of the human psyche that have been shaped by the turbulent and incestuous drama he called the "family romance."

To anyone familiar with the various suspicious interpretations of religion that have been proposed in Western culture, it seems odd that Ricoeur neglected to include the name of Ludwig Feuerbach among his master practitioners because there has never been a thinker in this culture so preoccupied with and devoted to the critique of religion. Within six years in the 1840s, he wrote four important books on the subject, one of them being the famous and influential *The Essence of Christianity*.[6] These books, in turn, are flanked by two works that stand like book ends to his entire corpus: *Thoughts on Death and Immortality*,[7]

---

[4] Karl Marx, "Critique of Hegel's Philosophy of Right," in Rodney Livingstone and Gregor Benton, trans. with an intro. by Lucio Colletti, *Karl Marx Early Writings* (New York: Random House, 1975), p. 244.

[5] Friedrich Nietzsche, *Twilight of the Idols*, in *The Portable Nietzsche*, trans. with an intro., prefaces, and notes by Walter Kaufmann (New York: Viking Press, 1954).

[6] *The Essence of Christianity*, trans. George Eliot, with an introductory essay by Karl Barth and foreword by H. Richard Niebuhr (New York: Harper & Row, 1957). See also *Das Wesen des Christentums*, ed. Werner Schuffenhauer and Wolfgang Harich, *Gesammelte Werke*, 19 vols., vol. v (Berlin: Akademie-Verlag, 1973).

[7] *Thoughts on Death and Immortality from the Papers of a Thinker, along with an Appendix of Theological-Satirical Epigrams, Edited by One of his Friends*, trans. with intro. and notes by James A. Massey (Berkeley: University of California Press, 1980). *Frühe Schriften, Kritiken und Reflexionen (1828–1834)*, in *Gesammelte Werke*, ed. Werner Schuffenhauer and Wolfgang Harich, with a foreword to the *Gesammelte Werke* by Werner Schuffenhauer, 19 vols. (Berlin: Akademie-Verlag, 1981), I.175–515.

his first major work, published in 1830, and *Theogonie*, his last work, published in 1857.[8] All of them are powerful exercises in the suspicious interpretation of religion.

These various works exhibit the four features that may be said to be characteristic of the hermeneutics of suspicion. There is, first of all, a theory of the origin of the gods. In *The Essence of Christianity*, Feuerbach's best-known work, these origins are explained in terms of a complex and subtle theory of consciousness. In the process of self-differentiation, it is claimed, the subject first projects its essential nature and then misconstrues this as an objective being. Feuerbach, of course, was not the first person to conceive of the idea of projection. As early as the sixth century BC, the Greek Xenophanes had cynically observed that the gods of the Ethiopians were inevitably black with flat noses while those of the Thracians were blond with blue eyes. So, too, many centuries later both Giambattista Vico and David Hume had argued that it was a universal tendency among humans to explain unknown events in terms of other beings like themselves. But Feuerbach was the first to employ the concept as the basis for a systematic critique of religion.

The second characteristic feature of most suspicious theories of religion is that the projection which explains the origin of the gods is part of a larger theoretical structure, something like what Ricoeur has called a "mediate science." In the early Feuerbach's case, the theory of consciousness which explains how projection occurred is heavily indebted to Hegel's philosophy of Spirit. In his later works, as I shall demonstrate in the chapters that follow, his explanations are part of a theory of the embodied self and its relationship to nature. These theories profess to explain not only how religious belief is generated but why it continues to have such a hold on the religious imagination. They also help to explain why religious beliefs take the form that they do.

A third and important structural feature of suspicious interpretations is that the underlying theories cast up a set of guiding interpretative principles that dictate the type of approach the investigator will take to religious symbols as well as providing a key to the relationship between their conscious and their unconscious meanings. And this, in turn, is closely related to the reason why these religious symbols and beliefs are so emotionally powerful.

And finally, Feuerbach's suspicious hermeneutics exemplifies that

---

[8] *Theogonie, nach den Quellen des klassichen, hebräischen und christlichen Altertums*, ed. Wolfgang Harich, *Gesammelte Werke*, 19 vols., vol. VII (Berlin: Akademie-Verlag, 1969).

feature which is at one and the same time so embarrassing to the objective scholar of religion and infuriating to the religious believer: a fervor for atheism that might itself be considered evangelical. The masters of suspicion did not regard their demystifying work primarily as an intellectual exercise; rather, they saw it as therapy. They thought of themselves as liberators of the human spirit, and their zeal was grounded in the assumption that belief in the gods was an illness, that it was stultifying to human beings. For Marx, religion was "false consciousness," an expression of an estranged social existence. For Nietzsche, it was a disorder of the instincts, a reaction to suffering and the longing for another, morally better, world. For Freud, religion was a collective neurosis. For Feuerbach, religion is the "alienation" produced when the self, in the process of differentiation from others, makes its own essential nature another objectified being. For all of these atheists, as Ricoeur has observed, their aim was not solely to destroy religion; rather, they wanted to "clear the horizon for a more authentic word, for a new reign of Truth, not only by means of a 'destructive' critique, but by the invention of an art of *interpreting*."[9] Consequently, they viewed themselves in quasi-religious terms: as prophets and evangels, as denouncers of mystification and heralds of good news.

Feuerbach's critique of religion is even more fervently evangelical than those of the other masters of suspicion, not because he hated religion more passionately but, paradoxically, because he felt that when religion was properly understood it would be seen to contain a liberating truth. In his early work he believed that atheism was the secret of religion. Consequently, his approach was more dialectical than those of the other masters of suspicion. Unlike Nietzsche, who rejected the substance of Christianity even when it was demystified, or Freud, who regarded theism as infantile and neurotic, Feuerbach believed that religion encoded the deepest and most profound insights into human nature and existence. Consequently, he did not think that it should be dismissed simply as false consciousness. For the author of *The Essence of Christianity*, as Karl Löwith has pointed out, religion was the detour (*Umweg*) by means of which humankind comes to self-awareness regarding its true nature.[10] This is why Feuerbach could make the otherwise paradoxical claim that he was

[9] Ricoeur, *Freud and Philosophy*, p. 33.
[10] Ludwig Feuerbach, *Das Wesen des Christentums*, with an afterword by Karl Löwith (Stuttgart: Philipp Reclam Jun., 1969), p. 528.

basically a friend and not an enemy of religion. However mystified
the form of religion, the substance of it, he believed, was profound,
even true; hence, the importance of a mode of interpretation that
would uncover and lay bare this truth. His sole concern, he once
wrote, was not to invent but to unveil existence, to "extricate its true
meaning from the web of contradictions and delusions called
theology."[11] One might say that he believed that religion was too
important a subject to leave to the theologians.

SOME REASONS WHY FEUERBACH IS NOT RANKED AMONG THE MASTERS OF SUSPICION

Despite all of the above, there are intelligible if not always valid
reasons why not only Ricoeur but many other scholars of religion do
not rank Feuerbach among the masters of suspicion; indeed, why
some even regard him as a marginal figure whose philosophy of
religion is not worthy of serious consideration.

In the first place, he simply did not have the massive impact on
modern Western culture that Marx, Nietzsche, and Freud did. It
could not be said of him, as it could be said of them, that our present
culture cannot be made fully intelligible without reference to his
work. If, for example, there were intelligent creatures from Mars who,
landing in our midst, were to ask us to explain the course of history in
the West since 1848 – the rise of Fascism and Communism, the Cold
War, and the emergence of certain institutions such as psychotherapy,
not to mention the ethos of the modern university – we would be
unable to give them an adequate account of this history without
making some reference to Marx and Freud and, to a lesser extent,
perhaps, Nietzsche. But we would not need to mention the name of
Feuerbach. There is no perduring and influential Feuerbachian
school of thought with its own discursive practices as there are
Marxist or Freudian schools. Although Feuerbach, it is true, flashed
like a comet across the cultural horizon of Continental Europe in the
1840s and 1850s, he had virtually disappeared by the 1870s. And
although his book *The Essence of Christianity* was a sensation and
immediately translated into English by no less than the famous
novelist George Eliot, and although it is still considered a nineteenth-
century classic and still read by countless university students, his

---

[11] Feuerbach, *Christianity*, p. xxxvi; *Christentums*, p. 17.

subsequent works have been largely unread and untranslated. When his name is mentioned, it is usually added that his significance lies in having helped to bring about the transition from Hegel to Marx. And if he is said to have had important ideas, it is noted that they have been absorbed into the thoughts of others such as Marx and Freud. To use the language of Ricoeur, Feuerbach is not an author one reads in the expectation of being addressed.

A second reason for not ranking Feuerbach among the masters is closely related to the first. Unlike the religious critiques of Marx or Freud, Feuerbach's was not part of a larger theoretical framework that was widely appropriated by secular intellectuals and integrated into what we now call the behavioral sciences. Marx's theory of religion, for example, was in fact only a minor element in a comprehensive sociological and economic theory, just as Freud's was only a small part of a larger psychological theory. Both of these more comprehensive theories have not only given rise to revolutionary practices but have spawned a number of research programs of a conventional intellectual sort.

Feuerbach, by contrast, was primarily interested in religion and philosophy, to which he turned again and again, and to the extent that his conception of religion was part of a larger intellectual system, it was Hegelianism. But however fruitful this intellectual system has proved to be in social and political theory,[12] the theory of self-consciousness which was at its core and to which Feuerbach's projection theory was linked has seemed to most contemporaries dated and arcane. At any rate, it has not given rise to a research program or therapeutic intervention such as psychoanalysis.

Feuerbach's failure to construct a larger intellectual system of his own has naturally aroused the suspicion that he was incapable of doing so, that unlike Marx and Freud he simply lacked the synthetic intellectual powers of his teacher Hegel. As evidence for this, one might point to his tendency to write short programmatic essays, or his penchant for aphorisms in contrast to sustained argument. How else can one explain his failure to meet the expectations of his own generation which had been stimulated by *The Essence of Christianity*? At the time, it was widely believed to be a work of genius. It was thought that it demonstrated not only his critical capacities but his

---

[12] Charles Taylor argues that Hegel's political philosophy remains interesting and relevant today even though his ontology of *Geist* is "close to incredible." See his *Hegel and Modern Society* (Cambridge: Cambridge University Press, 1979), p. 69.

capacity to lay the foundations for a new philosophical program based on naturalism that would supplant Hegelianism.

There are even indications that Feuerbach also felt that he had been prompted by fate to accomplish this historic task, because he immediately poured his considerable energies into the writing of a small book with the very pretentious title *Principles of the Philosophy of the Future*.[13] This book was clearly intended to be a harbinger of a larger project that would constitute the revolutionary breakthrough to a new philosophical era. But the greater part of it, unfortunately, is merely an analysis of the failure of the old idealism, and when the author finally and adventuresomely turned to enunciating the principles of this new philosophy, he was only able to create some imaginative but vague aphorisms. Even if these aphorisms had proved to be pregnant with meaning, it was vain to hope that they could constitute the basis of an intellectual program of the scope found in the works of the other masters of suspicion.

Some commentators have even argued that Feuerbach was a tragic figure because he did not ascend to the intellectual heights that were expected of him and which he might easily have achieved.[14] They note that just when he was at the height of his powers, he was denied an academic position that might have provided the institutional structure and the incentives he needed in order to develop philosophically. Retreating to the countryside, where he was supported by the profits of a porcelain factory owned by his wife, he turned away from philosophy. Convinced that science was the wave of the future, he dissipated his intellectual energies, delving into geology and mineralogy under the guidance of his close friend Christian Kapp. But as Saul Rawidowicz has pointed out, he could at most have become a gifted amateur in these sciences, and he never achieved the deep knowledge of nature which he so desired.[15]

---

[13] I have used the English translation by Manfred H. Vogel, Library of Liberal Arts (Indianapolis: Bobbs-Merrill, 1966). Because Vogel translated the first and not the second edition, there is a slight discrepancy between the paragraphs in the English translation and those of the critical edition. Consequently, I have cited the page number of the German critical edition. There is also a translation of the *Grundsätze* in *The Fiery Brook: Selected Writings of Ludwig Feuerbach*, trans. with an intro. by Zawar Hanfi (Garden City, N.Y.: Doubleday, 1972), pp. 175–245.

[14] S. Rawidowicz notes that while Windleband thought the tragedy lay in his development toward radicalism, it really lay deeper in his philosophical being itself. A divided mind, he could never push his thoughts to their logical completion. *Ludwig Feuerbachs Philosophie: Ursprung und Schicksal*, 2nd ed. (Berlin: Walter de Gruyter & Co., 1964), p. 307.

[15] Rawidowicz, *Ludwig Feuerbachs Philosophie*, p. 199.

Although Feuerbach himself acknowledged that he lacked the synthetic and constructive philosophical talents of a Hegel, and that he had disappointed the expectations of many of his friends and colleagues, he did not think of himself as a tragic figure. Rather, he believed that his own calling was not to systematize but to clarify. "My own spiritual nature," he once wrote, "does not consist in systematization but in clarification" ("Mein geistiges Wesen ist kein 'System' sondern eine Erklärungsweise").[16] And what he felt compelled to clarify was the phenomenon of religion, to which he returned again and again, modifying and refining what he had just previously written and published. His first major book, *Thoughts on Death and Immortality* (1830), written while he was still deeply influenced by Hegel, was about religion. And after the sensational success of *Christianity*, he turned back to religion again in 1845 with *Das Wesen der Religion.*[17] Then again, in 1848, when invited by the students of the University of Heidelberg to give a series of public lectures, he expanded further on the themes of the little book he had written in 1845. There followed still more essays during the 1850s, culminating in a last major effort in 1857, *Theogonie*, to come to terms with the subject matter. It is not surprising that he once said that despite the classification of his various writings, which included histories of modern philosophy, his one and only theme was "religion or theology and everything connected with it."[18] And it is for this same reason that the Protestant theologian Karl Barth could write that this ferocious atheist, Feuerbach, was in reality an unhappy lover of theology.[19]

But perhaps the greatest obstacle contemporaries have to taking Feuerbach seriously as a master of the suspicious interpretation of religion is an interrelated series of conventional scholarly judgments about him that have gone uncontested for several generations. First of all, his name and work are virtually identified with *The Essence of Christianity* and the concept of projection that is found in it. After 1846, it is sometimes claimed, his work ceases to be interesting.

---

[16] Quoted from the *Nachlass* by Rawidowicz, *Ludwig Feuerbachs Philosophie*, p. 116.
[17] Wolfgang Harich (ed.), *Kleinere Schriften III (1846–1850)*, *Gesammelte Werke*, 19 vols., vol. x (Berlin: Akademie-Verlag, 1971), pp. 3–79.
[18] Ludwig Feuerbach, *Lectures on the Essence of Christianity*, trans. Ralph Manheim (New York: Harper & Row, 1967), p. 5. See also Feuerbach, *Vorlesungen über das Wesen der Religion: Nebst Zusätzen und Anmerkungen*, ed. Wolfgang Harich, *Gesammelte Werke*, 19 vols., vol. vi (Berlin: Akademie-Verlag, 1967), p. 12.
[19] Karl Barth in "An Introductory Essay," in Feuerbach, *Christianity*, p. x.

Consequently, his later books on religion, especially *The Essence of Faith According to Luther*,[20] *Das Wesen der Religion*, and the *Lectures*, have been virtually ignored because it has been assumed that they were merely minor revisions of *Christianity* and have no lasting significance in themselves. Little or no consideration has been given to the possibility that these books not only are not a refinement of the views in *Christianity* but propose a much more interesting and persuasive theory of religion.

Second, even the early Feuerbach is regarded as significant primarily because of his creation of the "transformative method," which had such a profound influence on Karl Marx. This "transformative method" refers to Feuerbach's clever inversion of Hegel's philosophy of Spirit. Hegel, Feuerbach claimed, suffered from the inveterate tendency to treat abstract predicates as entities, especially the predicates of reason. Having construed some attribute as the essence of human existence, Hegel then converted this attribute into an individual being, this idea into a subject. Since this was the clue to understanding Hegel, it follows that whatever is valid in Hegel can be extracted simply by inverting the subject and the predicate and restoring them to their proper relationship. Instead of construing the predicate "thinking" as an entity, one simply transforms the equation and asserts that thinking is the activity of existing individuals. Feuerbach used this transformative method as the basis of his theory of projection, but Marx was impressed by this method because he could appropriate certain features of Hegel's philosophy – that the self objectified itself in its activity – without accepting Hegel's idealism. "Feuerbach," Marx wrote, "is the only person who has a *serious* and a *critical* attitude to the Hegelian dialectic and who has made real discoveries in this field. He is the true conqueror of the old philosophy."[21] And since Marx has proved to be one of the most influential figures in modern history, Feuerbach's significance for most historians lies in his having provided the bridge from Hegel to Marx.

This conventional view is, of course, not without its partial truths. Feuerbach's first book was indeed a masterpiece, a *tour de force*, and much of its impact on his own generation was due to his transformative

[20] Ludwig Feuerbach, *The Essence of Faith According to Luther*, trans. with an intro. by Melvin Cherno (New York: Harper & Row, 1967). The German text is found in Werner Schuffenhauer and Wolfgang Harich (eds.), *Kleinere Schriften II (1839–1846)*, *Gesammelte Werke*, 19 vols., vol. IX (Berlin: Akademie-Verlag, 1970), pp. 353–412.
[21] Livingstone and Benton (trans.), *Karl Marx Early Writings*, p. 381.

method, which enabled it to invert Hegel's philosophy, to "stand him on his head," as it were. If Hegel had argued that the cosmos is the "objectification" of the Absolute Spirit, then Feuerbach and his friends could argue that God could be shown to be the objectification of human spirit. And if Hegel had argued that the Absolute Spirit comes to self-consciousness by taking the objectified and alienated cosmos back into itself, then they could claim that human beings come to full self-consciousness by realizing that God is their own objectified activity. It is also true that Marx thought that Feuerbach's method of transformation was important, as was his view of religion as projection. Further, Feuerbach himself tended to minimize the difference between his later and earlier work on religion. The *Lectures*, for example, were only written, he had said, to fill an important gap in the earlier book.[22]

And finally, and most importantly, it does seem that when Feuerbach is interpreted in this conventional fashion his hermeneutics of suspicion can hardly be taken seriously by any contemporary student of religion because it is so tied to the now arcane Hegelian philosophy of consciousness. And even if one argued that there are profound elements in Hegel's philosophy of Spirit, as I would, this philosophy could not hope to have enjoyed the wide secular appeal of Marx's and Freud's theories. In more charitable terms, whatever was interesting and relevant in Feuerbach has been taken up and appropriated by Marx and Freud.

Nevertheless, I believe that all of these conventional judgments are partial and misleading truths, and the purpose of this book is to challenge and, if possible, to correct them. Consequently I shall argue in the pages that follow that it is a mistake to identify Feuerbach's critique of religion with *The Essence of Christianity*. Further, I shall claim that although the transformation or inversion of the Hegelian model of consciousness plays a crucial role in that work, it by no means plays the only role. There is a subordinate strand of argumentation – I will refer to it as the "existentialist paradigm" – that is also important and bears the weight of many of Feuerbach's most interesting insights. Moreover and more controversially, I believe that these insights do not stand or fall with the validity of the transformed Hegelian argumentation.

I shall argue that it is this existentialist strand of argumentation in

---

[22] Feuerbach, *Lectures*, p. 19; *Vorlesungen*, p. 26.

Christianity, which is subordinate to the Hegelian strand, that emerges as the major and dominant theme in Feuerbach's later work. These works should not be considered merely as extensions of his earlier work but as serious revisions of it. Consequently, contemporary religious studies is the poorer for having neglected them. Not only have we have hitherto lived with a truncated and distorted picture of Feuerbach's work and career, but we have been deprived of an interpretation of religion that is more interesting and suggestive than his earlier one even though it was not as brilliantly articulated. This later theory is less vulnerable to the objections commentators have traditionally made to the early theory and with which they justify their claim that his work is only of historical interest.

To understand the two strands of argument in *Christianity* and the concerns that underlie them is also to understand why it is mistaken to accept the conventional opinion that Feuerbach's best insights were mediated to modernity by Marx and Freud. Although there are obvious points of continuity between these two thinkers and Feuerbach, the discontinuities are even greater and, as I shall argue, more significant as regards the interpretation of religion. This is especially true of the concept of projection. Even though Marx thought he was indebted to Feuerbach for the insight that the gods arise out of a sense of privation and, hence, that religion would wither away when this privation was abolished, both the early and later Feuerbach believed that religion is rooted in something more primal and elemental in consciousness itself.

Although Freud, like Feuerbach, believed that religion arises from the helplessness of the creature confronted with the implacable powers of nature, Feuerbach's interpretation of this situation led to an entirely different conclusion. He believed that the religious projection arises out of the nature of human self-consciousness itself. This, I shall argue, is more like an ontological than a psychological claim and when developed in his later works had surprising consequences even for him. This claim, to be sure, was not entirely original because he was the inheritor of the long German idealistic tradition that has its roots in the philosophies of Kant, Fichte, and Hegel. But what Feuerbach attempted to do was demystify this tradition – one might say, to existentialize it – in the most interesting ways, ways that took him beyond it and that justify our view of him as a truly original mind as regards the interpretation of religion.

Feuerbach's view that religion is a function of the emergence of self-consciousness leads to a far more complex interpretation of religion than that practiced by the other three masters of suspicion, as I shall attempt to show. Indeed, it raises the fundamental question whether it is possible to make a sharp dichotomy between the hermeneutics of suspicion and the hermeneutics of charity. His conviction that religion is rooted in the drive for well-being as well as in the anxiety of the "I" in confrontation with the "not-I" led him to practice a type of interpretation that in many respects resembles the phenomenology of religion that Ricoeur takes to be the prime exemplar of the hermeneutics of recollection. Feuerbach, too, believed that the interpreter of religion should focus on and listen to the immediate utterances of ordinary believers rather than those of theologians, because it is in the expressions of naïve believers that the real desires and wishes of religion come to expression.

The interpreter who listens to the naïve expressions of the religious discovers that what they really desire is delivery from disease, suffering, and death. The ordinary believer wants a deliverer, a superhuman power that can set aside and overcome the inexorability of necessity and fate, that can save and redeem. The ordinary believer is not interested in abstract beliefs and doctrines, except in so far as these articulate the faith that the gods are committed to the well-being of the creatures. Consequently, the interpreter of religion must acknowledge that petitionary prayer and worship, belief in miracles and in deliverance from suffering and death, are the core of religion even if theologians are normally embarrassed by this naïve piety.

Because of his basic conviction that the investigator of religion should listen seriously to what religious believers actually say, Feuerbach, or so I shall argue in Chapter 2, cannot be so easily dismissed as a "reductionist," as has so often been done with other suspicious interpreters. Or more precisely, I shall maintain that the charge of reductionism is much too crude and roughhewn a designation to identify the type of interpretative method he employed. However unlikely it might seem for a master of suspicion, Feuerbach prided himself on taking as his object of analysis and interpretation whatever significance the religious believers themselves attributed to a belief or ritual. This is why he could claim that the first obligation of the interpreter was to let religion speak for itself. "I constitute myself only its listener and interpreter, not its prompter," he wrote.[23] Unlike

---

[23] Feuerbach, *Christianity*, p. xxxvi; *Christentums*, pp. 16f.

Nietzsche, Marx, or Freud, all of whom may be said to have had "tin ears" as regards religion, Feuerbach could legitimately claim that he was able to interpret religion because he had not just studied it in books but had

> become acquainted with it through life, not only through the life of others, who demonstrated to me the causes and effects of religion from its good as well as its bad side, but also through my own life. Religion was already an object of praxis for me before it became an object of theory.[24]

For some of us, finally, not even Feuerbach's lack of those systematic and constructive talents possessed by his teacher, Hegel, is a fatal defect. We have found a new respect for sustained reflection on more delimited phenomena like religion in contrast to the construction of grand intellectual systems, just as in matters of style we have acquired a new appreciation for the unsystematic and probing analyses of thinkers like Wittgenstein. It is just because Feuerbach returned to religion again and again, modifying and revising his previous views, that his work seems so suggestive. He never ceased to explore the meaning of religion for the human consciousness and, consequently, he never found it easy, as Marx and Freud did, to settle his accounts with it once and for all. Just because he was not concerned to construct an intellectual system in which religion had a fragmentary but well-defined place, he was constantly open to revision and correction and the deepening of insight. One cannot help but be impressed with the imaginativeness with which he continued to explore certain themes: the sense of the ego standing over against and yet participating in a boundless reality that seems alien to it yet inspires it with a sense of wonder; the confrontation of the self with others and the desire to be acknowledged by them; the sense of being a consciousness that must relate to the world through the body, through sensuousness; the apparent contradiction between one's Promethean desires and the apparent indifference of nature to those desires. All this is why his books cannot be read without a sense of being enriched and illumined.

THE PROJECT: A RATIONAL RECONSTRUCTION OF FEUERBACH

It is obvious from the above that my reinterpretation of Feuerbach's theory of religion is not only revisionary in intent but driven by the

---

[24] Ludwig Feuerbach, "Fragmente zur Charakteristik meines philosophischen curriculum vita," in *Kleinere Schriften III*, *GW* x.172. See also Hanfi (trans.), *The Fiery Brook*, p. 286.

conviction that his later works have something relevant and interesting to say to those in religious studies. Indeed, I believe that what Basil Willey once wrote about David Friedrich Strauss's *Life of Jesus* is also true of Feuerbach's work. "It is indeed a crucial difficulty in the study of the last century," Willey wrote,

that it continually embarrasses us, as a father often embarrasses a son, by stating with pertinence and superior knowledge positions which we had assumed, without having really examined them, to be obsolete or untenable. Remoter centuries have not this disturbing quality; we are not implicated in their absurdities, and can regard them with complacency. The nineteenth century compels us to define our own position, and as this is difficult and often painful, we have (until recently) avoided its society like prodigal sons, or by-passed it with superficial irony.[25]

Feuerbach's writings on religion also have this disturbing quality in full measure, and what follows in these pages is an attempt to present his later thought so that it cannot be waved aside as obsolete or by-passed with superficial irony.

It soon became clear to me that in order to realize this revisionary intent this book could not take the form of a traditional historical study. It could not take the form of placing Feuerbach's thought in its historical and cultural context or tracing the development of his mind as it was formed in conversations, letters, and arguments with his friends. My aims were more narrowly focused and yet constructive. They are narrowly focused, because I was concerned with his interpretation of religion and, even more narrowly, with the complexities of his argumentation, first in *Christianity* and then in the *Lectures*. I wanted to show how the subordinate and less familiar strands of argumentation in the former gradually came to preeminence in the latter. Moreover, since my interpretation seemed to be at odds with that of most commentators with whom I am familiar, it seemed necessary to analyze four of his works in this period in greater detail than is customarily done in standard intellectual histories. But my aim was also constructive, because I not only wanted to separate out and recover what I think valuable and interesting in his interpretation of religion but also wanted to show why it was so. This seemed to dictate an attempt to bring Feuerbach into a conversation with some contemporary figures in religious studies.

There are, of course, intellectual historians who regard a project

---

[25] Basil Willey, *Nineteenth Century Studies: Coleridge to Matthew Arnold* (London: Chatto & Windus, 1950), p. 220.

such as this one as anachronistic and fruitless. It is, they argue, one thing to attempt to set straight the historical record concerning a past thinker; but it is quite another to let one's constructive interests so shape and determine the inquiry that the resulting picture is not only one-sided but anachronistic. At best such a project can only involve putting questions to past thinkers that contain concepts and involve assumptions that these same thinkers could not have understood and for which their work, therefore, contains no answers. At worst, these types of inquiries lead to a modernization of the past for the purpose of making it acceptable to the present. This, it is claimed, is a mistake. The only legitimate approach to past thinkers is to situate them in their own cultural milieux and to describe faithfully the questions with which they were confronted and how they attempted to answer them.

But surely, it may be replied, it ought to be possible to accept the importance of traditional historiography without rejecting other legitimate ways of relating to past thinkers, as Richard Rorty has conveniently argued in a recent essay. In this essay, he identified and discussed four types of approaches to the past which scholars have taken: historical reconstruction, intellectual history, *Geistesgeschichte* (the attempt to trace important ideas and to fix a canon), and what he labeled "rational reconstruction."[26]

It was Rorty's distinction between historical and rational reconstruction that seemed most relevant for understanding what I was trying to do in this study of Feuerbach. Historical reconstruction refers to the type of history with which we are all familiar. It treats the dead on their own terms, so to speak, by imaginatively and faithfully reconstructing the social and intellectual context in which they lived, the texts that they read, the friends and companions to whom they wrote and with whom they argued and conversed. To use the language of R. G. Collingwood, historical reconstruction attempts to rethink the thoughts of past historical agents, to see the world as they must have seen and interpreted it.[27] Rational reconstruction, on the other hand, requires a different type of approach. Here the aim is not so much to recreate the past in its own terms as it is to conduct a profitable dialogue or conversation with it. There may be many

[26] Richard Rorty, "The Historiography of Philosophy: Four Genres," in Richard Rorty, J. B. Schneewind, and Quentin Skinner (eds.), *Philosophy in History* (Cambridge: Cambridge University Press, 1984), pp. 49–79.
[27] R. G. Collingwood, *The Idea of History* (Oxford: Clarendon Press, 1946), part v.

reasons for desiring such a dialogue: to prove oneself superior to the past, or to know whether some thinker could make certain points without necessarily being committed to others that are problematic. Or it may be that we wish to clarify our own thoughts on some matter important to us and about which some past thinker has had profound thoughts.

Rorty points to Peter Strawson's work on Kant as a splendid example of rational reconstruction.[28] Guided by the conviction that contemporary attempts to replace the common-sense Aristotelian framework of things with "events" and "stimuli" are as misguided as an earlier Humean atomism, Strawson turned to an analysis of Kant in order to demonstrate how he could properly reject this atomism without saying some other less plausible things. "Strawson's conversation with Kant is the sort one has with somebody who is brilliantly and originally right about something dear to one's heart, but who exasperatingly mixes up this topic with a lot of outdated foolishness."[29] Such a conversation may seem anachronistic in certain respects, but it may also prove to be extremely useful if pursued with a high degree of self-awareness.

Traditional historical reconstruction, of course, operates under certain constraints, as Quentin Skinner has pointed out, the most important of which is that "No agent can eventually be said to have meant or done something which he could never be brought to accept as a correct description of what he had meant or done."[30] One cannot, for example, anachronistically attribute categories, norms, criteria, and interests to someone in the past who could not, in the nature of the case, have possessed or employed them. Consequently, if we wish to have an account that observes this constraint, Rorty concludes, then

we shall have to confine ourselves to one which, at its ideal limit, tells us what they might have said in response to all the criticisms or questions which would have been aimed at them by their contemporaries (or, more precisely, by that selection of their contemporaries or near-contemporaries whose criticisms and questions they could have understood right off the bat – all the people who, roughly speaking, "spoke the same language."[31]

Rational reconstructions, like Strawson's, take a different form.

---

[28] P. F. Strawson, *The Bounds of Sense: An Essay on Kant's "Critique of Pure Reason"* (London: Methuen, 1966).

[29] Rorty, "The Historiography of Philosophy," p. 52.

[30] Quoted by Rorty, "The Historiography of Philosophy," p. 50.

[31] Rorty, "The Historiography of Philosophy," p. 50.

They usually contain four elements: the inquiry is most often confined to a relatively small portion of the past philosopher's work; it is dominated by questions that have come to prominence in some more recent philosophical work; it tends to be determined by the argument that the philosopher has some excellent ideas but could not get them straight; and the aim is to show that the answers given by the past thinker, though plausible and exciting, badly need restatement or, perhaps, a more precise refutation than they have hitherto received.

It is tempting for me to claim that what follows is a rational rather than an historical reconstruction of Feuerbach. But, alas, the issue is not so simple, because although my book most exemplifies the characteristics of a rational reconstruction, it is also an attempt to correct and reinterpret a widely accepted version of Feuerbach's thought, and, consequently, much of the book is an analysis of four of his important works and an attempt to show how his thought developed between 1842 and 1848. And to the extent that I have tried to do this, I have felt myself to be under many of the same constraints felt by more traditional historians. One cannot, for example, play fast and loose with the texts one is discussing; ignoring, for example, their location in the chronological development of the thinker and how this, in turn, must be taken into account when one assesses the relative importance of certain ideas and not others. In Chapter 4, for example, I argue that Feuerbach's book on Luther was crucial in enabling him to reformulate his views concerning the function of religion in *The Essence of Christianity* and, hence, allowed him to drop certain Hegelian interpretative principles that he had employed there and to emphasize others. This is basically an historical argument in the sense that it would constitute an anachronistic "howler" to attribute this later understanding of Luther to the author of the first edition of *Christianity*.

Or again, even if one is engaged in rational reconstruction in Rorty's sense, one must be faithful to the dynamics of argumentation in the texts being discussed; that is, which arguments seem to be the most fundamental and which are less so, etc. This, in turn, presupposes an historical knowledge of the intellectual context that determines the meanings of the specialized terms employed in those arguments. Since these meanings are inevitably public, the act of understanding them is inevitably an act of historical reconstruction. For example, Feuerbach's argument in *Christianity* is replete with terms that are intelligible only if one understands something about the debates occurring in Hegelian and neo-Hegelian circles at the time: *Entäusserung*, *Vergegenständlichung*, *Entfremdung*, *Gattung*, *Gattungswesen*, *Unendlichkeit*, and the like. Indeed, Professor Wartofsky has persuasively argued that one cannot really understand *The Essence of Christianity* without a prior knowledge of Hegel's famous *Phenomenology of Spirit*, upon which it is parasitical. In sum, even if one seeks to rationally reconstruct Feuerbach, this presupposes many of the constraints of historical reconstruction.

It could also be argued that even rational reconstruction presupposes the constraints of historical reconstruction even when one engages in that activity most peculiar to it; namely, the attempt to sort out the "outdated foolishness" from what now seems more valid, or the attempt to determine whether a past author could have embraced certain conclusions without embracing others. For how can an inquirer even identify "outdated foolishness" without first historically reconstructing the relationship of this foolishness to some past cultural context which is then said to be "outdated"? If, for example, a rational reconstructionist wishes to argue that Feuerbach's notion of projection in *Christianity* is compounded with the "outdated foolishness" of the notion of the "species concept," this argument requires a great deal of familiarity with the history of that concept, its relationship to Hegelianism, and its uses by the young Hegelians such as Marx. So, too, if the rational reconstructionist is interested in the question whether Feuerbach could have mounted a projection theory without this concept of the species and still retained his claim that religious faith was alienating, this also presupposes and requires a reconstruction of the logical relationships then obtaining between "self-consciousness," the idea of the species, and "alienation" as Feuerbach would have understood them.

Still, my book does have many of those characteristics Rorty attributes to rational rather than historical reconstruction. First of all, it is concerned with only a relatively small portion of Feuerbach's work, with that produced between 1842 and 1848. It does not attempt to deal with the earliest period of his thought, or with the latest. I do not, for example, discuss his very last work, *Theogonie*, which was published 1857, a work that is interesting in its own right. And even though confined to what might be called his "middle years," the book does not attempt to describe the important controversies and conversations that must have influenced his thought in the period under discussion. I am concerned almost solely with the development of his interpretation of religion from *The Essence of Christianity* to the *Lectures on the Essence of Religion*, and primarily the latter.

Why this limitation? This brings us to Rorty's second criterion for rational reconstructions: they are dominated by questions that have come to prominence in some recent work, and they tend to be determined by the argument that although the past philosopher had some excellent ideas, he/she could not get them straight. There is no question that my inquiry is dominated by questions that have only come to prominence in contemporary work; in this case in the field of religious studies in contrast to theology. I put the issue in this way not to depreciate theology but because, strangely enough, Feuerbach's work for the most part has been taken seriously only by Marxist philosophers and Protestant theologians and has been virtually neglected by scholars in religious studies. Some Protestant theologians in the 1960s, for example, saw in Feuerbach's formula "the secret of theology is anthropology" a harbinger of the short-lived "death of God" movement; and Karl Barth took Feuerbach seriously, but as a *reductio ad absurdum* of liberal theology since Schleiermacher.[32]

My concerns, however, are those which surface from time to time in religious studies: What is the nature and function of religion? What does it mean to say that religion is a projection? If religion is regarded as a projection, how does this claim yield principles that enable one to provide a suspicious interpretation? What, in fact, are the hermeneutical principles that guide such interpretations? Are such interpretations reductionistic? What is reductionism? What are the grounds for thinking that religious beliefs are unhealthy and "alienating"? What does it mean to say that a belief is alienating? If religions express the deepest wishes and longings of the human heart and they lighten the burden of existence, why aren't human beings justified in clinging to them even if they are false?

What, then, can be said about my project in the light of Rorty's third criterion – that rational reconstructions are determined by the assumption that although there are some excellent ideas propounded by past philosophers, these ideas for various reasons need restatement?

Here, too, my relation to the genre of rational reconstruction is more complex, as can be seen from the structure of my book. At the risk of oversimplification, it is my argument that in the case of

---

[32] Barth in "An Introductory Essay," in *Christianity*, pp. xixff.

Feuerbach we are not dealing with one but two positions, an earlier and a later. The earlier position in the *Essence of Christianity*, with which Feuerbach's name is usually identified, is basically woven together from two related but (we can now see) distinct argumentative strands: a dominant one, which, for the sake of simplicity, I shall name the Hegelian, and a subordinate strand, which I shall label the naturalist-existentialist. Taken together, these two strands or motifs make possible an imaginative, even brilliant, interpretation of religion, one which Sidney Hook argued "still remains the most comprehensive and persuasive hypothesis available for the study of comparative religion."[33] But despite such praise, Feuerbach's first position was one with which he, for good reasons, was not satisfied, and he reformulated it in two later works, *Das Wesen der Religion* and the *Lectures on the Essence of Religion*. In these later works, I contend, we find that the naturalist-existentialist motif, which was subordinate in *Christianity*, has now become dominant, and the dominant Hegelian theme plays virtually no role at all. It is this later interpretation of religion which has been ignored by most commentators and which needs restatement because, in my opinion, it is not entangled in the arcane and speculative theory of consciousness that mars *The Essence of Christianity*.

Since all of the above are controversial claims, the first three chapters of this book might be called a "critique of a critique," an attempt to sort out the various levels of argument in *Christianity* and to show how they constitute the basis for the interpretative strategy that he followed there. Without this analysis and demonstration it would be quite unconvincing to claim, as I do, that the later conception of religion differs in important respects from the earlier, and, further, that it lacks just those features that mar the earlier view and make it untenable for many of us in the contemporary world.

This "critique of a critique" culminates in Chapter 3 and yields what many Feuerbachian scholars will consider to be a controversial and ironical conclusion. The conclusion is that the idea with which Feuerbach's name is most closely associated – that belief in God is "alienation" – is only tenable if one first accepts the most arcane and problematical aspects of Feuerbach's projection theory; namely, that (Hegelian) thread of argumentation concerning the objectification of the species concept.

---

[33] Sidney Hook, *From Hegel to Marx: Studies in the Intellectual Development of Karl Marx* (New York: The Humanities Press, 1950), p. 221.

In Chapter 4, I argue that Feuerbach's most powerful criticism of religion is not, as is so often claimed, that it is alienating but that it contains inherent intellectual contradictions and, more importantly, produces an "inner disunion" in the believer, a disunion produced by the contradiction between faith and love. Whether this inner disunion might be considered a form of alienation or not is a terminological question; but whatever it is called, Feuerbach believed that there is a "malignant principle" in Christian faith because the self-esteem it confers upon the believer is bought at the price of an incredible narcissism and the exclusion of non-believers. Moreover, he believed that the Christian faith corrupts the respect or "sentiment" for truth, a criticism which has not been sufficiently appreciated in the literature. In short, by making love dependent upon faith, Feuerbach believed Christianity corrupted both.

Both of these arguments are linked not to the Hegelian strand in *The Essence of Christianity* but to the naturalist-existentialist motif. To accept this insight then makes it possible to understand why it is misleading for historians to argue that whatever was suggestive in Feuerbach's critique of religion was appropriated by Marx. This claim could only be made by someone who (a) accepted the legitimacy of the earlier Feuerbach's analysis of religious projection, (b) failed to identify the naturalist-existentialist strand, and (c) did not see that this naturalist-existentialist strand is what dominates the later Feuerbach's critique. My conclusions also make it possible to criticize those who dismiss Feuerbach's critique because it is so obviously compounded with what to them is now "outdated nonsense" about the "species being."

If the first three chapters of this book may be considered to be a "critique of Feuerbach's earliest critique of religion," then Chapters 5 and 6 represent an attempt to restate what I believe to be the more persuasive but ignored position of this later Feuerbach. Here one finds a conception of religion that is immune from the criticisms that I have leveled at *Christianity*. The reasons for the superiority of this later position, as I have suggested above, are, first, that the naturalist-existentialist theme that was subordinate in that earlier work has now become dominant and all that this entails; second, that Feuerbach reformulated his view to make nature the object of religion and so was able to explain in a way that his earlier theory did not why religious believers have such a sense of "otherness" of the divine. In *Christianity*, the religious object was the "species idea" that arises out of the

I–Thou encounter and which is then reified by the imagination. God is the idea of humanity made into an individual being. In *Religion*, by contrast, the real object of religion is all-encompassing nature, the sum of forces from within and without that impinge upon the self and upon which it is absolutely dependent. This reformulation, I argue, led Feuerbach to pursue a different interpretative strategy in his later works than he pursued in *Christianity*, which had been determined by the Hegelian paradigm.

In Chapter 4, which constitutes the transition to this interpretation of the later Feuerbach, I have tried to explain those factors that led Feuerbach to modify his views. The first of these, speaking generally, was Feuerbach's developing anthropological views whereby he came to reject Hegel's emphasis upon humanity as a bearer of reason in favor of a naturalism that begins with the human as an embodied being existing in relationship with other embodied beings. Feuerbach, like Kierkegaard, insisted that it was a mistake to tear the faculty of reason from the totality of the "real human being." But unlike Kierkegaard, he insisted on the importance of "sensuousness" and the social nature of the self. Human beings are related to the world and to other human beings through the body, but the self-consciousness which distinguishes the individual, the I, exists only in relation to Thous.

The second factor that played an important role in altering Feuerbach's interpretation of religion was his discovery and appropriation of the thoughts of the Protestant Reformer Martin Luther. The book *The Essence of Faith According to Luther*, which might initially have been written in response to the criticisms of *Christianity* made by Protestant theologians, was, I argue, an important step in Feuerbach's realization that the most important subjective feature driving religious belief was the rage to live, the *Glückseligkeitstrieb*, and the desire to transcend all of the conditions of human dependence and finitude. The secret of religion, he came to believe, is the Promethean desire to be free from all evils, from the oppression of matter, from death, and from the limitations of nature. It is the desire for blessedness.[34]

In the last two chapters of the book, I have attempted to bring the later Feuerbach's interpretation of religion into what might be called the modern conversation in religious studies concerning such issues as the theory of projection, anthropomorphism in religion, the function of religion, and other related issues. In order to focus the discussion I

---

[34] Feuerbach, *Luther*, p. 103; *Luther*, p. 403.

have turned to some contemporary theorists of religion who have utilized the concept of projection as both an explanatory and an hermeneutical device by means of which to interpret religion. In Chapter 7 I am particularly interested in how Feuerbach's later views may be compared to two contemporary types of projection theories of religion: those theories in which metaphors taken from the technology of the cinema or the magic lantern are dominant, on the one hand, and those theories, on the other, in which projection is conceived of as a type of conceptual or symbolic framework for the organization of all experience. As illustrations of the former, I consider some psychoanalytic theories. As representatives of the latter, I am interested in the views of the Dutch anthropologist Fokke Sierksma, and the American sociologist of religion Peter Berger.

Finally, in Chapter 8, I turn to what is sometimes called the neo-Tylorian theory that religion is basically anthropomorphism and that to acknowledge this does not require a theory of projection, as has recently been argued by the anthropologist Stewart Guthrie. Guthrie argues that anthropomorphism is a natural and inevitable element in all perception and cognition and that religion is simply a special case of this. Although he considers Feuerbach to be one of his predecessors in some sense, I argue that this view is incompatible with that naturalist-existentialist motif which is distinctive of the later Feuerbach. Feuerbach's views, on the contrary, are most like those of Ernest Becker, who, in his *The Denial of Death*, argued that the human being differs from other organisms by virtue of being an embodied consciousness absolutely dedicated to Eros but also able to envisage its own death. As conscious and free, it is continually confronted by possibility. As embodied and finite, it is bound to the earth and death. The roots of religion lie in this ontological structure of the human being: the loneliness and helplessness of the ego that participates in and confronts the forces and beings that impinge upon it; the anxiety of the psyche facing necessity and death; and, above all, the desire for recognition and self-esteem.

As a result of this conversation, I conclude, as I hope the reader will also, that even though Feuerbach lived before the age of the social-scientific study of religion and is considered by many to be an outdated nineteenth-century "armchair" theorist, he still has the power to compel us to define our own positions. If we think seriously about religion, then, to use of words of Basil Willey, we cannot avoid his society or by-pass him with superficial irony.

CHAPTER I

"Projection" in "The Essence of Christianity"

SELF-DIFFERENTIATION AND PROJECTION

If any text qualifies as an example of the suspicious interpretation of religion, surely it is *The Essence of Christianity*. Its basic premise is that the superhuman deities of religion are, in fact, involuntary projections of the essential attributes of human nature, and this projection, in turn, is explained by a theory of human consciousness heavily indebted to Hegel. Moreover, unlike most suspicious interpreters of religion who, like Marx, Freud, and Nietzsche, simply claim that religion is projection, Feuerbach sought to demonstrate the truth of his theory by systematically decoding the major doctrines and symbols of Christianity: the idea of a personal God, the doctrine of the Incarnation, the mystery of the Trinity, the idea of the Logos, the beliefs in providence, in miracles, in prayer, and, above all, in immortality.

When the conclusions of the book are baldly stated, it seems outrageous: the idea of God is really a composite of human predicates. What is worshiped as divine is really a synthesis of the human perfections. Theology is anthropology and, therefore, the hidden meaning of Christianity is atheism. And if all this were not outrageous enough, Feuerbach claimed that he had not imposed his own meaning on Christian symbols but had discovered this by letting religion speak for itself. "I constitute myself only its listener and interpreter, not its prompter," he wrote.[1]

The book was a *tour de force*, and it burst like a bombshell on the German intellectual scene in the early 1840s. Immediately translated into English by one of England's best-known authors, George Eliot, it became like a Bible to a group of revolutionary thinkers, including Arnold Ruge, the Bauers, Karl Marx, Richard Wagner, and

---

[1] Feuerbach, *Christianity*, p. xxxvi; *Christentums*, pp. 16f.

Friedrich Engels. David Friedrich Strauss, whose *Life of Jesus* had created a similar furor earlier, wrote that Feuerbach's book "was the truth of our time"; and Friedrich Engels, reminiscing many years later, reported that "at once we all became Feuerbachians."[2]

Strauss's comment contains the clue to understanding the enthusiasm which the book then generated in Germany, because the "truth of our time," so far as an entire generation of young German intellectuals was concerned, was to be able to appropriate the most important elements of Hegel's monumental philosophy of Spirit without accepting his metaphysics or the conservative political ideology with which his political philosophy had become identified. Feuerbach had accomplished this, as I have indicated in the Introduction, by applying his "transformative method" to Hegel's thought, a method that Karl Marx had hailed as Feuerbach's great contribution to philosophy.[3] This method was based on Feuerbach's conviction that Hegel's thought was the culmination of Western philosophy's preoccupation with the objective reality of essences or universals, a preoccupation initiated by Plato. Hegel's philosophy, Feuerbach argued, was based on the reification of abstract predicates like "thought" which were then treated as agencies. Since Feuerbach believed that this was the clue to understanding Hegel, it followed that if one wished to appropriate Hegel's insights, it was only necessary to invert the relationship between the subject and the predicate and restore them to their proper relationship. If, for example, Hegel had argued that the world is the objectification and unfolding of the divine mind, then this should be transformed to mean that the divine is the abstraction and reification of human thought.

Hegel's philosophy of Spirit had enormous implications for the philosophy of religion and for the understanding of Christianity. Since he regarded all of the various stages of human culture as "moments" in the unfolding of the Absolute Spirit, it followed that the various stages of religion, from animism to the ethical monotheism of Judaism and Christianity, could be seen as stages in the self-manifestations of this Spirit. In other words, the history of religion culminating in Christianity was a progressive revelation of the truth that the Absolute is not merely an impersonal substance but a Subject. Philosophy establishes that Christianity is the consummate

[2] Frederick Engels, *Ludwig Feuerbach and the End of Classical German Philosophy* (Peking: Foreign Languages Press, 1976), p. 14.
[3] Livingstone and Benton (trans.), *Karl Marx Early Writings*, p. 281.

or absolute religion. Through its cultic life and doctrines the ultimate truth about reality has come to its highest symbolic expression. In the Christian myth of creation, fall, and redemption, the religious mind has intuited in symbolic form the truths which the Hegelian philosopher has better grasped in precise concepts. They have both seen that the Infinite is perpetually pouring out its life in the finite world and then reconciling itself to this objectified world by taking it back into its own life again. In short, the Infinite comes to its own self-realization in and through the life of nature and creation.

By inverting Hegel's scheme, Feuerbach cast up an even more radical philosophy of religion. Instead of saying that the Absolute Spirit (God) achieves self-knowledge by objectifying itself in the finite world, he argued that the finite spirit comes to self-knowledge by externalizing or objectivizing itself in the idea of God. Religion is not, as Hegel thought, the revelation of the Infinite in the finite; rather, it is the self-discovery by the finite of its own infinite nature. God is the form in which the human spirit first discovers its own essential nature.

Man – this is the mystery of religion – projects (*vergegenständlicht sich*) his being into objectivity, and then again makes himself an *object* to this projected image of himself thus converted into a subject; he thinks of himself as an object to himself, but as *the object of an object*, of *another* being than himself.[4]

Hegel believed that Christianity was the absolute religion because the doctrine of the Incarnation symbolizes the metaphysical truth that the Absolute, after objectifying itself in the external world, reconciles itself to Its alienated creation. Feuerbach also claimed that Christianity was the absolute religion; but not for Hegel's reason. Rather, he argued that Christianity was the absolute religion because in the doctrine of the Incarnation is articulated the atheistic insight that humanity's well-being is more important than God's. It contains the insight that just as "God has renounced himself out of love, so we, out of love, should renounce God."[5]

This transformative method was not a cheap debater's trick but was the result of Feuerbach's long and profound struggle with German idealism in general and Hegel's version of it in particular, a struggle that culminated in a critique of Hegel in 1839 in which he had criticized the entire enterprise of speculative philosophy – the arbitrariness of Hegel's starting point in his *Logic*, his preoccupation

---

[4] Feuerbach, *Christianity*, pp. 29f.; *Christentums*, p. 71.
[5] *Christianity*, p. 53; *Christentums*, p. 109.

with temporality in contrast to space, his reification of abstractions, especially "Being," his identification of Being with thought and, consequently, his lack of recognition of the genuine otherness of nature, the system of secondary causes that only science and not metaphysics can understand.[6]

It was because Feuerbach's method was grounded in this profound intellectual struggle that his work excited so many members of his generation. Moreover, the transformative method had implications not only for the philosophy of religion and metaphysics but for the political life of Germans as well. Christianity was at the time the state-sponsored religion and often found its philosophical justification in Hegel's philosophy of Spirit. It was in defense of this religion that conservative state authorities censored anything critical of the state and its policies.[7] To argue, then, that religions were not "moments" in the unfolding of the Absolute but the way in which human beings in various cultures had objectified their images of themselves was at once to affirm that there was truth in Christianity, as Hegel had claimed, but that this truth was all-too-human and not metaphysical. In short, Feuerbach provided an entire generation with a critical counter-interpretation of religion.

The form as well as the content of *The Essence of Christianity* reflects this method of transformation. They reflect Feuerbach's purpose to help his reader achieve self-knowledge by seeing through the objectifications of Christian faith. Just as Hegel thought that the Infinite Spirit must reappropriate its alienated being (creation), so Feuerbach believed that the human spirit must reclaim its alienated image embodied in the idea of God.

Religion is the relation of man to his own nature, – therein lies its truth and its power of moral amelioration; – but to his nature not recognized as his

---

[6] For a learned study of this struggle see Charles A. Wilson, *Feuerbach and the Search for Otherness*, American University Series, Series v, Philosophy, vol. 76 (New York: Peter Lang, 1989). See also Claudio Cesa, "Feuerbach's Kritik des Idealismus und seine Versuche zu einer neuen Erkenntnistheorie," in Hermann Lübbe and Hans-Martin Sass (eds.), *Atheismus in der Diskussion: Kontroversen um Ludwig Feuerbach, Systematische Beiträge*, No. 17 (Munich: Chr. Kaiser Verlag, 1975), pp. 218–233.

[7] Marilyn Chapin Massey has suggested that the threat of censorship influenced both the style and the substance of the first edition of *The Essence of Christianity* in 1841. She argues that the scholarly paraphernalia and the boorish theological quotations, as well as the abstract language Feuerbach used and which he acknowledged to be "bad writing," were intended to fool the censor and mask its revolutionary thrust. They also obscured the elements of parody in the work. See "Censorship and the Language of Feuerbach's *Essence of Christianity (1841)*," *The Journal of Religion*, 65 (1985), 173–195.

own, but regarded as another nature, separate, nay, contradistinguished from his own: herein lies its untruth, its limitation, its contradiction to reason and morality; herein lies the noxious source of religious fanaticism.[8]

The structure of *Christianity* reflects Feuerbach's therapeutic aim. Part I of the book is called "The True or Anthropological Essence of Religion" and is devoted to showing how the theory of objectification or projection best explains the form as well as the content of the doctrines of Christianity. This part is described as "positive" because it claims to demonstrate that what has hitherto been depicted as divine is, in reality, profoundly human. It shows that the human predicates are the real objects of devotion in religion, and not a divine subject who possesses these predicates. Christianity really celebrates the perfections of the human species which humanity has not yet dared to attribute to itself.

Part II of the book, "The False or Theological Essence of Religion," is, in contrast to the first part, "negative," because it professes to show that when theologians take the original naïve objectifications of religion to be true, all sorts of bad consequences follow. If the book had only consisted of the second part, Feuerbach noted, then he might have been justly accused of being purely destructive. But the second part presupposes the first and has no independent significance. The first part is concerned with the development of religion and, hence, is calm and light; the second deals with theology and, hence, is vehement and, consequently, like fire *(Feuer)*. In the first part, the proof of the thesis is direct; in the second, indirect. The purpose of the second part is only "to show that the sense in which religion is interpreted in the previous part of the work must be the true one, because the contrary is absurd."[9]

There is, of course, something overly tidy about Feuerbach's view of the relationship between the two parts. It obscures, first of all, his own ambivalence towards naïve religion, the degree to which not only theology but religion itself manifests a "false consciousness," to use Marxist terminology. Second, it is logically questionable, because it does not follow that if theism is absurd, then Feuerbach's own theory must be true. It is a possibility that both theism and his theory are false.

Perhaps a better way to understand the relationship between the

---

[8] Feuerbach, *Christianity*, p. 197; *Christentums*, p. 334.
[9] Feuerbach, *Christianity*, p. xxxvii; *Christentums*, p. 18.

two parts is to view them as aspects of a single suspicious interpretation of religion. So considered, the idea of God arises when in the process of self-differentiation the imagination seizes upon the abstract predicates of human consciousness and combines them into the image of one superhuman subject, God. This hypothesis best explains the content of religious doctrine, the language that is used, as well as the practice of prayer. But at the same time, this also explains, negatively, why the idea of God is replete with contradictions, because it is impossible to attribute all human perfection to a single divine being without falling into contradictions. Once it is understood that theology is really mystified anthropology, human beings can begin to reclaim their own attributes. They can realize that the human species as a whole is the proper location for these perfections.

Although the enthusiasm with which the book was received by the young rebels in mid-nineteenth-century Germany is explicable in terms of its resolution of certain problems they had with Hegelianism, this does not explain why so many contemporary readers still find it fascinating and disturbing. The Hegelian project has long since become both unfamiliar and strange to them, and Feuerbach's thesis seems to have no obvious political significance. One of the reasons for this fascination, I suggest, lies in the way Feuerbach, though still writing in a strange vocabulary, anticipated so many themes of the twentieth century: a Marxist theory of alienation, the Freudian emphasis on the role of wishing and desire, the empiricist's stress on sense experience, the phenomenologist's concern with the body, and the existentialist concern with the confrontation of the consciousness with death and anxiety. Moreover, Feuerbach constructed his project on the foundation of a social theory of the self, his view that the I always emerges in relationship to a Thou. Feuerbach, as Manfred Vogel has noted, was "the philosophical anthropologist par excellence."[10]

A second reason why Feuerbach is still interesting is that despite his suspicious interpretation of religion, he cannot be dismissed, as so many other critics of religion can, as a religiously illiterate outsider. Despite his criticisms of religion, he had a basic sympathy with those human desires and longings that manifest themselves in religious belief. He understood the sense of futility the self feels in the face of an indifferent nature, the anxiety experienced in the face of death, the longing for some sense of recognition by a cosmic "other." Although

[10] Manfred Vogel in introduction to Ludwig Feuerbach, *Principles of the Philosophy of the Future*, p. viii.

Sigmund Freud also understood these things to some degree, he could only regard human faith as a manifestation of infantile helplessness, whereas Feuerbach believed that faith arises out of the structure of self-consciousness itself. Moreover, his critique of religion, unlike Freud's, was grounded in an extraordinary grasp of the history of the Christian religious tradition. He could claim with some legitimacy that he had arrived at his interpretation by letting the tradition speak for itself. This is what imparts a power and profundity to his suspicious interpretation of religion lacking in Ricoeur's other three "masters of suspicion."

What evokes the most contemporary interest in Feuerbach, however, is his theory that the gods are projections together with the ingenuity with which he used this theory to interpret Christian ideas. But unlike other projection theorists, he did not evaluate religion in a purely negative fashion. His treatment was inherently dialectical. Religion, to be sure, is a projection, but it also serves as "man's *earliest and also indirect* form of *self-knowledge.*"[11] As the objectification of human nature, it is alienating; but it is also the means by which human beings come to reappropriate love for others. Human beings first discover what human nature essentially is when it is projected in the form of another being. "Every advance in religion is therefore a deeper self-knowledge."[12]

The idea that religion is a projection has now, of course, become commonplace in religious studies, especially among psychologists. In his book *The Duality of Human Existence*, David Bakan endorses the claim that this idea, which was once only on the periphery of science, has become what

might be termed a credo. It is the belief that the evidence set forth by anthropologists and psychoanalysts, particularly by Frazer and Freud, in favor of the proposition that religions are the products of human imaginations revised by rationality, is so massive and persuasive that it adds up to a veritable discovery, potentially the most consequential discovery since Darwin's theory of evolution.[13]

Whether this discovery is the greatest since Darwin's may be questioned, but there can be no doubt that this credo underlies the interpretation of religion by an extraordinary number of scholars

---

[11] Feuerbach, *Christianity*, p. 13; *Christentums*, p. 47.
[12] *Christianity*, p. 13; *Christentums*, p. 47.
[13] Henry A. Murray quoted by David Bakan in *The Duality of Human Existence* (Chicago: Rand McNally, 1966), pp. 38f.

working in diverse methodologies. Indeed, it is probably not an exaggeration to write that the concept is close to the center of some of the most influential currents of modern thought: Freudian, Marxist, Durkheimian, Kantian, and, most recently, Nietzschean. As a metaphor applied to religion, the term "projection" is as much at home in positivistic modes of thought as it is in those that assume that reality is "socially constructed." Although the lay person tends to associate projection theories with the name of Freud, and hence, with hostile interpretations of religion, one also finds projection theories among psychologists, sociologists, philosophers, and anthropologists who are neither hostile to religion nor think of it as a delusion.

It is just because there is such a variety of projection theories, however, that we cannot immediately assume that we know what Feuerbach meant by the term. A technical term acquires its meaning from its associations and logical connections with other concepts in a theory. This is also true of Feuerbach's use of the term. In fact, he rarely used the German term *Projektion* but, rather, a host of terms, some of which were informal, that his English translator, George Eliot, rendered in English as "projection" or "to project." Moreover, the most often employed of these German terms, "to objectify" (*vergegenständlichen*), was primarily taken from Hegelian philosophy and has some connotations which the English verb "to project" does not have. The concept, in short, was a technical one, and readers unfamiliar with its Hegelian background will be frequently puzzled by the conceptual affinities the terms has with others; for example, that "projection" and "objectification" also entail "alienation."

But even if one were familiar with the Hegelian background, the concept of projection in Feuerbach's work is not easily understood. He was an original thinker and, in my opinion, his argument cannot be viewed simply as parasitical on Hegel's. As we shall see, he believed that the act of self-differentiation was mediated through a concrete and bodily encounter with another Thou, an idea which he thought was foreign to Hegel and which enabled him to take his own argument in a different direction. To fail to understand or to miss these original features in Feuerbach's version of the argument is, I believe, to miss what is most interesting in it. It is also to miss why Feuerbach's ideas still have appeal to many contemporary readers. But more importantly, it is to overlook just those aspects of his anthropology that enabled him to formulate his later theory of religion, a theory which has genuine discontinuities with the earlier argument and which, I shall argue, is more viable and lacks the entanglements with Hegelian idealism.

What I shall attempt to do in the remainder of this chapter, then, is to help the reader understand this very complex concept of projection in *The Essence of Christianity*. I shall attempt to show that the concept is far more complicated than most commentators have observed. In fact, Feuerbach's argument weaves together several threads of argumentation that initially seem inextricable from one another but which prove not to be. The dominant threads are, to be sure, Hegelian, but there are other subordinate threads that are un-Hegelian and important. Without them the pattern of interpretation Feuerbach proposes, which I shall explore in Chapter 3, could not have taken the form that it did. Since these subordinate threads of argumentation seem to be free of much of the "outdated nonsense" that makes the concept of projection so difficult for modern readers, I shall explore at least two of the ways in which it might seem feasible to "rationally reconstruct" Feuerbach's theory: the first along lines proposed by Freud, the second, by Alexandre Kojève. To anticipate, I shall argue that although the reconstruction inspired by Kojève is more faithful to Feuerbach's thought than that inspired by Freud, we cannot legitimately conclude that the threads of Feuerbach's argument in *Christianity* can be separated from the dominant Hegelian strand, because so much of Feuerbach's argument remains hidden. Nevertheless, the distinction between the several threads is an important one because it prepares us for my interpretation of Feuerbach's later thought, as we shall see in subsequent chapters.

THE COMPLEXITY OF THE MODEL

On the surface, Feuerbach's theory of projection seems deceptively simple: the idea of God is the unconscious projection of the essential human predicates, which is then regarded as a single, separate, heavenly being. But this simplicity immediately vanishes when the contemporary reader turns to the first chapter. There one is confronted with a line of argumentation and a terminology that are, by contemporary standards, extraordinarily obscure and speculative. In the initial two pages, for example, it is argued (a) that religion is identical with self-consciousness; that is, with the consciousness that a person has of his/her own nature, (b) that consciousness is in the strict sense identical with consciousness of the infinite nature of consciousness, and (c) that a limited consciousness is no consciousness. All these sweeping assertions are then interwoven with such claims as "man is nothing without an object," or that the object to which a subject necessarily relates is nothing else than that subject's own objective nature.[14] The lay reader, merely hoping to understand the ramifications of what initially appeared to be a simple thesis concerning how human beings create the gods, suddenly finds himself/herself wrestling with highly obscure and allusive arguments that seem to be but the tip of a conceptual iceberg largely hidden from view.

The analogy of an iceberg is particularly apt. Marx Wartofsky, who has written the most impressive work on Feuerbach in English, argues that the allusive nature of the book can be accounted for only if one understands that it is thoroughly imbedded in and only intelligible against its Hegelian background; more specifically, against the background of Hegel's great work *The Phenomenology of Spirit*. Not only does *Christianity* recapitulate the formal structure of Hegel's book, but the central model upon which everything depends – that the process of self-differentiation involves objectification, alienation, and reconciliation – is derived from the *Phenomenology*. This is also true of certain important supporting arguments: the infinitude of consciousness, the concept of the species, and the theory of the imagination. In fact, the unresolved tensions in Feuerbach's book arise, in Wartofsky's opinion, because he is thoroughly enmeshed in the Hegelian scheme but is struggling to break free of it and to achieve something new.

A further difficulty in understanding Feuerbach's theory of projection is that he decided, for complex reasons, not to spell out or develop those epistemological arguments that would have made it plausible. Nevertheless, these epistemological arguments are crucial to his view of both religion and philosophy. Consequently, Wartofsky argues, the book can be read at two levels. At the most popular level, it professes to show that humanity creates the divine in its own image. At a deeper level, there is an argument regarding how concepts are formulated in religion and philosophy. But since this deeper level is only implicit and is veiled from the reader, it has to be "dug out of the work" and reconstructed.[15] Unfortunately, few lay readers are in the position to do this.

Feuerbach's book begins with the judgment that the clue to the

[14] Feuerbach, *Christianity*, pp. 1–4; *Christentums*, pp. 28–32.
[15] Marx W. Wartofsky, *Feuerbach* (Cambridge: Cambridge University Press, 1977), pp. 198, 202.

nature of religion lies in that attribute which differentiates human beings from animals; namely, consciousness. Consciousness is distinctive because it can make the essential predicates of the human an object of thought. To be sure, animals have some feeling of self in the sense of possessing a common center of successive sensations, but they do not possess consciousness in the strict sense of the word. They have no awareness of being a member of a species. It is not only this sense of species consciousness that makes abstraction and speech possible, but the ability of one individual to imagine itself in the position of another. It is consciousness that makes it possible to be at once an I and a Thou.[16]

This argument is obviously a variation on a theme in Hegel's extraordinary analysis of consciousness and self-differentiation in *The Phenomenology of Spirit*, as Wartofsky has pointed out. Feuerbach accepted Hegel's argument that the condition of possibility of self-consciousness is the consciousness of another, which is to say that the I only comes into existence as a self-reflexive being over against a Thou for which it is an object. Feuerbach also accepted Hegel's view that an analysis of this interdependence of self and other contained an implicit awareness that the I shared essential characteristics with that other, not the least of which is the attribute of consciousness itself. Both Feuerbach and Hegel believed, Wartofsky observes, that "The achievement of self-consciousness is the achievement of knowledge of the other as *like* myself, *in terms of the quality of consciousness itself*. This constitutes *species* knowledge, knowledge of myself insofar as I am *species*-identical with the other."[17]

Despite these similarities, Feuerbach's arguments contain original features that not only serve to differentiate his views from Hegel's but lead him to conclusions that make it impossible to interpret his thought merely as an inversion of his teacher's. Feuerbach insisted that the self-differentiation of the I from the Thou was mediated through a bodily encounter and not merely through consciousness. The Thou is perceived to be another because it is embodied. The other stands over against the I and physically limits it.[18] Hegel, Feuerbach complained, always treated reality merely as a reflection of logic and of thought and, hence, could not do justice to concrete, individual existence. "*The Phenomenology*," he once wrote, is "nothing

[16] Feuerbach, *Christianity*, p. 2; *Christentums*, p. 29.
[17] Wartofsky, *Feuerbach*, p. 207.
[18] Feuerbach, *Christianity*, pp. 91f.; *Christentums*, p. 177.

but a phenomenological Logic. Only from this point of view can the chapter on sensuous certainty be excused."[19] Feuerbach's subject, by contrast, becomes aware of himself/herself in and through the encounter with an embodied, "flesh and blood," Thou.

Furthermore, it is this encounter with an embodied other that mediates the awareness of nature in general. Unlike Hegel's Absolute, which produces the otherness of nature as the first "moment" in its process of development towards self-conscious spirit, Feuerbach's human spirit first becomes aware of the otherness of nature and the world in and through its encounter with a sensuously perceived Thou.

The *first* object of man is man. The sense of Nature, which opens to us the consciousness of the world as a world, is a later product; for it first arises through the distinction of man from himself.[20]

It follows from this that the I–Thou relation is the focus for several dialectical mediating relationships. It mediates the sense of being an I over against an other, the sense that the other is like myself, the sense of an external nature; and it also constitutes the bond between the self and the world. "I am, and I feel myself dependent on the world, because I first feel dependent on other men."[21] This dependence is not merely a physical dependence, although it is that, but a dependence in the sense that the world is not empty and meaningless because other human beings help it to become clear to the I.

It is one of the curiosities – one might say the failings – of *The Essence of Christianity* that this emphasis on embodiedness and the mediation of the idea of nature is not emphasized or explicated in those first chapters of the book in which the basic thesis is presented but is only found in scattered passages throughout the book. In those early and important passages, Feuerbach is preoccupied only with that aspect of consciousness that is conscious of the unlimited and infinite nature of consciousness itself. "*Consciousness*, in the strict or proper sense," he wrote,

is identical with consciousness of the infinite; a *limited* consciousness is *no* consciousness; consciousness is essentially infinite in nature. The consciousness of the infinite is nothing else than the consciousness of the *infinity of the*

[19] Hanfi (trans.), *The Fiery Brook*, p. 7. "Zur Kritik der Hegelschen Philosophie," in *Kleinere Schriften* II, *GW* IX.45.
[20] Feuerbach, *Christianity*, pp. 82f.; *Christentums*, pp. 165f.
[21] Feuerbach, *Christianity*, p. 82; *Christentums*, p. 165.

consciousness; or, in the consciousness of the infinite, the conscious subject has for his object *the infinity of his own nature.*[22]

The consequence of this failure to stress the awareness of external nature as an ingredient in consciousness is that when Feuerbach turned to the crucial task of elucidating what was distinctive about human existence and, hence, what is projected, he tended to revert to the Hegelian preoccupation with consciousness alone; that is, he did just what he had criticized Hegel for doing – ignoring sensuousness, the body, and nature. Thus when Feuerbach argues that in self-differentiation the self becomes aware of being a member of a species, this is taken to mean that the self is aware of itself as a bearer of consciousness. And since the essence of consciousness is constituted by reason, will, and feeling, one can say either that the essential predicate of the species is consciousness or that its essential predicates are reason, will, and feeling. Consequently, the whole process of projection and, hence, the nature of religion tends to ignore nature. This was to become, as Feuerbach himself later acknowledged, a serious defect of the theory in *Christianity*.

The statement above that a limited consciousness is no consciousness is virtually unintelligible to most contemporary readers and reveals how much this theory of projection presupposes the Hegelian context. It presupposes, as Wartofsky has shown, a previous and highly technical discussion in Feuerbach's earlier *Dissertation* that was concerned with one of the central problems of Hegelian idealism, the relationship of the individual to the species. Basically the discussion there hinges on the analysis and definition of finitude and infinitude. In the idealistic framework, finitude was basically taken to refer to whatever is determined by something external to it, whereas infinitude meant self-related or undetermined by another. On these assumptions, the essence of any determinate being consists in all of its determining relationships. Consciousness could then be said to be infinite if it were determined by nothing beyond itself. Since Feuerbach regarded consciousness as essentially consciousness of the species, which he regarded as infinite, the term "infinity" in this connection suggests "the totality of relations in which human consciousness is the subject and human activity in every one of its modes is the object, each mode being without limit in its own sphere."[23]

---

[22] Feuerbach, *Christianity*, pp. 2f.; *Christentums*, p. 30.
[23] Wartofsky, *Feuerbach*, p. 272. I am indebted to Wartofsky's excellent clarification of these terms in chapter 9 of his book.

For someone for whom this Hegelian terminology is itself problematic, this clarification may not be sufficient to render the argument plausible, but at least it makes clear that Feuerbach's reference to the "infinity of consciousness" was not just a rhetorical flourish but presupposed the philosophical anthropology underlying his work.

There is also an important ancillary argument that will strike most readers as problematical. In the process by which the self comes to differentiate itself from the Thou and becomes aware that it is part of a species, the self also comes to feel that its own distinctive "species powers," those distinctive potentialities that constitute it as a member of a species, are absolute, and, hence, "perfections." By "absolute," Feuerbach meant that these distinctive powers constitute and determine what we can think, do, and feel and, hence, determine what the world is for us and how we shall exist in it. Our species powers determine the perspective from which we relate to the world.

The arguments backing this claim also seem abstruse by contemporary standards. Thus he can write that "the object to which a subject essentially, necessarily relates, is nothing else than this subject's own, but objective, nature."[24] This means, Feuerbach went on, that if an object is common to several individuals of the same species even though under distinct conditions, it still represents itself as their own nature. This argument can be made somewhat less abstruse if we translate it into more contemporary language like this: How any given organism relates to the world is a function of its own biologically distinctive cognitive apparatus. Each type of organism has its own unique "species perspective," so to speak, its own species-specific world of experience. An animal, for example, with a highly developed sense of smell but with no capacity for sight experiences a different world than an organism with sight but no olfactory organ. Every species has it own horizon which is determined by its distinctive natural powers. In this sense, any object to which a subject necessarily relates tells us about the objective nature of this subjective being.

The organism takes its powers not only as absolute but as perfections: absolute, because they are not only the conditions of all possible experience for the species; perfections, because the exercise of these powers brings health and joy. The human species is fulfilled, to use the terminology which Marx took over from Feuerbach, when it

---

[24] Feuerbach, *Christianity*, p. 4; *Christentums*, p. 33.

utilizes its own distinctive species powers.[25] It is truncated and alienated when, for some reason, it is deprived of the exercise of them. Since Feuerbach believed that reason, will, and feeling are the essential predicates of the species – Marx was later to modify this and claim that the distinctive activity of the "species being" was labor – then consciousness can be said to be *"self-verification, self-limitation, self-love,* joy *in one's own perfections."*[26]

Once the process of self-differentiation occurs and the self becomes latently aware that it is a member of the species whose attributes seem perfect, it is both enraptured by this perfection and aware that as an individual it is an inadequate representation of that perfection. The species is perfect, the individual imperfect. The species will endure, but the individual will die. It is in this gap or discrepancy between the individual and the species that Feuerbach believed religion first takes root. Because the individual feels limited and fated to die, it yearns to be free from the defects of its individuality and the fate of death. It yearns and longs for "the perfect type of his nature."[27] Not having any awareness of anything above itself, driven by its will to live and its longing for species perfection, the imagination, which is in the service of the feelings, seizes upon the essential predicates of consciousness – reason, will, and emotion – and transforms them into a transcendent, divine being. This projection so captivates the emotions that the individual worships it. God is the notion of the species transformed by the imagination into a perfect exemplar of the species, a conscious being with perfect knowledge, will, and, above all, feeling.

It is a peculiarity of the highly compressed first chapter of the book that Feuerbach did not attempt to explain in any detail how or why the feelings and the imagination are moved to reify this idea of the species; how, in short, the mechanism of projection, so to speak, works. We are only told that in the act of self-differentiation the I realizes that it is a member of the species and then objectifies these species predicates. It is only later that we are introduced to the two principal factors at work in the process of projection, the imagination and the feelings; and when these are introduced, it is not always clear how they are related to the concept of consciousness laid out in the initial chapter. And even when Feuerbach does, on occasion, actually

[25] This is the argument underlying Marx's "Economic and Philosophical Manuscripts of 1844." See Livingstone and Benton (trans.), *Karl Marx Early Writings,* pp. 322–334.
[26] Feuerbach, *Christianity,* p. 6; *Christentums,* p. 36.
[27] *Christianity,* p. 281; *Christentums,* p. 455.

describe the mechanism of projection, he brings forward a number of psychological arguments that do not seem, on the surface at least, to be intrinsically and logically related to the Hegelian paradigm. In these arguments he tells us how driven the human individual is to be free from the limitations of nature and death, and how powerful the feelings are in contrast to the reason, how prone the imagination is to trick the reason and serve the feelings, and how powerful is the wish to have a deity that can love the self. But it is not clear how all this fits together.

Some surmise about how these psychological arguments are related to the arguments about self-consciousness and species consciousness can only be made after we have examined the two categories that seem to be the primary organs at work in religion: the feelings and the imagination.

The concept of feeling is especially important because it is at this point that Feuerbach once again proposes a view that distinguishes him from Hegel so far as the interpretation of religion is concerned. Hegel had regarded religion as basically the apprehension of ideas in symbolic and mythological form, whereas Feuerbach, by contrast, believed that religion was principally a matter of feeling. In this regard, he seemed to be more appreciative of the views of Hegel's academic rival, Schleiermacher, than Hegel himself was. Schleiermacher had argued, particularly in his early work, *Speeches on Religion*, that the essence of religion was feeling, and although he had qualified that claim in his mature work, as we shall see in a later chapter, he never abandoned the view that it was a mistake to see religious doctrines as philosophical concepts in symbolic garb, as Hegel did. Moreover, Feuerbach was in general agreement with Schleiermacher that religious feeling is passive, although he did not think of it as the sense of being impinged upon by a larger whole, as Schleiermacher did. Rather, feeling is the capacity to be moved by and respond to others, and it manifests itself in longing and in wish. In contrast to Schleiermacher's view that religious feeling arises in connection with the awareness of being a part of a universal whole, Feuerbach believed that feeling recognizes no conditions or limits at all. "Feeling knows no other necessity than its own, than the necessity of feeling, than longing; it holds in extreme horror the necessity of Nature, the necessity of reason."[28]

[28] *Christianity*, p. 146; *Christentums*, p. 258.

Incidentally, any English reader of *The Essence of Christianity* interested in the details of Feuerbach's argument concerning the nature of feeling will be unnecessarily puzzled by Feuerbach's views. One of the reasons is that the translator, George Eliot, apparently assumed, with some justification, that since Feuerbach was writing for the layperson he was not concerned with overly technical distinctions. Consequently, she makes no effort to distinguish between the German terms *Empfindung*, *Gemüt*, and *Gefühl*, terms that are difficult to translate into English in any case. The result is that the reader will not know that *Empfindung* is translated as "feeling" in some chapters, as "sensation" in others, and then, confusingly, said to be inferior to *Gefühl* in an appendix.[29]

Nevertheless, the outlines of his position are relatively clear. Feeling (*Empfindung*) is the capacity of the human ego to feel both itself and the others that act upon it. It is, he writes, "the oblique case of the *ego*, the *ego in the accusative*."[30] Generally, it is unfettered by the reality principle; that is, either by reason or by the restraints of nature. It "breaks through all the limits of the understanding, which soars above all the boundaries of Nature."[31] It assumes that the deepest wishes of the heart are true, that what is wished for does, in fact, exist. And since there is no deeper human wish than that the Absolute be a being with a "sympathetical and tender, loving nature," the feelings rush to the judgment that there must be a deity that is personally concerned with the individual.

It is in the chapters dealing with feeling that Feuerbach strikes the modern reader as most contemporary, because what we find here is a picture of the human ego in the grip of the rage to live and, hence, longing for an ultimate reality that can grant its deepest wishes. The religious projection is the result of the "omnipotence of feeling," or what Feuerbach calls "unrestricted subjectivity." By this he meant that the inmost wishes of the heart are assumed to have objective validity and reality. Here the "whole world, with all its pomp and glory, *is nothing weighed against human feeling*."[32]

This unrestricted subjectivity manifests itself in several forms, all of which are encapsulated in Feuerbach's interpretation of Christian

---

[29] Eliot translates "Gefühl ist Sympathie; Gefühl entspringt nur in der Liebe des Menschen zum Menschen. Empfindungen hat der Mensch allein für sich, Gefühle nur in Gemeinschaft" as "Feeling is sympathy; feeling arises only in the love of man to man. *Sensations* [*sic*] man has in isolation; feelings only in community." *Christianity*, p. 283; *Christentums*, p. 458.

[30] Feuerbach, *Christianity*, p. 140; *Christentums*, p.248.

[31] *Christianity*, p. 125; *Christentums*, p. 226.   [32] *Christianity*, p. 121; *Christentums*, p. 220.

faith: faith in providence, which is but a form of confidence in the infinite value of one's own existence; faith in miracle, the confidence that the gods are unfettered by natural necessity and can realize our wishes in an instant; faith in immortality, the certainty that the gods will not permit us as individuals to perish; and, above all, faith in the existence of a loving God.

Longing is the *necessity of feeling*, and feeling longs for a personal God. But this longing after the personality of God is true, earnest, and profound only when it is the longing for *one* personality . . . That which to the feelings is a necessary being, is to them immediately a *real* being. Longing says: There must be a *personal* God, *i.e.*, it *cannot* be that there is *not*; satisfied feeling says: *He is*.[33]

It is because feeling is unrestrained by the reality principle and lives in the realm of desire and wish that Feuerbach liked to compare it with dreaming.

In dreaming, the active is the passive, the passive the active; in dreaming, I take the spontaneous action of my own mind for an action upon me from without, my emotions for events, my conceptions and sensations for true experiences apart from myself. I suffer what I also perform . . . It is the same ego, the same being in dreaming as in waking; the only distinction is, that in waking, the *ego acts on itself*; whereas in dreaming it is *acted on* by itself as by another being . . . Feeling is a dream with the eyes open; religion the dream of waking consciousness: dreaming is the key to religion.[34]

In both dream and religion, he notes, "we only see real things in the entrancing splendor of imagination and caprice, instead of in the simple daylight of reality and necessity."[35]

This distinction between "real things" and the "entrancing splendor of imagination" brings us to the second important element in the mechanism of projection, the imagination (*Phantasie*), which he argues is the original organ of religion.[36] It is original for two reasons. First of all, the imagination, unlike abstract thought, produces images that have the power to stir the feelings and the emotions. Human beings are sensuous and feeling creatures who require sensuous images as vehicles of their hopes and dreams. Thus the "imagination is the faculty which alone corresponds to personal feeling, because it sets aside all limits, all laws which are painful to the feelings, and thus makes objective to man the immediate, absolutely unlimited satisfaction

[33] *Christianity*, p. 146; *Christentums*, pp. 257f.   [34] *Christianity*, p. 140; *Christentums*, p. 248.
[35] *Christianity*, p. xxxix; *Christentums*, p. 20.   [36] *Christianity*, p. 214; *Christentums*, p. 360.

of his subjective wishes."[37] Second, the imagination, unlike feeling, can deal with abstractions taken from the real world. In this sense it is a mode of representation, but, unlike thought, drapes its abstractions in sensuous imagery. "Mind presenting itself as at once type-creating, emotional, and sensuous, is the *imagination*."[38] In this way, the imagination is peculiarly important for religion because it is the faculty that can make concepts available to feeling which is otherwise blind.

The imagination, however, is deceptive in the nature of the case, especially when it becomes allied with feeling and wishing. It can and often does cheat the reason. It can screen contradictions and set aside all limits and laws painful to the feelings. It is in the service of desire and wish. Above all, it can exercise its deceptive powers by confusing the abstract with the concrete, which is precisely what has happened in the Christian religion. It is the imagination that has taken the species characteristics of human consciousness (reason, will, and affection) and transformed them into the form of a single, perfect, divine being.

God is the idea of the species as an individual – the idea or essence of the species, which as a species, as universal being, *as the totality of all perfections*, of all attributes or realities, freed from all the limits which exist in the consciousness and feeling of the individual, is at the same time again an individual, *personal* being.[39]

The strategy of Feuerbach's book is to convince his readers that this hypothesis (although he would scarcely have used such a tentative word) best accounts for the form and content of Christian doctrines and practices as well as the contradictions that plague them. Thus, the greater part of the book is devoted to exegesis of these doctrines and practices, everything from the doctrine of the Trinity to the Sacraments. In Part I he attempts to show how each Christian doctrine is best understood as an objectification of some distinctively human predicate; in Part II he is concerned with the contradictions that arise because of this mystification. Normally, each chapter takes up a single Christian doctrine, although occasionally this pattern is broken by taking up some issue that Feuerbach thought was particularly instructive or illustrative of his argument, such as

---

[37] *Christianity*, p. 131; *Christentums*, p. 235.
[38] *Christianity*, p. 75; *Christentums*, p. 153.
[39] *Christianity*, p. 153; *Christentums*, pp. 268f.

mysticism, the relationship of Christianity to "heathen" religions, or the concept of nature in God.

A typical form of argumentation appears in the first three chapters of Part I. There Feuerbach attempts to illustrate the claim that the Christian concept of God is an objectification of the three essential predicates of the species being: reason, will, and feeling. The argument is complicated, but essentially looks like this: Since the reason or understanding – Feuerbach, in contrast to Kant, uses the German terms *Intelligenz, Vernunft,* and *Verstand* synonymously – is the impersonal part of our nature that is the source of logical identity and apprehends abstractions, necessities, and patterns, it is the source of all those metaphysical attributes, such as incorporeality, formlessness, and omniscience, which stand in contrast to the personal attributes. The intelligence, he writes, is that faculty that is impervious to desire, passion, and wants. It "is that part of our nature which is neutral, impassible, not to [be] bribed, not subject to illusions – the pure, passionless light of the intelligence."[40] Because it is concerned with abstractions, religious anthropomorphism is alien to it. Under the hegemony of this predicate, God is defined as Infinite Spirit.

Reason, however, is only one of the essential predicates of the human species, and a god who is primarily the objectification of reason cannot satisfy the wishes and desires of the individual heart. As infinite reason, God has no religious or, to use one of Feuerbach's favorite words, "practical" significance. Therefore, the human species requires a deity that also represents moral perfection, the absolutization of the faculty of the will. But this objectification also leads to an unhappy consciousness, to a sense of disunion with oneself, because when confronted with a perfect moral being, a person can only feel a chasm between his/her own state of being and God's moral perfection. How, then, shall this sense of disunion be overcome? The answer is to be found in the third attribute, the divine love, because "It is the consciousness of love by which man reconciles himself with God, or rather with his own nature as represented in the moral law."[41] Only when God is believed to be a subjective being who has sympathy with the individual can he/she experience that sense of liberation and freedom which is the aim of religion.

---

[40] *Christianity*, p. 34; *Christentums*, p. 77.
[41] *Christianity*, p. 50; *Christentums*, p. 101.

The law condemns; the heart has compassion even on the sinner. The law affirms me only as an abstract being, – love, as a real being. Love gives me the consciousness that I am a man; the law only the consciousness that I am a sinner, that I am worthless. The law holds man in bondage; love makes him free.[42]

The priority of the attribute of love then explains why Feuerbach believes that religions are inevitably anthropomorphic.

For every religion which has any claim to the name presupposes that God is not indifferent to the beings who worship him, that therefore what is human is not alien to him, that, as an object of human veneration, he is a human God.[43]

This tendency to anthropomorphism is most highly developed in Christianity, the central doctrine of which is the Incarnation. Here faith affirms quite explicitly that God becomes human. Moreover, this divine act of condescension is not merely a contingent act, as it is in those pagan religions in which the deity transforms itself into some finite creature. Rather, in Christianity human nature is intrinsically a part of the divine nature. One can see this best, Feuerbach argued, in that important doctrine that affirms that it was the second person of the Trinity who was incarnate in Jesus. "Man was already *in* God, was already *God himself*, before God became man, i.e., showed himself as man."[44] This same insight, Feuerbach cleverly observes, is reflected in the doctrine that God became human in order to deify humanity.

Feuerbach's claim that the idea of God is the absolutization and reification of the essential human predicates of reason, will, and feeling (love) became the basis for two additional and important arguments: (a) that there is an inherent contradiction between the metaphysical predicates of God derived from reason and the anthropomorphic predicates derived from feeling, a contradiction that arises when all human predicates are concentrated in one single being, and (b) that religious piety is far more interested in the predicates of deity than it is in some existing subject behind these predicates and which is the bearer of them.

I shall discuss the former argument in a subsequent chapter, but here it is important to note how crucial it was to Feuerbach's argument that religion generally and Christianity particularly fully

[42] *Christianity*, pp. 47f.; *Christentums*, p. 98.
[43] *Christianity*, p. 54; *Christentums*, p. 109.
[44] *Christianity*, p. 50; *Christentums*, pp. 101f.

confront the implications of anthropomorphism. Theologians, of course, have attempted to avoid anthropomorphism by making a distinction between the deity as it appears to humanity (for us) and the deity as it is in itself. Human beings, it is said, must necessarily talk in anthropomorphic terms, but this talk should be understood to be analogical or symbolical because the Deity is in itself unknowable. This distinction, Feuerbach argued, is untenable for several reasons. First of all, it is fatal to faith. Human beings assign to deity the predicates they do just because they believe that these predicates are absolute and divine. "The fact is not that a quality is divine because God has it, but that God has it because it is in itself divine: because without it God would be a defective being."[45] Humans attribute love to God, for example, because if they do not there will lurk in the background the possibility of a divine subject who could choose not to love. Consequently, where the divine–human predicates are not taken seriously unbelief has, in effect, triumphed over faith. "Hence he alone is the true atheist to whom the predicates of the Divine Being, – for example, love, wisdom, justice, – are nothing; not he to whom merely the subject of these predicates is nothing."[46] Indeed, as David Hume argued earlier in his *Dialogues on Natural Religion*, the proposition that God is unknowable, i.e., lacks determinate predicates, is indistinguishable from skepticism. "If thou doubtest the objective truth of the predicates, thou must also doubt the *objective truth of the subject* whose predicates they are. If thy predicates are anthropomorphisms, the subject of them is an anthropomorphism too."[47] And finally, the distinction is untenable because it violates one of Feuerbach's fundamental epistemological assumptions. One can make the distinction between an object as it is and how it appears "only where an object can really appear otherwise to me," which is impossible because how things appear is determined by our constitution. "The measure of the species is the *absolute* measure, law, and criterion of man."[48]

The refusal to permit the distinction between an unknowable subject and a deity with human predicates is crucial for Feuerbach's argument. For two reasons: it illumines what he believes to be the characteristic waffling of Christian theologians when confronted with

[45] *Christianity*, p. 21; *Christentums*, p. 59.
[46] *Christianity*, p. 21; *Christentums*, p. 58.
[47] *Christianity*, p. 17; *Christentums*, p. 53.
[48] *Christianity*, p. 16; *Christentums*, p. 52.

a particular dilemma, and it underlies Feuerbach's own radical demystification of the Christian doctrine of the Incarnation. The dilemma arises with the basic Christian affirmation "God is love." This affirmation, of course, presents us with a subject, God, and a predicate, love. But so formulated, the affirmation permits the doubt to arise that God could be a being who is not loving. Perhaps God is a subject who could choose either to love or not to love. Perhaps behind the predicate "love" there stands in the background an "unloving monster, a diabolical being, whose *personality* . . . delights in the *blood* of heretics and unbelievers, – the *phantom of religious fanaticism.*"[49]

Christian theologians have tended to waffle when confronted with this issue. On the one hand, the formula "God is love" has been taken to mean that God is an omnipotent being who could, as it were, choose not to save human beings. Love is, so to speak, an accidental predicate and "recedes and sinks into insignificance in the dark background – God."[50] On the other hand, if Christians reject the distinction between a hidden subject "behind" the predicate "love," they then seem to be committed to universal salvation. God, by virtue of His essential nature, has no option but to save the creatures. Unable to affirm the anthropomorphism but shrinking from the consequence of not doing so, the Christian tradition presents the predicate "love" to me, Feuerbach wrote, "at one moment . . . as something essential, at another, it vanishes again."[51]

But the most important reason why Feuerbach insisted that no distinction can be made between a hidden subject and the predicate love is that he believed that the Christian doctrine of the Incarnation is the objectified and mystified form of the insight that it is love and not the subject that is divine.

Love determined God to the renunciation of his divinity. Not because of his Godhead as such, according to which he is the *subject* in the proposition, God is love, but because of his love, of the *predicate*, is it that he renounced his Godhead; thus love is a higher power and truth than deity. *Love conquers God.* It was love to which God sacrificed his divine majesty.[52]

But if it was for love of human beings that God sacrificed his divine majesty, what could this mean other than the latent inference that love is more important than God? In one of those passages that strike

[49] *Christianity*, pp. 52f.; *Christentums*, p. 107.
[50] *Christianity*, p. 52; *Christentums*, p. 106.
[51] *Christianity*, p. 52; *Christentums*, p. 107.
[52] *Christianity*, p. 53; *Christentums*, pp. 107f.

Christians as blasphemous but sympathetic readers of Feuerbach as the most daring consequence of his hermeneutics of suspicion, he wrote:

Who then is our Saviour and Redeemer? God or Love? Love; for God as God has not saved us, but Love, which transcends the difference between the divine and human personality. As God has renounced himself out of love, so we, out of love, should renounce God; *for if we do not sacrifice God to love, we sacrifice love to God*, and, in spite of the predicate of love, we have the God – the evil being – of religious fanaticism.[53]

THE NATURALIST-EXISTENTIALIST STRAND (FREUD)

In the light of the previous discussion, it can be seen that the concept of projection in *The Essence of Christianity* is far more complex than we have been led to expect by the claim that it is simply an inversion of Hegel's philosophy of Spirit. It is a concept woven from many different threads. To be sure, the dominant thread is taken from Hegel's theory of self-differentiation, in which the self in its encounter with another comes to realize that it is a member of the species; but there are also other subordinate strands that are not Hegelian and that, as we shall see, stand in tension with the Hegelian and seem like they might be logically independent of it. There is, first of all, the claim that it is the "omnipotence of feeling" that leads to the "identity of the subjective and objective" or the idea of a personal god. Second, it is said that it is our social nature combined with our feelings of loneliness that generates the need for a social deity, a Trinity "in whom there is *society*, a union of beings fervently loving each another."[54] Third, there is the statement that there is no personality or consciousness without corporeality and, hence, without the distinction of sex.[55] Fourth, there is the argument that it is the flesh and blood encounter with another Thou that mediates the need for self-esteem, love, and recognition by another. And finally, there is the claim that it is our fear of death that determines our desire to transcend the necessities and indifference of nature.

Although Feuerbach undoubtedly believed that all of these arguments were inextricably interwoven and mutually supporting, in retrospect this is not clear. For example, it is not clear how the Hegelian argument that God is the objectification of the distinctive

---

[53] *Christianity*, p. 53; *Christentums*, p. 109.
[54] *Christianity*, p. 73; *Christentums*, p. 149.
[55] *Christianity*, p. 92; *Christentums*, p. 178.

attribute of the species, consciousness, is related to Feuerbach's view that the encounter with the other is always with an embodied other. If to be embodied is what is distinctive about human existence, as he argued against Hegel, then why does he identify the species idea with consciousness alone? Why is consciousness taken to be the "essence" of human nature rather than embodied subjectivity? If what is distinctive about human existence is being embodied, why doesn't the projected idea of God reflect this? Why doesn't God have a body? Feuerbach, of course, claims that Christians abhor the body and concentrate on spirit, but this does not explain why in those early passages discussing the essence of religion as anthropomorphism he concentrated entirely on predicates derived from consciousness. This explanation has to do with religion as such and not just Christianity.

Or again, even if we grant for the moment that the self–other differentiation contains implicitly the idea of being a member of the species, why should this species idea immediately be filled in with the attributes of reason, will, and feeling? Why shouldn't the I–Thou encounter simply lead to the less complex idea that the essence of the species is simply subjectivity as such? Why not project simply an infinite Thou without further characterizing it in terms of three predicates? Wouldn't it be less artificial to argue simply that the encounter with another subject together with the elements of feeling and the desire for recognition generates the belief in a cosmic person who recognizes and loves the I?

Or still again, how does the psychological argument concerning the omnipotence of feeling and wish essentially relate to the Hegelian argument concerning the objectification of the species idea? Doesn't the former argument have a slightly different logic than the latter? Why, for example, does one need to argue that religious longing is first attached to the species idea mediated through the I–Thou encounter when it seems as convincing to argue that the individual's sense of inadequacy and the desire for a personal god could as well be explained by the rage to live and the wish for a loving other not determined by the indifference of nature?

When one reflects on these diverse arguments in Feuerbach's *Christianity*, they seem roughly to fall into two groups or strands, a dominant and a subordinate. The dominant strand is, of course, Hegelian, where the emphasis is put on self-consciousness and consciousness of the species. The subordinate strand, for reasons of conceptual shorthand, I shall call the naturalist-existentialist strand or paradigm. The Hegelian contains the familiar pattern said to be intrinsic to the self-realization of Spirit: objectification–alienation–reappropriation. The naturalist-existentialist strand, by contrast, emphasizes (a) the embodiedness of the I–Thou relation; (b) the notion that the species is distinguished not only by consciousness but by sexuality; (c) that the encounter with nature is mediated through the I–Thou relation rather than being the first self-expression of spirit; (d) that nature is seen to be indifferent to the raging desire of the self for life; and (e) the omnipotence of feeling and wish, especially the wish for a personal god who will intervene in nature in the interests of the self. In this naturalist-existentialist strand, the human self is basically in the grip of feeling and desire but is confronted by the necessities of nature and, hence, death. The self longs to transcend this nature, to be saved from it. But it believes it can be saved only by a power that can transcend and intervene in nature, which can work miracles. It not only longs for such a power, but desires that this superhuman power be a personal subject.

Given these two strands, it is intelligible that contemporary readers should find the naturalist-existentialist strand to be more plausible than the Hegelian with its convoluted and arcane arguments about the infinitude of consciousness, the perfection and absoluteness of the species idea, and the like. Consequently, anyone interested in a rational reconstruction of the early Feuerbach, a reconstruction that involves sorting out those ideas that still seem plausible from those that now appear to be "outdated nonsense," will naturally tend to concentrate on that strand of argumentation which stresses the Promethean rage of the self to live, the sense of helplessness before nature and death, and the omnipotence of feeling. This, it will be claimed, is what is worth saving in Feuerbach.

It is, of course, just this type of argument which one finds in an abbreviated form in Sigmund Freud's best-known works on religion, in *Totem and Taboo* and *The Future of an Illusion*. Consequently it is not surprising that it should be claimed that what was most suggestive in Feuerbach's work has been taken up and appropriated by the first psychoanalyst. Here, it is said, we have Feuerbach's best insights without the "outdated nonsense" of the species idea. We have, in Paul Ricoeur's elegant phrase, an interpretation of religion as the working out of the "strategy of desire."[56] In *The Future of an Illusion*, for

---

[56] Ricoeur, *Freud and Philosophy*, chap. 3.

example, Freud argued that belief in the gods springs from two factors: the longing for a personal deity who can offer consolation, and the helplessness of human beings before nature and death. As regards the latter, the humanization of nature makes the universe less uncanny and threatening because one can at least attempt to cajole and appease the gods, whereas one can only accept the impersonal powers of nature. Such a replacement, he notes, can provide not only psychological relief but some further chance of mastering the situation.[57]

This human situation, moreover, recapitulates an infantile prototype that evokes powerful feelings. The helpless child also has reasons to fear the parents, especially the father, but it reposes its confidence in their ability to protect it against dangers and threats. It was natural then, Freud argued, to assimilate and fuse these motives of fear of the father and the longing for protection. Both in the mentality of children and in dreams it is normal for a person to transform the forces of nature not only into human-like beings "with whom he can associate as he would with equals" but into gods, who, like fathers, offer both protection and consolation.

Although the observation of regularities in nature made its infantile personification less and less tenable as civilization proceeded, the feelings of helplessness and the longing for a personal deity persisted. Moreover, the functions of religion in civilization shifted somewhat as it was increasingly associated with morality. It became the function of the gods to "even out the defects and evils of civilization, to attend to the sufferings which men inflict on one another in their life together and to watch over the fulfillment of the precepts of civilization, which men obey so imperfectly."[58] Now the gods exist to assure human beings that everything that happens in the world serves a higher purpose, that everything is ordered for the best. Most especially, death is not the final extinction of the person, because life on this earth is a prelude to a higher and better one. Moreover, human beings can have personal communion with this deity, can "recover the intimacy and intensity of the child's relations to his father."[59]

In Freudian theory, it is not difficult to find echoes of some of those major themes first articulated in *The Essence of Christianity*, albeit they are selectively chosen, to be sure, and expressed in the language of

---

[57] Sigmund Freud, *The Future of an Illusion*, trans. W. D. Robson-Scott, revised and newly edited by James Strachey (Garden City, N.Y.: Doubleday, 1964), p. 23.
[58] Freud, *The Future of an Illusion*, p. 25.   [59] Freud, *The Future of an Illusion*, p. 27.

psychology rather than philosophy. We find the urge to control nature as well as to attain communion with a personal deity, the emphasis on providence, and above all, the power of wishing. Indeed, Feuerbach's emphasis on the omnipotence of feeling and wishes even seems to have found a literal echo in Freud's earlier essay on animism in *Totem and Taboo*. In this essay, Freud was concerned with "applying the findings of psycho-analysis to topics in the field of mental science"; especially in anthropology and its preoccupation with animism, the notion that the world is peopled with spirits. He wanted to know how "primitive men" arrived at this system of thought, which he believed to be the first human *Weltanschauung* as well as the "foundation on which religions are later built."[60]

The key to the phenomenon of this type of projection, he proposed, lies in a suggestion by J. G. Frazer. In attempting to explain the origins of magic, Frazer had written that human beings mistook the order of their ideas for the order of nature and so believed that by controlling their ideas they could also control things. Freud reasoned that Frazer's suggestion was a good one but did not go deep enough. The clue lies in the immense importance that primitive people, like children, attribute to the power of wishes.

This, too, reflects an infantile prototype. (Many of the leading arguments in this book presuppose Freud's assumption that there are analogies between the mentality of children and those he calls "primitives."[61]) Freud had earlier written a paper in which he had suggested that children satisfy their wishes in a hallucinatory manner, a phenomenon that can be seen in their play. In "primitive" mentality, the importance attached to wishes together with the possibility of willful activity culminates in magic. "It may be said that the principle governing magic, the technique of the animistic mode of thinking, is the principle of the 'omnipotence of thoughts.' "[62] The child/"primitive" naïvely believes that what he/she thinks necessarily occurs.

This "omnipotence of thoughts" itself reflects, of course, a fundamental narcissism Freud believed "primitives" have in common with children and neurotics. This can be seen in the similarity

---

[60] Sigmund Freud, *Totem and Taboo: Some Points of Agreement between the Mental Lives of Savages and Neurotics*, trans. James Strachey (New York: Norton, 1950), p. 77.

[61] I have decided to employ the term "primitive" while expounding Freud's views, but have used quotation marks to signify my discomfiture.

[62] Freud, *Totem and Taboo*, p. 85.

between the obsessive acts of the neurotic and the magical practices of the "primitive." Both types of activities are defensive reactions, designed to ward off disaster or, more fundamentally, death. Like Schopenhauer, Freud believed that the problem of death stands at the outset of every philosophy and is also the source of belief in souls and demons. And since every person has, for the most part, a narcissistic organization of his/her ego, the threat of death is still behind those higher religions towards which animism is but the first step.

Even if we reconstruct Feuerbach's argument along these Freudian lines, it nevertheless lacks that one essential element which makes Feuerbach's argument unique: that projection is somehow tied up with self-differentiation, with the encounter of an I with a Thou. The Freudian appropriation of Feuerbach's argument lacks this crucial element. But perhaps we could correct this defect by amending the Freudian reconstruction with the help of the well-known theory of projection proposed by the anthropologist Weston La Barre. In his book *The Ghost Dance*, La Barre proposes a theory of the origins of religion that looks something like this: The human self comes to self-consciousness in relation to other selves, but we can best concretize these other selves as parents; first the nurturing mother and then, later, the father. Not only are these selves the others in relation to which the I comes into self-consciousness, but these parental others nurture the child through a long period of dependency, a period that exceeds that of any other mammal. The child thus becomes accustomed to calling on these figures in times of stress and danger. It is natural, then, that when danger and stress arise and no parent is available the child is driven to perceive the non-human environment in terms of this infantile prototype of "the Thou"; in short, to see it in anthropomorphic terms.

Ultimately, both magic and religion reflect the individual narcissism that insists, inalternatively, that somewhere there *must* be an omnipotence to minister to one's here wholly conscious and clear, categorically sanctioned, sacred id need. The environment *must* be what I, unself-questioningly, demand that it be. The absoluteness of the imperious id creates the Absolute.[63]

But to reconstruct Feuerbach's argument in this fashion is to suggest that religious faith is basically a regression to an infantile prototype. Although there are suggestions in Feuerbach's book that religion is a

---

[63] Weston La Barre, *The Ghost Dance: Origins of Religion* (New York: Dell, 1970), p. 110.

"childlike condition of humanity," nevertheless, he characteristically regards it as having its roots in self-differentiation as such, in the encounter of an I with the Thou and the reflex this encounter occasions, a reflex in which the self feels that there is a cosmic Thou who recognizes and loves the self and for whom the welfare of humankind is its greatest anxiety. When Feuerbach invokes the example of the child, as he does in the chapter on prayer, it is to illustrate not a sense of infantile helplessness but the need of the self to believe that the "infinite nature of the Father of men is a *sympathetic, tender, loving* nature, and that thus the dearest, most sacred emotions of man are divine realities."[64]

What, then, can we say in summary about this attempt to salvage Feuerbach's best insights by means of a Freudian reconstruction? The most obvious response is that although it does have striking similarities to important motifs in Feuerbach's work, it also has to jettison not only those "outmoded" ideas that play such a dominant role in the interpretation – the Hegelian schema of objectification–alienation–reappropriation – but the central idea that binds together the subordinate strands; namely, that religion is not merely grounded in wish and desire but in the structure of consciousness itself: the distinction between the I and the Thou and the mediation of nature through that encounter, a nature which is then perceived as indifferent to its deepest desires and which it wants to transcend. Without that notion, it is doubtful whether some of the most important arguments in *Christianity* can be salvaged at all. The Freudian reconstruction presents us with a theory that has striking affinities with many aspects of Feuerbach's theory; nevertheless, it is, finally, a different theory.

THE NATURALISTIC-EXISTENTIALIST STRAND (KOJEVE)

This less-than-successful attempt above to rationally reconstruct Feuerbach's argument along traditional Freudian lines suggests that Feuerbach's various arguments are so tightly interwoven that it may be impossible to abstract one of them without unraveling the whole. If this is true, then Professor Wartofsky is correct when he argues that not only is the Hegelian dialectical scheme of objectification, alienation, and reappropriation essential to the argument, but so also

---

[64] Feuerbach, *Christianity*, p. 124; *Christentums*, p. 224.

is the admittedly confused notion of species being as well as the related argument concerning the imagination.

Nevertheless, there are some historical and intellectual reasons for not yet abandoning the attempt to sort out the various threads of argument, to explore the logical relationships between the naturalist-existentialist thread and the Hegelian paradigm with its identification of the species attributes of reason, will, and feeling. Historically, for example, we know that throughout his book, Feuerbach was trying to break free from Hegel's influence, as Wartofsky has shown, and one of the main points at which he worked hardest at this was Hegel's excessive emphasis on consciousness in abstraction from the body. In retrospect, we also know that in his subsequent writings on religion, he relied less and less on the species motif and the Hegelian scheme of objectification–alienation–reappropriation and more and more on what I have called the naturalist-existentialist theme, which plays a subordinate role in *Christianity*. In his later works, we find an argument that emphasizes the self driven by the urge to happiness, its encounter with what he calls the "not-I" (all of the various external powers and beings that impinge on the self, including its own unconscious forces), and, finally, the desire to reduce the mysteriousness of these powers by personifying them. Intellectually, then, the issue is whether there is any indication that this subordinate naturalist-existentialist theme in *The Essence of Christianity* is logically independent of the convoluted arguments concerning self-consciousness becoming aware of its essential predicates reason, will, and feeling.

Perhaps we can begin to get a purchase on this issue by observing that the I–Thou encounter, which is the core of Feuerbach's argument, is described by him in at least four similar but nevertheless different ways: first, as the differentiation of the self as a conscious unity over against another for whom the I is an object-subject; second, as the differentiation of the I from the species, in which the distinctive attribute of the species is simply subjectivity without any further qualification; third, as the differentiation of the self from the species, in which the distinctive attribute is consciousness spelled out as reason, will, and feeling; and, finally, as differentiation from the species, whose distinctive characteristic it is to be embodied and sexually differentiated.

All of these various descriptions of the I–Thou encounter might appear on the surface, at least, to be the same claim qualified in slightly different ways; and Feuerbach and many of his interpreters have assumed this to be so. But those of us in religious studies who have been preoccupied with philosophical anthropology and who have had the benefit of scores of analyses of self-consciousness can no longer assume this to be the case. We can, for example, no longer equate the awareness of being a differentiated I in the world with the awareness of being a part of a species with certain essential predicates or essences that are the object of reason. We may concede that the I comes to itself over against other persons, to be sure, but we also believe that the categories that the self uses to relate itself to others are those given to it by its culture and language. The awareness of another Thou is probably first given to the child below the level of speech, just as there are also good reasons to believe, as Martin Buber has shown, that it also comes into being in adults without being conceptualized in essentialist terms. It is, then, one thing to argue, as Feuerbach does, that self-consciousness involves the self-differentiation of the I from the Thou, but quite another to argue that this necessarily involves the awareness of oneself as the bearer of the essential predicates of reason, will, and feeling. We confront others as subjects, but we do not necessarily conceptualize them in these essentialist terms.

We may put this matter in slightly different terms. There is a more fundamental and *less conceptualized* core encounter presupposed in Feuerbach's overly determined act of self-differentiation. The self-differentiation from the species presupposes this more fundamental encounter of I and Thou, but this fundamental encounter need not be conceptualized in all of the forms Feuerbach employs. The predicates of the species, for example, are not given in the act of self-differentiation but, like all predications, are social and cultural constructions. Indeed, this core experience of being a subject – or more precisely, the awareness of being a differentiated I over against a Thou – can be conceptualized in a number of different ways, as it has been in the history of culture. The faculty psychology that Feuerbach uncritically adopts is only one of many such cultural constructions.

An illustration of how it is possible to distinguish this core conception of the process of self-differentiation from its maximal elaboration in essentialist terms can be found in the writings of Alexandre Kojève, whose interpretation of Hegel earlier in this century had such a powerful effect on a generation of French philosophers, including Jean-Paul Sartre, and which paved the way for that unique synthesis of Hegel, Marx, and Heidegger that continues to have such an influence on the modern intellectual scene.[65] Kojève is particularly relevant for our purposes because, like Feuerbach, he was concerned with the importance and significance of the act of self-differentiation in Hegel's *Phenomenology* and how one might appropriate that analysis without also embracing Hegel's metaphysics.

Kojève argues that a phenomenological analysis of self-consciousness must begin, first, with the biological organism and its hierarchical synthesis of instincts and desires, a beginning, incidentally, that is similar to Feuerbach's analysis of embodiedness and sexuality that appears in later portions of *Christianity*, although not in the crucial initial chapters. The very being of the human presupposes desire because it is out of desire that action is born. Action is the attempt to quiet and to satisfy desire. "Generally speaking, the I of Desire is an emptiness that receives a real positive content only by negating action that satisfies Desire in destroying, transforming, and 'assimilating' the desired non-I."[66] Indeed, it is just because of this close relation between desire and action that we can, as Hegel did, characterize our being as action. But desire alone, Kojève took Hegel to mean, is a necessary but not a sufficient condition for self-consciousness. In order for a distinctive human reality to come into existence within the animal reality, there must be a herd, and for the herd to become a society there must not only be a multiplicity of desires but the desires of each member must be potentially directed, at least, towards the desires of others. Even in the case of the relationship between man and woman, each of them desires not just the body of the other but also his/her recognition, his/her desire. Each person wants to be recognized for his/her own distinctive being and value. So, too, even the desire for natural objects is "mediated" by the desires of others directed towards the same object. An otherwise "useless" object attains its value just by virtue of being desired by others.

Human desire is distinctive only in so far as it triumphs over or transcends merely animal desire. Distinctively human desire is to receive and to give recognition to others. "Indeed, the human being is formed only in terms of a Desire directed toward another Desire, that is – finally – in terms of a desire for recognition."[67] Life is the struggle for this recognition and the conferring of recognition. "In other

---

[65] Alexandre Kojève, *Introduction to the Reading of Hegel; Lectures on the Phenomenology of Spirit*, assembled by Raymond Queneau, ed. Allan Bloom and trans. James H. Nichols, Jr. (Ithaca: Cornell University Press, 1969).
[66] Kojève, *Introduction*, p. 4.   [67] Kojève, *Introduction*, p. 7.

words, all human, anthropogenic Desire – the Desire that generates
Self-Consciousness, the human reality – is, finally, a function of the
desire for 'recognition.' "[68]

Kojève then proceeded to provide his own exegesis of the famous
Master–Slave passages in the Hegel's *Phenomenology*, in which the
philosopher attempted to demonstrate how the development of
consciousness is necessarily reciprocal and social. But what is relevant
for our purposes is the way in which Kojève conceptualizes the
process of self-differentiation without having to invoke the concept of
the species or to characterize that concept further in terms of the three
faculties of reason, will, and feeling, a characterization that so
burdens Feuerbach's analysis of the same process.

With Kojève's interpretation in hand, it is an interesting exercise to
return to the text of *Christianity* in order to inquire whether there are
any passages in which something like Kojève's version of self-
differentiation can be found. In fact, there are, although they are not
brought together in any single unified argument as was the case with
the Hegelian model in the initial chapters of the book. In his
remarkable analysis of what he called the "mystery of the cosmogonical
principle" in chapter 8, for example, Feuerbach argued that the
theological distinction between God and the creator is really a
"mystic paraphrase of a psychological process, nothing else than the
unity of consciousness and self-consciousness made objective."[69] He meant
by this that self-consciousness is at once consciousness of another that
limits it, and in this relationship there is mediated the idea of the
world or nature which stands in contrast to its desire. In short, the
I–Thou encounter, which is the first moment of self-consciousness,
immediately tumbles over into the second, the idea of nature or the
world. "The *first* object of man is man. The sense of Nature, which
opens to us the consciousness of the world as a world, is a later
product, for it first arises through the distinction of man from himself
. . . The *ego*, then, attains to consciousness of the world through
consciousness of the *thou*."[70]

This interpretation of the I–Thou encounter is interesting for two
reasons: first of all, it is a clear departure from Hegel's view that
nature is the first self-objectification of Spirit, the first "moment" of
Spirit on its way to self-realization; but second, it provides a model of

[68] Kojève, *Introduction*, p. 7.
[69] Feuerbach, *Christianity*, p. 81; *Christentums*, p. 164.
[70] *Christianity*, pp. 82f.; *Christentums*, pp. 165f.

self-differentiation in which the I–Thou relationship becomes the basis not so much of the awareness of species predicates but simply of (a) one's own subjective unity, (b) the existence of another embodied subject, and (c) the existence of nature. Moreover, in his chapter on mysticism, in which Feuerbach is concerned with the idea of nature in God, the species consciousness is connected to the relationship to man and woman, which, in turn, is linked to nature. "Personality," he wrote, "is nothing without distinction of sex," which is to say, to nature, because "A personal being apart from Nature is nothing else than a being without sex, and conversely."[71] Thus we have in these and other scattered passages an analysis of the I–Thou relationship, self-differentiation, and even species consciousness set forward in a naturalist-existentialist mode that has many affinities with Kojève's analysis. And to this must be added the analyses in Chapters 10–15 in which Feuerbach was not so much concerned with demonstrating that the content of Christian dogma is the result of objectifying the essential faculties (reason, will, the imagination) as with showing that feeling and desire conspire with the imagination to seduce the self into believing in a deity who loves and recognizes it.

With these passages in hand, then, we might attempt to reconstruct this thread of Feuerbach's argument that, somewhat oversimplified, looks like this. The differentiation of the I from the Thou involves two "moments": first, the differentiation of the self from other selves, and second, the differentiation of the self from nature. This two-fold movement actually constitutes the structure of a self-conscious biological organism whose natural instinctual drive towards self-preservation is transformed into conscious desire. This desire, in turn, takes two forms that correspond to these two moments of self-differentiation. With respect to the differentiation from nature, which seems so indifferent to desire, it takes the form of wanting to assimilate it or to manipulate it in the interests of our needs or, even, to be free from the necessities of nature altogether. This is the element which Freud stressed in his analysis of magic in *Totem and Taboo*. With respect to the differentiation from other selves, however, desire takes the form of wanting recognition and love. The imagination, which is largely in the service of feeling and desire, conceives not only of the possibility of an individual existence free from the constraints of nature but of a superhuman being who can provide recognition and

---

[71] *Christianity*, p. 92; *Christentums*, p. 178.

love that is not contingent upon and subject to the vicissitudes of human fate. In the idea of God, these two moments of desire coalesce. God is not only the superhuman master of nature but the recognizer of the self.

It is possible to interpret much of what Feuerbach says about faith in terms of these two "moments." Consider the "moment" of desire to be free from nature and his analysis of faith as belief in providence, miracles, creation out of nothing, and immortality. All of them are manifestations of the natural narcissism of subjectivity and its desire to be freed from the constraints of natural necessity, a desire which Feuerbach believes reaches its apex in Christianity, with its emphasis on the individual person, an emphasis which ultimately isolates the human from nature and makes him/her an absolute being.[72] The belief in providence is the most fundamental religious conviction because here it is most clearly revealed what religion is about: to assure the individual subject that his/her welfare is the highest good.

Providence is a *privilege* of man. It expresses the *value* of man, in distinction from other natural beings and things; *it exempts him from the connection of the universe.* Providence is the conviction of man of the infinite value of his existence, – a conviction in which he renounces faith in the reality of external things; it is the idealism of religion.[73]

The doctrine of providence, which is grounded in the radical distinction between the individual and nature, soon becomes conceptually linked to the doctrine of creation, on the one hand, and miracles, on the other. Since the doctrine of providence assures the individual that human welfare is the highest good, any being who can secure this welfare must also have power over nature. Consequently, the Christian doctrine of creation out of nothing is but the culminating point of the principle of subjectivity because it is the highest expression of the omnipotence of feeling; that is, "subjectivity exempting itself from all objective conditions and limitations, and consecrating this exemption as the highest power and reality."[74] The doctrine of miracles is only an extension of the same principle. It is the proof of providence, the faith that wishes can become true in an instant, that providence can cancel the laws of nature and interrupt

[72] *Christianity*, p. 107; *Christentums*, p. 199.
[73] *Christianity*, p. 105; *Christentums*, p. 195.
[74] *Christianity*, pp. 101f.; *Christentums*, p. 191.

the path of necessity, that "iron bond which inevitably binds effects to causes."[75]

All of this reflects the natural narcissism of the organism grounded in the structure of self-conscious desire. Faith is the confidence that these desires will be fulfilled. For Feuerbach faith is, by definition, the confidence that the generalizations about nature drawn by reason will not hinder the gods from answering human prayer. Hence, the believer is continually exhorted to suppress and distrust reason, to bring his/her deepest desires to God in prayer in the confidence that they will be heard and fulfilled. Faith is the trust that with the gods all things are possible, that wishes can become reality. The person

wishes to be immortal, therefore he *is* immortal; he *wishes* for the existence of a being who can *do everything which is impossible to Nature and reason*, therefore such a being exists; he wishes for a world which corresponds to the desires of the heart, a world of *unlimited subjectivity*, i.e., of unperturbed feeling, of uninterrupted bliss, while *nevertheless* there exists a world the opposite of that subjective one, and hence this world *must pass away*, – as necessarily pass away as God, or absolute subjectivity, must remain.[76]

Feuerbach knew that many Christian theologians saw the dangers in tying faith too tightly to the fulfillment of personal desire and, consequently, that they often emphasized the importance of prayer as a discipline through which believers learn to surrender their own wills to the mystery of the divine will. But this is why when Feuerbach later discovered Luther, a theologian who had not played much of a role in the first edition of *Christianity*, he felt that his insights into Christian faith had been vindicated. For Luther stressed the primacy of faith, and he regarded faith as that which enables the believer to accomplish anything he/she desires. He continually juxtaposed faith to reason, and he exhorted the believer to trust that whatever is against the welfare of humankind cannot be from God. Because God is omnipotent and loving, He wishes us to ask for everything that is useful to us. And He will give us everything for which we ask. He is, in fact, the being that by definition is "for us." As we believe, so does it happen. Feuerbach saw in Luther the confirmation of his own analysis of faith, and it is not surprising, therefore, that in his introductory essay to the paperback edition of *Christianity*, Karl Barth shrewdly noted that

[75] *Christianity*, p. 103; *Christentums*, p. 193.
[76] *Christianity*, p. 128; *Christentums*, pp. 230f.

"after Feuerbach, one may no longer repeat these things from Luther without some caution."[77]

So far, we have considered only one of the two "moments" of self-differentiation, the self-differentiation from nature and its necessities. But there is an equally profound desire that arises from the first "moment" of differentiation from other selves: the desire for the recognition and love of the other. It is in this context that Feuerbach, although a master of suspicion, most clearly reveals his sensitivity to the religious consciousness. He understands that religious faith is not only the desire to be free from the limitations of an indifferent nature; it is also the desire to be acknowledged and affirmed by another human being. Religious feeling, he argues, longs for sympathy and compassion, for a "being who has, if not an *anatomical*, yet a psychical *human heart*."[78] All religions, he argues, contain this desire, but it is Christianity that has brought it to its most intense expression in its central doctrine of the passion of Christ.

Christ is God *known personally*; Christ, therefore, is the blessed certainty that God *is* what the soul desires and needs him to be. God, as the object of prayer, is indeed already a human being, since he sympathizes with human misery, grants human wishes; but still he is not yet an object to the religious consciousness as a real man. Hence, only in Christ is the last wish of religion realized, the mystery of religious feeling solved: – solved however in the language of imagery proper to religion, for what God is in *essence*, that Christ is in actual *appearance*. So far the Christian religion may justly be called the absolute religion.[79]

In this "moment," prayer is not so much the articulation of a petitionary wish as it is the longing for communion with a personal god. In prayer, though not the routine prayers after meals or "the ritual of animal egoism" but the prayer that arises from despair and ends in rapture,

man addresses God with the word of intimate affection – *Thou*; he thus declares articulately that God is his *alter ego*; he confesses to God, as the being nearest to him, his most *secret* thoughts, his deepest wishes, which otherwise he shrinks from uttering. But he expresses these wishes in the confidence, *in the certainty* that they will be fulfilled. How could he apply to a being that had no ear for his complaints? Thus what is prayer but the *wish of the heart* expressed with *confidence in its fulfillment*?[80]

[77] Barth, "An Introductory Essay," in Feuerbach, *Christianity*, p. xxiii.
[78] Feuerbach, *Christianity*, p. 55; *Christentums*, p. 112.
[79] *Christianity*, pp. 144f.; *Christentums*, p. 256.
[80] *Christianity*, p. 122; *Christentums*, p. 221.

CAN THE TWO STRANDS BE DISENTANGLED?

If, in the spirit of rational reconstruction, one were to extract this naturalist-existentialist thread of argumentation from the Hegelian schema with which it is interwoven, it might be summarized in this fashion: Religion can best be defined as a type of anthropomorphism rooted in the structure of self-consciousness; more precisely, in the two-fold differentiation of the self from nature, on the one hand, and persons, on the other. This two-fold distinction creates the correlative desires to be free from nature and to gain recognition from other subjects. The gods satisfy both structural desires uniquely. They can set aside the limits of nature by performing miracles, and they can offer a recognition that transcends that which can be given by any finite person. The attempt to persuade or coerce the gods to alter the patterns of nature is the source of magic; the attempt to seek recognition and love leads to various spiritual forms of religion. Religion is a spectrum on which there is magic at one end and personal communion at the other.

This rational reconstruction of Feuerbach's argument, it might be claimed, not only is free from some of the difficulties inherent in the Hegelian paradigm but has certain virtues as well. One of them is that it makes possible a less confused account of the relationships among religions than Feuerbach's own account is able to offer.

As Feuerbach was later to acknowledge, his discussions of the non-Christian religions and of their relationship to Christianity are one of the least satisfactory aspects of his book. They are unsatisfactory not only because the discussions there are inadequate but because he appeared to waver between two conflicting views. On the one hand, he seemed to suggest that the various religions of the world represent the variety of self-images by means of which human beings have defined themselves throughout history. No one of these images can be said to be better or truer than any other; each is simply one of the inexhaustible possibilities of the species. On the other hand, there are passages in the book that seem to suggest that the history of religion is the history of a progressive development regarding the concept of human nature and that Christianity is the consummate or absolute religion.

In the first alternative, he noted that various cultures will project different kinds of deities because the cultures embrace different images of humanity and, consequently, different ideals. Some cultures objectify physical strength, others, sexuality, still others, moral virtue. The possibilities, in fact, are endless because, as Feuerbach noted, the possibilities of self-definition are unlimited. "The mystery of the inexhaustible fulness of the divine predicates is therefore nothing else than the mystery of human nature considered as an infinitely varied, infinitely modifiable, but consequently, phenomenal being."[81]

In the second alternative, however, Feuerbach does not seem to be entirely free from the Hegelian view that religion is the history of progress in self-knowledge and that Christianity, although a form of error, is the highest form of self-knowledge not only because it has grasped the predicates of essential being but also because its doctrinal structure embodies the Hegelian schema of objectification–alienation–reappropriation. Indeed, as we shall see in Chapter 2, he believed that the Christian doctrine of the Incarnation is a mythical expression of the final moment in this Hegelian dialectic. In this "orientalism," which embodies the insight that God is willing to empty Himself of his godhead on behalf of humanity, there is the latent truth that the highest object of worship is the species. The hidden meaning of the Incarnation, in short, is atheism. Christianity is the penultimate stage to full self-knowledge.

The naturalist-existentialist paradigm is able to avoid this confusion because it makes a distinction between what we might call the core projection, the bare projection of subjectivity as such, and the images and values that are laid over this core projection by various cultures and religions. Every religion projects, as it were, a heavenly Thou, but the characteristics and predicates which are then assigned to this Thou will be cultural constructions. We do not need to claim, as Feuerbach does, that there is a progression in religion and that Christianity represents the highest development.

This rational reconstruction, incidentally, has interesting affinities with a position once advanced by the anthropologist-philosopher Robin Horton.[82] Horton, like Feuerbach, defines religion as patterned interaction with superhuman beings, and he argues that this definition is superior to others because it not only meets the criterion of common sense but has social-scientific utility as well. The utility is that when religion is so defined, the variables that have been found useful in the

[81] *Christianity*, p. 23; *Christentums*, p. 60.
[82] Robin Horton, "A Definition of Religion, and its Uses," *Journal of the Royal Anthropological Institute*, 90 (1960), 201–226.

analysis of person-to-person relationships will also be found useful in the analysis of person-to-deity relationships. One might find, for example, that in religions these person-to-deity relationships run the gamut from manipulation (magic) to communion just as they do in personal relationships. Given this possibility, one might then ask such questions as these: Under what sort of social and cultural conditions does one type of religion tend to prevail in contrast to the other? Does, for example, the prevalence and growth of science in Western culture tend to erode both kinds of religion or only one of them? Would the answer to this question cast any light on the persistence of religion in highly rationalized cultures? Are there societies in which both types of religion exist side by side? If so, are there any social factors that can account for this? How are these cultures different from those in which one type predominates?

After describing examples of both types of religion, Horton then explores this question: whether the type of relationships envisaged in these examples can be correlated with the types of human relationships that are made possible and fostered by the social institutions in which these religions flourish. After conceding that it is very difficult to come to any conclusions about societies in which relationships of communion are highly valued because so little research has been done in this area, he suggests that rationalistic and Freudian critics of religion have rarely asked why it is that some people actually give up satisfying communal relationships with other people in favor of relationships with the gods. Horton proposes that perhaps the variations in religious relationship along the manipulative–communion spectrum might be connected with changes in the importance attributed to scientific thinking in a given culture. The rationalist naturally believes that as empirical science flourishes religion will wane. But this may only be true of manipulative religion, and it may overlook the interest in religion as communion, which is not affected by science. Indeed, as this advance continues it may be that cultures put a greater premium on the importance of the communal aspect.

Even if this sort of reconstruction of Feuerbach's self-differentiation hypothesis did prove to have certain virtues, it seems only fair, in conclusion, to pose the same question to it that we posed to the Freudian reconstruction; namely, whether Feuerbach could have advanced most of the arguments that were dear to him without the Hegelian scheme of objectification–alienation–reappropriation. Is not the basic strategy of his book determined by the assumption that "in the religious systole man propels his own nature from himself, he throws himself outward; in the religious diastole he receives the rejected nature into his heart again"?[83] His argument is not just that the gods arise out of the differentiation of the I from the Thou; it is that this objectified divine image alienates the individual from the species and, finally, that this alienation is overcome only by restoring the predicates that have been misattributed to God back to the species where they rightly belong. Religion is a form of self-knowledge.

One of the difficulties in giving a confident answer to this question is that so much that would be necessary to answer it remains an iceberg in this fascinating work. Nevertheless, from what can be "dug out," it seems probable that Feuerbach himself believed that these various threads were inextricably interwoven, that one could not extract one of them without unraveling the entire garment. Without the inversion of the Hegelian philosophy of Spirit and without the objectification of the species being, it is difficult to understand how he could have analyzed the Christian dogmas in the way that he did, especially those about God, the Trinity, and the Logos. Perhaps one might still have been able to preserve some notion of a creator, a providential deity, even miracles, without the Hegelian paradigm, but one could not have salvaged those analyses upon which Feuerbach put so much weight. Still, it was important to have distinguished some of the various threads; otherwise, it would have been unintelligible why this book still has the fascination it does for so many contemporary readers despite the arcane framework within which everything is set.

[83] Feuerbach, *Christianity*, p. 31; *Christentums*, p. 73.

CHAPTER 2

The interpretative strategy informing "The Essence of Christianity"

THE BASIC PRINCIPLES

In the previous chapter, I tried to give some sense of the complexity of Feuerbach's theory of projection in *The Essence of Christianity*. Although the central argument rests on an inversion of Hegel's philosophy of Spirit, as most commentators have observed, it also incorporates elements that are both original and un-Hegelian. In fact, the theory is woven together from many different threads of argumentation.

It is important to recognize this fact if one is to fully understand Feuerbach's actual interpretative procedure in *The Essence of Christianity*, his exegesis of specific Christian doctrines and practices. As I shall attempt to show in this chapter, he does not in every case simply and woodenly invert Hegel but frequently invokes imaginative principles of his own. It is also important to sort out the distinctive threads in this text because I should like to prepare the ground for my own later argument that the naturalist-existentialist motif, which was subordinate to the Hegelian paradigm in *Christianity*, surfaces to become the dominant motif in his later writings, in *Religion* and the *Lectures on the Essence of Religion*. Finally, it is important to isolate the various threads because only then are we in a position to deal with the accusation frequently made against Feuerbach that he was a reductionist.

The complexity – some would say the richness – of Feuerbach's hermeneutics is easily obscured if one takes too seriously his own too-catchy formula "theology is anthropology" or regards the inversion of the Hegelian principle alone as the single clue to his project. This formula is deceptive because it suggests that all he attempted was to demonstrate that Christian doctrines are mystified claims about human nature, and thus it fails to illuminate those aspects of the interpretation that have little to do with Hegel's phenomenology of Spirit, inverted or otherwise. As will become apparent below, Feuerbach was so concerned to do justice to what Christians have traditionally believed that his interpretation was often richer and more perceptive than his own explicit explanatory principles allow. He exhibited an extraordinary and sensitive grasp of the Christian theological and religious tradition, as Karl Barth has himself noted. "In his writings – at least in those on the Bible, the Church Fathers, and especially on Luther – his theological skill places him above most modern philosophers."[1]

It is a characteristic feature of theories of projection that they contain both explanatory and interpretative elements. This is also true of Feuerbach's theory, and because explanation and interpretation are so closely related it might prove useful to set the five most important of these explanatory principles before the reader in an abbreviated form before we turn directly to his exegesis.

1. The most important of them, of course, is Feuerbach's version of the three-fold Hegelian schema of self-knowledge: objectification–alienation–reappropriation. In Feuerbach's version of this schema, the self, over against another Thou, realizes that it is a member of a species. Fascinated and entranced by the perfections of the species, the self objectifies or externalizes them in the idea of a perfect being. But in contemplating and revering this alienated other, in religion, the self comes to realize that this other is its own being mystified. This is the "religious systole and diastole" of human life.

2. The theme of the objectification or externalization of the self, which is the first "moment" in this Hegelian schema, is given three slightly different formulations which Feuerbach took to be synonymous but which I have argued in the previous chapter are not:

a. The self objectifies its own consciousness or bare subjectivity and thus believes itself to be in relation to another Thou.
b. The self objectifies the essential attributes of consciousness which are said to be reason, will, and feeling.
c. The self objectifies its social nature, hence the doctrine of the Trinity.

3. A third explanatory principle to which Feuerbach appeals and which plays an important role in his hermeneutics is the imagination. It is the imagination which, under the pressure of feeling, ignores the

---

[1] Karl Barth, "An Introductory Essay," in *Christianity*, p. x.

reality principle and seizes upon the concept of the species and clothes it in the form of image, symbol, and myth.

4. A fourth explanatory principle that is invoked again and again is the omnipotence of feeling, which Feuerbach tends to equate with wishing, desire, and longing. It is in the service of feeling rather than reason that the imagination labors.

5. Finally, to these four explanatory principles we should add still another which, though not strictly explanatory, functions as a powerful interpretative tool in Feuerbach's hermeneutics. The assumption is that the principal aim of religion is to secure the welfare or felicity of humanity in general and the self in particular. It is this "felicity principle" together with the emphasis on feeling and the social nature of the self that gives such an existentialist flavor to Feuerbach's enterprise. He emphasized again and again that religion has its roots in anxiety before death, suffering, and the longing for happiness and for recognition by another. The important Christian doctrines speak to these anxieties and these longings; which is to say, they were meant "for us and for our salvation." "The essential standpoint of religion is the practical or subjective. The end of religion is the welfare, the salvation, the ultimate felicity of man."[2]

These five principles, although distinguishable, often overlap and reinforce one another. For example, it is the concept of the species that is said to be objectified in the three-fold Hegelian schema of objectification–alienation–reappropriation. And this concept of the species is then sometimes identified with consciousness, sometimes with the three predicates of reason, will, and feeling, and sometimes with the social nature of the self. So, too, the objectification of the concept of the species, as we shall see in the next chapter, is at the heart of the concept of alienation. In Feuerbach's view, the projection of the species concept in the idea of God deprives existing human beings of their own essential (species) possibilities. "To enrich God, man must become poor; that God may be all, man must be nothing."[3] Or again, the role of the imagination is necessarily linked to the objectification of the species because it is Feuerbach's view that it is the imagination which seizes upon the idea of the species and, ignoring reason, projects it under the pressure of wish and desire.

Although these five basic principles overlap, the first three of them tend to play a greater role in the determination of the content of

[2] Feuerbach, *Christianity*, p. 185; *Christentums*, p. 316.
[3] *Christianity*, p. 26; *Christentums*, p. 65.

Christian dogma such as the doctrine of God, the Trinity, and the Incarnation than do the last two (feeling and the felicity principle), which are most characteristically invoked when Feuerbach is discussing not doctrines as such but beliefs in providence, miracle, prayer, and immortality. This is an important distinction to make because the arguments concerning providence, miracle, prayer, and immortality are what strike the contemporary reader as the most powerful, and, on the surface at least, they do not seem to depend on the Hegelian schema of objectification–alienation–reappropriation, nor do they seem to involve the notion of an objectification of the species, especially when that objectification is linked to the three predicates of reason, will, and feeling.

Of these five principles we could say that the Hegelian schema of self-differentiation – objectification–alienation–reappropriation – is probably the most important because it not only constitutes the basic premise of the book but also dictates the interpretative strategy of the author and, hence, the form of the work. The strategy is, in effect, to lead the reader through the various "moments" of the Hegelian dialectical schema until the culminating insight of atheism is grasped. The first moment is explicated in the opening chapters, where it is shown how the various Christian dogmas can best be interpreted as the objectification of human nature. The second Hegelian "moment" is "alienation," and, hence, it is important for Feuerbach to show that Christian dogmas and doctrines fall into absurdity and contradiction when they are made the object of reflection by theologians. This negative critique is pursued in the second half of the book, in which most of the chapter titles begin with the words "The Contradiction in the doctrine of." The last "moment," reappropriation, is not exemplified in any single section but informs all of the discussion, especially the discussion of the doctrine of the Incarnation. The aim here is to enable the readers to reappropriate the latent truth from which they have been alienated by virtue of having transferred their own predicates to an external divine being. With this reappropriation, self-knowledge is achieved. The readers have restored to them their relinquished selves.

This last step is probably the most important so far as Feuerbach's own self-understanding as an author is concerned because he believed that religion held the key to the liberation of humanity, but not as religious people believed that it did. Consequently, Feuerbach wanted to lead his readers to retrace, as it were, the dialectical process of objectification, alienation, and appropriation which was embodied in the structure of Christian dogma itself. He thought that once these doctrines were "seen through" his readers would be brought to the reappropriation of their own essential nature, to atheism. It was important to him, then, that his readers see that this atheism was implicit in the Christian faith – indeed, in the central dogma of that faith, the doctrine of the Incarnation. They should understand that in this doctrine Christians themselves confess, albeit in a mystified form, that God has sacrificed Himself for the welfare of humanity, that "love had conquered God." Thus to understand this central doctrine is to acknowledge that human welfare is more important than the divine. And this realization, he felt, is the birth of atheism, for it must surely follow that "As God has renounced himself out of love, so we, out of love, should renounce God."[4] Religion, in short, is the detour, the *Umweg*, by means of which humanity comes to realize its own essential nature and worth.

Although this last "moment" is, of course, what renders the book outrageous and even offensive to many Christian readers, it also reveals the extent to which Feuerbach conceived his interpretative task to be therapeutic and not merely critical.[5] Like Nietzsche, he thought of himself as a physician of culture who diagnoses its spiritual diseases and prescribes the appropriate therapy. But unlike Nietzsche, who saw no truth at all at the core of Christianity but only resentment, Feuerbach's therapy was, like that of later psychoanalysts, to lead Christian believers patiently through the details and structure of their own collective dream. His strategy, unlike Nietzsche's, was not to demean or ridicule the dream but to "see through it," to change the way it had been customarily viewed. He thought this would be a liberating practice, one that even had a continuity with the aims of the old religion. By recognizing that it was really human nature that was recognized and celebrated in the worship of deity, human beings could come to estimate their own worth and dignity properly.

The Hegelian schema together with Feuerbach's own view of the primacy of the imagination and feeling yielded two closely related

---

[4] *Christianity*, p. 53; *Christentums*, p. 109.
[5] Marilyn Massey argues that this therapeutic aim is what accounts for the rhetorical language in the book which Engels criticized as "sickly sentimental." Feuerbach exposed cultural contradictions through parodies of the religious pieties of the middle class and of powerful, conservative Prussians. "Censorship and the Language," pp. 173–195.

methodological rules that are important to single out. The first of
these is that since religion is humanity's "earliest and indirect form of
self-knowledge," the most immediate and earliest expressions of the
religious consciousness should be taken as the most revelatory and
authentic. The second rule is that "the nearer religion stands to its
origin, the truer, the more genuine it is, the less is its true nature
disguised because in the origin of religion there is no *qualitative* or
essential distinction between God and man. And the religious man is
not shocked at this identification."[6]

These two rules, taken together, reflect Feuerbach's attempt to
reconcile the different postures that Hegel and Schleiermacher took
to religion, the two intellectual giants who represented the theological
alternatives of the time. With Hegel, Feuerbach agreed that religion
is distinguished from philosophy because its distinctive mode of
expression is image and symbol, in contrast to philosophy, which
employs abstract concepts and ideas. Also like Hegel, he believed
that the imagination is the "original organ of religion" because it is
the mediator between perception, which deals with the individual
and concrete, and abstraction, which deals with ideas. It grasps the
concrete but not yet as idea and, hence, it represents the concrete in
the form of the image. Thus the imagination seizes on the idea of the
species but presents it to the feelings in the image of a single
individual. It follows from this that "religion everywhere precedes
philosophy, as in the history of the race, so also in that of the
individual."[7]

With Schleiermacher, however, Feuerbach insisted that the
immediate utterances of the religious consciousness are revelatory of
feeling. Although both Hegel and Schleiermacher held that the
immediate utterances are imaginative and poetic in form, Hegel
thought that these utterances contained speculative truth, whereas
Schleiermacher believed that they were an expression of the religious
emotions of a specific historic community and did not convey
knowledge or, at least, not speculative knowledge.

Feuerbach attempted to have the best of both positions. With
Schleiermacher he held that religion was primarily a surrender to
what he called the omnipotence of feeling and not a rudimentary
form of speculative truth. But with Hegel he believed that what
arouses and sustains this feeling is the imagination's grasp of the idea

---

[6] Feuerbach, *Christianity*, p. 197; *Christentums*, pp. 335f.
[7] *Christianity*, p. 13; *Christentums*, p. 47.

of the species. Imagination presents this confused abstraction to the feelings, which are entranced and enthralled by it.

Both of these two beliefs converge to yield the interpretative principle that the investigator should regard religion as prior to theology, which is to be understood as the reflection on and the rationalizing of religion. This principle, taken by itself, could be understood in a relatively uncontroversial way, as simply articulating a position that many Christian theologians have assumed in the past; namely, that theology is "faith seeking understanding." But the principle becomes controversial in Feuerbach's hands when it is combined with his second methodological rule: the nearer religion stands to its origin the less its true anthropomorphic nature is disguised. This rule means that the religious interpreter should regard the earliest and most naïve utterances of the believer, however supernaturalistic, as the key to the true nature of that religion. All later intellectual reflection (theology) is a rationalization and falsification of that original naïvete. Naïve religion longs for a personal god who can intervene in nature, make the sun stand still, defeat enemies, and deliver the believer from death. Consequently, providence and miracle are of the essence of religious faith and not merely accidental to it. It is only the theologian who, embarrassed by this crude supernaturalism, attempts to eliminate this anthropomorphism by bringing faith in conformity with reason.

Most Christian theologians, especially liberal Protestants, have rejected this view. They have argued that it presents theologians with a false and intolerable dilemma: either fundamentalism or atheism. If the theologians attempt in any way to eliminate the anthropomorphism and supernaturalism of the religion, then they are accused of not dealing with "real religion." If, on the other hand, they accept anthropomorphism, they are ridiculed as obscurantists. Christian and Jewish theologians have used a number of strategies to avoid this "no-win" situation. They have argued that the anthropomorphic utterances are symbolic and analogical; or they have tried, as classical liberal Protestantism has done, to distinguish between a timeless and valid religious "kernel," which is thought to be both religiously meaningful and intellectually acceptable, and a mythological "husk," in which the timeless religious message is imbedded but which can be shucked off. Or, more recently, Protestant theologians have sought to "demythologize" the Christian message: that is, to argue that mythological language itself expresses a way of understanding oneself in the world that is not itself supernaturalistic and which can be appropriated.

This issue is not easily resolved, in favor of either Feuerbach or the theologians. Indeed, one might argue that the history of both Christianity and Judaism since the Enlightenment has been a series of unstable attempts to do so. To the degree that traditionalists have attempted to preserve the supernaturalistic and anthropomorphic origins of the faith, liberals have rejected it as intellectually untenable. But to the degree that liberals and demythologizers have sought to make the faith compatible with our modern conception of the world, they seem to have eliminated just those elements that constitute its appeal to the ordinary, unsophisticated person.

Feuerbach himself believed that the liberal Christianity of his time had, in fact, emasculated traditional Christianity and, hence, constituted a decisive break with its supernaturalistic origins. As Nietzsche was later to do, he poured his scorn and sarcasm on that which passed for Christian theology in his own time.

Religion has disappeared, and for it has been substituted, even among Protestants, the *appearance* of religion – the Church – in order at least that "the faith" may be imparted to the ignorant and indiscriminating multitude . . . the faith of the modern world is only an ostensible faith, a faith which does not believe what it fancies that it believes, and is only an undecided, pusillanimous unbelief. . . Hence the simulated religious indignation of the present age, the age of shows and illusion, concerning my analysis."[8]

EXAMPLE I: THE DOCTRINE OF THE TRINITY

By skillfully weaving together the various explanatory themes and motifs Feuerbach was able to bring a complex set of interpretative principles to bear on the entire range of Christian doctrine and belief. His aim was three-fold: (a) to account for the form and content of the doctrine; (b) to exhibit the intellectual tensions and contradictions that result when a doctrine becomes a matter of theological reflection; and (c) to exhibit what he called "the characteristic illusion of the religious consciousness," the illusion that attributes everything to God and nothing to human nature but is unaware that it is, in fact, human nature which determines what and how God can work.

The clearest example of this illusion is the doctrine of revelation. Christians claim that the natural mind can know nothing about God

---

[8] *Christianity*, p. xxxix; *Christentums*, pp. 20f.

and, consequently, that God must reveal everything. Nevertheless, what God reveals must necessarily be made comprehensible to human nature. Consequently, it turns out, He cannot reveal what He wishes, but only what humans can comprehend. Thus, between the divine revelation and so-called human reason there is no more than an illusory distinction because the contents of divine revelation, it appears, do not proceed from "God as God," but from God *as determined by human reason*, [and] *human wants*.[9]

In order to illustrate the manner in which Feuerbach often invoked several principles when treating such a relatively simple example of projection as the doctrine of God, let us consider this doctrine and its distinctively Christian version, the doctrine of the Trinity. As was usually the case when interpreting a dogma, in contrast to a practical religious belief, he relied primarily on the Hegelian notion of objectification – the first "moment" in the schema – and the concept of the species.

As we have already seen in the previous chapter, when Feuerbach first treated the doctrine of God he simply explained it as the objectification of the three human faculties, of reason, will, and feeling (*Empfindung*), the essential predicates of the species. The so-called metaphysical, nonanthropomorphic attributes – self-subsistence, unlimitedness, self-sufficiency, absolute unity, infinitude, omniscience, and necessary being – were regarded as objectifications of the reason, just as the moral attributes were derived from the will and love from the feelings. The Christian doctrine of God, however, is not a simple exemplification of monotheism but is distinctive in that it posits three "persons" in the godhead, a Trinity. Thus when in Chapter 6, "The Mystery of the Trinity and the Mother of God," Feuerbach turned to explaining the distinctiveness of this Christian form of monotheism, it is interesting that he did not rely heavily upon the objectification of the predicates of the species, as one might have expected, but, first, on the nature of self-consciousness itself and then on its social structure.

He began by observing that the first thing an interpreter might expect to confront when approaching the doctrine of the Trinity is some element that represents the objectification of self-consciousness itself. Because human beings cannot conceive of themselves as lacking consciousness, and because this self-consciousness is absolute for

---

[9] *Christianity*, p. 207; *Christentums*, pp. 351f.

them, they cannot conceive of God without it. And this is, in fact, what one finds. "God thinks, God loves; and, moreover, he thinks, he loves himself; the object thought, known, loved, is God himself. The objectivity of self-consciousness is the first thing we meet with in the Trinity."[10]

But this explanation, depending as it does upon the objectification of consciousness alone, would seem to explain only monotheism, not Trinitarianism. It generates only a solitary God, an abstract consciousness. How, then, can it explain the doctrine of the Trinity? To understand how this doctrine emerged, Feuerbach invoked the principle that religion mirrors concrete and lived human relationships. And in concrete and lived human relationships self-consciousness always arises in relationship to other selves. The I is always found together with a Thou. Consequently, just as the human "I" cannot exist in solitude, neither can it worship a deity existing in solitude. Thus, the religious mind projects first the abstract and absolute being of God but then immediately posits along with it an "other," a Thou, with whom this God is in relation. This practical duality is then objectified in the images of a divine Father and a Son. The solitary and generative I is the Father, and the Thou is a Son.

God the Father is *I*, God the Son *Thou*. The *I* is understanding, the *Thou* love. But love with understanding and understanding with love is mind, and mind is the totality of man as such – the total man.[11]

But even this duality does not fully express the human need for a fuller communal relationship between the I and the Thou. Since only a *"Participated life is alone true, self-satisfying divine life,"* the differentiation of the I from the Thou generates a third person, the Holy Spirit, which is the "love of the two divine Persons towards each other; it is the unity of the Son and the Father, the idea of community, strangely enough regarded in its turn as a special personal being."[12]

That this Holy Spirit primarily designates a relationship between two concrete images of persons explains, Feuerbach perceptively suggested, why the concept of the Holy Spirit has always been so vague and undifferentiated in the history of Christianity; why, in the practical life of Christians, the nature of God has primarily been seen

[10] *Christianity*, p. 65; *Christentums*, p. 131.
[11] *Christianity*, p. 67; *Christentums*, p. 136. In the third edition Feuerbach substituted *Geist* for *Verstand* in this quotation.
[12] *Christianity*, p. 67; *Christentums*, p. 137.

as a duality and not a Trinity.[13] Given this fact, Feuerbach continued, it should not be surprising why in Roman Catholicism the religious imagination has feminized this vague relation and articulated it in the form of a divine mother. "Where the Son is, the Mother cannot be absent; the Son is the only-begotten of the Father, but the Mother is the concomitant of the Son."[14] Protestants, to be sure, have rejected this feminization of the deity in an effort to minimize the obvious anthropomorphism which is at work, but for that same reason, Feuerbach argued, Protestantism should have been consistent and courageous enough to give up the Father and Son duality, which is only a half-way house, so to speak. Actually, the triune deity of the Catholic faith meets a profound and heart-felt necessity in a religion that also elevates the anchorite, the monk, and the nun.

The triune God has a *substantial* meaning only where there is an abstraction from the *substance* of real life. The more *empty life* is, the *fuller*, the more concrete is *God*. The impoverishing of the real world and the enriching of God is one act . . . God springs out of the *feeling of a want*; what man *is in need of*, whether this be a definite and therefore conscious, or an unconscious need, – that is *God*. Thus the disconsolate feeling of a void, of loneliness, needed a God in whom there is *society*, a union of beings fervently loving each other.[15]

Feuerbach's exegesis of the doctrine of the Trinity illustrates how much more complicated his interpretative practice is than the mere formula "theology is anthropology" would lead us to expect. The idea of God is regarded, first, as an objectification of self-consciousness, then of the three faculties, then of the social structure of concrete human life, and this social structure then receives the greatest emphasis because of the principle that religion deals with practical life. Furthermore, at the end of the argument he invokes still another principle: that religious doctrines reflect some impoverishment of life, some need.

As I have argued in the previous chapter, to objectify the three faculties of consciousness – intellect, will, and feeling – is not the same thing as to objectify subjectivity as such, and it is not surprising, therefore, that we can see a certain tension between Feuerbach's treatment of the idea of God as subject, on the one hand, and his

---

[13] This is the conclusion Cyril Charles Ritchardson reached in his *The Doctrine of the Trinity* (New York: Abingdon Press, 1958).
[14] Feuerbach, *Christianity*, p. 71; *Christentums*, p. 145.
[15] *Christianity*, p. 73; *Christentums*, pp. 148f.

treatment of the Trinity, on the other. In the early chapters, for example, the idea of God was treated as if it were an objectification of the three human faculties of reason, will, and feeling (*Empfindung*). The reader might have expected, then, that Feuerbach would correlate each of these species predicates with the three persons of the Trinity. Presumably the Father would be correlated with the faculty of reason, the Son with the will, and the Holy Spirit with feeling.

Feuerbach did, in fact, begin to make such a correlation. He wrote that "Man's consciousness of himself in his *totality* is the consciousness of the Trinity. The Trinity knits together the qualities or power which were before regarded separately into unity, and thereby reduces the universal being of the understanding, i.e., God as God, to a special being, a special faculty."[16] But he had barely finished writing the first two paragraphs of the chapter devoted to the Trinity when he abandoned the pursuit of this correlation and shifted the discussion to how the duality of the I–Thou relationship is decisive for the emergence of the doctrine of the Trinity.

The reason he cannot convincingly pursue the original line of argument will be obvious to anyone familiar with the long history of doctrinal struggles surrounding the doctrine of the Trinity. Although it would seem to be a relatively simple matter to correlate the human faculties of intellect, will, and feeling with the divine attributes of omniscience, justice, and love, the fact is that the Christian doctrinal tradition has not correlated the persons with these predicates in this way. Further, if the reason were to be correlated with the Father and feeling with the Son, as Feuerbach first suggested, then the Holy Spirit would have to be linked with the will. But to do this would be disastrous for the Christian dogma.

Not only would Feuerbach's original pattern of exegesis not have explained the traditional doctrine of the Trinity; it would also have created intolerable problems for his own interpretation of the doctrine of creation through the Logos. How can the "person" of the Father, for example, be equated solely with the faculty of reason when the Logos, the second "person," is the active agent in creation, that is, the will? As if sensing that his original parallelism breaks down, Feuerbach abandoned the attempt to correlate the attributes of God with the various predicates of the species and turned instead to the concrete human I–Thou relationship, correlating the I with the

---

[16] *Christianity*, p. 65; *Christentums*, p. 131.

Father, the Thou with the Son, and the Holy Spirit with the love between them.

This abandonment of the attempt to correlate the Trinity with the three "faculties" of consciousness is only one of the interesting examples in which Feuerbach himself in effect makes the distinction I previously made between asserting (a) that God is an objectification of the perfections of the species and (b) that God is the objectification of some concrete human situation; in this case, the I–Thou relationship. The two claims are by no means synonymous.

But this is not the only interpretative problem that arises by virtue of his claiming that the Trinity is an objectification of the social structure of the self. If the doctrine of the Trinity follows from the practical relationship between the I and the Thou, and this is a universal structure of human existence, why is it that the doctrine of the Trinity is unique to Christianity? Why is the objectification of this basic structure of human nature not also reflected in all of the monotheistic religions? Feuerbach never addressed or attempted to answer this question. Indeed, he would have been unable to do so as long as he insisted that religion is the projection of the predicates of the species rather than, more minimally, that the gods arise out of the differentiation of the self from others from whom they then seek recognition.

EXAMPLE 2: THE DOCTRINE OF THE LOGOS

The interpretation of the doctrine of the Trinity is one of the least complicated examples of Feuerbach's interpretative procedure, combining as it does only the objectification thesis and the species motif. A much more complicated and less predictable exegesis of a Christian doctrine occurs in the chapter devoted to "The Mystery of the Logos and the Divine Image." This exegesis is less predictable because it is governed by Feuerbach's highly technical theory of the imagination, a theory upon which his views not only changed over the years but which is never spelled out or defended in this work. Moreover, this theory was central to Feuerbach's epistemology and, hence, his philosophy of religion. It plays a central role in his views on the relationship of the imagination to feeling, on the one hand, and to thought, on the other. Consequently, the lay reader who is not privy to the theory will not only be puzzled by the exegesis but find it unconvincing.

The Logos doctrine with which Feuerbach was concerned arose in the second and third centuries when the apologetic theologians of the Christian Church turned to Greek philosophy as an aid in articulating the theological relationship between God and Christ. Indeed, the doctrine probably represents the synthesis of several more ancient strains of thought: the Greek idea of the divine mind (*Nous*) which informs all created things; the Jewish conception of the preexistent Wisdom that contains the archetype of the Law; and the Near Eastern idea of a preexistent heavenly man who represents the embodiment of all human perfection. In its Christian form, the Logos was taken to be the preexistent mind or reason, the second "hypostasis" (which Latin theologians translated as "person") of the incomprehensible divine source (*Monas*) from which it issues. This Logos was then said to be the perfect expression or mirror of the source (the Father). The Logos is the image, the Son, the Word – all these metaphors were used – and it is the means by which the truth has been revealed to human creatures from Moses to Plato. This eternal Logos is, of course, believed by Christians to have been incarnate in the man Jesus of Nazareth, the Word made flesh.

Because the Logos is, in principle, derived from the divine Source – the Source (Father) cannot be said to be derived from the Logos – furious debates raged within the Early Church over whether the Logos was in some sense inferior to the Source (Father) or was coequal to it, a debate that had, in turn, enormous consequences for the issue whether Jesus was fully divine or an intermediate and inferior being. These debates persisted over decades, even centuries, but were finally resolved with the orthodox formula that the Second Person of the Trinity, the Logos, was not only "like" the Father (*homoiousia*), as the Arians proposed, but was of the same essential nature (*homoousia*) with the Father, as Athanasius argued. Although these debates now seem to be artificial and hair-splitting, they were extremely important theologically because, as Feuerbach perceptively noted, nothing less was at stake than the status of the image of the Second Person as both divine and fully human.

It is not surprising, then, that both Christian piety and doctrine concentrate their interest on this Second Person of the Trinity. Piety, because "The *real* God of any religion is the *so-called Mediator*, because he alone is the *immediate* object of religion";[17] doctrine, because the

---

[17] *Christianity*, p. 74; *Christentums*, p. 150.

Second Person of the Trinity, in contrast to the remote and abstract Father, is so obviously the embodiment of love, the corollary of the faculty of feeling (*Empfindung*).

It is a basic principle of Feuerbach's view of human nature that the human creature is primarily a sensuous, emotional creature and, therefore, that it is more entranced by dramatic images than by abstract ideas. The imagination (*Phantasie*) is the organ that works in combination with the feelings to satisfy this need for images. Since religion basically springs out of feeling, it is not surprising that it should, in general, traffic in images, and in the case of Christianity, the image of the Second Person as a son.

It is important to understand that Feuerbach does not merely claim here that the Son meets the human need to think in terms of images. Rather, he claims that the Son is itself an image and, further, that this image is the objectification of the human faculty of the imagination. It is not just that human beings find it more satisfying to symbolize the mysterious being of God as a father; it is that the imagination is itself projected or made objective. It is not just that the religious mind needs to transform the abstract being of the reason into an object of sense and imagination; it is that this image must itself be regarded as divine.

And it is in fact no devised, no arbitrary image; for it expresses the necessity of the imagination, the necessity of affirming the imagination as a divine power. The Son is the reflected splendor of the imagination, the image dearest to the heart; but for the very reason that he is only an object of the imagination, he is only the nature of the imagination made objective (*das gegenständlich Wesen der Phantasie*).[18]

Feuerbach was aware that just as theologians have wanted to distinguish between the deity-in-itself and the predicates that have been applied to this deity, so also they have attempted to distinguish between the Son as a metaphysical reality and the image of the Son. But just as the former move is indefensible, so is the latter. He argued that it is the image itself that is important for the religious consciousness; and in a flurry of rhetoric he defended image worship, even the worship of images of the saints, because they "are only the optical multicopies of one and the same image."

If God loves his Image *as himself*, why should not I also love the *Image* of God *as* I love *God himself*? If the Image of God is God himself, why should not the

18 *Christianity*, p. 75; *Christentums*, p. 154.

image of the saint be the saint himself? If it is no superstition to believe that the image which God makes of himself is no image, no mere conception . . . why should it be a superstition to believe that the image of the saint is the sensitive substance of the saint?[19]

The second half of the chapter on the Logos doctrine deals with a related image, the Word of God. A word, Feuerbach claimed, is really nothing but an abstract image, or, one might say, an imagined thought, and hence is also a product of the imagination. Thought, too, expresses itself only in images and words, and the power of words is the power of the imagination. Given this power of words, it is not surprising that the ancients believed the word to be a "mysterious, magically powerful being," a pale echo of which exists in the way modern people are bewitched by words and speech.

In this way, Feuerbach then connected the objectification of the imagination with the objectification of the Word, especially as it occurs, first, in the Biblical tradition, where the Word is said to make the blind see, the lame walk, and the dead return to life, and, second, in the Lutheran tradition, where "God reveals himself to us as the Speaker."

As we can conceive nothing else as a Divine Being than the Rational which we think, the Good which we love, the Beautiful which we perceive; so we know no higher spiritually operative power and expression of power than the power of the Word. *God is the sum of all reality.* All that man feels or knows as a reality he must place in God or regard as God. Religion must therefore be conscious of the power of the word as a divine power. The *Word of God* is the *divinity* of the word, as it becomes an object to man within the sphere of religion, – the true nature of the human word.[20]

In this interpretation of the doctrine of the Logos, we can see that Feuerbach has combined the first "moment" of the Hegelian schema, objectification, with the third principle, the importance of the imagination. Once again, it should be observed, he does not try to interpret the doctrine as an objectification of some species predicate, nor does he invoke what I have called the "felicity principle," the "pro me" motif. In fact, it is because he does not utilize the notion of the species predicates that certain questions arise about his procedure.

The first of these questions concerns how we are to understand the relationship of the imagination to the other three faculties of the

---

[19] *Christianity,* p. 77; *Christentums,* p. 157.
[20] *Christianity,* p. 79; *Christentums,* p. 161.

reason, will, and feeling that supposedly comprise the three essential predicates of the "species." Is the imagination, for example, still a fourth faculty alongside of reason, will, and feeling? If so, how are we then to understand the derivation of the idea of God in the first few chapters because this depended so heavily upon the three-fold distinctions of reason, will, and feeling? What happens to this earlier argument if there is now introduced another essential power, the imagination, which, when objectified, produces its own dynamism in the interpretation of the doctrine of God? Why is the Christian deity triune rather than quadripartite?

This question raises another. Even were we to grant that the imagination is an objectified faculty alongside of reason, will, and feeling, why is it that the other two monotheistic religions, Judaism and Islam, have not produced a deity in whom images play equally important roles? There is in the Jewish tradition, for example, the notion of Sophia or Wisdom that has, in some respects, an ontological status similar to that of the Logos in the Christian tradition. Why, then, does Trinitarianism not also arise here? Or, if not Trinitarianism, why is it that this Sophia does not take on the same characteristics that attach to the Logos by virtue of the objectification of the imagination? How does Feuerbach explain this?

Since Feuerbach did not provide any explicit and detailed account of the relation of the imagination to the three predicates of the species, it is difficult to know how he would have responded to these questions had they been put to him. But one possible line of response consistent with his position immediately suggests itself. Following Hegel's philosophy of Spirit, why not argue that in the act whereby God first thinks Himself He also necessarily generates the Logos (the structure of all things) and, hence, the world and all of its possibilities? The imagination, then, would be the Logos in the form of a concrete image, the Second Person of the Trinity. There need not be four persons corresponding to four faculties, but only three persons, since the imagination is the image of the Son. So conceived, it is the organ that mediates between the abstract and the concrete, between idea and perception.

At any rate, it seems clear from these discussions of the doctrines of the Trinity and the Logos that Feuerbach relied less on the principle of the objectification of the predicates of the species – reason, will, and feeling – than he did on the social nature of the self, the necessity of an I having a Thou, and the role of the imagination. And to the degree that this is the case, it also seems clear that when he turned to the central dogmas of Christianity, the objectification of the species did not always play a central role. This is, I believe, an important observation because it suggests that even though he thought all of his various versions of the objectification principle were synonymous, it turns out that in practice, he implicitly concedes that they are not.

THE FELICITY PRINCIPLE

If one were to compare Feuerbach's various hermeneutic principles with a set of workman's tools, then one would observe that his use of them, like the workman's, was selective – utilizing first this one to perform a certain interpretative task, and then that one to perform a different exegetical chore. When interpreting Christian dogma – God, the Trinity, the Logos – he was most apt to depend upon the objectification thesis. When explaining the symbolic form of religious expressions or the way in which the reason has been tricked, he appealed to the role of the imagination. But when treating those beliefs and practices that are the heart and soul of ordinary religious piety, he almost always appealed to the priority of feelings and, especially, to the felicity principle. And since, unlike Hegel, he was primarily concerned with the existential, in contrast to the theoretical, function of religion, it is not surprising that this principle was the tool for which he reached again and again. He believed that the essential standpoint of religion, its primary goal or end (*Zweck*), is the well-being, the salvation, of humankind, and, consequently, it was his aim to demonstrate this.

Although he believed that this felicity principle underlies all religion, he thought it had achieved its most intense form in Christianity, where the whole of creation culminates in the creation of humanity. In Christianity, nature itself is subordinated to human destiny and God even sacrifices his own Son in order to save humanity from the consequences of sin. This "utilism" in Christianity has, in turn, its source in its parent religion, Judaism, in which the most fundamental doctrine was that of creation out of nothing. Judaism was from the beginning, Feuerbach argued, dominated by the practical in contrast to the aesthetic or theoretical standpoint. Whereas some cultures tend to think of nature as an end in itself or, as in Greece, an object of theoretical reflection, Judaism made the world of nature the vassal of its self-interest. The world was thought to be created as an instrument of its own will and pleasure, and "Nature was a mere means towards achieving the end of egoism, a mere object of Will."[21]

For those interested, as I am, in the question whether any or some of Feuerbach's hermeneutical principles can be abstracted from the "outdated nonsense" concerning the objectification of the species idea, the felicity principle, of course, offers itself as a prime candidate. For by appealing to it, one can make sense of those driving existential issues – the longing for recognition and need to trust in a providential order – that find expression in the ideas of God and Christ but which do not require the Hegelian schema of objectification, alienation, and reappropriation. It is not surprising, then, that contemporary readers will find those chapters in which Feuerbach appeals to the felicity principle to be the most convincing in the book.

Before turning to his interpretation of these religious beliefs, however, it seems important to pause momentarily and consider his derogatory comments about Judaism, that unlike Greek religion it had made nature into a vassal of its own self-interest and egoism. From the standpoint of the late twentieth century, these passages now make painful reading because they seem to embody those characteristic anti-Judaic prejudices of mid-nineteenth-century Germany that were to prove so disastrous in the twentieth. Even Marx Wartofsky, in his otherwise extremely charitable book, has noted that they are similar in character, language, and metaphor to Karl Marx's "On the Jewish Question," and he does not hesitate to refer to Feuerbach's "anti-Semitism."[22]

There is no point in denying that even the most important Protestant theologians and philosophers in Germany, such as Schleiermacher and Hegel, regarded Judaism at best as a religion inferior to Christianity.[23] But to apply the label "anti-Semitism" to these remarks of Feuerbach, in my opinion, is very misleading. In the first place, his remarks, unlike Marx's, were not directed at a "race"

---

[21] *Christianity*, p. 115; *Christentums*, pp. 211f.

[22] Wartofsky, *Feuerbach*, p. 319.

[23] Although many of Schleiermacher's dearest friends in Berlin were Jews, he could write in the fifth of his famous speeches that Judaism "is long since dead." See his *On Religion: Speeches to the Cultured among its Despisers*, trans. John Oman (New York: Harper, 1958), p. 238. So, too, in Hegel's early writings, the figure of Abraham was the figure of a person deeply alienated from nature. See G. W. F. Hegel, *Early Theological Writings*, trans. T. M. Knox, with intro. and fragments trans. Richard Kroner (Philadelphia: University of Pennsylvania Press, 1971), pp. 182–190. For a nuanced view of Schleiermacher's views on Judaism see Joseph W. Pickle, "Schleiermacher on Judaism," *The Journal of Religion*, 60, 2 (1980), 115–137.

or ethnic group but at a religion, and second, unlike Schleiermacher or Hegel, he was not making an invidious comparison of Judaism with Christianity but, on the contrary, was making the point, quite unrepresentative of the time, that Christianity as a religion has simply radicalized and individualized the egoism already present in Judaism.

> Israel is the historical definition of the specific nature of the religious consciousness, save only that here this consciousness was circumscribed by the limits of a particular, a national interest. Hence, we need only let these limits fall, and we have the Christian religion. Judaism *is worldly Christianity*; Christianity, *spiritual Judaism*. The Christian religion is the Jewish religion purified from national egoism.[24]

The point underlying Feuerbach's analysis of both Christianity and Judaism is that there exists a deep and disturbing conceptual relationship among the doctrines of creation *ex nihilo*, providence, miracles, prayer, and faith. The link that binds them all is that the aim of creation itself is the well-being of the human species in general and the blessed survival of the individual in particular. Judaism is singled out because of its doctrine of creation out of nothing. This doctrine, Feuerbach argued, asserts that the world of nature has been created by an arbitrary act of the will and, hence, has no being in its own right. The significance of nature lies solely in its utility for human beings. It is not conceived as a being with its own integrity, a "mother" or a matrix out of which human life emerges, but as an arbitrary creation of a transcendent being who is primarily concerned with a specific tribal community, in the case of Judaism, or with individuals, in the case of Christianity. In both cases, nature has no intrinsic values but is simply the backdrop against which the drama of the divine–human relationship is being played out, a setting in which human history occurs.

We need not consider this criticism of Judaism to be anti-Semitic any more than we consider the complaint that the Christian attitude towards nature has been disastrous for the environment to be anti-Christian. The complaint has often been made by Christian theologians themselves. In this connection, incidentally, Feuerbach had some very interesting things to say about Israel's condemnation of idolatry, the worship of natural objects. This idolatry, Feuerbach argued, is basically the worship of nature in a naïve mode just as monotheism is the worship of the human spirit in a naïve mode. When

---

[24] Feuerbach, *Christianity*, p. 120; *Christentums*, pp. 217f.

the Hebrews thus raised themselves above the worship of idols to the worship of the creator, they were, in effect, turning their backs on a type of piety that contains within it the seeds of an incipient theoretic and aesthetic contemplation of nature, a piety that stands in contrast to the incipient narcissism of anthropomorphic religion. In embracing the doctrine of creation, then, Jews and Christians both embrace the purely practical or egoistic point of view.

But let us return to our main concern – Feuerbach's employment of the felicity principle to interpret the anthropocentrism of religion as well as its corollaries: the belief in providence, miracles, prayer, and immortality. We have already touched upon the doctrine of providence in the previous chapter, but it is important to stress here that Feuerbach believed that this doctrine expresses the conviction that everything in the universe is intended for the well-being of humanity in general and the individual in particular. This conviction, he argued, is implicit in any view that puts such a premium on what he calls "personalism" or "subjectivity." For personalism arises, in the nature of the case, out of the differentiation of consciousness from nature. "Personalism *isolates, separates,* him from Nature; converts him from a part into the *whole,* into an *absolute* being [*Wesen*] *for himself.*"[25] But when this self-differentiation is linked with the doctrine of creation *ex nihilo,* then this subjectivity is made absolute and there arises an incipient hostility to nature, as can be seen in Christianity's hostility to pantheism.

Thus the creation of the world expresses nothing else than subjectivity, assuring itself of its own reality and infinity through the consciousness that the world is *created,* is a *product of will,* i.e., a *dependent, powerless, unsubstantial existence.*[26]

The Christian depreciation of nature is reflected in its attitude towards the realm of intermediary or secondary causes. Since the felicity of human beings is, from the religious point of view, dependent upon an immediate relation with the creator, the world of nature is at best of no significance, destined to fall away in the after life, and, at worse, a barrier, because it is the realm of necessity resistant to the individual's wishes. Consequently, for the Christian, everything that effects the subjective feelings, whether good or evil, comes not from nature but from an external power; either from the creator or from a

---

[25] *Christianity,* p. 107; *Christentums,* p. 199 (my translation).
[26] *Christianity,* p. 109; *Christentums,* p. 202.

malevolent power. Inspiration and spiritual ecstasy are the "work of the Holy Spirit," but temptations and evil inclinations are from the Devil.

Man is good or wicked by no means through himself, his own power, his will; but through that complete synthesis of hidden and evident determinations of things which, because they rest on no evident necessity, we ascribe to the power of "*chance* . . . " Divine grace is the power of chance beclouded with additional mystery.[27]

Because the religious ideal is an unmediated relationship to the personal Spirit that stands hidden and behind the creation, the nexus of intermediate natural causes is regarded as a hindrance to that relationship, as something that will pass away in the life to come. This attitude towards nature comes to clearest expression in the close conceptual relationships that exist among faith, prayer, and belief in miracles. Since faith is the conviction that the omnipotent creator's deepest intention is the happiness of the believer, it also holds that God can set aside the necessities of nature in order to secure that for which the believer prays. Thus the ordinary believer comes to regard the belief in the possibility of miracles as a test of true faith in the power of the creator; indeed, in the existence of a creator at all.

The natural expression of this faith is the practice of prayer, because in it believers turn directly to God and express the deepest wishes and desires of their hearts. Believers do not pray for spiritual gifts alone but for those things that seemingly lie within the power of nature, a power which it is the very object of prayer to overcome.[28] Faith is the conviction that God will answer these prayers, that He will fulfill these deepest desires and wishes. Hence, the believer is exhorted to believe that prayer itself has the power to "move mountains," to overcome any obstacle in nature.

Thus God is to him the *immediate* cause, the fulfillment of prayer, the power which realizes prayer. But an immediate act of God is a miracle; hence miracle is essential to the religious view. Religion explains everything *miraculously*.[29]

As was pointed out in the previous chapter, Feuerbach argued that prayer not only is a heartfelt plea for the creator to intervene in the order of secondary causes but also expresses the "unconditional trust

[27] *Christianity*, pp. 187f.; *Christentums*, p. 320.
[28] *Christianity*, chap. xiii; *Christentums*, pp. 226–240.
[29] *Christianity*, p. 194; *Christentums*, pp. 329f.

of the heart, untroubled by all thought of compulsive need."[30] It is an expression of the faith that "the almighty, infinite nature of the Father of men is a *sympathetic, tender, loving nature*, and that thus the dearest, most sacred emotions of man are divine realities."[31] Religion, in short, is not "utilism" in the crudest sense but at bottom the longing for a sense of one's own dignity and worth, an assurance that the isolated self is an object of the creator's love.

This assurance is imparted to Christians in and through a series of related doctrines: that God is person, that God suffers, but, above all, that God has descended to earth in Jesus Christ. The figure of Jesus Christ is the confidence that "I am thought by God," that God not only is as the soul desires and needs Him to be but will grant that wish which above all motivates all human beings, the wish not to die. Christ is "the last wish of religion realized, the mystery of religious feeling solved: – solved however in the language of imagery proper to religion, for what God is *in essence*, that Christ is in actual *appearance*."[32] This wish not to die, which Feuerbach thought was originally identical with the natural instinct of self-preservation, has become compounded in human beings with self-consciousness, the distinction of the individual from the species. The individual, suffering the vicissitudes of finitude, longs for a better life after death. Religious faith does not merely represent this longing but has as its content the certainty that this wish will be realized. Since reason cannot produce this certainty, faith requires a practical demonstration.

This can only be given to me by the fact of a dead person, whose death has been previously certified, rising again from the grave; and he must be no indifferent person, but, on the contrary, the type and representative of all others, so that his resurrection also may be the type, the guarantee of theirs.[33]

The Christian doctrine of the Incarnation thus proves to be the central doctrine of Christianity not only for the Hegelian reasons given earlier but because this doctrine guarantees the power of God to set aside the necessities of nature. It is also the deepest confirmation of the felicity principle. It conveys certitude to the deepest wish of humankind to enjoy a life of bliss forever. Thus, the Second Person of the Trinity is, in fact, "the sole, *true, first* person in religion."[34] It

---

[30] *Christianity*, p. 124; *Christentums*, p. 224.
[31] *Christianity*, p. 124; *Christentums*, p. 224.
[32] *Christianity*, p. 145; *Christentums*, p. 256.
[33] *Christianity*, p. 135; *Christentums*, p. 241.
[34] *Christianity*, p. 51; *Christentums*, p. 104.

answers that longing which belongs "more or less to every religion as such."[35]

For every religion which has any claim to the name presupposes that God is not indifferent to the beings who worship him, that therefore what is human is not alien to him, that, as an object of human veneration, he is a human God. Every prayer discloses the secret of the Incarnation, *every prayer is in fact an incarnation of God.*[36]

WAS FEUERBACH A REDUCTIONIST?

There are many interpreters of religion who are fundamentally opposed to any suspicious interpretation of religion and who accuse its practitioners of being reductionists. Sometimes this accusation is formulated relatively crudely, as in the case of the British anthropologist Evans-Pritchard, who, in criticizing the various theories of primitive religion cast up in the nineteenth century, claimed that all of these theories simply reflected the atheism of the theorists themselves. Unable to explain "how everywhere and at all times men have been stupid enough to believe" in spiritual beings, the investigators were driven to put forward biological, psychological, and sociological explanations of their own. If the investigators had been able to accept the reality of these spiritual beings, then there would have been no need to explain them away, because "He who accepts the reality of spiritual being does not feel the same need for such explanations."[37]

More often, the charge of reductionism is formulated with greater sophistication. The criticism is not that the suspicious interpreters of religion are hostile to religion but that they fail to see that understanding a religious belief is necessarily incompatible with explaining it. The failure is conceptual, not attitudinal, although the former may spring from the latter. Moreover, it is alleged, the attempt to explain religious belief by using social-scientific methods compounds the confusion because the methods of the social sciences are fundamentally incompatible with those of the humanities. The natural sciences, it is claimed, explain natural events deductively. They explain individual natural events as instances of general laws. Cultural sciences, including religious studies, make human events intelligible not by appealing to laws but by grasping sympathetically the intentions and attitudes that have motivated personal agents.

---

[35] *Christianity*, p. 54; *Christentums*, p. 109.   [36] *Christianity*, p. 54; *Christentums*, p. 109.
[37] E. E. Evans-Pritchard, *Theories of Primitive Religion* (Oxford: Clarendon Press, 1965), p. 121.

Natural events have no "inside," so to speak, no intentions that must be understood in order to explain them; consequently, the methods of the natural sciences are appropriate here. But human events, by contrast, have an "inside." They are the outcome of the convictions, passions, reasons, and beliefs from which they spring. Consequently, if one is to understand persons, one must grasp the convictions, passions, reasons, and beliefs that animate them. And in order to do this, one must "get inside" the minds and hearts of these actors, so to speak. One must attempt to see the world as they must have seen it. Only then can we understand why they acted or thought as they did. Explanation, it is said, will never yield such an understanding. This is especially true of religious experience and belief. It is simply not the sort of experience that can be explained, in contrast to being understood.

This line of argumentation goes back to a theory of interpretation first proposed by Schleiermacher which was then systematically developed by the philosopher of history Wilhelm Dilthey. It has been further refined by a number of theologians and philosophers in the early decades of this century. It found a powerful exponent in Max Weber, the sociologist of religion, and was taken up in the work of such influential scholars in religious studies as Rudolf Otto and Joachim Wach. A modified form of the argument is found in the work of the phenomenologist of religion Cornelius van der Leeuw and of the comparativist Mircea Eliade. Under the influences of these two scholars, the phenomenologists of religion have now become the chief opponents of any attempt to explain religion in contrast to understanding it; hence their opposition to the hermeneutics of suspicion. So much is this the case that one commentator on the contemporary scene in religious studies has recently written that the phenomenological view has even won over the "old deluder sociology" in the persons of two well-known contemporary sociologists of religion, Robert Bellah and Peter Berger.[38] For Bellah has conceded that he is

now prepared to claim that, as Durkheim said of society, religion is a reality *sui generis*. To put it bluntly, religion is true. This is not to say that every religious symbol is equally valid any more than every scientific theory is equally valid. But it does mean that, since religious symbolization and religious experience are inherent in the structure of human existence, all reductionism must be abandoned.[39]

---

[38] Daniel Pals, "Reductionism and Belief: An Appraisal of Recent Attacks on the Doctrine of Irreducible Religion," *The Journal of Religion*, 66, 1 (1986), 19.

[39] Robert N. Bellah, "Christianity and Symbolic Realism," *Journal for the Scientific Study of Religion*, 9, 2 (1970), 93.

So, also, Peter Berger has recommended

that the scientific study of religion return to a perspective on the phenomenon "from within," that is, to viewing it in terms of the meanings intended by the religious consciousness. I rather doubt that, so far as the definitional delineation of religion is concerned, it will be possible to go very far beyond the contributions of the phenomenological school. Indeed, I think that one could do worse than return to Otto's starting point in the matter.[40]

As any perusal of the enormous literature on this topic will confirm, there are a number of difficult philosophical issues at stake, and it is tempting to interrupt our discussion of Feuerbach's interpretative practice at this point in order to engage them: Is there, as Schleiermacher suggests in his early writings, an immediate religious experience below the level of concept, belief, and language? Can religious experience be adequately characterized as an encounter with the sacred or holy, as Rudolf Otto contended? More generally, is there a special method of understanding unique to the cultural sciences and, hence, to religion? Is the method of *Verstehen*, the attempt to "enter in" and relive (*nacherleben*) the subjectivity of the person, the most adequate way to describe that method? Is the cause of a belief utterly irrelevant to the assessment of its significance, as William James and others have argued? Is all explanation necessarily incompatible with understanding? Should religious utterances be taken at "face value"? How does one know when one has accurately understood the religious consciousness?

However important these questions are, there are two closely related reasons why I think it wise not to turn aside from our discussion of Feuerbach's interpretative practice in an attempt to answer them. The first is that Feuerbach's mode of interpretation does not easily fit either of the two alternatives normally proposed: explanation, on the one hand, and "getting inside" the religious consciousness (*Verstehen*), on the other. As any charitable reader of the preface to the second edition of *The Essence of Christianity* will immediately discern, Feuerbach claimed that he differed from other radical critics of Christianity just because he, unlike them, had decided to let the believers speak for themselves. "I constitute myself," he wrote, "only its listener and interpreter, not its prompter.

40 Peter Berger, "Some Second Thoughts on Substantive versus Functional Definitions of Religion," *Journal for the Scientific Study of Religion*, 13, 2 (1974), 129.

Not to invent, but to discover, 'to unveil existence,' has been my sole object; to see correctly my sole endeavor."[41]

The second reason lies in a recent book by Wayne Proudfoot, which deals with many of the above issues.[42] In this book, Proudfoot's overall concern is to examine and assess the large role which the relatively recent appeal to religious experience has played in modern religious studies: how it has shaped the conception of the nature of religion – an allegedly immediate and non-conceptualized experience which occurs across cultures, and how this conception of religion has, in turn, undergirded the methodological arguments concerning how this experience can be understood.

The burden of his argument, greatly oversimplified, goes something like this: Schleiermacher is at once the founding figure of the hermeneutical tradition that is opposed to any type of explanation in contrast to "understanding" and the author of the view that religious experience is immediate and independent of all concepts, thoughts, and beliefs. Proudfoot argues that in so far as Schleiermacher attempted to hold both of these ideas simultaneously his position is incoherent. On the one hand, he argued that there is an experience below the level of concepts and thought, while on the other, he contended that we can only grasp another person's religious subjectivity through the medium of concept and thought. But more importantly, we now know that Schleiermacher's claim about religious experience is false.[43] It goes against what has virtually become a consensus in both the cultural and the behavioral sciences; namely, that we cannot even ascribe emotions to ourselves or to others without concepts and beliefs, that we employ emotion words not as simple descriptions but as interpretations and explanations of the phenomena.[44] We might even go so far as to say that emotions themselves arise out of or are functions of interpretations, as Aristotle himself noted long ago and as has been recently confirmed in the ingenious experiments of the social psychologist Stanley Schachter. Just as there are no theory-free

---

[41] Feuerbach, *Christianity*, p. xxxvi; *Christentums*, p. 167.
[42] Wayne Proudfoot, *Religious Experience* (Berkeley: University of California Press, 1985).
[43] Proudfoot's criticism of Schleiermacher's position in the *Speeches on Religion* is less controversial than his treatment of the mature Schleiermacher, whose position on the relationship of feeling to cognition is much more complicated. In rehearsing Proudfoot's position on the relationship of religious experience to language I do not mean to endorse without qualification his reading of the mature Schleiermacher's position.
[44] Proudfoot, *Religious Experience*, pp. 93f.

perceptions, so also there are no uninterpreted emotions. We have learned that interpretation "goes all the way down," so to speak.

Not only are everyday emotions saturated with interpretation, but there is reason to believe that the religious emotions are also. One might go further and even claim that the religious "sense" which William James explored so profoundly in his *Varieties of Religious Experience* itself contains an implied explanation because this sense is alleged to arise out of or to have been caused by contact with an unseen presence, a "More." James argued that religious judgments are, in fact, similar to perceptual judgments because the religious believer has the vivid sense of being in direct relation to the Unseen. But just as perceptual judgments are corrigible and possibly erroneous, Proudfoot argues, so too are religious judgments. We can be mistaken when we say that we have seen such and such, and it follows that we can also be mistaken if we believe that our religious feelings have been caused by an encounter with an unseen presence. But if religious feelings, like perceptual judgments, are interpretations and contain implied claims about their causes, Proudfoot goes on, we cannot then argue, as James did, for the sharp disjunction between understanding and explaining, because religious judgments themselves involve explanation.

Proudfoot's argument is crucial for the discipline of religious studies because it is essential that an investigator have some way of understanding religious experience without necessarily agreeing with its implied claims. Otherwise, a Buddhist investigator could not understand Judaism, a Muslim could not understand Judaism, or a Christian, ancestor worship. Understanding cannot be identified with agreement if there is to be any intellectual enterprise named religious studies. And the first condition of understanding, he continues, is that the investigator must be able to describe the experience in terms that can be plausibly ascribed to the subject who has them. One cannot claim to have understood, much less explain, any human experience if the subject being investigated cannot even recognize his/her own experience in the descriptions the investigator gives of it. In this respect, Proudfoot embraces the hermeneutical tradition of Schleiermacher and Dilthey, who argue that the aim of interpretation is to be able to "make sense" of the experience of others. And to do this requires, in the nature of the case, the ability to understand the way in which these others have correlated certain emotions with certain concepts and beliefs.

Proudfoot's most important conclusion, so far as our discussion of Feuerbach is concerned, is this: Although it is true that in order to understand a religious experience we should be able to describe it in ways that can be plausibly ascribed to the one who has had it, there is no reason to argue that such an understanding precludes trying to explain it as well. There is no reason to dismiss such an attempt as reductionism. In fact, he argues, the term "reductionism" is itself too rough-hewn to do justice to what is at issue.

We really need to distinguish between two types of reductionism. On the one hand, there is "descriptive reductionism," which is the failure to identify an experience under a description that can plausibly be ascribed to the subject having it. This sort of reductionism Proudfoot thinks is a bad thing, and in this sense he agrees with the phenomenologists. But there is also an "explanatory reductionism," which is an explanation of an experience in terms which the subject might not use or even recognize. Understanding another person's experience requires that we avoid descriptive reductionism, but it is not incompatible with explanatory reductionism. In ordinary life, we frequently attempt to understand experiences while at the same time attempting to explain them, and there is nothing illegitimate in this.

Proudfoot argues that the failure to distinguish between these two types of reductionism is what leads the phenomenologist to claim that any account of religious experience must be restricted to the perspective of the experiencing subject. This claim derives whatever plausibility it has from examples of descriptive reductionism but is then extended to explanatory reductionism. But when it is extended in this fashion, it becomes an apologetic and defensive strategy. "The subject's identifying description becomes normative for purposes of explanation, and inquiry is blocked to insure that the subject's own explanation of his experience is not contested."[45]

Proudfoot's book, especially the distinction between descriptive and explanatory reductionism, helps us clarify what should be said about the charge that Feuerbach is a reductionist. It also makes possible a more discriminating line of inquiry concerning the contrast between his own type of descriptive and explanatory judgments and those of other masters of suspicion like, say, Nietzsche.

Perhaps the reader will have anticipated my conclusion that it is difficult to justify the charge that Feuerbach was a descriptive

---

[45] Proudfoot, *Religious Experience*, p.197.

reductionist, if only because his enterprise was, in the first instance, so heavily dependent upon Hegel's *Phenomenology of Spirit*. Both of these enterprises are attempts to illumine the structure of consciousness "from the inside," so to speak. But Feuerbach went even further. It was just because he believed that Hegel had overemphasized the conceptual content of religion and ignored the role of feeling that he believed it necessary to appeal to the actual, concrete, living religious consciousness of believers. His complaint against Hegel was not merely that he was mistaken as regards the importance of feeling in religion; it was that Hegel's speculative theory of religion had led to bad interpretation. Speculation, he charged, necessarily has to make "religion say only what it has *itself* thought, and expressed far better than religion; it assigns a meaning to religion without any reference to the *actual* meaning of religion."[46]

In order, then, to avoid Hegel's error, Feuerbach, the alleged reductionist, felt it necessary to argue in the same fashion in which contemporary phenomenologists now argue; namely, that the interpreter of religion should first listen carefully to what the religious people themselves say. Consequently, he considered himself to be a realist in the domain of religion, "a natural philosopher in the domain of the mind" in contrast to the speculative philosopher who has everywhere ordered the materials to fit his speculative scheme.[47]

The complaints Feuerbach lodged against the radical debunkers of Christianity in his own time are revealing in this respect. For example, against one historian's attempt to claim that the origins of the Lord's Supper or Eucharist could be traced back to blood sacrifice, Feuerbach responded that he was only interested in the view of it sanctioned in Christianity.

I, on the contrary, take as the object of my analysis and reduction only the Christian significance of the rite, that view of it which is sanctioned in Christianity, and I proceed on the supposition that only that significance which a dogma or institution has in Christianity (of course in ancient Christianity, not modern), whether it may present itself in other religions or not, is also the true origin of that dogma or institution in so far as it is Christian.[48]

And against his own fellow "Left-wing Hegelians" David Friedrich Strauss and Bruno Bauer, who had laboriously tried to distinguish between a real historical Jesus and the Biblical Christ, Feuerbach

[46] Feuerbach, *Christianity*, p. xxxv; *Christentums*, p. 16.
[47] *Christianity*, p. xxxiv; *Christentums*, p. 15.
[48] *Christianity*, p. xli; *Christentums*, pp. 22f.

wrote that he had no interest in a project that seeks to distinguish the historical from the supernatural Christ, or that attempts to separate out historical facts from miracles. "I do not . . . inquire," he wrote,

what the real, natural Christ was or may have been in distinction from what he has been made or has become in Supernaturalism; on the contrary, I accept the Christ of religion, but I show that this superhuman being is nothing else than a product and reflex of the supernatural human mind.[49]

That Feuerbach could write in one and the same sentence that he accepts the Christ of religion and that this Christ is "nothing but" a reflex of the human mind illustrates how difficult it is to classify him easily either as someone who lets religion speak for itself or as a reductionist. Using Proudfoot's categories, it would be far more discriminating to say that he was an explanatory but not a descriptive reductionist. His first interpretative move was to make sure that his descriptions corresponded with what believers themselves had said. But he also explained what they had said in terms that they would not have accepted. The issue, then, is whether this explanation is somehow illegitimate. Proudfoot argues that it is not necessarily so, that such explanatory reductionisms, like those claims of the religious mind itself, cannot be judged wholesale but only on the special arguments and reasons that can be brought forward for and against them.

It might be responded that reductionism is not merely the offering of explanations for religious belief but the problem of claiming that a conscious meaning of a religious confession is really a function of an unconscious meaning. The issue is not so much that of causation as it is of meaning. The charitable interpreter takes religious symbols at their face value; the suspicious interpreter professes to find a hidden or latent meaning within the manifest meaning.

This allegation also raises complex hermeneutical issues. Paul Ricoeur, hardly a defender of suspicious hermeneutics, has argued that we are dealing here with the problem of language, the discovery by Ernst Cassirer and others of the difference between the literal sign and the symbol. We are dealing with the fact that symbols, in the nature of the case, have multiple meanings and, hence, can be interpreted differently. It was because Freud understood this multiplicity of meanings of symbols, Ricoeur argues, that he also saw the possibility of a hidden, latent level of meaning in every human

---

[49] *Christianity*, p. xli; *Christentums*, p. 23.

expression. Thus he extended the scope of the interpretative process to include not only written texts but dreams, neurotic symptoms, and slips of the tongue. He saw that religious symbols were no more exempt from the possibility of having latent and unconscious levels of meaning than other modes of symbolism. It was this possibility, Ricoeur concludes, that constitutes "our entire hermeneutical problem."[50]

There is still a deeper reason than the multiplicity of meanings that makes possible diverse interpretations of symbols. This reason was best articulated by the sociologist Peter Berger in his *Invitation to Sociology*, a book written before his endorsement of the phenomenology of religion. In this book, which attempts to explain the practice of professional sociologists, Berger argued that once the subject matter of sociology itself has been identified – it has to do with the abstractions that characterize systems of interactions among people and how these interactions are organized by institutions – its method necessarily requires that we do not take human expressions at face value. "It can be said," Berger writes, "that the first wisdom of sociology is this – things are not what they seem."[51] Consequently, this first wisdom requires the exercise of suspicion.

The reason why sociologists assume that "things are not what they seem" is rooted in their understanding of the role that society plays in determining and influencing the tacit definitions, values, expectations, desires, and roles that structure the social interactions between persons, a role that most persons are unaware of. Moreover, these self-definitions, values, and roles do not simply structure external actions but are internalized by consciousness itself. Thus the enterprise of understanding these interrelationships "presupposes a certain awareness that human events have different levels of meaning, some of which are hidden from the consciousness of everyday life."[52] It is just by virtue of this assumption that sociologists are suspicious of official explanations of events by authorities, whether they be political, juridical, or religious. And it is also by virtue of this assumption that no sociologist or psychologist would take at face value a statement of a person's deepest beliefs. Indeed, this assumption involves nothing less than "a transformation of consciousness" in the modern Western intellectual world. The aim of the investigator is to

[50] Ricoeur, *Freud and Philosophy*, p. 17.
[51] Peter Berger, *Invitation to Sociology: A Humanistic Perspective* (New York: Penguin, 1966), p. 34.
[52] Berger, *Invitation to Sociology*, p. 41.

"see through" the façade of human institutions and to "look behind" the expressed rationalizations of action.[53]

In this sense, the hermeneutics of suspicion is a result of our modernity. Any given action or expression or system of thought and belief will inevitably solicit different interpretations. All interpreters, including the phenomenologists, will offer explanations and latent meanings, and it is no longer convincing to dismiss those with whom we disagree as "reductionists."

This said, however, it is worthwhile to emphasize that Feuerbach's interpretative practice differed in one important respect from that employed by the other masters of suspicion, a difference that Proudfoot's distinction between descriptive and explanatory reductionism throws into relief. Feuerbach, at least in those passages dealing with the felicity principle, argued that only someone who ignored the manifest meaning of believers could deny that what they most deeply wanted is a suffering deity who recognizes and loves them and can intervene miraculously on their behalf. In other words, the latent meaning of their religious expressions is not something that stands in contradiction to the manifest meaning, but is simply an extension of its not fully conscious meaning. The comparison with Nietzsche in this respect is instructive. In his view of religion the latent meaning can be said to be in direct contradiction with the manifest meaning. Thus, in his analysis of the Christian notion of love, Nietzsche argues that love is really an expression of resentment, that it became a virtue among the powerless as a way of expression of their own will to power over the noble classes. It is the way the slave class deceives itself into thinking that it is morally superior to the noble classes. Nietzsche, in short, was a descriptive as well as an explanatory reductionist. Feuerbach, by contrast, argued that what Christians said about love should be taken seriously, so seriously that it raised questions about its compatibility with faith, as we shall see in the next chapter.

The contrast between the two types of suspicion is a significant one because it bears on the issue of how one attempts to justify an interpretation. Feuerbach, presumably, would actually find it important to argue that a given interpretation does more justice to what believers really say than a competing interpretation; hence, his long and detailed analysis of the piety of ordinary Christians. The logic of

[53] Berger, *Invitation to Sociology*, pp. 41–61.

his interpretation is not to say, as a Nietzschean would, "Look at this religious expression and you will see it as a manifestation of the will to power." Rather, his logic would be, "This is what Christians really say about God sacrificing his only Son for us. I have not put words into their mouths, and it is implicit in this creedal confession that God values the welfare of humankind more than his own being." His explanation, in short, is the attempt to understand both how Christians could believe what they do and, at the same time, be committed, as he thinks they are, to the contradictions that follow when what they have said is made into an object of intellectual belief.

CHAPTER 3

The criticism of religion in
"The Essence of Christianity"

CHRISTIANITY AS ALIENATION

I have been attempting to sort out the various argumentative threads woven together by Feuerbach to construct his complex and problematic projection theory in *The Essence of Christianity*. To understand these various threads and how they are related to one another helps to explain the curious impression the book often makes on contemporary readers who pick it up for the first time. They ask how it is that there are passages that read as if they were written only yesterday and yet these passages seem to be built upon an intellectual structure that seems incredibly speculative and arcane, a structure in which the central category is the concept of the "species" and in which self-consciousness is consciousness of "the infinitude of the species."

To differentiate these various argumentative threads and to understand how they are related to one another is also to cast light on the various hermeneutical principles which Feuerbach employed, principles he then applied to specific Christian doctrines and practices. Many of these principles were derived from Feuerbach's clever inversion of Hegel's philosophy of Spirit, not only the central thesis that theology is anthropology but also the overall interpretative strategy of reappropriating the inner truth of the projection. But many of these principles are Feuerbach's own and are not derived from his transformative method.

It is important to turn now to that aspect of the book which seems so characteristic of suspicious hermeneutics generally and which naturally disturbs the religious reader: the apparent hostility to religion. Like Nietzsche, Marx, and Freud, Feuerbach was, on the surface at least, contemptuous of Christianity. But even though he was as savage in his criticism of Christianity as these other masters of suspicion, he differed from them in one crucial respect: he believed that the new age of which he was the prophet would only emerge if the deepest values of Christianity were preserved. If Nietzsche believed that Christianity was the disease that had infected the body of Western culture and had to be surgically removed with whatever instrument was at hand, Feuerbach wanted to preserve the content of Christianity, but not its form. If he criticized Christianity, it was in the service of the same human values Christianity itself recognized and fostered. If the Trinity was to be rejected as a reified myth, this rejection was in the name of a genuine human family bound by ties of love and mutuality. If the dogma of the Incarnation was exhibited in all of its falsity, it was with the aim of reducing this supernatural mystery "to a *simple* truth *inherent* in human nature: – a truth which does not belong to the Christian religion alone, but which, implicitly at least, belongs more or less to every religion as such."[1] As Karl Löwith has noted, Feuerbach was no ordinary atheist because his only aim "was to remove the 'subject' of religious predicates, God, but in no way did he seek to remove the predicates themselves in their distinctive human meaning."[2]

This particular aspect of Feuerbach's hermeneutics of suspicion is a function of his concept of alienation, which, in turn, is dependent upon the Hegelian model of Spirit or consciousness. If for Hegel the Absolute Spirit objectifies itself in the finite creation and then finds itself alienated from its creation, for Feuerbach, the human spirit objectifies itself in the idea of God and alienates itself from its own essential nature. Although, in both cases, alienation is a "moment" in the dialectical process by means of which self-consciousness is realized, Feuerbach attempted to provide a psychological explanation of what occurs. By placing all human perfections in a transcendent being, he explained, the human species in the nature of the case deprives itself of these same perfections. "The reason of this is, that as what is *positive* in the conception of the divine being can only be human, the conception of man, as an object of consciousness, can only be *negative*. To enrich God, man must become poor; that God may be all, man must be nothing."[3] As G. Petrovic has observed,

Feuerbach accepted Hegel's view that man can be alienated from himself, but he rejected both the view that nature is a self-alienated form of Absolute

[1] Feuerbach, *Christianity*, p. 54; *Christentums*, p. 109.
[2] Feuerbach, *Das Wesen des Christentums, Nachwort von Karl Löwith*, p. 531.
[3] Feuerbach, *Christianity*, p. 26; *Christentums*, p. 65.

Mind and the view that man is Absolute Mind in the process of dealienation. Man is not self-alienated God. On the contrary, God is self-alienated man; he is man's essence absolutized and estranged from man.[4]

Consequently, the Christian religion, paradoxically, is both the manifestation of human alienation and the vehicle for overcoming it. It is through reflection on this religion that the human reappropriates its relinquished nature. If Hegel had provided a metaphysical justification for Christianity and by demythologizing it had permitted it to remain in place (a religion for those who could not philosophize), then Feuerbach had provided a naturalistic justification of Christianity, but one that required the jettisoning of its dogmatic form.

It is ironical that the concept of alienation, which is so central to the interpretative strategy of *The Essence of Christianity* and has inspired generations of Marxist critics of religion, should seem to many contemporary readers to be one of the least plausible ideas in Feuerbach's book. How many contemporary atheists would now argue that belief in a transcendent personal being is intrinsically alienating? They might criticize Christianity as irrelevant, meaningless, or even false, but few would use the term "alienation" in the technical sense in which Feuerbach used it.

There are at least three reasons that contemporary atheists would not use this language. First of all, we live in an era that has witnessed what Philip Rieff has called the "triumph of the therapeutic," an era that judges any religious belief in terms of its value as an aid to personal happiness and "peace of mind." If a religious belief brings psychological comfort, if it enables someone to get through the night, so to speak, not many contemporaries would call it alienating. Second, the notion of a universal human essence from which an individual could become alienated has itself become problematical to many. And third, the specific assumptions that made Feuerbach's idea of alienation plausible in his time are no longer in place in our own. He worked out his theory against the background of Hegelian philosophy, in which it was assumed that the human essence could only be exemplified in the totality of human history.

It seems important, then, to attempt to make Feuerbach's theory of alienation as plausible as one can. But this is not a simple task. First of all, although it is clearly indebted to Hegel's objectification–alienation–reappropriation schema, Feuerbach added certain conceptual elements

[4] G. Petrovic, "Alienation," in Paul Edwards (ed.), *The Encyclopedia of Philosophy*, 8 vols. (New York: Macmillan and the Free Press, 1967), 1.77.

of his own to it. Furthermore, although the concept governs the overall interpretative strategy of his book, it is, oddly, never systematically discussed. Indeed, the two German words that figure so largely in Hegel's discussion of it in *The Phenomenology*, *Entfremdung* and *Entäusserung* (the former usually translated as either "alienation" or "estrangement" and the latter as "externalization" or "divestment"), occur in only two or three isolated passages in Feuerbach's book. This absence of any systematic discussion of the term "alienation" is especially surprising when we consider that one of the major controversies swirling around Hegel's philosophy of Spirit at the time was whether he had identified "objectification" with alienation, as Karl Marx had charged in his *Economic and Philosophic Manuscripts of 1844*. Marx claimed that Hegel had derived the objectivity of things from the self-alienation of Spirit and thus regarded all objective things produced by human activity as alienated. Marx, by contrast, argued that the self naturally has objects independent of it and that these objects are indispensable "to the exercise and confirmation of . . . [its] . . . essential powers."[5] A being without objects, he claimed, was a non-being. In short, objectification was not alienation.

It is probable that the lack of any systematic discussion of the concept of alienation in *Christianity* is related to the absence of any discussion of the process of concept formation upon which it is parasitical and which, as Wartofsky has argued, is the unarticulated but deep thesis underlying Feuerbach's concept of projection. For just as the concept of projection or objectification is related to the formation of the concept of the species, so is the concept of alienation. Alienation refers to the discrepancy that arises between the individual and his/her essential potentialities when these potentialities are attributed to God and not to the species. Since the process of concept formation is only implicit in Feuerbach's work and has to be dug out, the same applies to the notion of alienation.

It seems important, then, to say something, however brief and necessarily inadequate, about the Hegelian background of the idea. I write that it is "necessarily inadequate" because any satisfactory summary of Hegel's concept of alienation would have to take account not only of the intellectually rich treatment of the "self-alienation of Spirit" in the *Phenomenology*, where the concept is used and developed in a discussion of classical Greek civilization, the Middle Ages, the

---

[5] Livingstone and Benton (trans.), *Karl Marx Early Writings*, pp. 388–390.

Reformation, the Enlightenment, and the French Revolution, but also his analysis of labor as *Veräusserung* in *The Philosophy of Right* as well as his discussion of Original Sin as *Entfremdung* (estrangement) in the *Lectures on the Philosophy of Religion*. As if this were not complicated enough, there are formidable problems surrounding Hegel's characteristic terminology: *Veräusserung, Entäusserung,* and *Entfremdung*.[6]

It might prove helpful to distinguish two contexts in which Hegel employs the concept of alienation (*Entfremdung*). The first is the more familiar metaphysical notion in which alienation is one of the "moments" through which the Absolute Spirit necessarily moves towards its self-actualization. This is the use that explicitly informs Hegel's philosophy of religion but is implicit in all of his writings. In the 1828 version of his *Lectures on the Philosophy of Religion*, for example, there is a section entitled "Knowledge, Alienation, and Evil" in which Hegel refers to the cleavage or rupture introduced into the finite order because of Adam's and Eve's acquisition of the knowledge of good and evil. Here the term is used to refer to the loss of humanity's original goodness; hence its alienation from God. But it also implies that God, the Absolute Spirit, has been alienated from that which is really his own.[7]

The second context in which *Entfremdung* plays a major role is the *Phenomenology*, in which the term is used in very complex ways. Richard Schacht has argued that there are basically two related but distinct meanings of the word there.[8] In the first case, the term "self-alienation" refers to the loss of the immediate unity with the culture or social substance that occurs when the self-consciousness of the individual first arises. The emerging consciousness feels that the culture is something alien and strange to it, something with which it is not identified but to which it must conform. But since the social substance (the cultural values and norms) contains the universality to which an individual subject essentially belongs (that which enables it to participate in the social nature of human life), this alienation from the society can be said to involve an inner discord with oneself as well.

---

[6] It is regrettable that there is not more agreement among English translators regarding the rendering of these important terms.

[7] Georg Wilhelm Friedrich Hegel, *Lectures on the Philosophy of Religion, One-volume Edition, the Lectures of 1827*, ed. Peter C. Hodgson, trans. R. F. Brown, P. C. Hodgson, and J. M. Stewart with the assistance of H. S. Harris (Berkeley: University of California Press, 1988).

[8] I am indebted to Professor Schacht's discussion of the idea, although I have some reservations about his view of Feuerbach's relationship to Hegel, on the one hand, and to Marx, on the other. See his *Alienation* with an introductory essay by Walter Kaufmann (Garden City, N.Y.: Doubleday, 1971).

Thus Hegel uses the term "self-alienation." But since the social substance or culture is understood by Hegel to be the objectification of Spirit, it can be also be said that objectified Spirit is alienated from the individual. But whether we speak of self-alienation or alienated spirit, both forms of alienation have in common a discordant relationship between the self and that to which it belongs.

In the second case, the word "alienation" refers to the surrender or renunciation of the individual that is necessary for alienation in the first sense to be overcome. The self has to give up its own autonomy to the social substance from which it had been estranged. Schacht takes Hegel to mean that the individual consciousness makes itself one with the social substance only through the alienation of itself.[9]

This two-fold use of the term "alienation" actually reflects two dominant strands of meaning in the Latin root of the English word. The term *alienatio* was used in a variety of related contexts in classical Latin to signify transformation, separation, and transferral.[10] It could be used neutrally to refer to the separation of one item from another, or it could acquire both negative and positive associations. It could signify the transfer of ownership and, by extension, could designate the loss of personality or insanity. In a religious context, Plotinus and Augustine both used it to signify the alienation of the mind from the body (*alienatio mentis a corpore*) which they believed to be the essence of mystical unity with the One. It could also be used in a negative sense, as it was in the Latin Vulgate, to refer to separation of the individual from God, as in Ephesians 4:18. The Protestant Reformer John Calvin also used the term to refer to the spiritual death of the soul because of God's rejection of it.

A second classical strand of meaning, however, refers to the transfer of property or rights, and this strand was especially important for Social Contract political theory, first in Grotius and later in Rousseau, whose views were important for Hegel. Grotius argued that political authority gets its charter from those who transfer (alienate) to it certain rights. It is this meaning, incidentally, that lies behind that remarkable belief articulated in the American Declaration of Independence that there are certain self-evident and "inalienable rights," which is to say, certain rights that can never be legitimately surrendered to another.

---

[9] Schacht, *Alienation*, pp. 54f.
[10] For a useful discussion of the concept of alienation and its metamorphoses see Nathan Rotenstreich, *Basic Problems of Marx's Philosophy* (Indianapolis: Bobbs-Merrill, 1965), chap. 7.

Given this brief background of the term, perhaps we are now in a position to see more clearly how Feuerbach's notion of alienation is related to Hegel's. Although both theories have the emergence of self-consciousness (spirit) as their theme, Feuerbach, unlike Hegel, was not concerned with the emergence of the self from the culture or social substance but, rather, with emergence of the self as an individual within the species and the subsequent loss of unity with that species by virtue of the projection of the species attributes onto God. Consequently, Feuerbach did not use the concept of alienation as Hegel did to analyze the various stages of the relationship between the self and society. Feuerbach's notion of alienation is in many ways much more formal and ontological and hence, as Marx argued, less historical than Hegel's. Basically it has to do with an alleged discrepancy between existence and essence that occurs when the distinctive human predicates are attributed to a deity believed to be a separate, transcendent being. Still, this usage has an important and fundamental affinity with Hegel's in the *Phenomenology* because both of them viewed "alienation" as a loss of something universal, something that inherently belongs to one's nature. In Hegel, the self is alienated from the universality that is inherent in the social substance; in Feuerbach, it is alienated from the universality that pertains to the species as such.

Feuerbach's argument that the religious projection alienates the self from the species has two foci which, though closely related, need to be considered separately. The first is his claim that the very act of attributing human predicates to an external divine being necessarily withdraws these same predicates from the human race to which they properly belong. The second is that when individual feeling is the focus of religion there is a loss of species consciousness and, consequently, a loss of unity with nature and other human beings. It involves a discrepancy between a given individual and his/her essential human nature. It is the second of these foci, as we shall see, upon which Feuerbach puts the greatest weight.

The first argument follows from the general principle that the misplaced attribution of human predicates to some external and nonhuman being necessarily deprives the human being of those potentialities that he/she should claim as his/her own. Consequently, the human being contemplates his/her own nature as something foreign or alien. In this respect, the very "core of religion"

is that in proportion as the divine subject is in *reality* human, the greater is the *apparent difference* between God and man; that is, the more, by reflection on religion, by theology, is the identity of the divine and human denied, and the human, considered *as such*, is *depreciated*.[11]

This depreciation is especially extreme, the argument continues, when human perfections are attributed to the deity, for then not only is the identity of the divine and human rejected, but the divine has predicated of it what is essentially human. The human denies to himself/herself only what he/she attributes to God.[12]

Feuerbach brought forward a number of examples to illustrate this process. The human, sensing that reason is one of his/her distinctive predicates, projects a divine being that is infinitely wise. The result of this then leads, dialectically, to the corollary that compared with the divine, human reason is imperfect and weak, so inadequate that it can only know what God chooses to reveal to it. Or again, humanity projects its innate sense of dignity onto the divine and then claims that it has no worth of its own except in the eyes of the divine. The logic of the projecting process is that because God is the perfect exemplification of human nature, existing individual persons are imperfect and evil. Because God is just, the human must be unjust. In short, human beings project their essence into objectivity and then construe themselves as unworthy objects of this projected image. "God is, *per se*, his relinquished self."[13]

This argument is sometimes combined with a second, somewhat different though related, argument; namely, that what human beings renounce in themselves they then only enjoy in "an incomparably higher and fuller measure in God."[14] Thus the ascetic monk who has made a vow of chastity to God has an image of woman and love in the form of the Virgin Mary. "They could the more easily dispense with real woman in proportion as an ideal woman was an object of love to them."[15] Or again, the higher the value placed on some faculty or sense, the more likely it is to be restored in the picture of God.

Man denies as to himself only what he attributes to God. Religion abstracts from man, from the world; but it can only abstract from the limitations, from the phenomena; in short, from the negative, not from the essence, the positive, of the world and humanity: hence, in the very abstraction and

---

[11] Feuerbach, *Christianity*, p. 26; *Christentums*, p. 64.
[12] *Christianity*, p. 27; *Christentums*, p. 66.
[13] *Christianity*, p. 31; *Christentums*, p. 73.
[14] *Christianity*, p. 26; *Christentums*, p. 65.
[15] *Christianity*, p. 26; *Christentums*, p. 65.

negation it must recover that from which it abstracts, or believes itself to abstract. And thus, in reality, whatever religion consciously denies . . . it unconsciously restores in God.[16]

I write that this argument is somewhat different because it is one thing to contend that human beings project their species perfections on the divine and thereby deprive themselves of these perfections; it is quite another to say that *because* human beings feel themselves deprived of some predicate, they attribute this to the divine. The logic of the first argument is that just because human beings feel that reason and love are their own perfections, they attribute them to the divine to which they then compare themselves invidiously. The logic of the second argument is that because human beings feel that they lack this or that predicate, they attribute it to the divine. Although the difference between these two arguments is a subtle one, they nevertheless lead to different theories of religion, as can be seen in the differences between Karl Marx's and Feuerbach's. In Marx, religion reflects a previous deprivation of some sort. In Feuerbach, the act of religious projection itself creates the alienation. In Marx, deprivation is the cause of religion; in Feuerbach, religion is the cause of deprivation.

Even when one tends to view Feuerbach's objectification–alienation–reappropriation schema as simply an inversion of Hegel's, it is important not to obscure certain important differences between them. Nathan Rotenstreich has contended, for example, that Hegel attributed certain constitutive powers to spirit whereas Feuerbach did not. For Hegel, the finite world is in some sense created by the Absolute Spirit just as society and culture are the creations of the finite spirit. Feuerbach, however, believed that the religious objectification of the human spirit was purely fictitious, the reification of an abstraction. Hegel saw alienation as the necessary instrument of the realization of spirit and objectification, therefore, had a positive value. For Feuerbach, Rotenstreich claims, the objectification had an implied negative significance. At best, religion can only serve as a means for self-knowledge.[17]

There is some validity in Rotenstreich's comparison between the two thinkers, but I also think that Feuerbach's view is more complex and ambiguous in certain respects than Rotenstreich's interpretation suggests. It is true that Feuerbach regards the religious objectification

---

[16] *Christianity*, p. 27; *Christentums*, pp. 66f.
[17] Rotenstreich, *Basic Problems of Marx's Philosophy*, pp. 155f.

as fictitious, but it is less clear that it only has a negative significance. On the one hand, there are passages in *Christianity* that support the view that religion does serve a positive function, that it is "man's earliest and indirect form of self-knowledge." He wrote that every advance in religion is an advance in humanity's conception of itself. To the degree that this is true, religion does have a positive function. Even Christianity can be given a positive evaluation because it has encapsulated the most adequate picture of essential human predicates: reason, will, and love. On the other hand, Feuerbach seems unclear whether this religious detour to self-knowledge is a necessary one or whether this self-knowledge could have been achieved in some other way and thus avoided the alienation intrinsic to it. It is also unclear whether Christianity is the last and best religion, the culmination of self-knowledge, as Hegel claimed, or whether it is inferior to certain religions because it has elevated the individual over the species.

The second focal point of Feuerbach's theory of alienation is the way in which the religious projection involves a loss of species consciousness, which, in turn, he interpreted as alienation from one's essential nature and other human beings.

To understand this argument, it is necessary to recapitulate Feuerbach's view of the religious projection briefly. The I, in distinguishing itself from the Thou, dimly apprehends that the other person is like itself, that both the I and the Thou share an essential human nature. Both possess consciousness and have the predicates of reason, will, and feeling. In this act of self-differentiation, the individual I experiences a powerful inrush of two types of feeling: on the one hand, a painful feeling of limitation and inadequacy over against the unlimitedness of the species and, on the other, an ecstatic sense of the attractiveness of the species, an attractiveness grounded in the individual's joy in the exercise of his/her own distinctive powers. But because the idea of the species is an abstraction and as such has very little emotional power, it is seized upon by the imagination and transformed into the idea of a single divine being. The individual, driven by his/her desire to live and his/her sense of finitude, finds in the perfection of the divine being a substitute for the true bearer of these predicates, the species, as well as an assurance of his/her own worthiness and immortality as an individual.

This argument, as I have shown in a previous chapter, gets much of its force from Feuerbach's conception of the relationships among reason, feeling, and the imagination. Reason is the faculty that entertains concepts; hence the idea of the species is its appropriate object. The reason is, he writes, "the self-consciousness of the species as such."[18] Feeling, by contrast, is linked to the desires and sensations of the individual. It is the "self-consciousness of the individual." Reason is linked to abstraction, whereas feeling is "the partisan of the individual." Since the imagination is an instrument of the feelings, it cheats the reason of its proper object by dressing up the idea of the species in the costume of a perfect (divine) human being. The result of this conspiracy between feeling and imagination against the reason is the creation of a religious object in which, on the human side, the individual is raised above the species and, on the divine side, the species is made into an individual. In both cases, religion involves alienation and estrangement: a discrepancy between individual existence and the essential nature to which it belongs.

Feuerbach believed that the subordination of the species to the individual has reached its most extreme form in Christianity, and that it provides an illustration of the alienating propensities of anthropomorphic religion generally. In it, Feuerbach argued, the human individual has been made into a self-sufficing whole, an individual soul that is destined for immortality and for whom, therefore, the relationships to nature and other human beings are regarded as accidental rather than constitutive. In contrast to followers of the "heathen religions," which do not shut nature out of their self-understandings, Christians view themselves as independent of nature and its necessities. Whereas heathens consider humanity to be essentially constituted by the relation to nature, Christians believe that the individual transcends nature. Heathens subordinate the part to the whole.

Christianity, on the contrary, cared nothing for the species, and had only the individual in its eye and mind. *Christianity* – not, certainly, the Christianity of the present day, which has incorporated with itself the culture of heathenism, and has preserved only the name and some general positions of Christianity – is the *direct opposite of heathenism*, and only when it is regarded as such is it *truly* comprehended . . . The ancients sacrificed the individual to the species; the Christians sacrificed the species to the individual.[19]

This subordination of the species to the individual manifests itself in a number of ways: in the Christian attitude not only towards nature in

---

[18] Feuerbach, *Christianity*, p. 285; *Christentums*, p. 475.
[19] *Christianity*, pp. 151f.; *Christentums*, p. 265.

general but towards sex, death, and, as we shall see later, in its doctrine of Original Sin.

Feuerbach's argument that the Christian attitude towards sex is an example of its subordination of the individual to the species is particularly revelatory of what he means by species consciousness. It also illustrates an interesting departure from Hegel's notion of alienation. Nothing more clearly reveals the inherent connection between the individual and the species, Feuerbach contended, than the love between the sexes. In love, one reckons another as part of his/her own being. In love, men and women are seen and known to be the complement of one another, and "thus united they first present the species, the perfect man (. . . *erst die Gattung, den vollkommnen Menschen darzustellen*)."[20] In love, one declares that the life one has "through love to be the truly human life, corresponding to the idea . . . of the species."[21]

The individual is defective, imperfect, weak, needy; but love is strong, perfect, contented, free from wants, self-sufficing, *infinite*; because in it the self-consciousness of the individuality is the mysterious self-consciousness of the perfection of the race.[22]

It follows that the Christian depreciation of sexuality is a reflection of this elevation of individual subjectivity over the species, and this has been manifested in the asceticism and monasticism which have broken out again and again in the history of Christianity from its beginnings. This monasticism, Feuerbach argued, was not an importation from the East, as has sometimes been alleged, but is derived from the innermost impulses of Christianity itself. It is a necessary consequence of the view that "The individual man attains his end by himself alone; he attains it in God . . . but God is present to each individual separately."[23] Persons who live for an eternal life can only believe in the "worthlessness and nothingness of this life." Their basic orientation in life is to resist being captivated by the transitory values of this world in order to pursue the values of the next. It follows from such a self-understanding that marriage is at best a concession to the weakness of the flesh, and unmarried life is regarded as more saintly. Consequently, even when the Christian believes in the resurrection of the body, "the *principle of sexual love is excluded* from

[20] *Christianity*, p. 156; *Christentums*, p. 273.
[21] *Christianity*, p. 156; *Christentums*, p. 274.
[22] *Christianity*, p. 156; *Christentums*, p. 274.
[23] *Christianity*, p. 160; *Christentums*, p. 279.

heaven as an *earthly, worldly* principle . . . the heavenly life is the *true,* perfected, eternal life of the Christian."[24]

But it is the Christian preoccupation with death and the doctrine of individual immortality that it generates, Feuerbach argued, in which one sees most clearly the elevation of the individual over the species. There is, he argued, a monumental and scarcely disguised egoism at the core of Christianity, an egoism that finds expression in the doctrines of individual salvation, personal providence, and resurrection.

This argument, which plays a minor but powerful role in *Christianity,* is a variation on a major theme that Feuerbach had already developed in his earliest book, *Thoughts on Death and Immortality,* the publication of which had been the reason for his rejection by the theological faculty at the University of Erlangen. In that book, he had argued that the Christianity of his time was a religion of "pure self," a religion in which the individual was the sole source of meaning and value. Preoccupied with personal salvation, this religion leads to a fundamental misunderstanding of the communal nature of human life. And with this rejection of communal life it also rejects the structures of finitude under which life is lived and, hence, life itself. Consequently, he engaged in a slashing attack on this religion of "pure self" and, especially, on its rejection of individual death. All of his rhetoric is calculated to change the human attitude towards death. As John Massey has written in his perceptive introduction to the English edition of the book, Feuerbach wished to show that the "inexhaustible quality of the limited time that we have is far superior to a life that would be defined primarily by its eternal duration."[25]

In that earlier book, Feuerbach had clothed his appeal for the acceptance of finitude, community, and death in the language of an idealistic philosophy. As persons, he had said, we are all participants in an Infinite Spirit, and our "essence demands other essences." In existence, personhood is a boundary between ourselves and these other essences, a boundary we are always having to overcome. But in death we shall all pass into Infinite Spirit, where this boundary is finally canceled.

In death, the result of this process, those boundaries for the cancellation of which you have worked in and by Spirit throughout your entire life

---

[24] *Christianity,* p. 165; *Christentums,* p. 287.
[25] Massey in introduction to Feuerbach, *Thoughts,* p. xxvii.

completely disappear. The last word that you speak is death, in which you totally express yourself and impart yourself to others. Death is the ultimate act of communication.[26]

In *Christianity*, however, this appeal to participation in Infinite Spirit has vanished and only the language about the infinitude and perfection of the species remains. Now it is the species alone that justifies the existence of the individual, and it is in loving the species that individuals rediscover their own true nature. Further, this species is no mere abstraction, but

it exists in feeling, in the moral sentiment, in the energy of love. It is the species which infuses love into me. A loving heart is the heart of the species throbbing in the individual. Thus Christ, as the *consciousness of love*, is the *consciousness of the species* . . . Thus, where there arises the consciousness of the species as a species, the idea of humanity as a whole, Christ disappears, without, however, his true nature disappearing; for he was the substitute for the consciousness of the species, the image under which it was made present to the people, and became the *law* of the popular life.[27]

Paradoxically, Christians who worship Christ cannot see through His image to the reality behind it, the species. Swayed by feeling and deceived by the imagination, their natural instinctual urge for self-preservation is transformed into nothing less than a Promethean demand for individual immortality. Everything that links the self to nature and to the species is seen as a hindrance to eternal life; consequently, faith in the future life is "the *freedom of subjectivity from the limits of Nature*."[28]

A charitable interpreter of Feuerbach's theory of alienation might argue that despite the arcane language about devotion to the species in which this theory is couched, there is nothing inherently implausible about it, even for contemporaries. Basically, it could be said, Feuerbach was arguing that Christianity puts such an excessive premium on the individual that it leads to a rejection of the basic conditions of finitude itself, especially the condition that we are social creatures. It rejects any meaning to life except on the condition that the individual survive death and enjoy eternal life. All this could be said, it might be claimed, without appealing to the outdated nonsense about devotion to the species.

[26] Feuerbach, *Thoughts*, p. 121; *Gedanken über Tod und Unsterblichkeit*, in *Frühe Schriften, Kritiken und Reflexionen (1828–1834)*, *GW* I, p. 336.
[27] Feuerbach, *Christianity*, pp. 268f.; *Christentums*, pp. 442f.
[28] *Christianity*, p. 184; *Christentums*, p. 314.

Even though this charitable reconstruction has the virtue of trying to make Feuerbach's notion of alienation plausible to contemporaries, it is extremely doubtful whether it does justice to the "historical Feuerbach's" view, because the notion of the species is not incidental but fundamental to it. It is the idea of the species that is projected and then transformed into the idea of God; it is the species from which the individual is alienated; and it is the species that is the proper object of veneration and worship. Wartofsky is surely correct when, in summarizing Feuerbach's thought, he writes:

The fundamental distinction in his work is that between the existing individual man as the finite and incomplete instance of the species, and human nature as such, which is the infinite character of the species, its essence, or that unlimited potentiality or capacity humanity has for being "truly" human.[29]

Consequently, Feuerbach believed that the real object of human piety should be humankind, the species, and what he desired, Wartofsky concludes, is that "an 'authentic humanity' be fully realized in every individual."[30]

Wartofsky's summary is not only correct but revelatory, for one need only reflect on this summary in order to discover the inherent difficulties in Feuerbach's concept of alienation. On the one hand, it seems to refer to some alleged gap or discrepancy between an individual's existence and "the infinite character of the species," which, as we shall see below, also means the totality of human beings. On the other hand, alienation seems to refer to the failure of an individual to be "truly human," that is, to realize in his/her own life those distinctive potentialities which define him/her as human. The first meaning contrasts the individual with the totality of the species; the second contrasts the individual with some standard of human health he/she can achieve by realizing his/her own inherent potentialities.

There are some contemporary philosophers who would argue that both of these notions are unintelligible: the first because it makes no sense to contrast an individual with the "infinitude" and totality of the species; the second because it makes no sense to talk in essentialist terms about some universal human nature.

But unless one is prepared to reject any notion of distinctively human potentialities that can be lost or forfeited, there does not seem

[29] Wartofsky, *Feuerbach*, p. 209.   [30] Wartofsky, *Feuerbach*, p. 209.

to be anything implausible about the second notion of alienation. Everything depends on how the notion of essence or human nature is specified. Indeed, one might argue that some such notion is found in many forms of contemporary discourse: in psychotherapy, Marxist and socialist criticisms of capitalism, classical libertarian criticism of Marxist and socialistic societies, various forms of existentialism, and even in some feminist philosophy. All of these presuppose some idea that human beings can fail to achieve what they essentially are.

Moreover, some of these forms of discourse are able to conceptualize alienation with a minimal commitment to essentialism as it is normally construed. Kierkegaard, for example, argued that human beings are unique by virtue of being gifted with "spirit" or selfhood, which he sometimes described in terms of degrees of consciousness.[31] The more consciousness, the more self. He then went on to argue that God has placed the demand upon the individual to achieve as great a degree of consciousness as possible. God's command is that we become fully conscious selves. This conception of human nature then became the basis for his attack on the Philistinism of his age, in which the individual self lives in conformity with the expectations of others. Heidegger, whose indebtedness to Kierkegaard was as great as it was unacknowledged, secularized Kierkegaard's view. He employed the notion of alienation to describe the "inauthenticity" that results when the individual (*Dasein*) accepts unquestioningly the assumptions of the taken-for-granted world. The taken-for-granted world, he argued, smothers "the call" of conscience to take responsibility for one's "ownmost" possibilities of being, the most important of which is death. Both Kierkegaard and Heidegger, especially the latter, attempted to avoid all essentialist language and yet utilize the concept of alienation.

It could even be argued, as the theologian Paul Tillich has, that some such discrepancy between essence and existence is fundamental to all those religions of the world that are oriented to "salvation" and enlightenment. They all assume that human beings have forfeited or lost some original state of being to which they need to be restored. Like Hegel and Kierkegaard, Tillich himself interpreted the Christian myth of Original Sin in these terms. Although it is doubtful whether this particular idea is found in the Hebrew Bible, Christians have used

---

[31] Søren Kierkegaard, *Sickness Unto Death: A Christian Psychological Exposition for Upbuilding and Awakening*, ed. and trans. with intro. and notes by Howard V. Hong and Edna H. Hong (Princeton: Princeton University Press, 1980).

the terms "alienation" and "estrangement" to describe the human state after the expulsion of Adam and Eve from the Garden of Eden. The profundity of this idea, Tillich wrote, lies in the idea that the human being is

> not what it essentially is and ought to be. He is estranged from his true being . . . that one belongs essentially to that from which one is estranged. Man is not a stranger to his true being for he belongs to it. He is judged by it but cannot completely be separated [from it], even if he is hostile to it.[32]

But as Richard Schacht has pointed out, the plausibility of this idea is dependent upon the concept of essence itself, and "any lack of clarity as to what constitutes man's essence results in a lack of clarity with regard to the precise nature of estrangement."[33] One finds this lack of clarity in Feuerbach's view. The difficulty is that his idea of the human essence or species includes at least two logically distinct ideas: first, the notion of the human essence refers to those inherent potentialities the realization of which constitutes the "truly human"; second, it refers to the species taken as a totality. The first idea is still plausible to most contemporary readers; the second is so only if one can accept the Hegelian assumption, held by Feuerbach and some of his contemporaries like David F. Strauss, that the idea of the species cannot be exemplified in any one individual but only in the totality of all individuals, in which the multiplicity of exemplars complement one another.

It is this Hegelian assumption, incidentally, that is the basis for Strauss's criticism of Hegel's demythologization of the doctrine of the Incarnation, just as it is for Feuerbach's assumption that Christ is the image under which the species idea is made present to the populace. Strauss argued against Hegel that the Idea (the essence) "is not wont to lavish all its fulness on one exemplar." Consequently, the "key to the whole of Christology" is "that, as subject of the predicate which the church assigns to Christ, we place, instead of an individual, an idea." It is Humanity that is the union of two natures, and that dies and rises again.[34]

It is the fusion of these two ideas that explains the feeling

---

[32] Paul Tillich, *Systematic Theology*, vol. II, *Existence and the Christ* (Chicago: University of Chicago Press, 1957), p. 45.

[33] Schacht, *Alienation*, p. 216.

[34] David Friedrich Strauss, *The Life of Jesus Critically Examined*, ed. with intro. by Peter C. Hodgson, trans. George Eliot, Lives of Jesus Series, 4th ed. (Philadelphia: Fortress Press, 1972), p. 780.

contemporary readers of *Christianity* frequently have that Feuerbach has articulated a profound insight but that there is something unintelligible about the implications he draws from it. The first formulation enables us to understand Feuerbach's objection that Christianity alienates because it elevates the individual to such an extent as to deny his/her species nature; which is to say, it denies the I–Thou structure of human life. The second formulation, however, seems arcane and strange because we can make no sense of alienation as a failure to regard the totality of humanity as perfect.

These problems in Feuerbach's conception of the species as the proper human object of religious veneration come out most clearly in the chapter entitled "The Distinction between Christianity and Heathenism." This chapter, incidentally, also raises the question whether the religious projection is intrinsically alienating or whether Christianity is only a special case. In any event, he argued that heathens, at least, consider human beings to be essentially connected with one another, whereas Christianity has elevated the individual beyond the bonds and laws of nature. The Christian error, he claimed, is "the total absence of the idea of the species," an error he thought was best seen in the Christian doctrine of the universal sinfulness of all human beings.

Feuerbach took this Christian doctrine of Original Sin to mean that Christians felt themselves to be guilty or sinful because they fail to be perfect; which is to say, they assume that as individuals they could have adequately represented the perfections of the species. But this is an error, he concluded, because "only men taken together are what man should and can be."[35] Feuerbach's conclusion is so confused at this point that I feel that I should quote it at length lest I be accused of parodying his view.

All men are sinners. Granted; but they are not all sinners in the same way; on the contrary, there exists a great and essential difference between them. One man is inclined to falsehood, another is not; he would rather give up his life than break his word or tell a lie; the third has a propensity to intoxication, the fourth to licentiousness; while the fifth, whether by favour of Nature, or from the energy of his character, exhibits none of these vices. Thus, in the *moral* as well as the physical and intellectual elements, men *compensate* for each other, so that, taken as a whole, they are as they should be, they present the perfect man.[36]

---

[35] Feuerbach, *Christianity*, p. 155; *Christentums*, p. 272.
[36] *Christianity*, pp. 155f.; *Christentums*, p. 272.

This argument is confused because, first of all, if one were to add up all the defects of countless individuals the result would not be a picture of the "the perfect man." A countless but large number of individual defects can only justify the conclusion that human beings are defective, albeit in different ways. It is also confused because it undercuts any possibility of achieving the aim which Wartofsky attributes to Feuerbach; namely, that authentic humanity be fully realized in every individual. If any person could argue that any of his/her actions, however defective – as liar, thief, even rejecter of the Thou – contributed to the perfection of the whole, then the normative demand upon each human individual to become "authentically human" would be meaningless.

The argument that the sum total of individuals constitutes "a perfect man" occurs later in the same chapter, and from this Feuerbach draws the incredible conclusion that all the sins of individual persons will vanish in the idea of the species itself. This argument is also so revealing that it seems important to quote it at length.

Hence the lamentation over sin is found only where the human individual regards himself in his individuality *as a perfect, complete being, not needing others* for the realization of the species, of the perfect man; where *instead of the consciousness of the species* has been substituted the *exclusive self-consciousness of the individual*; where the individual does not recognize himself as *a part* of mankind, but identifies himself with the species, and for this reason makes his own sins, limits and weaknesses, the sins, limits, and weaknesses of mankind in general. Nevertheless man cannot lose the consciousness of the species, for his self-consciousness is essentially united to his consciousness of another than himself. Where therefore the species is not an object to him *as a species*, it will be an object to him *as God*. He supplies the absence of the idea of the species by the idea of God, as the being who is free from the limits and wants which oppress the individual, and, in his opinion (since he identifies the species with the individual), the species itself. But this perfect being, free from the limits of the individual, is nothing else than the species, which reveals the infinitude of its nature in this, that it is realized in infinitely numerous and various individuals.[37]

Kierkegaard poured out his biting sarcasm on this idea of the perfection of the species, and although sarcasm does not qualify as intellectual criticism, it will nevertheless strike many contemporary readers as justified in this case. With this faith that the species is

---

[37] *Christianity*, p. 157; *Christentums*, pp. 275f.

divine, he wrote, idealistic philosophy has sunk so low that the mob has become the God-man.[38]

THE CONTRADICTIONS OF CHRISTIANITY

Since most commentators have interpreted Feuerbach's theory of alienation as simply an inversion of the Hegelian schema of objectification–alienation–reappropriation, those readers who find this schema unconvincing will naturally be disposed to dismiss his critique of religion as an interesting but antiquated episode in the history of atheism. As I have attempted to demonstrate, this would be a mistake, even though there are aspects of the theory that are clearly untenable.

It is a mistake for still another reason: it ignores a number of serious criticisms both of religion and theology that are quite independent of the theory of alienation. The crucial negative term here is not "alienation" but "contradiction."

The term "contradiction," it soon becomes evident, was loosely employed by Feuerbach to cover a number of diverse things to which he objected: doctrines with which he simply disagreed; doctrines that seem to exhibit what he thought to be characteristic of the "religious illusion"; mutually inconsistent attributes of God; and, finally, virtues that seem to be incompatible. Most of these contradictions are attributed not to religion but to theology. Whereas religion is the first "involuntary, childlike, simple act of the mind" that no sooner separates God from humanity than it identifies them again, theology makes this unintentional and involuntary act into an "intentional, excogitated separation, which has no other object than to banish again from the consciousness this identity which has already entered there."[39] It is religion, then, that contains the "true essence of religion," and it is theology that embodies the "false essence of religion." Religion is relatively harmless, but theology alienates.

Initially, this distinction between religion and theology seems to be both simple and unproblematic. It enabled Feuerbach to identify religion with feeling and theology with dogma and, hence, to regard the former as relatively harmless until corrupted by the latter. But when one analyzes this distinction in all of its ramifications, it becomes clear that it is more problematic than it initially appears.

---

[38] Kierkegaard, *Sickness Unto Death*, p. 118.
[39] Feuerbach, *Christianity*, p. 197; *Christentums*, pp. 334f.

Some of this is due to Feuerbach's own complex relationship to Hegel at the time. He was indebted to him but increasingly critical of him.

It had been basic to the Hegel's philosophy of culture that all of the various expressions of human consciousness – art, religion, philosophy – be seen as vehicles through which the Absolute Spirit gradually comes to self-conscious freedom in the course of human history. Religion, Hegel argued, was the penultimate stage of this developmental process because, unlike philosophy, which articulates the truth in the form of concepts (*Begriffe*), religion clothes these same truths in the form of images (*Vorstellungen*). Of the various religions, Christianity is the absolute religion because it embodies the deepest metaphysical truths in its myths and symbols. The doctrine of creation symbolizes the going forth of the Infinite into the finite, and the doctrine of the Incarnation symbolizes the reconciliation of the Infinite with this estranged "otherness."

Although Feuerbach turned this Hegelian metaphysical schema upside down, so to speak, he nevertheless retained certain elements of Hegel's developmental schema. He, too, shared the view that religion clothes abstractions in the form of images – that religion is penultimate to philosophy – and he too believed that religion is a necessary step in the evolution of self-consciousness, although in his case this self-consciousness entailed atheism. Thus Feuerbach could claim that religion is a "childlike condition of humanity" in which "a man is an object to himself, under the form of another man." Just as the child develops, so, also, "the historical progress of religion consists in this: that what by an earlier religion was regarded as objective, is now recognized as subjective; that is, what was formerly contemplated and worshipped *as God* is now perceived to be something *human*." What earlier was regarded as religion is later seen as idolatry. Each religion, then, is an advance, and "every advance in religion is therefore a deeper self-knowledge."[40]

Given this developmental view of religion, Feuerbach also seemed to regard Christianity as the most highly developed form of religion. But whereas Hegel justified this evaluation on the grounds that Christianity taught the reconciliation of the Infinite with the finite, Feuerbach justified it on the grounds that it taught that God had renounced his divinity out of love for humanity. Christianity, in short, implicitly contains the insight that humanity is really more important

---

[40] *Christianity*, p. 13; *Christentums*, p. 47.

than God, hence atheism. "Is not then the proposition, 'God loves man' an orientalism (religion is essentially oriental), which in plain speech means, the highest is the love of man?"[41]

Hence, only in Christ is the last wish of religion realized, the mystery of religious feeling solved: – solved however in the language of imagery proper to religion, for what God is in *essence*, that Christ is in actual *appearance*. So far the Christian religion may justly be called the absolute religion.[42]

Even though Feuerbach adopted certain aspects of Hegel's developmental schema, his theory of religion, as we have seen, also contained genuinely new and anti-Hegelian elements, and it is not surprising, therefore, that the latter, in turn, put severe conceptual strains on the former.

Consider this example. The Hegelian developmental paradigm tends to view theology as necessary for the full development of self-consciousness, whereas Feuerbach's position would seem to be that it would have been better for humanity had theology never emerged at all. But if theology with its inherent contradictions had never emerged at all, how would the human consciousness have ever been led to the insight that the inner meaning of religion is atheism? Theology and its contradictions are just those things that invite the "deconstruction" performed on it by the atheistic thinker, that justify the claim that "What yesterday was still religion is no longer such to-day; and what to-day is atheism, tomorrow will be religion."[43] But just in so far as theology is necessary for this atheistic insight, what sense is there in saying that theology is more corrupting than religion? Both would seem to be dialectically necessary. Just as the race must pass through childhood and adolescence before achieving maturity, so also it must go through the education of both religion and theology.

To complicate this matter, the sharp distinction between an innocent religion and a corrupt theology is further blurred by an argument in which religion appears to be much less harmless than the metaphor of childlike innocence suggests. If theology is the mistaken reification of the species with its subsequent contradictions, then religion is the expression of the inherent narcissism of the individual self, the omnipotence of the wish. Indeed, it is ironic that one of the most revealing chapters on the corrupting tendencies of religion

---

[41] *Christianity*, p. 58; *Christentums*, p. 116.
[42] *Christianity*, p. 145; *Christentums*, p. 256.
[43] *Christianity*, p. 32; *Christentums*, p. 74.

appears in part II, which is devoted to a criticism of theology.[44] Here Feuerbach repeats the argument he had made earlier that the practical and subjective standpoint of religion is dominated by the wish to exempt the self from all objective conditions and limitations, as can be seen in intercessory prayer and belief in miracle. Like Kierkegaard, Feuerbach believed that the essence of the faith was belief in possibility, the confidence that God could set aside all of the necessities of nature when the well-being of the individual subject was at stake. Consequently, the practical religious standpoint is basically inimical to the theoretical point of view and, hence, to knowledge in general and science in particular. The religious view, rather, considers the world entirely from the standpoint of the narrow aims of the self and is hostile to the acquisition of knowledge concerning the realm of external causes and effects.

This anti-intellectual thrust of religion, Feuerbach argued, is visible in the religious believer's view both of his/her inner life and of external nature. In the inner life, for example, anything which the religious spirit experiences involuntarily is immediately assumed to come from some external source. Evil thoughts and impulses stem from evil powers, whereas the

involuntary movements of inspiration and ecstasy appear to it as the work of the Good Being, God, of the Holy Spirit or of grace. Hence the arbitrariness of grace – the complaint of the pious that grace at one time visits and blesses them, at another forsakes and rejects them.[45]

So too, in the realm of physical nature, the basic narcissism of wishing reveals itself in the hostility to the search for explanations in terms of secondary causes. Naïve religion, in fact, knows nothing of a realm of secondary causes, and when the awareness of such causes intrudes itself upon the consciousness, there is a diminution of belief in a divine cause. "Second causes are a capitulation of the unbelieving intellect with the still believing heart."[46] As the awareness of secondary causes develops, God becomes more and more a hypothetical being who created the world in some remote past time or an explanation for the inexplicable. "[God] . . . is the ignorance which *solves* all doubt by *repressing* it . . . Darkness (*Die Nacht*) is the mother of religion."[47] In a sentence that might as easily come from Nietzsche,

[44] *Christianity*, chapter 19, "The Essential Standpoint of Religion."
[45] *Christianity*, p. 187; *Christentums*, p. 319.
[46] *Christianity*, p. 189; *Christentums*, p. 323.
[47] *Christianity*, p. 193; *Christentums*, p. 329.

Feuerbach wrote that "In relation to the inner life, grace may be defined as *religious genius*; in relation to the outer life as *religious chance*."[48]

This depiction of the subjective standpoint of religion hardly justifies the attribution of harmlessness to religion and corruption to theology.

From the standpoint of religious studies, another problem that results from Feuerbach's ambivalence towards Hegel is his ambiguity regarding the relation of Christianity to the other religions. On the one hand, he seems to have adopted the Hegelian view that Christianity is the absolute religion, although his un-Hegelian reason is that it simply brings to expression the anthropomorphic tendencies in all religion. On the other hand, he often compares Christianity invidiously with paganism because of its absolutization of feeling and wish and the resultant elevation of the individual over the species. When adopting the former developmental schema, he tended to interchange the words "religion" and "Christianity" and to move easily from one to the other. When adopting the latter view, he argued that Christianity is inferior to heathen religions because, unlike them, it does not have a consciousness of the species, of being linked to nature and other human beings. The result, as he was later to confess, is a basic unclarity regarding the distinction between Christianity and other religions. This unclarity, in turn, results in a basic ambiguity regarding the alienating propensity of religion. Does it occur only in a theological religion, like Christianity, or is it endemic to religion as such?

This tendency to interchange "religion" and "Christianity" is most evident in part II of the book, which is devoted to a consideration of the "falsehoods, illusions, contradictions, sophisms" that arise when the religious projection of human nature is made into an object of reflection (theology). For it is not the religious projections of the non-Christian religions that are criticized, but those of Christianity. Thus a section of the book devoted to the "false essence of religion" is really a section devoted to the contradictions of Christian theology.

Two of these contradictions are worth discussing. The first of them is, as the word suggests, intellectual; the second concerns the depths of personal existence and is more interesting.

The most fundamental intellectual contradiction of Christian theology is two-fold, Feuerbach contended, in that it attempts to

---

[48] *Christianity*, p. 187; *Christentums*, p. 320.

combine in one notion of God two mutually incompatible types of predicates – metaphysical, on the one hand, and personal, on the other – and then rationalizes the resulting contradictions with the assertion that the divine being is incomprehensible to the human intellect. On the one hand, the divine being is said to be omniscient, omnipresent, omnipotent, and impassible; on the other hand, this God is a loving and compassionate being who is moved by human suffering. As Feuerbach regarded it, "The fundamental idea is a contradiction which can be concealed only by sophisms."[49]

This criticism, of course, was not original with Feuerbach, nor is it a criticism that has been made only by skeptics and unbelievers. With Pascal, reflective Christians have always been troubled by the enormous discrepancy between what he called "the god of Abraham, Isaac, and Jacob" and the "god of the philosophers."[50] The God of Abraham is a personal, compassionate being and concerned even with the fall of the sparrow, whereas the God of the philosophers, by contrast, is an unchangeable being who sees the world in a timeless act of vision and who, by definition, cannot be affected or "suffer" in any way by what it sees.

Pascal's formulation of the discrepancy too easily suggests that the conflict is simply between personal religious piety, on the one hand, and philosophy, on the other, when in fact it has been Christian theologians themselves, not philosophers, who have attributed to God impassibility, omniscience, omnipotence, and the like. The conflict is not so much between faith and philosophy as between ordinary Christian belief in the God of the Bible, on the one hand, and the dominant Christian intellectual tradition of the West, on the other.

Contemporary readers will recognize in Feuerbach's criticism an anticipation of a similar criticism that has been leveled against classical theism in our own time by a number of philosophical theologians, including F. R. Tennant, Alfred North Whitehead, and, most comprehensively, by Charles Hartshorne, whose criticisms of classical theism have had such an influence on Process Theology.[51] In

---

[49] *Christianity*, p. 213; *Christentums*, p. 359.

[50] This criticism is most typically made by non-Catholic theologians and philosophers of religion. Beginning with Luther, the list of those who have noted this contradiction and wrestled with it is impressive: Nicholas Berdyaev, F. R. Tennant, Karl Barth, Emil Brunner, Rudolf Bultmann, Freidrich Gogarten, Reinhold Niebuhr, Gustaf Aulen, Schubert Ogden, Gordon Kaufman, John Cobb, and many others.

[51] See especially the works of John Cobb and Schubert Ogden. One should also note that Karl Barth has made a similar criticism of classical theism, but on the grounds that these metaphysical categories are not implicit in or given with revelation.

his many books Hartshorne has argued that classical Christian theology has, to its own detriment, systematically avoided or explained away the intuitions of ordinary Christian believers that God is a personal being whose own life is enriched and even changed by its experience of the created world. The reasons Christians have not incorporated these religious intuitions into their doctrines are due, first, to the tendencies of believers to celebrate sovereignty and power, and second, to the uncritical acceptance of classical Greek philosophical categories by Christian theologians. In Greek philosophy, which Christian theologians began to employ systematically in the first few centuries after Christ, perfection was equated with change-lessness (impassibility) and imperfection with change. God as perfect being was said to be "pure actuality," while imperfect finite being was said to characterized by the change from potentiality to actuality. Since knowledge of whatever kind involves being affected by objects, God, the perfect being, could not, it was argued, either "know" or be acted upon.

To demonstrate that he has not caricatured the Christian tradition in this respect, Hartshorne is fond of turning to those classical Christian texts that are particularly revelatory of this internal contradiction. One of the most revealing of these comes from the hand of St. Anselm of Canterbury, one of the great medieval exemplars of both Christian piety and theological imagination. In his famous work *Proslogium*, Anselm hoped to produce a single argument for the existence of God and for what might reasonably be believed about God's nature. After the first four chapters, in which Anselm offers the famous Ontological Argument, he turned to those attributes that might fairly be predicated of that being "than which nothing greater can be conceived": for example, the attributes of omnipotence, compassion, and passionlessness. This discourse, however, is suddenly interrupted by the appearance of a conundrum: How can God be both compassionate and passionless? That the discourse is written in the form of a prayer only adds to the pathos of his reasoning.

But how art thou compassionate, and, at the same time, passionless? For, if thou art passionless, thou dost not feel sympathy; and if thou dost not feel sympathy, thy heart is not wretched from sympathy for the wretched; but this it is to be compassionate. But if thou art not compassionate, whence cometh so great consolation to the wretched? How, then, art thou compassionate and not compassionate, O Lord, unless because thou art compassionate in terms of our experience, and not compassionate in terms of thy being?

Truly, thou art so in terms of our experience, but thou art not so in terms of thine own. For, when thou beholdest us in our wretchedness, we experience the effect of compassion, but thou dost not experience the feeling. Therefore, thou art both compassionate, because thou dost save the wretched, and spare those who sin against thee; and not compassionate, because thou art affected by no sympathy for wretchedness.[52]

Both Feuerbach and Hartshorne could have agreed that the intellectual contortions that appear in Anselm's prayer – Thou art compassionate in terms of our own experience and not compassionate in terms of Thy being – are the tortured results of attempting to reconcile the intuitions of the Christian heart with theology. But whereas Hartshorne would have argued that Anselm's problems stem from his attempt to articulate faith in terms of Greek categories, Feuerbach would have contended that the contradiction arises from the absolutization of the predicates of intellect and feeling and their combination in one transcendent being. The imagination thinks of the projected other as quantitatively greater than any finite being. This divine being not only exists but exists at all times and in all places; it loves but loves to a superlative degree; it knows but knows everything, past and future. Theology, in short, transforms the quantitative limits of the imagination into qualitative limits as well. The intellect then becomes puzzled by the apparent contradictions and takes refuge in the notion of the divine incomprehensibility, a move that has the effect of doing away with the similarity of the divine and the human. The favorite expression of theological apologetics, Feuerbach remarks, "is, that we can indeed know concerning God that he has such and such attributes, but not *how* he has them."[53] The result of this appeal to divine incomprehensibility, paradoxically, is to deny "precisely that determination or quality which makes a thing *what it is*."[54] The concept of God, in short, is the "central point of Christian sophistry."[55]

A typical example of this procedure, Feuerbach believed, was the way in which the notion of divine activity has been mystified and made unintelligible in the history of Christianity. Just as ordinary believers think of God as knowing and loving, so also they think of God as acting, as intervening in nature and history. But all human

---

[52] St. Anselm, *Proslogium; Monologium; An Appendix in Behalf of the Fool by Gaunilon; and Cur Deus Homo*, trans. Sidney Norton Deane (LaSalle: Open Court, 1948), pp. 13f.
[53] Feuerbach, *Christianity*, p. 217; *Christentums*, p. 365.
[54] *Christianity*, p. 221; *Christentums*, p. 370. [55] *Christianity*, p. 213; *Christentums*, p. 359.

productive activity is determinate and issues in a specific result. The divine activity, by contrast, must be thought of as manifested in everything, as omnipresent. As a result the notion of activity is emptied of any content:

> it is a necessary consequence . . . [of this] . . . that the *mode in which* God has produced the All is incomprehensible, because this activity is no *mode* of activity, because the *question concerning the how is here an absurdity*, a question which is excluded by the *fundamental idea of unlimited activity*.[56]

THE INNER CONFLICT BETWEEN FAITH AND LOVE

The last of the seven chapters devoted to unmasking the "False or Theological Essence of Religion" is not concerned with intellectual contradictions but with a conflict between the two basic dispositions that determine the subjective life of the Christian believer: faith and love. The conflict has to do not with *what* is believed but with an "inward disunion" in the believer, a disunion that inevitably expresses itself in an outer disunion as well.[57] Although Feuerbach, characteristically, first states the argument in his own technical terms – the latent essence of religion is the *identity* of the divine being with the human, but the form of religion consists in the distinction between them – he soon moves to a very straightforward statement of what he believed to be a dilemma that arises from Christian faith itself. If love is the fundamental virtue that leads Christians to identify themselves with others, faith forces them not only to distinguish themselves but to anathematize and condemn others. Love is universal; faith is partial. Love unifies the self; faith "produces in man an *inward* disunion, *a disunion with himself*, and by consequence an outward disunion also."[58] Since this contradiction arises from the pitting of one Christian virtue against another, it is not surprising that many readers, confronting this text for the first time, find this chapter, "The Contradiction of Faith with Love," to be the most disturbing in the book.[59]

The argument turns on regarding the Christian faith not as some generalized trust in a deity but as a determinate intellectual judgment as to what is true and, hence, what is false. The Christian faith is a response to a specific revelation, and knowledge so revealed is a

---

[56] *Christianity*, p. 218; *Christentums*, p. 366.
[57] *Christianity*, p. 247; *Christentums*, p. 409. [58] *Christianity*, p. 247; *Christentums*, p. 409.
[59] Over many decades, I have discovered that university students are invariably more shaken by this chapter than any other.

saving knowledge. It follows that those who do not accept this revelation are not merely in ignorance and error but in perdition. Consequently, Christians have a special responsibility not only to communicate this saving knowledge but to protect it from error, and this is accomplished by formulating it in the form of dogma. Dogma is not something extrinsic to faith but is an expression of its inner nature, the necessity of separating truth from error. Christianity, in the nature of the case, is dogmatic, exclusive, scrupulously particular, and intolerant, and it would not have survived without these qualities.[60]

To those familiar with the history of skepticism and free thought, especially in the eighteenth century, Feuerbach's criticisms of the intolerance of traditional Christian faith are, taken by themselves, scarcely original. This literature is replete with accusations that the damnation of heretics and unbelievers is a necessary and logical consequence of Christian exclusivism. What distinguishes Feuerbach's criticisms from most others is the rich and "suspicious" analysis of the psychology of faith that underlies this exclusivism, his view that the "hostile dispositions" of faith arise from the peculiar combination of dignity, arrogance, humility, and fanaticism inherent in the conviction that one has been singled out for salvation by the divine.

Although there are passages that lend themselves to the view that Feuerbach tended to equate faith with intellectual assent, it soon becomes clear in the course of the chapter that the attractiveness and power of faith consist in something far more fundamental: the dignity, the sense of worth, it confers upon the believer. Religious faith is not simply the desire to be saved or to be free from the limitations and necessities of nature; it is also the desire to be acknowledged and affirmed by a divine Thou. If the recognition by a finite other gives one a sense of worth, then the recognition and acceptance by an infinite other gives "man a *peculiar sense of his own dignity and importance*."[61]

In this respect, Feuerbach's view of faith is similar to that of another young thinker who also felt it necessary to revolt against Hegel's understanding of religion, Søren Kierkegaard. In one of his most powerful "Christian" writings, *Sickness Unto Death*, Kierkegaard also observed that the distinctive element in Christian faith lies in this,

---

[60] Feuerbach, *Christianity*, pp. 251–256; *Christentums*, pp. 416–424.
[61] *Christianity*, p. 249; *Christentums*, p. 413.

that a human being should have this reality: that as an *individual* human being a person is directly before God and consequently, as a corollary, that a person's sin should be of concern to God.[62]

Some people think Christianity is dark and gloomy, he went on, but the real reason it offends the intellect is "that it is too high, because its goal is not man's goal, because it wants to make man into something so extraordinary that he cannot grasp the thought."[63] It is as if a day-laborer in a kingdom ruled by a mighty king should learn that this king had wished to have him for his son-in-law. It would be understandable if the day-laborer were to excuse himself and say that such an invitation was "too high" for him, that he could not get it into his head. And yet this is precisely the Christian claim:

Christianity teaches that this individual human being – and thus every single individual human being, no matter whether man, woman, servant girl, cabinet minister, merchant, barber, student, or whatever – this individual human being exists *before God*, this individual human being who perhaps would be proud of having spoken with the king once in his life, this human being who does not have the slightest illusion of being on intimate terms with this one or that one, this human being exists before God, may speak with God any time he wants to, assured of being heard by him – in short, this person is invited to live on the most intimate terms with God! Furthermore, for this person's sake, also for this very person's sake, God comes to the world, allows himself to be born, to suffer, to die, and this suffering God – he almost implores and beseeches this person to accept the help that is offered to him![64]

Kierkegaard believed that this claim constituted the "offense" of Christianity and was essential for understanding that religion. Feuerbach also believed this, except that, unlike Kierkegaard, he believed that the needs of the narcissistic individual ego could scarcely have found a more satisfying gospel than the fantastic claim that the individual believer exists face to face with the creator. Moreover, he thought that a peculiarly sadistic twist can be given to this sense of having been singled out by the Divine; namely, that others have not been elected. An essential element in the story of the day-laborer, to return to Kierkegaard's parable, is that the king has passed over and ignored others. "The believer," wrote Feuerbach, "finds himself distinguished above other men, exalted above the *natural* man." She/he is an aristocrat among plebeians.[65] The

---

[62] Kierkegaard, *Sickness Unto Death*, p. 83.
[63] Kierkegaard, *Sickness Unto Death*, p. 83.   [64] Kierkegaard, *Sickness Unto Death*, p. 85.
[65] Feuerbach, *Christianity*, p. 249; *Christentums*, p. 413.

Christian "knows" God personally; the heathen does not. The Christian has a secret which the heathen does not share. He/she has knowledge and they are ignorant. The Christian, to be sure, can be said to "exist for the heathen; but *mediately*, on condition that they cease to be heathens and become Christians."[66]

The key to understanding the defect in what might otherwise be considered a good thing in the psychology of the Christian, Feuerbach believed, is this: Although faith brings with it a sense of dignity and self-worth, this dignity is conveyed circuitously, as it were. Believers do not possess dignity in themselves, but only acquire it mediately through a deity that is distinct from them. Just as a servant sometimes identifies himself with the social class of his employer, so, too, the believer's superior status is a derived status. Indeed, it is because this dignity is borrowed that we can account for one of the revealing psychological paradoxes of religious faith; namely, that what the believer experiences as humility appears to others as arrogance. In a passage that anticipates the "suspicion" of Nietzsche, Feuerbach concluded:

In fact, we have here the characteristic principle of religion, that it changes that which is naturally active into the passive. The heathen elevates himself, the Christian feels himself elevated. The Christian converts into a matter of feeling, of receptivity, what to the heathen is a matter of spontaneity. The humility of the believer is an inverted arrogance, – an arrogance none the less because it has not the *appearance*, the external characteristics of arrogance. He feels himself pre-eminent: this pre-eminence, however, is not a result of his activity, but a matter of grace.[67]

This sense of self-worth is made even more dangerous by the conviction that faith leads to the eternal salvation of the soul. It is not just that the individual soul stands face to face before the creator and so receives cosmic recognition; it is that the soul is saved from perdition. This inevitably involves the judgment that those who are passed over remain enemies of the divine. Not only does the Christian faith involve the belief that one possesses a knowledge that others do not have, but when these others do not respond to the message of salvation, the Church feels justified in condemning them, to attributing their unbelief to moral weakness and pride. As always, Feuerbach was happy to document this condemnation with copious quotations from Christian theologians throughout the ages. "*In faith*," he concluded,

[66] *Christianity*, p. 249; *Christentums*, p. 413.
[67] *Christianity*, p. 250; *Christentums*, p. 414.

"*there lies a malignant principle.*"[68] And because the Christian's dignity is passive in character, the condemnation of the unbelievers possesses a peculiarly fanatical quality: "*its cause* is the *cause of God, its honor his honor.*"[69]

It is on the basis of this complex analysis of the psychology of faith that Feuerbach brought forward that criticism of Christianity now so familiar to readers of humanistic literature: that faith corrupts both the moral and the truth sense. The corruption of the moral sense consists simply in the fact that faith is preeminent above all natural moral considerations. It "makes salvation dependent on *itself*, not on the fulfillment of *common* human duties."[70] Indeed, believers frequently experience what they think is a conflict between common human duties and faith. This is understandable, Feuerbach claimed, because

there is no natural, inherent connection between faith and the moral disposition, that, on the contrary, it lies *in the nature of faith* that it is *indifferent* to moral duties, that it sacrifices *the love* of man to the *honour* of God, – *for this reason* it is required that faith should have good works as its consequence, that it should prove itself by love.[71]

So, too, Feuerbach argued, faith corrupts the "sentiment of truth."[72] Any faith that rests on the conviction that God revealed himself only at a particular time and place and to certain individuals rather than "universal man" necessarily leads to superstition and, above all, sophistry. Where a single Scripture is believed to be inspired and above criticism, one has superstition; where the defense of the Bible rests on the use of present standards of probability and evidence, one has sophistry, a "*disingenuous, sophistical, tortuous* mode of thought, which is occupied only with groundless distinctions and subterfuges, with ignominious tricks and evasions."[73]

Faith, Feuerbach concluded, is the opposite of love, and this theoretical contradiction necessarily manifests itself as a practical contradiction. A love that is limited by faith is not a universal love but a "narrow-hearted and false love," as one can see, for example, in the "diabolical sophisms" to which St. Augustine is driven in his apologia for the persecution of heretics. Love is by nature universal.

So long as Christian love does not renounce its qualification of Christian, does not make love, simply, its highest law, so long is it a love which is

---

[68] *Christianity*, p. 252; *Christentums*, p. 418.   [69] *Christianity*, p. 255; *Christentums*, p. 422.
[70] *Christianity*, p. 261; *Christentums*, p. 430.   [71] *Christianity*, p. 261; *Christentums*, pp. 431f.
[72] *Christianity*, p. 209; *Christentums*, p. 355.   [73] *Christianity*, p. 212; *Christentums*, p. 358.

injurious to the sense of truth, for the very office of love is to abolish the distinction between Christianity and so-called heathenism – so long is it a love which by its particularity is in contradiction with the nature of love, an abnormal, loveless love, which has therefore long been justly an object of sarcasm. True love is *sufficient to itself*; it needs no special title, no authority.[74]

Christianity, to be sure, is an intense manifestation of this new principle of love, but it makes "love collateral to faith" and thereby places itself in contradiction to universal love, the universal love embodied in the image of Christ. True veneration of this image would be doing what Christ did, loving humanity as a whole, the species. Hence, "where there arises the consciousness of the species as a species, the idea of humanity as a whole, Christ disappears, without, however, his true nature disappearing; for he was the substitute for the consciousness of the species, the image under which it was made present to the people, and became the *law* of the popular life."[75]

[74] *Christianity*, pp. 265f.; *Christentums*, p. 438.   [75] *Christianity*, p. 269; *Christentums*, pp. 442f.

CHAPTER 4

Feuerbach's intellectual development

THE IMPETUS TO REVISION

Although flawed in certain respects, *The Essence of Christianity* was one of the first attempts to construct a genuinely critical theory of religion, a theory that interprets the origins and persistence of religion in terms of the structure of the human psyche. It endeavored to answer certain fundamental questions: Why is it that religion is a universal phenomenon? Why are certain ideas and forms of religious practice found in it? Why are these ideas at once so emotionally powerful but conceptually problematical when made the object of rational inquiry? And even though this theory is inherently suspicious, it does not just dismiss religion as superstition but regards it as an "acoustical illusion" of consciousness, an illusion that arises naturally in the process of self-differentiation and that meets certain fundamental human desires. Because each religion is the dreamlike projection of a given culture's ideal image of humanity, it should also be regarded as a necessary stage in the human development towards self-knowledge. The suspicious interpreter, consequently, should not be regarded as an enemy of religion, a rationalistic debunker, but as someone who opens human eyes to its real meaning, who changes "the object as it is in the imagination into the object as it is in reality."[1]

There were then as now many criticisms made of the book. At the time, they came from two sources: quite expectedly from Protestant and Catholic theologians; quite unexpectedly from members of the circle of radical Young Hegelians who had gathered around the Bauer brothers in Berlin and with whom Feuerbach was himself ideologically identified. I write "unexpectedly" because Karl Marx, a member of that circle, had obviously been deeply impressed by Feuerbach's work and wrote that Feuerbach was "the only person

[1] Feuerbach, *Christianity*, p. xxxix; *Christentums*, p. 20.

who has a *serious* and a *critical* attitude toward the Hegelian dialectic"
and whose magnitude of achievement, as well as the quiet simplicity
with which he wrote, stood in marked contrast to other critics of
Hegel. "He is," Marx concluded, "the true conqueror of the old
philosophy."[2] Yet despite these words of praise, Marx also believed
that Feuerbach was still too much mired in the theoretical criticism of
philosophy and theology and, hence, could never dissipate the fog of
mystification that Hegel had spread over these issues. Although
Feuerbach's materialism was superior to previous materialisms
because of his emphasis on concrete relationships between persons, he
remained in the realm of pure theory and had nothing to say about
existing social conditions, which make persons what they are. He
tried to resolve the religious projection into the human essence, to
dissolve the holy family into the secular family, but he failed to see
that the human essence is "no abstraction inherent in each single
individual" but is an "ensemble of the social relations." He talked
about the religious sentiment, but did not understand that it was a
social product and not a universal disposition. He did not see that the
aim of philosophy is not to attempt to understand but to change the
world.[3]

So, too, Max Stirner, also a member of the circle, argued that
despite Feuerbach's criticism of abstract idealism, he had only
substituted still another abstraction, the species. Moreover, he had
mystified this abstraction by making it an object of religious
veneration. A consistent atheism, Stirner complained, would not only
have avoided the appeal to any sort of universal like the species but
would have avoided any reintroduction of religious feeling with
respect to it. He felt that Feuerbach was still too religious. And finally,
Bruno Bauer echoed this criticism by labeling Feuerbach "the
greatest mystic of all times."[4]

These criticisms might have troubled Feuerbach more than they
did were it not that his own restless mind was already rethinking and
reformulating his position. This continual intellectual movement, as
Charles Wilson has shown, characterized Feuerbach's mental life
from the outset.[5] In this case, it led to still another reformulation of the

---

[2] See Livingstone and Benton (trans.), *Karl Marx Early Writings*, p. 381.
[3] Livingstone and Benton (trans.), *Karl Marx Early Writings*, pp. 421–423.
[4] Cited in Hans-Martin Sass, *Ludwig Feuerbach in Selbstzeugnissen und Bilddokumenten dargestellt* (Hamburg: Rowohlt Taschenbuch Verlag, 1978), p. 77.
[5] See Wilson, *Feuerbach and the Search for Otherness*.

theory of religion that not only enabled him to answer more satisfactorily some of the criticisms made at the time but, as I shall attempt to demonstrate, led him to a position that is less vulnerable to contemporary objections: for example, that the theory of projection in *Christianity* is too dependent upon the objectification of the species idea; that the species idea, in turn, is too identified with a type of essentialism in which reason, will, and feeling are made the predicates of human nature; that the theory of projection never really explains the believer's sense that the gods are real, external realities; that Christianity is too identified with religion; and, finally, that religion must inevitably develop into philosophy.

The pattern of Feuerbach's development may be seen in three documents published in the years 1842–1844: *Preliminary Theses on the Reform of Philosophy* (1842); *Principles of the Philosophy of the Future* (1843); and *The Essence of Faith According to Luther* (1844). In this chapter I should like to discuss these three books because they constitute the necessary background for understanding a genuine shift in Feuerbach's conception of religion.

THE "NEW PHILOSOPHY" BASED ON SENSUOUSNESS

The *Principles of the Philosophy of the Future* is a reformulation and elaboration of the *Preliminary Theses on the Reform of Philosophy*, which, despite the adjective "Preliminary," was aimed at nothing less than the overthrow of Hegelianism. (Feuerbach had more brashly entitled the first edition *The Reformation of Philosophy*.) Both monographs are rather brief; the first consisting of sixty-nine paragraphs, many of which are no longer than a single sentence, and the second of only sixty-five paragraphs, most of which are two or three pages long. In both texts Feuerbach argues that Hegel's philosophy is the logical culmination of the movement towards the pantheism of which Spinoza had been "the Moses," and that the "realization" of Hegel's philosophy, in turn, is Feuerbach's own materialism and atheism. Both documents call for a "new philosophy" that will forsake the abstractions of Hegel's philosophy and concern itself with the embodied human individual and its concrete feelings and needs.

The second document, the *Principles*, though longer, is more complex and less well organized than the first and is, as commentators have noted, both difficult and confusing for most readers. Although ostensibly a statement of principles, a manifesto, more than half of the book (paragraphs 1–30) is a very compressed and highly selective history of the development of modern philosophy on the issues of pantheism and materialism together with an analysis of the alleged contradictions in Hegel's philosophy. To this is then added a series of paragraphs (31–65), often in the form of aphorisms, that treat the most difficult philosophical issues in tantalizing brevity and, hence, raise as many questions about the new as the old philosophy. One commentator, Manfred Vogel, blames the unsatisfactory nature of the text on the fact that Feuerbach had originally intended to write, or perhaps had already written, a larger book that, by his own admission, he had then cut "like a barbarian" out of fear of state censorship. But even though he had severely cut the text, he did nothing to revise the structure of what remained in order to make it correspond with the new aphoristic form.[6] Consequently, the historical section is too compressed to be convincing as history, and certain important principles of the new philosophy are announced in too rhetorical and aphoristic a manner to be persuasive as philosophy: for example, "Love is objectively as well as subjectively the criterion of Being, of truth, and of reality."[7]

Nevertheless, the document is especially useful for enabling us to understand those ideas that led him to reformulate his theory of religion. There is, first of all, his own understanding of his place in the intellectual history of the West. It is clear that he did not think of himself as just another free-thinker who objects to the hegemony of Christianity over Western culture but as a leader of a new humanistic movement that he believed was the inevitable outcome of the Protestant Reformation. Christianity, he argued, has suffered both a practical and a theoretical "dissolution." On the practical side, Luther had dissolved theology into anthropology by claiming that it was of no concern to the believer what God is "in and for Himself" but only what He is "for us." On the theoretical side, speculative theology had inadvertently led to the same end by moving from pantheism to Hegelianism. Feuerbach saw himself as the "realization" (culmination) of Luther's religious revolution, on the one hand, and of Hegel's philosophy, on the other.

The argument of the book is so severely compressed as to be almost unintelligible to present lay readers, but may be summarized in some

---

[6] Vogel, introduction to Feuerbach, *Principles*, pp. lxxf.
[7] *Principles*, para. 35, p. 54; *Grundsätze der Philosophie der Zukunft*, in *Kleinere Schriften II (1839–1846)*, *GW* ix, p. 319.

fashion such as this. Speculative philosophy, by which he means the metaphysical theism of Descartes, Leibniz, and their contemporaries, is really the intellectual successor in the West to Christian theism. It is, in fact, simply the consistent working out of this theism. The personal deity of naïve piety first evolved in the hands of medieval theologians into an infinite mind – an omniscient, infinite, "necessary being." But whereas this theism still permitted the naïve believer to think of God as a sensuous being who loves and is moved by the creatures, the god of the metaphysicians, Descartes and Leibniz, is a pure mind abstracted and separated from all material things. For them, God is defined primarily as a thinking being, and what it thinks are its own thoughts because its thinking is not distinguished from its being. God is in reality thought thinking itself. Thus the essence of logic is the essence of God.

Both this theism and speculative philosophy are, however, embarrassed by the existence of matter, which is conceived as the opposite of spirit. Further, they are perplexed by the question how it is possible to conceive of God as Infinite Spirit and yet acknowledge that this deity is limited in some way by an external material world.

The only consistent answer to these questions, Feuerbach argued, was Spinoza's pantheism, in which matter and spirit were viewed as two of the infinite number of divine attributes. In short, Feuerbach argued, pantheism is the inevitable development of theism. "All the conceptions of theism, when grasped, seriously considered, carried out, and realized, lead necessarily to pantheism. Pantheism is *consistent* theism."[8] But if pantheism is the inevitable and logical development of theism, it is also indistinguishable from atheism even though naïve believers continue to use personalistic symbols when they worship. It is atheism because "he who makes matter into an attribute of God declares matter to be a *divine being*."[9] Matter, which was originally the great problem for theology, has been co-opted and made divine. Theism, which had considered God to be an immaterial being, has been transformed into "theological materialism," in which God is simply a name for everything there is taken as a "divine" whole.

The theoretical development that culminated in Spinoza, Feuerbach contended, was accompanied by an even more radical shift in practical attitude brought about by the success of the physical sciences. If Spinoza is the theoretical negation of theology, then the

[8] *Principles*, para. 14, p. 20; *Grundsätze*, p. 283.
[9] *Principles*, para. 15, p. 22; *Grundsätze*, p. 285.

empiricism implicit in modern science is its practical negation because God is no longer practically regarded as a deity who intervenes in human affairs or who figures in any answer to a scientific problem about nature.

Thus, mankind in the modern era lost the organs for the supernatural world and its secrets only because it lost together with the faith also the disposition toward the supernatural world, because its essential tendency was anti-Christian and antitheological; that is, it was an anthropological, cosmic, realistic, and materialistic tendency.[10]

So far, Feuerbach's rehearsal of the theoretical and practical shifts in the sensibility of the West, although compressed, does not differ in important respects from the picture of the secularization of the West one finds in some intellectual histories even now. It differs only in the importance that is attributed to Hegel's philosophy in this development. Feuerbach regarded it as the culmination and synthesis of all those streams of thought he labeled "modern philosophy." It was Hegel, he claimed, who was able to forge an intellectual synthesis that seemed to do justice to theism, speculative philosophy, pantheism, and idealism. And he accomplished this by conceiving of all reality, matter included, as "the only true and absolute being" and, moreover, as Subject.

The most ingenious aspect of Hegel's synthesis, Feuerbach argued, was his treatment of matter, the Achilles' heel of all idealistic conceptions of reality. Hegel dealt with this issue by arguing that the divine Subject first objectifies itself in nature (matter) and then struggles with this matter in order to achieve self-conscious freedom. Matter is the self-expression (*Selbstentäusserung*) of Spirit. "Thus, matter itself receives spirit and mind; it is taken up into the absolute being as a moment in its life, growth, and development."[11] Whereas speculative theologians had regarded the divine being as separated from matter and placed the responsibility for the self-liberation of spirit from matter on the shoulders of humanity, Hegel proposed that God himself "undertake this labor and, like the heroes of paganism, fight through virtue for his divinity."[12]

But however ingenious this Hegelian solution might appear to be, it was, Feuerbach believed, inherently unstable. On the one hand,

---

[10] *Principles*, para. 15, p. 23; *Grundsätze*, p. 286.
[11] *Principles*, para. 21, p. 32; *Grundsätze*, p. 296.
[12] *Principles*, para. 21, p. 32; *Grundsätze*, p. 296.

Hegel may be read as an atheist who recognized the truth of materialism by viewing the history of nature and humanity as the life of God. On the other hand, he may be seen as a friend of theology because he negates the truth of atheism by having God take up matter into His own life. He "negates the negation," and this negation of the negation is the true affirmation. God becomes God only as He overcomes and negates matter. Thus, Feuerbach concluded, we are in the end once more back where we started from – "in the bosom of Christian theology."[13]

The Hegelian philosophy is the last magnificent attempt to restore Christianity, which was lost and wrecked, through philosophy and, indeed, to restore Christianity – as is generally done in the modern era – by *identifying* it with the *negation* of Christianity. The much-praised speculative identity of mind and matter, of the infinite and the finite, and of the divine and the human is nothing more than the unfortunate contradiction of the modern era. It is the identity of faith and disbelief, theology and philosophy, religion and atheism, Christianity and paganism, placed on its highest summit, on the summit of metaphysics.[14]

It follows from this analysis that the "new philosophy," the principles of which Feuerbach propounded, has as its first task the criticism of Hegel and, as its second, the demonstration that the new philosophy is the "realization" of Hegel's philosophy, a realization that is at the same time its negation.

In addition to his criticism of Hegel's idealism as an unstable amalgam of spirit and matter, theism and materialism, Feuerbach leveled a second more specific accusation against his old teacher, an accusation that was to anticipate a similar criticism made two or three years later by Søren Kierkegaard: Hegel, they charged, had confused thought with being, logic with existence, possibility with actuality. Both of them believed that this identification was implicit in Hegel's view that the divine Spirit logically unfolds in human history and, hence, that what is rational becomes actual and what is actual is therefore rational. Feuerbach believed that this identification of thought and being was a consequence of the speculative idea that God's essence contains existence, a formula which he thought was but another way of proclaiming the divinity of reason, that "*reason is the absolute* being, the *comprehensive unity of all truth* and reality, that there is nothing *in contrast* to reason, rather that reason is everything just as

---

[13] *Principles*, para. 21, p. 33; *Grundsätze*, p. 297.
[14] *Principles*, para. 21, p. 34; *Grundsätze*, pp. 297f.

God is, in strict theology, everything, that is, all essential and true being."[15]

Even though Feuerbach's criticisms of Hegel's identification of thought and being do not have the stylistic elegance of Kierkegaard's, some of his arguments are similar: for example, that the noun "being" is not a name but a concept, and that the existence of an object cannot be included in its essence. In other words, existence is not a predicate. Consequently, it is meaningless to say that God is a necessary being. A thing either does or does not exist, and a fly exists as much as the deity does.[16]

The similarity of Feuerbach's and Kierkegaard's logical arguments reflects a more fundamental commonality between the two young anti-Hegelian thinkers. They both put a premium on the spatial and temporal situation of any given human individual and his/her encounters with other such conditioned beings. For both of them logic at best could only provide a formal criterion for reality and truth. A real object, Feuerbach argued, "is given to me only where a being that affects me is given to me and where my self-activity – when I start from the viewpoint of thought – finds its *boundary* or resistance in the activity of another being."[17] These real sensuous encounters with objects and beings occur in space and time, where space is not understood as merely a "negative determination" (Hegel) but the determinative mode for existence itself. In a passage that seems remarkable in retrospect Feuerbach wrote that "To-be here (*Dasein*) is the primary being, the primary determination. *Here* I am – this is the first sign of a *real living* being . . . Where there is no space, there is also no room for *any system*. The *first determination of reason* on which every subsequent determination can rest is to *situate* things."[18]

It follows from this that one should not think of the self as merely a bearer of reason but as an embodied being in concrete and sensuous relationships with other embodied beings. In a passage that might equally have been written by Kierkegaard, he wrote,

Desire not to be a philosopher, *as distinct from a man*; be nothing else than a *thinking man*. Do not think *as a thinker*, that is, with a *faculty torn* from the *totality* of the real human being and *isolated* for itself; think as a *living and real* being, as

---

[15] *Principles*, para. 24, p. 38; *Grundsätze*, p. 302 (my translation).
[16] See Søren Kierkegaard, *Philosophical Fragments or A Fragment of Philosophy*, trans. with intro. and notes by David F. Swenson (Princeton: Princeton University Press, 1936), pp. 59–73.
[17] *Principles*, para. 32, p. 51; *Grundsätze*, p. 316.
[18] *Principles*, para. 44, p. 61; *Grundsätze*, p. 327.

one exposed to the vivifying and refreshing waves of the world's oceans. Think *in* existence, *in* the world as a member of it, not in the vacuum of abstraction as a solitary monad, as an absolute monarch, as an indifferent, superworldly God; then you can be sure that your ideas are unities of being and thought.[19]

But if Feuerbach shared this assumption with Kierkegaard, he also differed from him in important respects: first, on the importance of sensuousness (*Sinnlichkeit*), and second, on the social nature of the self. Feuerbach believed that human beings are related to the world and to other human beings through the body and the senses (*Sinne*), and that the "I" only exists in relation to a Thou. "The truth . . . [is] . . .," he wrote, "that *no being*, whether it is called man, God, spirit, or ego (*Ich*), *is for itself alone* a *true, perfect, absolute* being, that *truth* and *perfection* are alone the union and unity of two beings similar in essence."[20]

Feuerbach's notion that sensuousness is the unique way in which persons relate to the world is at once his most distinctive idea and the most difficult to render philosophically precise. It is not surprising, therefore, that commentators have assessed it quite differently. Some German interpreters of his thought, such as Alfred Schmidt, H. J. Braun, and Michael von Gagern, tend to regard this idea as Feuerbach's most important contribution to modern philosophy. The title of Alfred Schmidt's book, for instance, is *Emancipatory Sensuousness*.[21] But others, like Wartofsky, argue that although there is an interesting core of Feuerbach's argument that can be salvaged, the category of sensuousness is treated so loosely by him that it is inconsistent at the most crucial points.[22] This difference of opinion can partly be accounted for by Feuerbach's aphoristic and cryptic presentation of his ideas. For some commentators, these aphorisms elicit elaboration and refinement; for others, they are not much more than a series of dogmatic statements rather than arguments and can only be rendered philosophically intelligible, not to say plausible, by elaboration, extension, and guess work.

Nevertheless, the overall outline of his position seems more or less clear. The human body is the way in which the self is in the world. It is through the body that the "I" is related to the environment impinging upon it. This body, moreover, is always situated in some

---

[19] *Principles*, para. 51, p. 67; *Grundsätze*, p. 334.
[20] *Principles*, para. 63, p. 72; *Grundsätze*, p. 340 (my translation).
[21] *Emanzipatorische Sinnlichkeit: Ludwig Feuerbachs anthropologischer Materialismus, Reihe Hanser* 109 (Munich: Carl Hanser Verlag, 1973).   [22] Wartofsky, *Feuerbach*, p. 367.

definite time and space, some concrete situation. Consequently, it would not be inappropriate to call this self-body *Dasein*, being-there, even if it is difficult to rid that term of its Heideggerian overtones. And *Dasein*, in turn, is constituted by its own unique constellation of senses for mediating the world to consciousness. One might even say that the body is constituted in its mode of being as feeling (*Empfindung*).[23] Each human sense organ has its own unique need for satisfaction and, hence, experiences joy as well as pain, and each is an instrument of consciousness. *Sinnlichkeit*, then, is the link between the body and the psyche.

Even though *Dasein* is embodied in the world and has this world given to it through the senses, Feuerbach argued that the human being, unlike the animal, is not a "particular" but a "universal" being. It is a universal being because as conscious it is not a "limited and restricted being but rather an unlimited and free being, for universality, unlimitedness (*Unbeschränktheit*), and freedom are inseparable."[24]

Although this language of "universality" and "unlimitedness" still reflect to some degree his idealistic background, Feuerbach wanted to block the idealistic interpretation of it that grounded this "universality" in reason alone. Consequently, he claimed that this universality did not consist in some special faculty such as reason but that "this freedom and this universality extend themselves over man's *total* being"[25] because consciousness informs all the senses; or better, the senses penetrate consciousness.

Since this language now strikes modern readers as arcane, it might prove fruitful to linger over it somewhat. We find remarkably similar language in the young Karl Marx's *Economic and Philosophic Manuscripts*, which were written only one year after the *Principles* and, arguably, were heavily influenced by it.[26] But even if they were not so

---

23 See Hans-Jürg Braun, *Ludwig Feuerbachs Lehre vom Menschen* (Stuttgart-Bad Cannstatt: Friedrich Frommann Verlag, 1971), pp. 92–96.
24 *Principles*, para. 53, p. 69; *Grundsätze*, pp. 335f. Vogel translates *Unbeschränktheit* as "absoluteness" at one point but as "unlimitedness" at another. I have consistently rendered it as "unlimitedness," which is the better meaning.
25 *Principles*, para. 53, p. 69; *Grundsätze*, p. 336.
26 There is every possibility that Marx's formulation was indebted to Feuerbach's, although scholars have recognized that the relationship between the two is extremely complex. Some think the influence is profound; others think that all Marx found useful in Feuerbach was the "inversion principle" he applied to Hegel. Still others, with whom I agree, think that despite his later criticism of Feuerbach in his "Theses on Feuerbach," Marx was fleshing out in the *Paris Manuscripts* his own version of Feuerbach's notion of the species, which Marx calls "species being" (*Gattungswesen*). Marx's discussion in the section entitled "Alienated Labor"

influenced, it seems safe to assume that both of these Young Hegelians were groping for a way of speaking about human nature that took more account of the body and materiality than they thought Hegel did. The concern with "the species" as both sensuous and "universal" was their attempt to do this.

Marx's discussion of the "universality" of the human "species being" (*Gattungswesen*) appears in a section of the *Manuscripts* in which he discussed "alienated labor," his terms for the way in which he believed capitalism distorted and truncated human nature. In order to show how capitalism does this it was necessary for him to provide a sketch of authentic human being: that is, a sketch of what he believed were those inherent potentialities of the human that when realized constitute the "species being." He argued that although human beings, like the animals, are physical beings and live in relation to inorganic nature, they also possess consciousness, and therefore the realm in which man lives is more universal.[27] Marx meant by this that all of "inorganic nature" can be assimilated by human consciousness and transformed into an object of natural science and art so that it becomes integral to human life and activity. The "universality" of the human species consists in the fact that the whole of nature can become the "inorganic body" of the human in that it serves not only as a direct means of life but as the object and instrument of its own distinctive life activity. The animal, he stated, is "immediately one with its life activity." One might even say that it is its life activity, whereas "Man makes his life activity itself into an object of his will and consciousness."[28]

This interpenetration of the senses and consciousness is also what Feuerbach meant by "universality." "Man," he wrote, "is not a particular being like the animals; but is a *universal* being," which means that any given sense is elevated by consciousness above its bondage to a particular need and attains "independent and theoretical significance." Even the lowest senses of smell and taste, he wrote, "elevate themselves in man to intellectual and scientific activities."[29]

has clear parallels to paragraph 53 of the English and paragraph 54 of the second German edition of the *Principles*. In his introduction to the early writings of Marx, Lucio Colletti notes that in March of 1843, Marx wrote to Arnold Ruge saying that he had read Feuerbach's *Principles* and agreed with it wholeheartedly except for the exaggerated importance Feuerbach put on natural philosophy in contrast to history and politics. See Livingstone and Benton (trans.), *Karl Marx Early Writings*, pp. 22–24.

27 Livingstone and Benton (trans.), *Karl Marx Early Writings*, p. 327.
28 Livingstone and Benton (trans.), *Karl Marx Early Writings*, p. 328.
29 Feuerbach, *Principles*, para. 53, p. 69; *Grundsätze*, p. 336.

Although the overall outline of Feuerbach's view of the embodied self is relatively clear, what is less so is how he understood the relationship of sensuousness to thought. Sometimes, as in his criticism of Hegel's rejection of sense certainty in the early pages of the *Phenomenology*, he seemed to be saying that the senses provide immediate knowledge. He could even write somewhat carelessly that "The real *so far as its reality* is concerned, as *real*, is the reality *as an object of the senses* – the *sensuous. Truth, reality* and sensuousness are identical."[30] In other places, as we shall see below, he wrote as if there could be no uninterpreted perceptions, that all knowledge is, as Hegel also argued, mediated by thought.

Since Feuerbach tended in his critique of Hegel to counterpose "sensuousness" to "thought," it is tempting to interpret the concept of *Sinnlichkeit* anachronistically; that is, as a nineteenth-century version of what some recent empiricists call "sense data." Although it is clear that the entire thrust of Feuerbach's text is, roughly speaking, towards an empiricism of some sort, it is also obvious that "sensuousness" cannot mean what people now call "sense data" but includes much more. It includes, for example, what we normally call perception and sensation, but it also encompasses much that could not so easily be classified: for example, feelings and even the apprehension of the feelings and intentions of others. He argued, for example, that it is not only external objects that are experienced by the senses but *"Man, too, is given to himself only through the senses*; he is an object of himself only as an object of the senses."[31] Or again, "We feel not only stones and lumber, flesh and bones; we also feel feelings, in that we press the hands or lips of a feeling being."[32] He stated that not only flesh but the mind and "the I" are objects of the senses. "Everything is, therefore, sensuously perceptible," he wrote in a rhetorical flourish, "and although not always immediately so, yet it is perceived through mediation."[33]

The terms "immediately" and "mediation" in that last quotation are, of course, the terms that Hegel had used in the early sections of the *Phenomenology*, in which he had argued that there is no such thing as immediate knowledge given by the senses because knowledge can only be mediated through concepts and thought. In an earlier section

[30] *Principles*, para. 32, p. 51; *Grundsätze*, p. 316.
[31] *Principles*, para. 41, p. 58; *Grundsätze*, p. 323.
[32] *Principles*, para. 41, p. 58; *Grundsätze*, p. 324.
[33] *Principles*, para. 41, p. 58; *Grundsätze*, p. 324.

of the *Principles*, Feuerbach had tried to refute this argument and to claim some sort of immediate certainty given to the senses.[34] But in the section where he wrote that the sensuously perceptible is "perceived only through mediation" he also seems to suggest that human perception is interpenetrated with thought. It is this oscillation between immediacy and mediation that led Wartofsky to argue that his position is basically unsatisfactory.

Perhaps the most charitable interpretation of Feuerbach's position is to say that he faced the same problem that modern empiricism faces: how, on the one hand, to do justice to a certain "givenness" of the external world, the fact that impressions force themselves upon us willy-nilly, as William James might have said, and, on the other, to acknowledge that there is no uninterpreted experience, no "brute data" that "speak for themselves," as some empiricists used to say. It seems clear that, for the most part, Feuerbach believed that both perception (*Anschauung*) and thought (*Denken*), although "opponents," are required for knowledge.

Perception *enlightens* the mind, but *determines* and *decides nothing*; thought *determines* but also often *narrows* the mind. Perception for itself has *no principles*, whereas thought for itself has *no life* . . . Hence, just as only perception that is *determined* by thought is true perception, so conversely only thought that is *broadened* and *opened* by perception is true thought corresponding to the essence (*dem Wesen*) of reality.[35]

But even though both thought and perception are required for knowledge, he believed that they are in contact with something impinging upon the self from without, not in the sense that this something is "uninterpreted" but in the sense that interpretation and knowledge have the sensuously given as their materials.

This more generous interpretation of Feuerbach's position has at least the virtue of accounting for one of the most puzzling and controversial sections of the *Principles*, in which he argued that by "sensuousness" he did not mean what speculative philosophy had meant by "immediate," namely, "the *profane*, *obvious*, and thoughtless that is *understood by itself*." Rather, "Immediate, sensuous perception comes much later than the imagination and fantasy" and can only be achieved through education and training. The first perceptions of uneducated persons are dominated by the imagination, and they only

---

[34] *Principles*, paras. 28, 29.
[35] *Principles*, para. 48, p. 65; *Grundsätze*, p. 331f.

see objects "*as they appear to them* and not as they are." Thus the task of philosophy and science consists in *leading toward the sensuous*.

Only now, in the modern era, has mankind arrived again – as once in Greece after the demise of the Oriental dream world – at the *sensuous*, that is, the *unfalsified* and *objective* perception of the sensuous, that is, of the real; precisely with this, however, it also came *to itself*; for a man who devotes himself only to entities of the imagination or of abstract thought is himself only an abstract or fantastic, but not a *real* and true human being.[36]

THE DISCOVERY OF LUTHER

It is intelligible why in 1844 Ludwig Feuerbach was the object of so much adulation and hope, why so many young intellectuals thought that he would be the "new Hegel" of German philosophy. In *The Essence of Christianity* he had cut the Gordian knot that identified Hegelianism with Christianity, and in the *Principles* he had produced the manifesto calling for the separation of Hegelianism from philosophy. He had done nothing less than provide the guidelines for an humanistic and democratic German philosophy of the future. Given his energetic talents and philosophical imagination, it seemed quite probable that he might be the philosopher of that future, a philosopher who thought as a "whole person" and proposed a politics based on communal life, a philosopher who believed that "The highest and last principle of philosophy is, therefore, *the unity of man with man*."[37] Imagine, then, the disappointment among many of his fellow revolutionaries when, after issuing the promissory notes of his new philosophy, Feuerbach suddenly seemed to turn his back on philosophy and politics and returned once again to the safe and familiar territory of religion by writing a small book entitled *The Essence of Faith According to Luther: A Supplement to the Essence of Christianity*.

The reasons for this retreat to the interpretation of religion has puzzled many scholars, especially those who have assumed that Feuerbach had only been concerned with religion in the first place because he thought it was a barrier to political progress. Moreover, they point out that his correspondence to his friends in the period after the publication of *Christianity* reveals that he was developing an amateurish but deep interest in the physical sciences. Why, then, having set his mind on the reform of philosophy, should he return to

---

[36] *Principles*, para. 43, pp. 59f.; *Grundsätze*, pp. 325f.
[37] *Principles*, para. 63, p. 72; *Grundsätze*, p. 340.

the interpretation of religion at all? And if he was to return, why should it have been to the religion of the Protestant Reformer Luther; that is, to just that type of religionist, a theologian, whom he had earlier claimed was the systematizer and corrupter of religion?

Perhaps the most widely accepted answer to this question is that Feuerbach's interest in Luther was prompted by the harsh critical reviews of the first edition of *Christianity* that had been published by Lutheran theologians, especially the long review (approximately one hundred pages) by the professor of Christian theology at the University of Halle, Julius Müller. Among other things, Müller had argued that Feuerbach's thesis, dependent as it was upon patristic, medieval, and mystical-pietistic sources, could at best apply only to Roman Catholicism but not to the Protestantism of Martin Luther, to which, he noted, Feuerbach had scarcely referred in the first edition of the book. Feuerbach wrote the book on Luther, so the hypothesis goes, because he wanted to prove Müller wrong. He wanted to show that the same criticisms that applied to Roman Catholic Christianity applied to Protestantism as well. This explains, then, why, after Müller published his criticisms, Feuerbach turned to an intensive study of Luther's sermons, Biblical commentaries, and theological treatises. This study culminated in a fifty-page reply to Müller, a revision of the first edition of *Christianity* that added extensive Luther material to the main body of the text as well as appendices, and a monograph on Luther. Whereas the first edition of *Christianity* does not indicate any special acquaintance with Luther, the second reflects a deep immersion in the Reformer's writings and a profound grasp of the dynamics of his theology.[38]

Recently, this widely held hypothesis for explaining Feuerbach's turn to Luther has been challenged by John Glasse. Citing personal letters in which Feuerbach stated that with *Christianity* he had put theology behind him forever and was now intending to study natural science, Glasse suggests that the real reason for the Luther book was his fear of censorship by the political authorities.[39] Along with the

---

[38] Professor John Glasse has noted that Luther was cited on only ten pages out of four hundred and fifty in the first edition as compared with an average of one in four in the second. Moreover, whereas he had not cited primary material in the first edition, the second has representative passages from the twenty-one-volume Leipzig edition of 1728–1740. In three-fourths of the appendices of the first edition, he added Luther material, and to those new appendices in the second, three-fourths also contain Luther material. See "Why did Feuerbach Concern himself with Luther?," *Revue internationale de philosophie*, 26, 101 (1972), 370f.

[39] Glasse,'Why did Feuerbach Concern himself?," pp. 38off.

other radical Young Hegelians, Feuerbach was concerned with the freedom of the press, not merely as a matter of political conviction but because he and his friends had suffered numerous acts of harassment and suppression by both the censors and the police. In 1841 Feuerbach's *Christianity* had been banned in Austria, and in 1842 a daily newspaper edited by Karl Marx, the *Rheinische Zeitung*, had been suppressed. In the same year, Arnold Ruge's *Deutsche Jahrbücher* had been so harassed by the censors that it had been forced to move to Paris, where it became the *Deutsch-Französische Jahrbücher* with Marx as editor. Feuerbach's *Theses* was one of the articles in which the censors had taken a special interest, so much so that Feuerbach felt compelled to publish it as well as the *Principles* in Switzerland. These threats of censorship seemed especially ominous because they indicated that the authorities were not only intolerant of anything critical of the state religion, Christianity, but were becoming increasingly interested in unorthodox philosophy as well.

For Feuerbach, the crowning blow came in April of 1843 when the authorities, hoping to find evidence of his connection with a young radical named Hermann Kriege whom they had under surveillance, invaded his home and rifled through his correspondence and papers. Feuerbach was outraged and traumatized, and when, two years later, he learned that the police were still harassing this young radical, he burned a great deal of his correspondence and vowed that he would never again permit political authorities to invade his privacy. He wrote to a friend that the Christian-German state system had become a den of pickpockets and highway robbers.[40]

The result of all this, Glasse argues, was that Feuerbach became convinced that it was necessary to state his radical views indirectly rather than directly. And since theology was still an accepted mode for discourse in Germany, he felt that it could serve as the vehicle by means of which he could convey his philosophical opinions. Moreover, the theology of Luther was especially suitable for this purpose because Luther was the "paradigmatic Protestant and a German hero," and if the censors chose to suppress Feuerbach's views of Christianity, then they would also have to suppress their hero. Glasse concludes:

In sum, I suggest that Feuerbach's use of Luther, both in revising *Das Wesen des Christentums* and in writing his Luther book, exemplifies this very strategy of survival and persuasion. Note that he came to articulate this strategy not

[40] Glasse, "Why did Feuerbach Concern himself?," p. 382.

in response to a scholarly book review but rather in reacting to a censor's suppression of the most forthright expression of his new philosophy that he had yet ventured.[41]

This is an interesting and suggestive hypothesis; but it would be a mistake, I believe, to conclude that there were no intrinsic intellectual reasons why Feuerbach turned to Luther, or that the immersion in Luther's writings contributed nothing to his intellectual development. By stinging Feuerbach into the serious reading of Luther, his critic, Julius Müller, had inadvertently led him to realize, first, that the Reformer was a major figure in the development of modern thought generally and second, that Protestantism was a practical proof of his major thesis that theology was anthropology. Feuerbach came to believe that Protestantism was not merely Catholic Christianity under a different name but a "practical" harbinger of the development that was to work itself out theoretically in the realm of philosophy. Luther, in short, was more than another illustrative figure of the Christian faith whom Feuerbach had neglected to cite in the first edition of *Christianity*; rather, his theology was the first stage in a spiritual and intellectual movement of which Feuerbach believed himself to be the "realization."

Even more important, however, was that Feuerbach's reflections on Luther led him to consolidate and to apply to religion the insights that he had come to in philosophy and that were articulated in the *Principles*. He had been criticized by Max Stirner and others, it will be recalled, for his excessive abstractness, for his preoccupation with the idea of the species, which was the central idea of *Christianity*. In the process of writing the Luther book he came to realize that the persistence and power of Christianity need not be explained in terms of these abstractions but, as will be seen below, by appealing to the desires of the individual in the grip of the rage-to-live, the desire to overcome death. Luther, Feuerbach believed, stood quite apart from Catholic theologians because he saw that the words "for us" were the most important words of the Nicene Creed. He understood more powerfully than any other theologian that faith was based on the felicity principle. He understood that it was crucial for practical Christian faith that there be no distinction between the idea of God in-and-for-Himself and God for us, that there be no possibility of doubt that what was revealed in Christ was the essence of God. He

---

[41] Glasse, "Why did Feuerbach Concern himself?," p. 383.

understood, in short, that "*Nothing is in God which is not in Christ*; Christ is the manifest (i.e., the *open, unreserved*) God,"[42] and this God is a human being.

So far as the theory of religion is concerned, this insight meant that Feuerbach could increasingly minimize the Hegelian paradigm of the objectification of the idea of the species and concentrate more heavily on that naturalist-existentialist theme which had been subordinated to the Hegelian in *Christianity*. He could now explore the implications for religion and philosophy of a philosophical anthropology in which the individual is seen as a creature haunted by death and in the grip of the desire for happiness, a creature who longs for contact with sensuous objects, on the one hand, and desire for recognition, on the other. We can see this new perspective in a passage Feuerbach wrote in 1846 when, looking back on his work, he noted in that quaint style he sometimes adopted when writing about himself:

You were still haunted by the abstract Rational Being, the being of philosophy, as distinct from the actual sensuous being of nature and humanity. Your *Essence of Christianity* was, at least partially, written when you still looked at things in this contradictory manner. Only in your *Luther* – which thus is by no means a mere "supplement," as the title says, but had independent significance – was this contradiction fully overcome. Only there did you fully "shake off" the philosopher and cause the philosopher to give way to the man.[43]

The Luther book, so far as length is concerned, is slight. It contains fewer than sixty pages in the German edition, and much of it consists of extensive quotations from Luther's work. Feuerbach's strategy is to construct an argumentative pattern each step of which is then illustrated with numerous supporting quotations from the Reformer's work, a strategy, unfortunately, that lends itself to the criticism that the quotations from Luther have been taken out of context and had an alien argumentative framework superimposed on them. Feuerbach himself was unhappy with the work, as he confessed in a letter to his friend Friedrich Kapp.[44] He felt it was too short and that his central theme had not been as clearly laid out for the readers as it should have been. Consequently, he felt that it would be misunderstood and give offense to many of them. All this is true, but Feuerbach's point was not to claim that Luther was consciously a proto-Feuerbachian, but

---

[42] Feuerbach, *Luther*, p. 88; *Luther*, p. 392.   [43] *Kleinere Schriften III*, *GW* x.188.

[44] Ludwig Feuerbach, *Briefwechsel II (1840–1844)*, ed. Werner Schuffenhauer, *Gesammelte Werke*, 19 vols., vol. xviii (Berlin: Akademie-Verlag, 1988), p. 396.

that in and through Luther's traditional affirmations one can see that the central affirmation is that "God – or the divine being – is simply the being who expresses, promises, and objectifies human (or, rather, Christian) wishes, the focus of which is the wish for blessedness."[45]

The first step of Feuerbach's argument is to acknowledge that Luther's distinctive teaching seems, on the surface at least, to refute the central argument of *Christianity*; namely, that God is simply the objectified nature of man. Luther attempted in every way to draw a radical contrast between the divine and the human. This contrast is not so much metaphysical, although it is that, but moral. Man is unjust, deceitful, sinful, and depraved, while God is everything good and just. Whatever can be attributed to God must be denied of humanity, and what humanity possesses must be rejected in God. So great is this contrast that Luther wrote that it was a condition of true religion that "If you want to have God, therefore, give up man; if you want to have man, reject God – or else you have *neither* of the two. *The nullity of man* is the *presupposition* of the *reality* of God."[46]

To say that the acknowledgment of this contrast is a condition of "true religion" is, of course, to say that it is implicit in Luther's understanding of Biblical faith; more particularly, of the Apostle Paul's understanding of faith. Feuerbach thought that this contrast was contained not only in Paul's paradoxical claim that God's strength was manifested in human weakness but also in his distinctive doctrine of justification by faith and not by works. This latter doctrine means that the believer cannot bring anything in the way of human worth and merit to the relationship with God; indeed, faith begins with the acknowledgment that there is no such thing as merit, that human righteousness is as "filthy rags." Luther believed, Feuerbach noted, that grace abolishes merit and merit abolishes grace, and it was this doctrine that "is the foundation on which Luther erected his edifice and shattered the Roman Catholic Church."[47] Luther declared himself entirely and unqualifiedly for God and against man.

But even though Luther's thought began with this utter contrast between God and man, it does not end with it. Although he attacked all self-esteem and took away any possible claim that humans might make for themselves, he restored in God a hundred-fold of what he

---

[45] *Luther*, p. 112; *Luther*, p. 409.
[46] *Luther*, p. 33; *Luther*, p. 354.
[47] *Luther*, p. 38; *Luther*, p. 358.

had taken from men. "Luther is inhuman toward man only because he has a *humane (humanen)* God."[48] God, so to speak, fills the place of man. Since God loves and cares for the individual, the individual does not have to love or care for himself/herself. In a characteristically vivid passage, Luther wrote:

Go away, you loathsome Devil! You want to encourage me *to care for myself*, although God says everywhere, "I will care for him Myself," and says, "I am your God"; that is to say, "*I will care for you*; consider Me thus and let Me take care of you." As Saint Peter says, "*Throw all your cares on Him, for He cares for you*" . . . The loathsome Devil, who is the enemy of God and Christ, wants to force us *upon ourselves* and *our own care*, so that we might undertake *God's office* (which is to care for us and to be our God).[49]

Although it might superficially appear that the Lutheran faith is basically similar to the Catholic because both affirm the words of the Nicene Creed that God became man, suffered, and was crucified "for us and our salvation," there is, in fact, Feuerbach claimed, a radical difference between them. The difference lies in the emphasis which Luther put upon the words "for us" and what I have called the felicity principle. To be sure, Catholics (and, one might have added, Calvinists) also believe that Christ suffered for humanity, but they do not make of this the practical truth which Luther did when he wrote, "It is therefore not enough that a man believe that there is a God, that Christ suffered, etc., but he must firmly believe that God is *a God for his blessedness*, that Christ suffered *for him*."[50] The real secret of Christian faith according to Luther, Feuerbach claimed, lies in the conviction that "God is by his *very nature* concerned with man, the *belief* that God is a being existing not for himself or against us, but rather *for us*, a *good* being, good to *us men*."[51]

It would be easy for readers who think themselves familiar with Christian teaching to overlook the radical implications Feuerbach saw in this Lutheran emphasis on the "for us." Christian theology, while stressing the centrality of the Incarnation, has nevertheless traditionally made an important distinction between God's being independent from the creation (in-and-for-Himself before all worlds) and God's relationship to the creation. This distinction serves several purposes. First of all, it stresses that what human beings can know

---

[48] *Luther*, p. 43; *Luther*, p. 362.
[49] Luther quoted by Feuerbach, *Luther*, p. 44; *Luther*, p. 362.
[50] Luther quoted by Feuerbach, *Luther*, p. 49; *Luther*, p. 365.
[51] *Luther*, p. 51; *Luther*, pp. 366f.

about God only approximates the real, ineffable nature of God. Second, it makes clear that the nature of God would have been the same had there been no creation at all, that creating the world was a free, gracious act. Finally, it emphasizes that God's purposes transcend creation and are not exhausted by those realized in it.

Feuerbach believed that Luther had consciously challenged this traditional view. He did not believe that God is first of all a being-for-Himself and only then, as a matter of free decision, a being-for-us. Rather, faith insists that God is, *by definition*, a being-for-us. It cannot entertain, as theologians like Calvin have, that the divine Subject might have some mysterious purpose different than the well-being of the creatures. It cannot permit the suspicion to arise that the salvation of humanity is only one among many divine purposes. This is, in fact, what it means to say that God is "good" or that God opposes "evil." For "good" can only mean "good for us" just as "evil" can only mean "evil for us." "What does it mean," Luther wrote in a famous passage, "to have a God; or, what is God?"

Answer. A *God* is that from Whom one should expect all *good*, and in Whom one should take *refuge* in times of *need*. Therefore, to have a God is simply *to believe in and trust in Him from the heart*; as I have often said, trust and faith of the heart create both God and false God. Whatever you hang your heart upon and trust, that is actually *your God* . . . Therefore I am pleased that we Germans should call *God* by the ancient name (finer and more appropriate than any other), "Good," as the One Who is an eternal source overflowing with superabundant good and from Whom everything which is *good*, and is called *good*, flows.[52]

One can perhaps understand how radical this felicity principle is when one considers its implications for the derivation of the attributes of God. Traditionally, Christian theologians have made a distinction between the metaphysical attributes of necessity, omnipotence, unlimitedness, omniscience, and the like, and those attributes derived from the Incarnation. The former, it has sometimes been claimed, can be discovered by natural reason reflecting on the structures of finite creation, while the latter are only given in revelation. Luther, Feuerbach argued, necessarily rejected this distinction and derived all the attributes of God from the attribute of benevolence, which, in turn, is but a restatement of the "for us." If God is the source of all our good, the one who can save us from all evils, then this God must

---

[52] Luther quoted by Feuerbach, *Luther*, p. 51; *Luther*, p. 367.

Himself be a being without needs and, hence, one who can selflessly secure ours. He will be unchangeable in goodness, omniscient in knowing our needs, omnipresent in being able to help us in all places, and omnipotent in being able to accomplish all that He has promised.

Even the doctrine of creation reflects Luther's felicity principle. To be an omnipotent creator means that the creation itself is for our benefit, that God is not the creator of nature for its own sake but has created it for ours. Were we to think of the creator simply as the omnipotent power behind the universe, then we might also legitimately infer that God could, if He so willed, also destroy the world and us. But God's power is defined by His goodness and "goodness" is defined in relation to human well-being:

God can do everything, *but* only wishes to do *good*.

God is *omnipotent*; *therefore He wishes* us to ask for everything which is *useful* to us.

Since He (God) is omnipotent, what *can I lack which He cannot give me or do for me?* Since He is Creator of heaven and earth and Lord of all things, *who will take anything from me or harm* anything of mine? Indeed, how will all things *not be for my benefit* and *serve* me if the one to whom they are *all obedient* and *subjected* grants goodness to me?[53]

The real issue for Christian faith, Feuerbach took Luther to argue, is not whether the sole emphasis ought to be laid on the felicity principle but the *right* of human beings to make such an anthropocentric claim about God. How, then, do human beings arrive at the certainty of this belief? The answer, of course, lies in the appearance of Christ. In the humanity of Christ, the human-mindedness of God is placed beyond doubt. But it is placed beyond doubt because it has become an object to the human senses. "Only a sensuous being favors and satisfies man and can be a *beneficent* being; for only a sensuous being is an *incontrovertible* and a *certain* being. And without certainty there is no beneficence."[54] The revelation of God has not been given merely to thought, nor does it rest on mere belief. "The *pledge* and *truth* of the goodness and mercy (humanness) of God lie therefore in Christ as the *sensuous essence* of God."[55]

With this emphasis on the sensuousness of the revelation in Christ, Feuerbach was able to bring his theory of religion into closer

---

[53] Luther quoted by Feuerbach, *Luther*, p. 57; *Luther*, p. 371.
[54] *Luther*, pp. 65f.; *Luther*, p. 377. Cherno uses the English word "sensual" to translate the German *sinnliches*, but I have chosen to use "sensuous" because "sensual" has increasingly acquired sexual connotations in ordinary speech.   [55] *Luther*, p. 64; *Luther*, p. 376.

relationship to the principles of his new philosophy. He had, to be sure, emphasized sensuousness to some degree in *The Essence of Christianity*, but he had linked it there primarily to the imagination and to feeling's need for images. In the Luther book, sensuousness is linked to the certainty that something exists and is real. Christians achieve certainty as to the object of faith not because an image ravishes their feelings but because they are confronted by a real sensuous being, something external. A sensuous being comes from without and not from within the head. "It is given to me; my senses have revealed it to me. It is no product of human reason, as is the God of the philosophers, but neither is it a product of human hands, as is Jupiter of Phidias. It is an *independent* being, which is consequently given to me not through me but *through itself*."[56] It were as if God were saying to Himself, Luther wrote,

> From a God Who is not revealed, I wish to become a *revealed* God, and yet I wish to remain the same God. I *wish to become a Man* or to send My Son; and thus I want to fulfill your desire and satisfy what you want to know – whether you are elected (predestined to blessedness) or not . . . No one has ever seen God. And yet God has revealed Himself to us out of *great mercy* . . . He has presented us with a *visible exact image*, and has said, "Behold, you have My Son; whoever hears Him and will be baptized is inscribed in the book of life. This I reveal to you through My Son, Whom you can touch *with your hands* and *see with your eyes*."[57]

Sensuousness, it should be noted, not only is the basis of the believer's certainty in Christ but also reinforces the "for us" principle. To believe in Christ is to believe that there is no possible distinction between Christ-in-Himself and Christ for us; or, in other words, that the Christian finds in the man, Christ, that the invisible being of God has been made into a visible and sensuously perceptible being. It is to believe that all the mysteries of the divine being have been disclosed and, hence, that there is no ground for mistrust and suspicion, that God is not different than He has revealed Himself to be. Christ is nothing in Himself which He is not "for us." Thus Luther could write:

> For this reason, one must first of all and above all things try to learn to trust the goodness of God which He has shown us in Christ, His Son, Whom He gave us because of our sins and death. For otherwise there arises a habit and tendency toward *mistrust of God*, which becomes insuperable.[58]

---

[56] *Luther*, p. 67; *Luther*, p. 378.
[57] Luther quoted by Feuerbach, *Luther*, p. 69; *Luther*, pp. 379f.
[58] Luther quoted by Feuerbach, *Luther*, p. 93; *Luther*, pp. 396f.

The thoughts about God's majesty, Luther was fond of saying, "are very dangerous. For an evil spirit can put himself in the form of majesty; but *he can never put himself in the form of the cross.*"[59]

It is important for my argument that throughout the book on Luther Feuerbach made no attempt to explain the idea of God in terms of the projection of the species concept that arises in the process of self-differentiation. Although self-differentiation is presupposed, to be sure, the emphasis of the book falls entirely on the self-love or egoism of the individual, the rage to live and to transcend all the conditions of dependence and finitude. And this motif reaches a crescendo in the last few pages of the book, which, like *Christianity*, contain a series of reflections on the inherent conflicts between the Christian virtues of faith and love. In *The Essence of Christianity*, as we have already seen, Feuerbach had contrasted the two in the starkest of terms: faith was fanatical and separatist; love was tolerant and unifying. In the Luther book, this contrast is less stark and, one might add, more profound. Here he acknowledged that for Luther the object of faith was, in fact, love.

The object of faith is, as we have seen, *love*; the supreme article of faith – the only decisive one, the one which encompasses everything – is the proposition "God is love." But love *for whom*? After all, love in itself and without an object is a chimera. The answer is, "*love for man.*" So, in truth, man is *the object of faith also. Philanthropy* – love of man – is also the mystery of faith. It is *distinguished from love* only in that *another* man is the object of love, whereas [in faith] *I myself* am the object of [love]. In love I love; in faith I am loved. But loving humbles me, for in this case I subordinate and subjugate myself to another being; being loved exalts me. What I lose in love, I receive again manyfold in being loved. The awareness of being loved is self-awareness, self-esteem; and the higher the being by whom I know myself loved, so much higher is my self-esteem. To know oneself loved by the supreme being is therefore the expression of the highest – indeed, divine – self-esteem. So the distinction between faith and love consists only in the fact that in faith man is a heavenly, divine, infinite being, but in love he is an earthly, finite, human being. "Through faith," says Luther, "man becomes God"; "In faith we are gods, but in love we are men."[60]

Luther took the Gospel to mean that God calls upon us to love ourselves, that "the object of faith is the inviolable holiness of self-love," that "being loved is the law of self-love." But this, in turn, raises the issue of the relationship of this self-love to love of others. Is

---

[59] Luther quoted by Feuerbach, *Luther*, p. 93; *Luther*, p. 396.
[60] *Luther*, pp. 99ff.; *Luther*, pp. 400f.

the quest for one's own salvation superior to the love of the neighbor? Luther argued that it was, because faith has to do with the fight against the Devil and for God; it has to do with death, eternal life, sin, and forgiveness. Consequently,

one compares with these weighty matters *love*, which has to do with *minor matters*, such as serving people, helping them with advice and deeds, consoling them, who would not see that *faith is much higher than love* and is to be willingly preferred to it? For how can you *even compare God with men*? How can you even compare *helping* and advising a man with that which helps us overcome *eternal death*?[61]

To say that Luther finally ranked faith above love, however, is also to say that he basically ranked self-love above love for others. To be sure, Feuerbach conceded, there is something psychologically valid in this ranking of the virtues because, he asked, how can one esteem others without having first been convinced of one's own worth? One must care for oneself before one can care for others. I must "make myself an end before I can make myself a means for others."[62] Nevertheless, faith is basically the belief in one's own salvation or blessedness, the satisfaction of one's own wishes and desires in God.

But what is your wish and your desire? Freedom from all evils, freedom from sin . . . freedom from the irresistible power and necessity of sensuous drives, freedom from the oppression of matter (which binds you with the chains of gravity to the soil of the earthy), freedom from death, freedom, in general, from the limitations of nature – in one word, *blessedness*.[63]

That blessedness is necessarily individual self-love is best seen, Feuerbach argued, in the centrality of the doctrine of the Resurrection, or to put it in its negative terms, the doctrine that death is not the inevitable extinction of one's own personal psychic life. It is death that is "the most perceptible expression of our finitude and dependence upon another being outside us; namely, nature."[64] Moreover, the fear of death necessarily and radically individualizes the self because one must suffer it alone. It is one's own individual death, then, against which the religious person needs some defense; consequently, blessedness, the overcoming of death, is also individualistically conceived, Feuerbach argued.

[61] Luther quoted by Feuerbach, *Luther*, p. 101; *Luther*, p. 402.
[62] *Luther*, p. 102; *Luther*, p. 403.
[63] *Luther*, p. 103; *Luther*, p. 403.
[64] *Luther*, p. 126; *Luther*, p. 425.

Just as no one can believe for another, so no one can be blessed for another. There can be no sin without something outside me – an object. But for blessedness there need be nothing but myself. One can sin only in human society, but one can be blessed quite alone . . . Of course, I wish blessedness for others, but only because it is the supreme object for me and I presuppose the same sentiment in others.[65]

It is no accident, then, Feuerbach concluded, that in Lutheran as well as in orthodox Christianity generally, the doctrine of the Resurrection should be the central theological doctrine; indeed, that "All theological disputations should see to and be directed to this point."[66] But to believe in such a doctrine, Feuerbach argued, is to believe in nothing less than that all the conditions of finitude will finally be set aside, that the self will become a god. As Luther wrote, the Christian must be able to say that just as Christ is a king, so am I. *"Just as He is a lord, I am also a lord, for what He has I also have."*[67] The Christian must be confident that "As you believe, so it occurs to you."

What can these words of Luther mean, Feuerbach asked rhetorically, except that

To believe is but to change the "There is a God and a Christ" into the "I *am* a God and a Christ." The mere belief "There is a God" or "God is God" is a moribund, vain, and empty belief. I only *believe* if I believe that God is *my* God. But if God is mine, then all divine possessions are my property; that is, all God's attributes are my attributes. To believe is to make God a man and man a God.[68]

Although the Luther book represents a distinct shift away from the abstractness of *The Essence of Christianity* – or, more precisely, represents the replacement of an earlier dominant theme (the objectification of the species idea) by a subordinate theme (the drive of the sentient individual for freedom from the limitations of nature and death) – we still have in this book not so much a theory of religion as a theory of Christianity. The issue then becomes whether this modified interpretation of Christianity also requires some modification in the theory of religion that lay behind the earlier work. If Christianity is no longer to be explained in terms of the Hegelian paradigm of self-consciousness and the objectification of the species idea, what should be done about the theory of religion that had also been cast in these terms? And if one no longer appeals to the

---

[65] *Luther*, p. 115; *Luther*, p. 411.   [66] *Luther*, p. 105; *Luther*, p. 405.
[67] Luther quoted by Feuerbach, *Luther*, pp. 106f.; *Luther*, p. 405.
[68] *Luther*, pp. 106f.; *Luther*, pp. 405f.

objectification of the species, does one also discard those suggestive insights and motifs which Feuerbach thought were inherent in that idea; namely, the self-differentiation from nature and the desire for recognition by others?

In my opinion, there is no more important evidence that Feuerbach's writings about religion were not merely an indirect way of conveying his (allegedly more important) political and philosophical opinions than the fact that upon completion of the Luther book he immediately turned once again to the theory of religion and completed what is perhaps his best book, *Das Wesen der Religion*, that he then added to this a "supplement and explanation" (*Ergänzungen und Erläuterungen zum "Wesen der Religion"*) in the same year, and that he returned once again to it in 1848 with his *Lectures on the Essence of Religion*. Like a tongue worrying a sore tooth, Feuerbach could not seem to leave religion alone. As he was to confess in 1848, although he had written books both in the history of philosophy and in religion, in all of these books, philosophical or religious, he was preoccupied with only one theme: "religion or theology and everything connected with it."[69] It is not surprising that Karl Barth should call him an unhappy lover of theology.

[69] *Lectures on the Essence of Religion*, p. 5; *Vorlesungen*, p. 12.

CHAPTER 5

The new bipolar model of religion

THE REFORMULATION

Given Feuerbach's intellectual development, described in the previous chapter, it is obvious that despite the sensational reception of *The Essence of Christianity*, it no longer adequately expressed the principles of his "new philosophy." He realized that in that earlier work he had been guilty of the same excessive abstractionism of which he had been so critical when practiced by Hegel. By claiming that the species as a whole was perfect and infinite, he had in effect deified humanity as a whole, as his critics never hesitated to remind him. Moreover, even though he claimed that Hegel's philosophy had foundered on the idea of nature, his own analysis of religion in *Christianity* could scarcely be said to have made nature central to the religious consciousness. Although he had not completely ignored the relation to nature, he had largely treated it as something the self wanted to transcend in its yearning to be infinite.

What was needed, then, was a reformulation of the theory of religion that would take account of the principles of his new philosophy and that would shuck off any remaining dependence upon Hegel. So, in 1845, only one year after the publication of the book on Luther, Feuerbach turned to this task. The result was a little book entitled *The Essence of Religion* (*Das Wesen der Religion*), published in 1846.[1] This book, in turn, became the basis in 1848 for a series of thirty lectures entitled *Lectures on the Essence of Religion*, published in 1851. Taken together, these two books present a much more complex, multi-causal theory of religion than is found in *Christianity*. Moreover,

---

[1] For a detailed analysis of the construction of this book see Francesco Tomasoni, *Ludwig Feuerbach und die nicht-menschliche Natur. Das Wesen der Religion: Die Entstehungsgeschichte des Werks, rekonstruiert auf der Grundlage unveröffentlichter Manuskripte*, Spekulation und Erfahrung, Texte und Untersuchungen zum Deutschen Idealismus, part II, vol. XX (Stuttgart-Bad Cannstatt: Frommann-Holzboog, 1990).

unlike *Christianity*, which was primarily a critique of the Christian religion, they are less concerned with Christianity than with religion generally. And religion, in turn, is no longer explained in terms of self-consciousness alone but in terms of a contingent self confronted with an all-encompassing nature upon which it is absolutely dependent. If in *Christianity* readers find a monopolar theory in which the gods are objectifications of consciousness, in these two books they will discover a theory revolving around two poles: nature, on the one hand, and human subjectivity, on the other. Moreover, the description of the subjective pole does not so much focus on the process of self-consciousness as on a number of psychological factors: human dependence upon and fascination with nature, the imagination, anxiety, human finitude, and, finally, human desire itself. The result, as we shall see, is a significantly different theory of projection.

The two books, although closely related conceptually, are quite different in form. *Religion* is quite brief (the German edition is only seventy-six pages), consisting of only fifty-five numbered paragraphs ranging in length from thirty-five to approximately seven hundred words. The fifty-five paragraphs themselves fall roughly into four natural groups, although there are no headings in the text itself to suggest such a division. The first group (paragraphs 1–25) is concerned with the central theme of the new paradigm; namely, that religion has to do with the feeling of dependency upon nature. "*Nature* is the *first, original object of religion*, as is amply confirmed by the history of all religions and peoples."[2] The second group (paragraphs 26–40) deals with the way in which the encounter with nature gives rise to belief in spiritual beings or gods. The third (paragraphs 41–50) attempts to show that theism necessarily presupposes (erroneously) a teleological view of nature and this, in turn, leads to the last five paragraphs, which deal with themes familiar to the readers of *Christianity*: the notions of providence, miracle, and the wish for immortality, all of which are fundamental to theism.

The book *Religion*, like the *Principles*, is written in a declarative mode; that is, there are hardly any arguments in contrast to assertions. And although Feuerbach later described the book as "a succinct intellectual or philosophical history of human religion," it is virtually unrelieved by concrete examples and illustrations.[3] Nevertheless, as discerning a critic as Marx Wartofsky has stated that it is

---

[2] Feuerbach, *Religion*, para. 2, p. 4.   [3] *Lectures*, p. 22; *Vorlesungen*, p. 29.

the best-written, the least technical, and the most "readily available to popular comprehension" of Feuerbach's works.[4] It is a pity, then, that unlike most of Feuerbach's other works, this one has never been translated into English except in an abridged form, and has been out of print for over a century.[5]

The *Lectures*, by contrast, is a longer and more informal work, not surprisingly given the context in which it was written. Feuerbach, who had retreated to private life after his dismissal from the University of Erlangen, had been invited by the student body organization of Heidelberg University to give a series of private lectures in the auditorium of the city hall after the university authorities and the Culture Ministry of Bavaria had refused to consider a student petition calling for his appointment as professor of philosophy at the university. Beginning in December of 1848, he lectured every Wednesday, Friday, and Saturday evening until March of 1849. He had no time to write out a complete manuscript in advance but used the earlier book, *Religion*, as a basis for his remarks.[6] The lectures not only read as if they were spoken – "in my last lecture I said" – but are dotted with personal asides and even an occasional apology. Thus in the last lecture he asked his audience to excuse his lack of brevity and to remember that he was not an academician accustomed to lecturing. "I had no finished text before me," he confessed, "and consequently was unable to measure my material by the yardstick of academic schedules, and organize it accordingly."[7]

Despite these defects in form, the *Lectures*, in my opinion, is superior to *Religion* in several respects. Not only does Feuerbach provide numerous examples from the history of religion to illustrate his points, but, more important, he often advances and develops significant ideas that had only been cursorily stated in *Religion*. As the lectures proceed, one can almost visualize Feuerbach rethinking and developing his position, seeing inadequacies here and clarifying obscurities there. This is especially true of his discussion of the subjective pole of the self–nature polarity. For example, in *Religion* the claim that the feeling of dependence is the source of religion is made in a brief paragraph or two. In the *Lectures* Feuerbach seems to have realized

---

[4] Wartofsky, *Feuerbach*, p. 388.
[5] An abridged translation by Alexander Loos was published in New York in 1873.
[6] Hans-Martin Sass reports that at first he was without a manuscript, but as the lectures progressed he was able to have his wife send him materials that enabled him to begin to write them out word for word. See *Ludwig Feuerbach*, p. 110.
[7] Feuerbach, *Lectures*, p. 276; *Vorlesungen*, p. 310.

that this was too narrow a basis to support what he wanted to say about religious subjectivity, and, consequently, he devoted chapters 4–10 to the development of this idea and its connection with what he calls "Egoism" (*Egoismus*) and the drive-to-happiness (*Glückseligkeitstrieb*). The *Lectures* is a far less elegant work than either *Christianity* or *Religion*, but for the student of religion, at least, it does greater justice to the complex phenomenon of religion.

THE OBJECTIVE POLE: NATURE

The most obvious factor that differentiates the new from the old model is the claim that religion has its basis in the dependency upon nature and not in objectification of the species idea. The gods are not generated out of consciousness reflecting on itself but by the impingement of external forces upon the self, forces that both nourish and threaten it. This new claim is put forward with deceptive simplicity in the second paragraph of *Religion*:

The feeling of dependency in human beings is the *basis* (*der Grund*) of religion; but the object of this dependency, that upon which they are and feel themselves dependent, is originally, nothing other than nature. *Nature* is the *first, original object of religion*, as is amply confirmed by the history of all religions and peoples.[8]

I write that this claim is deceptively simple because the characterization neither of the subjective nor of the objective pole in *Religion* gives the reader much sense of how complex each of these factors will prove to be as they are more fully developed in the *Lectures*. The feeling of dependency, as we shall soon see, will be expanded to include wishes, egoism, the fear of death, and the drive-to-happiness; and "nature" will sometimes refer to individual beings, sometimes to nature taken as a whole, and sometimes to the encompassing horizon of being, the "not-I" from which the "I" differentiates itself.

If in *Christianity* the basic structural situation in which religion arises is the I coming to consciousness over against a Thou, then in *Religion* it is the already conscious human being confronted by nature: by the light, air, water, and food upon which he/she is dependent. In animals, this dependency on nature is not reflected upon; in *Dasein*, it never leaves the consciousness. Religion, Feuerbach argued, simply brings to expression what we know ourselves to be.

[8] *Religion*, para. 2, p. 4.

In its earliest and archaic form of life, *Dasein* naturally regarded other beings as sensitive, living beings like itself. There are two reasons for this, Feuerbach suggested. The first is that *Dasein* is basically a being who relates to the world through affect and emotion, and it regards those beings who create good emotions in us as benign and those who cause bad feelings as evil. The second is that *Dasein* wishes to feel "at home" in the world and accomplishes this best by transforming natural beings (*Naturwesen*) into feeling beings (*Gemütswesen*), which is to say subjective human beings.[9]

In affect – and religion is rooted in affect and feeling – man places his being outside of himself (*setzt sich der Mensch sein Wesen ausser sich*). He treats the lifeless as living, the involuntary as voluntary, and he ensouls the object with his own sigh because it is impossible for him to appeal in affect to a feelingless being.[10]

This tendency to personify nature is reinforced by the inherent changeableness of nature itself, a changeableness that suggests agency, intention, and willfullness.[11] The sun burns and gives its light by day only to give way to the night with its unknown terrors. This changeability not only creates unrest and anxiety in the body-self but suggests that the agents causing this unrest and anxiety can be cajoled and assuaged. Since certain changes in nature will effect *Dasein* more than others, it naturally seeks to modify these changes in the interest of its own well-being; hence, the universal practice of magic, religious petitionary practices of various sorts, and, above all, sacrifice. In sacrifice, Feuerbach argued, we see most clearly the essential nature of religion, the mixture of anxiety, joy, affirmation, and doubt as to whether the gods will look kindly on human undertakings or not.[12] In it we see that religion is the activity in which human beings seek to make less mysterious the nature in which they live, move, and have their being.

The term "nature" is, of course, somewhat general, even vague, as Feuerbach acknowledged in a footnote to the first paragraph of *Religion*. Like the word "spirit," it is "nothing more than a general word (*ein allgemeines Wort*) to refer to those beings, things, and objects from which human beings distinguish themselves and their products; but not so general as to include personified and mystified beings that

---

[9] *Religion*, para. 26, p. 30.   [10] *Religion*, para. 32, p. 37.   [11] *Religion*, para. 31.
[12] *Religion*, para. 28; cf. *Lectures*, lecture 9.

are abstracted and separated from real beings."[13] Later in the *Lectures*, Feuerbach reendorsed this definition but stipulated that in practical terms it simply means that

nature is everything which man, notwithstanding the supernaturalist whisperings of theistic faith, experiences directly and sensuously as the ground and substance of his life. Nature is light, electricity, magnetism, air, water, fire, earth, animals, plants; nature is man, insofar as he is a being who acts instinctively and unconsciously.[14]

Or again, nature is "every visible thing that is not the product of human hand or human thought."[15] Or still again, but more problematically,

nature is the being, or the sum of beings and things, whose manifestations, expressions, or effects, in which its existence and essence consist and are revealed, have their ground not in thoughts or purposes or acts of will, but in astronomical or cosmic, mechanical, chemical, physical, physiological, or organic forces or causes.[16]

Although Feuerbach is frequently given to generality and lack of precision in the use of terms, it serves a purpose in this case. He wanted to claim that the religious consciousness was a response to real external powers upon which it is dependent, but he also wished to acknowledge that these external powers were differently conceived from culture to culture. Nature lends itself to different conceptual schemes and imaginings. For the archaic person directly dependent on certain beings and things, nature is alive and filled with benign and evil beings. For an ancient Greek intellectual, it is a marvelous display of purpose and teleology. And for Feuerbach's contemporaries, it was the sphere of scientific law. In short, how the world and nature appear to human beings, he claimed, depends upon their conceptions (*Vorstellungen*) and feelings (*Gefühle*) because these conceptions and feelings are unconsciously but immediately the measure of truth and reality.[17] The general term "nature" preserves the objectivity of nature but also acknowledges that how it is perceived is relative to culture.

The generality of the term "nature" also permitted Feuerbach to distinguish between two levels of consciousness: the awareness of being dependent upon concrete beings and the more general sense of

[13] *Religion*, note to para. 1, p. 4.   [14] *Lectures*, p. 91; *Vorlesungen*, pp. 104f.
[15] *Lectures*, p. 91; *Vorlesungen*, p. 105.   [16] *Lectures*, p. 91; *Vorlesungen*, p. 105.
[17] *Religion*, para. 40, p. 48.

being dependent upon an all-encompassing reality. Nature is not only the original object of religion but also its enduring though hidden background (*fortwährende, wenn auch verborgene, Hintergrund*).[18] It is this ever present but hidden background that creates the sense in us that the gods are external to human beings, that they are objective and independent. And it is the consciousness that our being always presupposes the existence of this independent "other" that is transformed into the faith that God, too, is the perduring and independent ground of existence. If the rationalistic theologians want to claim that the dignity of the divine lies in its independence of human being, Feuerbach remarked, then they should reflect on the fact that this same dignity is attributed to the gods by the "blind heathen."

The replacement of the concept of the species with nature as the object of religion is a significant shift in Feuerbach's thought. How significant can best be seen below when I compare the two models and, especially, contrast the way in which the attributes of God were said to arise in *Christianity* with the explanation given in *Religion*. In the *Lectures*, to anticipate, both the metaphysical and the moral attributes of the divine are abstractions from nature, whereas in *Christianity* they were abstractions from consciousness.

Given this new conception in which the object of religion is nature, the question naturally arises how it is that human beings ever came to believe in personal gods who transcend nature. How does belief in these gods arise if religious feeling is directed towards the impassible nature upon which humans are dependent?

There are several somewhat different answers proposed to these questions in *Religion*, but because of the brevity of the book and its declamatory style, the reader cannot always be sure how they are related. The first answer is that religion presupposes a gulf between wishes and their fulfillment, between intention and consequences. In venerating nature, human beings really venerate an impersonal object that does not meet their subjective needs. In fact, nature worship always runs the risk of disappointment and disenchantment because, he suggested, it is like making love to a statue. Since religion springs out of wishes and affect, and since affect cannot find satisfaction in an affectless being, the person is inevitably driven to posit "subjects" that transcend nature.[19] Deeply desiring such a subjective being, the human imagination transforms the unfeeling,

---

[18] *Religion*, para. 10, pp. 10f.   [19] *Religion*, paras. 35, 36.

indifferent being of nature into an invisible subject behind nature, a being who requires faith to apprehend it.

A second, related, answer is that although human beings are dependent upon nature, they also wish to be free of this dependency, and only a deity who is itself free, who can master and control nature, can satisfy this wish.

A third, more profound, answer to the question why transcendent gods appear stems from Feuerbach's conviction, which he shared with Hegel, that the gods are themselves reflections of *Dasein*'s own self-understanding, a self-understanding that undergoes historical development and is expressed in culture. As human beings become conscious of their own independence from nature and are "elevated above nature by their own wills and reason," they construct gods who are also elevated above nature.[20] As human beings become lords of nature so, too, will the gods. And as this lordship over nature reflects itself in more complex cultures and societies in which new anxieties and concerns arise, the gods, too, acquire different functions and roles. As human beings, for example, turn from hunting and gathering to establishing towns and cities, they will also adopt new forms of life in which new anxieties and needs occur. These, in turn, will be reflected in different expectations concerning the gods. If the anxieties and needs of tribal peoples revolved around nature, those of a more socialized *Dasein* will be political, moral, and legal.[21] This transition, Feuerbach claimed, can actually be seen in the ways in which the gods of Greece and Israel developed. Both Zeus and Yahweh, who were both originally nature gods, gradually became transformed into deities presiding over the moral and civic order. Their domains became attached to those of kings and rulers.

By making the encounter with a sensuously perceived nature fundamental to the religious consciousness, Feuerbach felt not only that he had filled in a large gap in his earlier theory of religion, as he later described it, but, more fundamentally, that he had been able to make nature and sensuousness, those stumbling blocks upon which Hegel had foundered, the keystone in the arch of his own interpretation of religion. Flattering as it must have been to him to have had *The Essence of Christianity* praised by Marx and others for its clever inversion of Hegel's philosophy of Spirit, this praise still presupposed

---

[20] *Religion*, para. 41, pp. 48f.   [21] *Religion*, para. 34, pp. 43-46.

that his work was in some sense parasitical on his teacher's. This could not be said of his new position, which was truly original.

The new emphasis on nature also enabled him to make some theoretical advances. He could not only give a better account of nature religions than he had done, but could treat the Christian religion as just one of the many variations on this theme. He need not regard it, as he had done in *Christianity*, as the absolute religion. Indeed, by virtue of its own flight from nature and sensuousness, perhaps the Christian religion could be seen as inferior to the religions of nature.

Nevertheless, the new model employed in *Religion* raises questions of its own. Many of these arise because the feeling of dependency, taken by itself, hardly seems capable of bearing the explanatory weight that Feuerbach forces it to bear. How are we to understand the relation of the feeling of dependency to wishes and to the desire to reduce the mysteriousness of nature, to feel at home in the world? Indeed, how does the appeal to the feeling of dependency justify the term "projection" at all, if by that term we mean some sort of involuntary reflex of the self in which the concept of the species is unconsciously objectified? Why not simply call religious belief a misinterpretation of nature?

These questions arise in part because the book *Religion* is primarily concerned with explaining how nature gives rise to religion and does not attempt to present a unified picture of the religious consciousness. Whereas in *Christianity*, Feuerbach had lavished his attention on the subjective pole and ignored nature, the opposite is the case in *Religion*. Consequently, this little book, suggestive as it is, has no answer to these questions.

There is, however, a more fundamental question that any careful reader of this book must ask: What is the relation of this new model to the old? The question arises because the author of *Religion* is strangely silent about those ideas which were most fundamental to the Hegelian paradigm governing the presentation in *Christianity*. As in the Luther book, there is here no appeal to consciousness becoming aware of its own infinite nature. Nor is there any notion of the veneration of the latent concept of species. There is, in fact, no employment of the Hegelian paradigm at all, the paradigm that explained the form, substance, and interpretative strategy of the earlier work. Instead we have the argument that anthropomorphism can best be explained by a combination of factors: the feeling of dependency, the changeability of nature, ignorance of the real causes at work in nature, and, of course, the desire to make nature less uncanny and mysterious. But these various factors are never brought together and synthesized into one unified conception of the religious consciousness. Given this lack of a unified conception, the reader naturally wants to know whether Feuerbach still believed that the anthropomorphizing of nature is the result of consciousness becoming aware of its nature or simply the result of ignorance and wishful thinking.

How these questions are answered is extremely important for any theory of religion because they determine, first, how one conceives of the substance or subject matter of religion, and, second, how one regards its function in human life. Both of these will determine which interpretative principles are brought to bear on it. In Feuerbach's earlier model, religion was necessarily regarded as an anthropomorphism because the gods are the involuntary objectification of the idea of the human species latent in the process of self-differentiation. In the later model, by contrast, there seems to be no comparable mechanism or cause of the projection. One can, for example, feel absolutely dependent upon nature and wish for a personal deity, but neither of these in themselves involuntarily generates or produces an anthropomorphic supernatural being.

So, too, consider the issue of the function of religion. In the earlier model, the theory dictates that the individual is necessarily enraptured by the idea of the species and finds in it an object of devotion that overcomes the individual's sense of inadequacy in comparison with it. The newer model, by contrast, is basically silent about this comparison of the individual with the species and suggests, rather, that religion is grounded in the fear or veneration of concrete beings in nature upon which the individual is dependent. But the newer model is unclear whether the anthropomorphic interpretation of nature is the result of ignorance of nature or rooted in some deeper need and desire.

Finally, how one answers these questions is important for the interpretation of religion. If the function of religion is the explanation and control of nature, as the later model suggests and some theorists have argued, then religion will be seen as a precursor of science. It would then follow that as human beings are able to discover and manipulate the real causes of natural events they will need religion less. The decline of religion would then be directly proportionate to the growth of knowledge. If, on the other hand, the religious projection is grounded in some deep-seated psychic need – for example, the need for recognition or communion – then religion will persist independently of the degree of knowledge and control of nature.

Feuerbach was certainly aware of the apparent differences between his old and his new theory, and, as we shall see, he attempted to minimize them early in his *Lectures*. But we can only assess the adequacy of this attempt after we have dealt in greater detail with those lectures in which he begins to relate the feeling of dependency to the notions of egoism, the drive to happiness, and the imagination (chapters 4–10 and 20–23). To anticipate, I shall attempt to show that the new description of the religious consciousness requires some very important but subtle shifts in the way projection is conceived and religion interpreted. Moreover, to the degree that this new theory has continuities with the old, these continuities are not so much with the dominant motifs of the Hegelian paradigm – consciousness becoming aware of itself – as they are with those existentialist motifs that were implicit in but subordinate to it. In short, my view is that the subordinate themes of *The Essence of Christianity* have become the dominant motifs in *Lectures on the Essence of Religion*.

THE SUBJECTIVE POLE: FEELING, EGOISM, AND THE DRIVE-TO-HAPPINESS

Feuerbach began the discussion of the religious consciousness in the fourth lecture by repeating the formula he had proposed in *Religion*: the foundation of religion is the feeling of dependency, and the first object of that feeling is nature. By so characterizing religion, he felt that he had found the "only truly universal name and concept by which to designate and explain the psychological or subjective ground of religion."[22] It had the advantage, in the first instance, of being a relational term. Religion is the characteristic of a being who "necessarily considers [itself] in relation to another being."[23] The gods, by contrast, are independent and immortal. Consequently, they do not need religion. Second, the feeling of dependency includes the notions of contingency and death. "If man did not die, if he lived forever, if there were no such thing as death, there would be no religion."[24] And finally, by its very generality the "feeling of dependency" has the advantage that it could incorporate many

[22] *Lectures*, p. 31; *Vorlesungen*, p. 39.
[23] *Lectures*, p. 33; *Vorlesungen*, p. 41.
[24] *Lectures*, p. 33, *Vorlesungen*, p. 41.

emotions, not only fear, which was the basis of many Enlightenment theories of religion, but other emotions as well, such as admiration and reverence. Of course fear plays an important role in religion, Feuerbach acknowledged; nevertheless, all those Enlightenment theories that attributed religion to fear, including that of the revered Spinoza, are too one-sided. They cite only the negative grounds for religion and ignore the positive. They fail to see that fear is too ephemeral an emotion to constitute the basis of religion and that feelings of joy, delight, and love have sometimes been attached to the object that is feared.[25]

Informed readers at the time must have surmised that by selecting "the feeling of dependency" as the term for the source of religion, Feuerbach was adding insult as well as injury to the Hegelians because this term was identified with the philosophy of religion of Hegel's principal rival, Friedrich Schleiermacher. In the fully matured version of his systematic theology Schleiermacher had argued that all religions have at their core "the feeling of absolute dependence" that is then modified or determined in different ways by each religion. Hegel, believing that religion was basically rooted in cognition, was openly contemptuous of Schleiermacher's view.[26] Feuerbach was aware of the similarity of his terminology and Schleiermacher's, so much so that he took some pains to disassociate himself explicitly from the latter. He criticized Schleiermacher's definition of religious feeling as theological, nebulous, indeterminate, and abstract compared to his own, which referred to concrete and specific feelings mediated through the senses. Archaic peoples, he claimed, do not have some vague general sense of being a part of a cosmic whole, as he thought Schleiermacher had argued. They have feelings of fear, awe, and gratitude towards specific animals, lands, crops, and the like. Realizing that their physical welfare depends upon these beings, archaic human beings worship and venerate them. The first definition of a god, Feuerbach announced, is simply "what man requires for his existence, and specifically for his physical existence, which is the foundation of his spiritual existence."[27]

One of the virtues of the informal style of the *Lectures* is that it permitted Feuerbach to dwell on examples that illustrated his points,

---

[25] *Lectures*, lecture 4.
[26] For a discussion of the Schleiermacher–Hegel disputes see Richard Crouter, "Hegel and Schleiermacher at Berlin: A Many-sided Debate," *Journal of the American Academy of Religion*, 48 (March 1980), 19–43.   [27] *Lectures*, p. 294; *Vorlesungen*, p. 330.

a practice that had been precluded by the dense, aphoristic style of *Religion*. In chapter 6, for example, he devoted an entire chapter to the phenomenon of animal cults. After acknowledging the scholarly differences of opinion surrounding the worship and veneration of animals, he concluded that there is no reason to doubt that this type of worship flourished among the ancient Egyptians as well as among the peoples of America, Asia, and Africa; and the primary reason for it, he suggested, seems to lie in the indispensability of certain animals for humankind in "the period of nascent civilization."[28]

On the other hand, he was often remarkably willing to concede the limitations of his formula and to consider phenomena that did not seem to fit it. He conceded, for example, that it is finally inadequate to explain the worship of animals purely in terms of their indispensability because the emotions of awe, admiration, and love become attached to them for reasons that are now entirely opaque. The imagination, for reasons that are accidental and unknown to us, attributes magical influence to some beings and not others. "Indeed, things and beings," he wrote,

> may be worshipped for no other identifiable reason than a special *sympathy* or *idiosyncrasy* . . . All the strange and conspicuous phenomena in nature, everything that strikes and captivates man's eye, surprises and enchants his ear, fires his imagination, induces wonderment, affects him in a special, unusual, to him inexplicable way, may contribute to the formation of religion and even provide an object of worship.[29]

Rivers may be worshiped for their beauty, cats for their mysteriousness, dogs for their vigilance and fidelity, even stones for their impenetrability and solidity. All these emotions are elements with which the religious scholar must reckon.

In describing the ways in which natural beings and objects become sacred and venerated, it would be an exaggeration to claim that Feuerbach anticipated the views of the contemporary historian of religion Mircea Eliade, who theorized that the archaic religious consciousness seizes upon beings and objects and then regards them as hierophanies of the sacred; that is, as revealing or manifesting the structure of life itself. For Eliade, the religious consciousness is preoccupied with certain micro–macrocosmic correspondences: human birth with divine birth, human sexuality with cosmic fecundity, human death with death in nature. The power of religious symbolism

---

[28] *Lectures*, p. 42; *Vorlesungen*, p. 50.   [29] *Lectures*, p. 45; *Vorlesungen*, p. 55.

lies in its double significance, its power to express simultaneously certain modalities of human existence and analogous structures of the world. The waxing and waning of the moon, for example, can become a cipher for time, change, and decay as well as for many other modalities that lend themselves naturally to cyclical interpretations. The moon can thus become the organizing center of a religious symbolism that dominates the mind of an entire people. The same could be said for powerful agricultural symbolisms; for example, those oriented around the tree. In this fashion, Eliade concluded, the world no longer appears to the archaic mind as chaotic and meaningless, a mere aggregate of unrelated elements, but is bound together by the same rhythms as human life.[30]

Nevertheless, there is something like Eliade's notion of hierophany in Feuerbach's treatment of natural religions. He suggested, for example, that the veneration of animals and concrete beings can only rise to "a true, permanent, historical religion expressing itself in a formal cult" when their attributes remind human beings of their continual dependence on nature, that they are nothing without nature. The sun, then, only becomes the center of a true cult when it is worshiped not only for its radiance but as "the supreme principle of agriculture, as the measure of time, as the source of natural and civil order, as the manifest and intelligible ground of human life, in short, for its necessity, its beneficence."[31] When this happens, religion becomes an historical factor and an object of interest to the student of the history of religion.

To the degree that Feuerbach affirmed this sense of contingency to be the core of religion, we can see a shift away from his earlier treatment of finitude. In *Christianity*, the sense of the inadequacy of the individual arises in comparison with the perfection of the species, and the doctrine of immortality expresses the longing for an ideal embodiment of this species. In the *Lectures*, by contrast, the sense of absolute dependency is concentrated in the fear of death, and religion is viewed as a defense against death. The most sensitive and painful of man's feelings, he writes,

is the feeling or awareness that he will one day end, that he will die. If man did not die, if he lived forever, if there were *no* such thing as *death*, there would

---

[30] Mircea Eliade, *The Sacred and the Profane: The Nature of Religion*, trans. Willard R. Trask (New York: Harper & Row, 1961). See also his "Methodological Remarks on Religious Symbolism," in *The History of Religions: Essays in Methodology*, ed. Mircea Eliade and Joseph M. Kitagawa with a preface by Jerald C. Brauer (Chicago: Chicago University Press, 1959), pp. 86–107.   [31] *Lectures*, p. 46; *Vorlesungen*, p. 56.

be *no religion* . . . That is why I say in my notes on *The Essence of Religion* that man's tomb is the sole birthplace of the gods.[32]

With the argument that religion not only is grounded in the feeling of dependence upon nature but is also a defense against death, the reader has the growing sense that the category "feeling of dependency" is being asked to bear more conceptual weight than it can. The category itself only suggests passivity and not the active attempt to defend against it. As a formula, then, it cannot do full justice to those drives to transcend nature that Feuerbach had acknowledged in *The Essence of Christianity* but that become the driving force of religion in the book on Luther. In that book, it will be remembered, he had dropped the appeal to the Hegelian paradigm of self-differentiation and argued that religion is really based on the felicity principle (human well-being), and the book had ended with the conclusion that the Christian faith as Luther expounded it was a manifestation of the desire to become an infinite being. God, he had concluded, is the wish to be free from the oppression of matter and all evil; above all, to be free from death. He is the satisfied urge to happiness, the divine being "who expresses, promises, and objectifies human (or, rather, Christian) wishes, the focus of which is the wish for blessedness."[33]

As if sensing the inadequacy of the "feeling of dependency" as a general formula for religion, Feuerbach, who tended to propose overly simplified formulas for complex ideas, proposed still another. In the seventh chapter of the *Lectures* we are told that egoism (*Egoismus*) is the hidden ground and essence of religion.[34]

The choice of this term was not a happy one, and its sudden appearance in the *Lectures* must have been puzzling even to his friendly readers. Given the commonly accepted identification of egoism with selfishness, Feuerbach must have seemed to have reversed his earlier position that the demystified core of religion is the love of the human species; that is, altruism. He had himself publicly traded on the pejorative meaning of the term "egoism" in *The Essence of Christianity*, where he had argued that Judaism was an egoistic religion.[35] He had also used the term in its pejorative sense in his diaries, as revealed in this entry written in the mid thirties: "There is only one evil – egoism; and only one good, it is love."[36] Furthermore, if egoism is taken to be a vice, then to say that it is the foundation of

[32] *Lectures*, p. 33; *Vorlesungen*, p. 41.   [33] *Luther*, p. 112; *Luther*, p. 409.
[34] *Lectures*, p. 49; *Vorlesungen*, p. 60.   [35] *Christianity*, chap. 11.
[36] *Kleinere Schriften III*, *GW* x.164.

religion leads the reader to expect a totally negative evaluation of all religions.

Feuerbach was aware of the difficulties with the term, and he attempted to deal with it by redefining egoism. We are not to understand the word as it is ordinarily used, "as anyone with an ounce of critical faculty can gather" from the context, he wrote somewhat testily.[37] Rather, the word refers to the aggregate of all human drives, needs, and predispositions, to

that necessary, indispensable egoism – not moral but metaphysical, i.e., grounded in man's essence without his knowledge or will – the egoism without which man cannot live . . . that egoism inherent in the very organism, which appropriates those substances that are assimilable and excretes those that are not.[38]

Egoism is simply the natural self-love that spurs human beings on "to satisfy and develop all the impulses and tendencies without whose satisfaction and development [one] neither is nor can be a true, complete person."[39] It is the "self-assertion of the person in accordance with its nature and consequently with reason."[40] It includes, however, the individual's love for other human beings because the self is nothing without other selves and, therefore, presupposes an "indirect self-love."[41] It is the egoism whose satisfaction is ultimately not in the hands of man, the egoism that fastens on whatever can alleviate its dependence and save the self from death.

How, the reader might ask, does the introduction of egoism relate to the feeling of dependency and especially to the notion of sacrifice, which was said to be so important to religion? Is the notion of sacrifice compatible with egoism and self-interest? Feuerbach's answer to the first question is to claim that even a cursory analysis of fear and beneficence, which arise out of the feeling of dependency, presuppose egoism in the broader sense because "*Where there is no egoism there is no feeling of dependency.*"[42] As for sacrifice, it is just the wider notion of egoism that makes it intelligible. Even in the case of those so-called "high religions" which stress self-abnegation, it is superficial to overlook the self-love that underlies these practices because they aim at gaining the favor of the gods, who can grant the soul what it so deeply desires. Self-abnegation is only a form of

37 *Lectures*, p. 50; *Vorlesungen*, p. 60.   38 *Lectures*, p. 50; *Vorlesungen*, p. 61.
39 *Lectures*, p. 50; *Vorlesungen*, p. 60.   40 *Lectures*, p. 50; *Vorlesungen*, p. 61.
41 *Lectures*, p. 50; *Vorlesungen*, p. 61.   42 *Lectures*, p. 80; *Vorlesungen*, p. 92.

self-affirmation, of self-love.[43] Moreover, sacrifice is predicated upon the principle that one sacrifices that which is most valuable in order to avoid misfortune or to give thanks for good fortune. Even sacrifice for a great human good presupposes self-affirmation, that is, egoism.

For Feuerbach, it seems clear, egoism is not so much a psychological as an ontological category, and the choice of this term to describe "the ground and essence of religion" is illustrative of the shift that has taken place in Feuerbach's conception of the source of religious belief. Not only has the object of religion been reconceived, but the emphasis now falls almost entirely on the individual's rage-to-live rather than some perceived discrepancy between the individual and the perfection of the species. In the grip of the *Glückseligkeitstrieb* but confronted with powers and beings upon which it is dependent, human beings worship those that they believe can satisfy that drive.

A God is essentially a being who fulfills man's desires. And the most heartfelt desire, at least *of those* men whose desires are not curtailed by natural necessity, is the desire not to die, to live forever; this is indeed man's highest and ultimate desire, the desire of all desires just as life is the epitome of all blessings for that very reason.[44]

It could be argued that this formulation represents not only a definite shift in Feuerbach's own thought but a shift in the surrounding cultural sensibility. The *Lectures* may be seen not as the final development of German idealism but as the first budding of that "Life Philosophy" which flowered in the late nineteenth century. Beginning with Schopenhauer and continuing through Nietzsche, Dilthey, Bergson, Schweitzer, and, even, Freud, we see a number of thinkers developing a philosophical anthropology that was an alternative to both rationalism, in which the human being was regarded as a "mind in a machine," and idealism, in which nature and mind were both grounded in some unified cosmic spirit. These Life-philosophers, by contrast, all regarded the human organism as a constellation of unconscious instincts and drives (will, will-to-power, libido), guided by consciousness to their proper satisfaction. They differed from one another largely in how they envisaged the relationship between the consciousness and these drives and, hence, what could be said to be the proper satisfaction of human desire. Schopenhauer, for example, wanted to cauterize and negate the incessant will to life because he

---

[43] *Lectures*, p. 67; *Vorlesungen*, p. 79.   [44] *Lectures*, p. 269; *Vorlesungen*, p. 302.

believed that this will was the source of human suffering. Nietzsche, on the other hand, wanted to affirm the will-to-power and the conflict and pain that accompanied it. Freud, by contrast, believed it was the function of the ego to mediate between the demands of the instincts (the libido) and the prohibitions of the super-ego or conscience in order to achieve as much pleasure as possible. Feuerbach, too, could write that I am "*a real sensuous being* and, *indeed, the body in its totality is my ego, my being (Wesen) itself.*"[45] But unlike the other Life-philosophers, especially Nietzsche, he also believed that the human organism is in the grip of an egoism that can find its true fulfillment only in community with other human beings and an acknowledgment of one's contingency and dependence upon nature.

There are, of course, serious conceptual problems associated with Feuerbach's appeal to egoism as the constellation of human instincts and drives, especially when it is defined as broadly as he defines it. The term, in fact, is systematically vague until one has clarified the conceptual relationships between what we normally designate as egoism, self-interest, and selfishness, on the one hand, and altruism, disinterestedness, and benevolence, on the other. As a historian of philosophy, Feuerbach must have known, for example, that there was a long philosophical tradition of egoism stemming from Thomas Hobbes in which human society was seen as a social compact among competitive and aggressive individuals who surrender some of their desires in order to secure collective protection against the predatory egoism of others. In this tradition, altruism, which is normally regarded as the opposite of egoism, is often regarded simply as a hidden manifestation of it, which is to say that there are no purely other-regarding motives. And Feuerbach must have also known that if egoism is construed in this fashion, then this would be difficult to reconcile with his own "new philosophy," in which "Love is objectively as well as subjectively the criterion of being, of truth, and of reality."[46]

Unfortunately, Feuerbach's treatment of this problem in the *Lectures* is not very satisfactory. On the one hand, he attempted to distinguish his own views from those which would define all motives as egoistic, and he made a distinction between a "natural" and an "unnatural egoism." A natural egoism, we are told, is in conformity with human nature and reason and is the natural self-love that animates all

[45] *Principles*, para. 36, p. 54; *Grundsätze*, p. 320.
[46] *Principles*, para. 35, p. 54; *Grundsätze*, p. 319.

creatures. It is the egoism which finds satisfaction in giving happiness to others. An unnatural egoism, by contrast, is manifest where persons act as if their own well-being could be realized in abstraction from the well-being of others. The good, then, "is merely what falls in with the egoism of all men, and evil is simply what falls in with the egoism of certain classes of men at the expense of others."[47] On the other hand, there are passages in the *Lectures* that come perilously close to the purely egoistic formulation. He argued, for instance, that egoism may really be considered the source of virtue and the law because "My egoism may permit me to steal, but my fellow man's egoism will sternly forbid me; left to myself I may know nothing of unselfishness, but the selfishness of others will teach me the virtue of unselfishness."[48]

These passages, unfortunately, rank among the least satisfactory in Feuerbach's *Lectures*, and it is with some relief, then, that the reader greets Feuerbach's replacement of egoism with a less prejudicial term, the drive-to-happiness or *Glückseligkeitstrieb*. Although this term is also not without its conceptual problems, at least it does not have the disadvantage, as does egoism, of immediately generating those paradoxes that usually arise when a term with a commonly accepted meaning, like individual selfishness, is redefined and stretched to include its commonly accepted opposite meaning, altruism. *Glückseligkeitstrieb* is meant to include not only that natural self-love that spurs the organism to develop its distinctive potentialities and powers (egoism), but, given Feuerbach's social view of the self, the drive to form human community. Because the essence of man is contained only in the community, the drive-to-happiness is fully realized only in interpersonal relationships. This is why Feuerbach could argue in the *Principles* that the Christian doctrine of the Trinity was not only the "highest mystery and the focal point of absolute philosophy and religion" but also the secret of communal and social life. The Trinity

is the secret of the *necessity of the "thou" for an "I"*; it is the truth that *no being* – be it man, God, mind or ego – *is for itself alone* a *true, perfect*, and *absolute* being, that *truth* and *perfection* are only the *connection* and *unity* of beings equal in their essence. The highest and last principle of philosophy is, therefore, the *unity of men with men*.[49]

Feuerbach grew increasingly fond of the term *Glückseligkeitstrieb*, and it soon became the central category not only in his last work on

---

[47] *Lectures*, p. 307; *Vorlesungen*, p. 345.   [48] *Lectures*, p. 303; *Vorlesungen*, p. 341.
[49] *Principles*, para. 63, p. 72; *Grundsätze*, pp. 339f.

religion, *Theogonie* (1857), but in his ethics as well, *Zur Ethik: Der Eudamonismus* (1867–1869), in which he took up with much greater philosophical sophistication those issues he had handled poorly in the *Lectures*: How, if the drive-to-happiness is said to be egoistic, should it be related to the sense of duty? How is this drive related to conscience (the co-presence of a Thou)? How, if it is understood as grounded in biology, should one understand the phenomenon of suicide and the tendency of nature to preserve the species rather than the individual?[50]

What emerges in the later Feuerbach is the picture of the human organism in the grip of this natural desire to live and to flourish but confronted by powers in nature upon which it is absolutely dependent. Fearful and anxious, it is seduced by the imagination with the thought that there are supernatural powers that can grant its desires and wishes.

But man wants to live; his life is his most precious possession. Impelled by his instinct of self-preservation, his love of life, he instinctively transforms this desire into a being capable of granting it, a being with human eyes to see his tears, with human ears to hear his complaints. For nature cannot grant this desire; nature, in reality, is not a personal being; it has no heart, it is blind and deaf to the desires and complaints of man.[51]

THE SUBJECTIVE POLE: THE IMAGINATION

So far, we have discussed three major concepts around which Feuerbach organized his analysis of the subjective pole of religion: the feeling of dependency, egoism, and the drive-to-happiness. But none of these categories in themselves or taken together explain why *Dasein* personifies nature. One may feel dependent and be driven by the rage-to-live but not necessarily personify nature. In short, in this new model there appears to be no projecting mechanism as there was in *The Essence of Christianity*. There is nothing corresponding to an involuntary reflex of self-consciousness that occurs when the I differentiates itself from the Thou and seizes upon the concept of the species. All we seem to have in the *Lectures* is the self transforming the beings or the whole of nature itself into a personal being under the pressures of anxiety and desire. We have, in effect, the argument that religion is the result of wishful thinking.

[50] See *Schriften zur Ethik und Nachgelassene Aphorismen*, in *Sämtliche Werke*, ed. Friedrich Jodl, 12 vols. (Stuttgart-Bad Cannstatt: Frommann Verlag, 1960), x.91–293.
[51] *Lectures*, p. 202; *Vorlesungen*, p. 227.

Feuerbach only turned his attention to the "theoretical cause" of this personification of nature in the nineteenth lecture, a somewhat tardy discussion when we recall that the theory of projection had been the first item on his agenda in *Christianity*. There, the theory of self-consciousness proved to be the foundation for everything that followed. When in the *Lectures* Feuerbach finally got around to a discussion of the issue, the missing link turned out to be the imagination (*Einbildungskraft*) or fantasy (*Phantasie*), the same "faculty" that had played such a large role in *Christianity* as an instrument of the feelings and the emotions. The imagination, which is rooted in feeling and emotion, is the organ or power that creates a world without reference to the reality principle. Unrestrained by reason and moved by impressive beings and powers in nature, the imagination seizes upon and hypostasizes them. It is the imagination "that makes an object appear to us differently from which it really is," that has "bathed nature in the enchanting, dazzling light for which human language has coined the term divinity."[52] It is the imagination that is "The theoretical cause (*die theoretische Ursache*) or source (*Quelle*) of religion and its object, God."[53]

Although the concept of the imagination plays an important role in the *Lectures*, as it did in *Christianity*, it is not treated any more systematically in the latter, unfortunately, than in the former. In both cases, the concept of the imagination is part of a larger epistemological iceberg, so to speak, that lies under and informs the writings but is never made explicit. In *Christianity*, it is possible to make out its outlines more or less, as Wartofsky has done, because of the deep structural parallels with Hegel's *Phenomenology*; but this is a more difficult task in the case of the *Lectures* because this book was written after Feuerbach had repudiated his Hegelian past and constructed his "new philosophy." Moreover, because only the rudiments of this new epistemology were put forward in the unsatisfactory form of programmatic sketches and aphorisms, some of the most important epistemological issues are not addressed, such as the relation of the imagination to the abstractions of thought, on the one hand, and to sensuousness, on the other.

Nevertheless, one can make informed conjectures about the shape of Feuerbach's iceberg even if important details are obscure, and this shape has some interesting parallels with attempts in our own

[52] *Lectures*, p. 177; *Vorlesungen*, p. 200.   [53] *Lectures*, p. 178; *Vorlesungen*, p. 201.

century, such as Ernst Cassirer's, to delineate the nature of mythic thought.[54] In *Dasein* we have an embodied, conscious, sensuous being immersed in a field of natural beings that impinge on it and upon which it is dependent. Because *Dasein* does not first relate to nature through abstract thought but is concerned with those qualities of nature that strike it emotionally, it does not perceive an "objective nature," if by that one means nature as determined by physical laws, but the "physiognomic character" of things, to use the language of Cassirer.[55] This is not to say that these qualities are merely subjective, because one can argue, as John Dewey has done, that "empirically things are poignant, tragic, beautiful, humorous, settled, disturbed, comfortable, annoying, barren, harsh, consoling, splendid, fearful; are such immediately and in their own right."[56] Indeed, it takes considerable social conditioning and education for these perceived qualities of nature to be treated as "merely subjective," as they are in natural science; and under certain conditions even so-called "civilized" persons can perceive the world in these dramatic terms. But the imagination or *Phantasie* of archaic humanity fastens on these immediate qualities and under the pressure of desire and wish transforms nature into the image of the human.[57]

Subjectively, the superimposition of a human image on nature by the imagination is prompted, as we have seen, primarily by anxiety, on the one hand, and desire, on the other. Thrown into a world in which it does not feel at home, *Dasein* wishes to "change the uncanny (*unheimlich*) being of nature into a known and comfortable nature."[58] Just as the "heart is always in motion and never ceases to beat," the feeling of dependency and the anxiety it creates drive the imagination:

at every step he takes, some harm may befall him, every object, however trifling, threatens injury and even death. This feeling of anxiety, of uncertainty, this fear of harm that always accompanies man, is the root of the religious imagination; and since religious man ascribes every evil he encounters to wicked beings or spirits, the fear of ghosts and spooks is, at least in uneducated persons and peoples, the essence of the religious imagination.[59]

---

[54] See Ernst Cassirer, *The Philosophy of Symbolic Forms*, vol. II, *Mythic Thought*, trans. Ralph Manheim with intro. note by Charles W. Hendel (New Haven: Yale University Press, 1955). See also his *Essay on Man: An Introduction to a Philosophy of Human Culture* (Garden City, N.Y.: Doubleday, 1944), chap. 7.   [55] Cassirer, *An Essay on Man*, p. 102.

[56] Dewey as quoted in Cassirer, *ibid.*, p. 104.

[57] Feuerbach, *Lectures*, p. 190; *Vorlesungen*, p. 214.   [58] *Religion*, para. 34, p. 40.

[59] *Lectures*, p. 196; *Vorlesungen*, p. 221.

In this respect, Feuerbach also anticipated Freud's argument some seven decades later: *Dasein* naturally believes that the impersonal forces of nature will seem less remote and less mysterious if they can be understood as having the same passions and desires as human beings. If the beings of nature can be thought to resemble human beings, if death and suffering are the acts of an evil will, then, Freud wrote, the human can breathe more freely and "can feel at home in the uncanny and can deal by psychical means without our senseless anxiety. We are still defenceless, perhaps, but we are no longer helplessly paralyzed; we can at least react."[60]

A second tendency towards personification derives from the fact that the imagination is in the service of egoism and the drive-to-happiness and, hence, wish and desire. Impelled by the love of life, *Dasein* instinctively transforms this desire into a being capable of granting it, into a subjective, feeling being.[61] Human beings cannot love and revere a natural force. A god is essentially a being who fulfills human desires; and the heart's desire is to be the object of a being who exercises providential care, who will protect the self from evil and death.

Because the imagination is driven by desire and wish, it is, as we saw in our previous discussion of *The Essence of Christianity*, the source of the religious belief in miracles, which, in turn, is a manifestation of the basic narcissistic orientation of religious faith. Religious faith is basically the confidence that the gods are concerned with the well-being of human beings in general and the religious person in particular. It is for this reason Feuerbach thought that he could identify the imagination with faith itself, an identification he thought was vindicated by the writings of Luther. It was the Protestant Reformer who had argued that faith brings into being the impossible, that it renders the invisible visible. It is faith that believes what cannot be demonstrated and that clings to things that cannot be seen. All the works of faith, Feuerbach wrote, are works of the imagination.

On the other hand, the imagination, although not restricted by the reality principle, does not create *ex nihilo*. It requires raw materials upon which to work, whether these be the impressionable events and beings in nature, sense impressions, or even abstractions that the mind has drawn from sensuous experience. In fact, the differences among religions are in part due to the difference in the raw materials

---

[60] Sigmund Freud, *The Future of an Illusion*, trans. W. D. Robson-Scott, revised and newly edited by James Strachey (Garden City, N.Y.: Doubleday, 1964), p. 22.
[61] Feuerbach, *Lectures*, p. 202; *Vorlesungen*, p. 227.

upon which the imagination works. In archaic times, the imagination took flight from the natural objects and beings – earth, fire, animals, and astronomical bodies – upon which human beings felt dependent and which made a forceful impression upon them. But the imagination can also be fueled by historical personages, such as the Buddha or Jesus, or, indeed, by abstractions themselves, such as the notion of "the whole" or even "Being as such." For example, Feuerbach explained the difference between polytheism and monotheism as a result of the imagination being fascinated by the multiplicity of beings, in the former case, and in the latter, by the coherence and unity of the world that "man, by his thought and imagination, has shaped into a unified whole."[62]

There are even different ways in which a given abstraction, such as the coherence and unity of nature, can provide fuel for the imagination. One can, for example, distinguish two types of monotheism: the metaphysical, which is characteristic of Christianity, and the practical-poetic, which is characteristic of the Hebrew Bible and of the Qur;an. In both the Hebrew Bible and the Qu;ran, the activity of God is indistinguishable from the activity of nature so that it is indifferent whether one says that God or nature provides food, makes the rain to fall, endows creatures with sight, and brings the living back from the dead. The workings of God are the workings of nature. Because nature is omnipresent, God is omnipresent; because nature is all-powerful, God is all-powerful. God is simply nature made into a subjective being by the imagination; which is to say that the imagination regards the workings of nature as the work of an unconditioned and unlimited being for which nothing is impossible.[63]

Feuerbach even argued that the major difference between Christian monotheism and the Jewish and Islamic forms of it is that the latter base their conceptions directly on the perception of nature. The Christian imagination, by contrast, closes its eyes, separates the personified essence of nature entirely from sense perception, and transforms what was originally nature into an abstract metaphysical being. Consequently, there is something lively and animated about Yahweh and Allah, whereas the God of the Christians is a "withered, dried-out God in whom all traces of His origin in nature is effaced."[64] The deity of the Muslim and the Jew is the union of imagination with

[62] *Lectures*, p. 192; *Vorlesungen*, p. 216.
[63] *Lectures*, p. 321; *Vorlesungen*, pp. 361ff.
[64] *Lectures*, p. 321; *Vorlesungen*, p. 362.

nature; the Christian God, the union of the imagination with the abstractions of thought. The latter is a metaphysical God, which is to say a compendium of the most universal attributes abstracted from nature and made into a personal subject. God is "Being itself" given a personal name.

THE EARLIER AND LATER MODELS CONTRASTED

If in *The Essence of Christianity* we found a theoretically elegant but flawed theory of projection, the objectification of the species idea implicit in the self-differentiation of the I from the Thou, we have in the *Lectures* a less elegant but more suggestive theory. It abandons some of the more problematic aspects of the Hegelian paradigm, and it does more justice to the many causal forces at work on the religious consciousness. It views religion as an overdetermined phenomenon and does not attempt to explain everything in terms of the consciousness becoming aware of its own essential nature.

Feuerbach, whose public identity was virtually based on *The Essence of Christianity*, quite naturally attempted to minimize any inconsistency between the later and the earlier theory. He conceded that by ignoring nature in that earlier work he had left a large gap (*eine grosse Lücke*) that had given rise to the "preposterous misunderstandings" on the part of his critics, who had claimed that a theory of religion based on the deification of man was incompatible with a theory based on the feeling of dependency on nature. But this gap, he rationalized, only mirrored the gap in the Christian religion itself, which, like idealism, had ignored nature and was preoccupied only with humankind as a moral and spiritual being. Since he had been only concerned to criticize Christianity it had been impossible for him to give a complete exposition of his view and doctrine. "Inevitably," he wrote, "I disregarded God's other half, His physical attributes, with which I was obliged to deal in another work."[65]

This other work was, of course, *The Essence of Religion*. If in the earlier work his formula had been "theology is anthropology," in the later it was "theology is anthropology plus physiology."

My doctrine or view can therefore be summed up in two words: *nature* and *man*. The being which in my thinking man presupposes, the being which is the *cause* or *ground* of man, to which he owes his origin and existence, is *not God*

---

[65] *Lectures*, pp. 19-21; *Vorlesungen*, pp. 26f.

– a mystical, indeterminate, ambiguous word – but *nature*, a clear sensuous, unambiguous word and thing. And the being in whom nature becomes personal, conscious, and rational is man. To my mind, unconscious nature is the eternal, uncreated being, the first being – first, that is, in time but not in rank, *physically* but not *morally*; man with his consciousness is for me second in time, but in rank the first.[66]

Feuerbach's attempt to minimize the discontinuities between the two models is not very convincing. He only claims that there are none but makes no attempt to clarify how nature rather than the concept of the species can be the object of religion without modifying his previous analysis. Are we to assume, for example, that the idea of God in the new model is still derived in the manner described in *Christianity*, that the species idea is projected onto nature? If so, how does he explain that some of the abstract attributes of God that were earlier derived from the "infinitude of consciousness" are now said to be derived from nature? Or again, can the notion of the unity of God be derived from the unity of consciousness alone, or is it necessary to achieve the abstraction of the unity of nature first? And what do we make out of the fact that the sense of the inadequacy of the individual in the earlier work arose in comparison with the perfection of the species, whereas in the latter it arises in the encounter with an all-encompassing nature? And finally, how do we account for the lack of any mention or use of the Hegelian paradigm of self-differentiation and objectification in the later works?

Some commentators seem to have accepted at face value Feuerbach's attempt to minimize the differences between the two theories of projection. F. C. Copleston, for example, has argued that the two versions can easily be reconciled in this fashion:

Man, conscious of his dependence on external reality, begins by venerating the forces of Nature and particular natural phenomena. But he does not rise to the concept of personal gods or of God without self-projection. In polytheism the qualities which differentiate man from nature are deified in the form of a multiplicity of anthropomorphic deities, each with his or her peculiar characteristics. In monotheism it is that which unifies men, namely the essence of man as such, which is projected into a transcendent sphere and deified.[67]

[66] *Lectures*, p. 21; *Vorlesungen*, pp. 28f.
[67] F. C. Copleston, *A History of Philosophy*, vol. vii, part 2 (Garden City, N.Y.: Doubleday, 1963), p. 63.

There are one or two passages in the *Lectures* that may seem to support this view, and I do not deny that there are remnants left over from the old theory.[68] But this attempt to reconcile the two views fails to throw any light on the discontinuities between them; for example, the difference in the way self-differentiation is conceived and how this, in turn, alters not only Feuerbach's interpretation of monotheism but his entire interpretative strategy. In the *Lectures*, there is very little trace of the Hegelian schema with its associated notion of an involuntary objectification of the latent concept of the species. We have in its stead the naturalist-existentialist model, in which the conscious self confronted by nature and haunted by anxiety transforms nature into a personal being who recognizes it and saves it from death. This, in turn, leads to a different account of the derivation of the divine attributes and a different interpretative strategy. It even led Feuerbach to a different classification of religion in which Christianity, as a religion of spirit, is inferior to natural religion. These arguments, I claim, would have been impossible under the old schema.

Compare, for example, the important differences in the way in which self-differentiation is conceived in the two theories. In *Christianity*, the religious projection is explained as an unconscious objectification of the latent idea of an essential (and perfect) human nature. The attributes of God are simply the magnification of the essential predicates of the human species: the understanding, will, and feelings. In the *Lectures*, by contrast, self-differentiation is still at the root of religion but is conceived in a quite different manner. The self, after differentiating itself from not-I, seizes on some aspect of nature – some quality, being, abstraction, or even nature as a whole – and personifies it. The "other," however conceived, is regarded as a subject. We may want to say with Copleston that this is still a projection of the "essence of man," but it is important to note that all reference to the essential predicates of which Feuerbach had earlier made so much has been dropped. Moreover, this essence is conceived in the most minimal terms; namely, as bare subjectivity, as a Thou. In short, there is some continuity between the earlier and later works as

---

[68] Feuerbach, *Lectures*, pp. 273ff.; *Vorlesungen*, pp. 306ff. Here Feuerbach repeats the thesis of *Christianity* and claims that some of the attributes of God, such as omniscience and ubiquity, are the projection of human desires, but he merely asserts this to be the case and does not attempt to reconcile these claims with his previous analysis, in which these same attributes are derived from nature.

regards personification, but the Hegelian paraphernalia of a perfect species has been dropped, as well as the associated notions of alienation and reappropriation.

The most powerful and illuminating statement which throws into relief the difference between the two conceptions of projection occurs, interestingly enough, not in the main body of the text but in an extended appendix to the fifth lecture. It is so revealing that it deserves to be quoted at some length. It occurs after a sentence explaining that the nature which is the object of religion includes not only external but one's own internal and unconscious nature, a nature that functions independently of our will.

This statement brings us to our most crucial point, the true seat and source of religion. The ultimate secret of religion is the *relationship* between the *conscious* and *unconscious*, the *voluntary* and *involuntary in one and the same individual*. Man wills, but often he does so unwillingly – how often he envies the beings who have no will; he is conscious yet achieves consciousness unconsciously . . . He lives, and yet he is without power over the beginning and end of his life; he is the outcome of a process of development, yet once he exists, it seems to him as though he had come into being through a unique act of creation . . . He has a body, in every experience of pleasure or pain he feels it to be his own, and yet he is a stranger in his own house . . . Every pain is an undeserved punishment; in happy moments he feels that life is a gift he has not asked for . . .
Man with his ego or consciousness stands at the brink of a bottomless abyss; that abyss is his own unconscious being, which seems alien to him and inspires him with a feeling which expresses itself in words of wonderment such as: What am I? Where have I come from? To what end? And this feeling that I am nothing without a *not-I* which is distinct from me yet intimately related to me, something *other*, which is at the same time my *own* being, is the religious feeling. But what part of me is I and what part is not-I?[69]

This is a remarkable passage, and had we not known that it was written in the mid nineteenth century, we might easily have attributed it to any number of contemporary writers: to Ernest Becker, for example, whose own writings, in turn, were indebted to Freud, Otto Rank, Kierkegaard, and others. *Dasein*, as we have seen, is an embodied consciousness driven to realize its distinctive powers, to expand and to flourish. As a physical body, it is fated to die; as conscious, it is aware that it will die. In the grip of the rage-to-live, it is driven to rebel against its natural limitations. As a social creature, it longs for recognition and affirmation by another subject. Although

---

[69] *Lectures*, pp. 310f.; *Vorlesungen*, pp. 349f.

the I wills, it does so unwillingly; although it is conscious, it achieves consciousness unconsciously. Pain appears phenomenologically to be like punishment; and joy, like a gracious gift. Feuerbach even suggested, as Nietzsche was to do later, that the inrushes of unconscious forces such as epilepsy or ecstasy "have been looked upon as divine revelations or manifestations."[70] Thus, the fusion of the I and not-I is at once the foundation of individuality and also the root of religious feeling. It is the source of pride as well as humility in which the individual recognizes "that [it] did *not* obtain *from itself* what [it] is and has, that [it] does not possess life and being but merely holds a lease on them and can therefore be deprived of them at any moment."[71]

There is another important difference between the two models. In *Christianity*, the concept of nature plays a very minor role in how the attributes of God are derived. Feuerbach could even write that the divine is nothing other than human nature freed from all limitations, that "All the attributes of the divine nature are, therefore, attributes of human nature."[72] Consequently, in the case of monotheism, the attributes of God were all derived from human consciousness alone. Even the metaphysical attributes – infinitude, self-subsistence, necessary being, and First Cause – were derived from the human understanding or reason. The understanding, it was said, was that part of our nature which was impassible, incorporeal, incomprehensive, without limits, the source of identity, necessity, and law. The moral attributes, on the other hand, were derived from the objectification of the will because moral perfection was said to depend on the perfection of the will rather than on nature. And finally, the notion that God was compassion or love was derived from the objectification of the feelings.

In *Religion* and the *Lectures*, however, the gods are composite beings, some of their attributes being derived from nature and others from human consciousness. Moreover, many of the metaphysical attributes that had previously been derived from self-consciousness are now said explicitly to be derived from nature. If the monotheist thinks of God as necessary existence, this is because nature is so. If God is believed to be self-subsistent, it is because nature is as well. And if God is thought to be the First Cause, this is because nature is the source of all things. Even the attribute of unity, which Feuerbach had once derived from the unity of consciousness, is now said to be an abstraction from the

---

[70] *Lectures*, p. 311; *Vorlesungen*, p. 350.
[71] *Lectures*, p. 313; *Vorlesungen*, p. 352.
[72] *Christianity*, p. 14; *Christentums*, pp. 48f.

causal nexus of nature. How could it be otherwise, he asked rhetorically, because nature is "everything which man . . . experiences directly and sensuously as the ground and substance of his life."[73] It is no wonder, then, that nature is the source of fear, awe, and gratitude, so that human beings should worship it. "Even today," Feuerbach confessed, "I find *within myself* the motives of nature religion, motives which, if they were not countered by culture, science, and philosophy, would still make me a nature worshiper today."[74]

More surprising is that some of the moral attributes which Feuerbach had previously claimed were derived from human consciousness are now said to have their origins in nature. Even the attribute of justice does not arise out of insight into the moral nature of human beings but from the experience of evils that befall us in nature. For the polytheist who has not achieved the notion of the world as a whole, the occurrence of evil leads to the postulation of evil beings alongside the good. But for the monotheist, the occurrence of evil is interpreted as an expression of the wrath of the one god. And since in human life, anger is directed against those who have harmed us, so too the evils that befall us in nature are thought to be the result of some transgression against God. And finally, even the notion of God's goodness is not derived from human nature but is

merely abstracted from those beings and phenomena in nature which are useful, good, and helpful to man, which give him the feeling or consciousness that life, existence, is a good thing, a blessing. God's goodness is merely the utility of nature, ennobled by the imagination, by the poetry of man's emotions, personified and transformed into an active force.[75]

Finally, the elimination of the appeal to the projection of an essential human nature is reflected in Feuerbach's rough classification of religions. Although in *The Essence of Christianity* he did not seriously attempt to classify the religions as Hegel had done, he did make the Hegelian claim that the Christian religion was superior to the religions of nature; indeed, that it should be regarded as the "absolute religion" because "only in Christ is the last wish of religion realized, the mystery of religious feeling solved."[76] In the *Lectures*, however, Feuerbach shockingly proposed that the nature religions are superior to religions of the spirit, including Christianity, because they, at least, are sensuously in touch with the earth and nature, whereas Christianity

---

[73] *Lectures*, p. 91; *Vorlesungen*, p. 104.   [74] *Lectures*, p. 90; *Vorlesungen*, p. 104.
[75] *Lectures*, p. 111; *Vorlesungen*, p. 126.   [76] *Christianity*, p. 145; *Christentums*, p. 256.

abstracts from nature and makes God a separate, nonsensuous, spiritual being. One can, he argued, at least sympathize with nature worship and appreciate the sensuous impressions it makes upon the imagination, but in Christianity we can see "how God and nature, the love of God and the love of man, are in contradiction, how the activity of God on the one hand and that of man and nature on the other cannot be reconciled except by sophistry. Either God or nature!"[77]

FAITH AS (MIS)INTERPRETATION OF THE NOT-I

If we were to step back and reflect in contemporary language on the theoretical significance of the differences between the earlier and the later models of religion, we might say that Feuerbach seems to have quietly dropped the idea that religious belief is projection, the notion that the gods are the involuntary objectifications of the essential predicates of human nature, in favor of a view in which the self, driven by feeling, anxiety, and desire, abstracts certain qualities from nature and personifies them or, in the case of monotheism, unifies all the abstractions into one and personifies it. The gods are composite beings. The element of self-differentiation is still present, but in a different form from that described in *Christianity*. In the *Lectures*, the I finds itself confronted by a not-I that seems both to include it and to stand over against it. This confrontation inspires the feeling that the I is nothing without the not-I which is distinct from and yet intimately related to it, something *other* which is at the same time its own being. The imagination under the pressure of desire and wish personifies this not-I. Religion is not to be regarded, then, as a necessary stage or detour (*Umweg*) to self-knowledge but as an erroneous interpretation of the encompassing mysterious powers impinging upon the self and upon which it is dependent.

On the surface, this shift from one model to another might seem to be slight; but actually, it not only alters the way in which the content of religious ideas is explained and interpreted but, as I shall show in the next chapter, alters the logic or the overall strategy of interpretation itself. For example, when using the new model, the suspicious interpreters of religion will no longer take the Hegelian schema of objectification–alienation–reappropriation as the overarching hermeneutical framework. The gods will not be regarded as the alienated

[77] *Lectures*, p. 161; *Vorlesungen*, p. 183.

objectification of essential human predicates and, consequently, the goal of interpretation will not be to help religious believers reclaim the (lost) divine predicates as their own. In short, one can assume neither that every advance in religion is an advance in self-knowledge nor that religion itself is the vehicle to a higher self-knowledge. Rather, the suspicious interpreter assumes that religion springs out of *Dasein*'s confrontation with nature and the task will be to expose the distortions of life that result when the imagination operating under the pressures of anxiety, fear of death, and desire personifies nature.

Since in both the earlier and the later models the gods are personifications, and "projection" is often the term that is used to refer to personification, it might prove useful to pause momentarily and reflect on (a) the differences in meaning between the term "projection" and the term "religious belief" and (b) the appropriateness of assigning these terms respectively to the two models.

The first and obvious difference is that the term "projection" usually has an implicit pejorative meaning, while the term "religious belief" is more neutral. The reason for this is that the term "projection" normally includes four distinct but closely related strands of meaning. It suggests, first of all, that whatever features are attributed to the gods are nothing but the objectification of the traits of the believing subject and in no way reflect a cognitive response to something external. Some subjective trait has been objectified and applied to something believed to be external to oneself. Second, because the attributes assigned to the gods are not believed to be a cognitive response to an external reality, it is assumed that there must be some psychological mechanism generating the projection. Psychological theories like Freud's and Jung's, for example, appeal to repressed drives or archetypal instinctual patterns as causes of religious belief. Third, since the projection is to be explained in terms of some unconscious psychological process, the projection is obviously untrue or an illusion. Consequently, to call a religious conviction a "projection" naturally seems prejudicial and pejorative to the religious believer. And finally, once the psychological causes have been postulated, this then becomes the basis for a reductive interpretation of some sort. The interpreter treats religious symbolism as a semiotic code for conveying some latent, unconscious meaning.

The term "religious belief," by contrast, is more neutral. Although like "projection" it may suggest that belief is not knowledge in the sense of being a cognitive response to a perceived reality, it does not imply that the belief is caused by some internal and involuntary psychological process of which the believer is unaware. On the contrary, it even leaves open the possibility that believers may have reasons for what they believe even though an external observer may not think these reasons to be good reasons. Consequently, to use the term "religious belief" rather than "religious projection" invites no search for unconscious meanings that are supposed to be the real content of religious belief. Nor does the term imply that religious belief is in the nature of the case false or illusory.

Given these conceptual differences between the two terms, it is understandable why the theory of religion Feuerbach proposed in *The Essence of Christianity* is so universally and appropriately referred to as a projection theory of religion. Some Hegelian philosophers, to be sure, might object that this term obscures some of the uniqueness of the theory, but, nevertheless, it is more accurate to label it a projection theory than a theory of religious belief. The gods are the involuntary objectification of the essential predicates of human nature; the process of self-differentiation explains how the projection necessarily occurs; the projection must in the nature of the case be said to be an illusion; and, finally, the assumption that the gods are projections dictates the interpretative strategy; that is, how the content of religious ideas are explained and interpreted, why they alienate believers from their essential nature, and why, then, they should be reappropriated in a demystified form.

To call the theory of religion in the *Lectures* a projection theory simply because the gods are anthropomorphic beings, by contrast, is to obscure Feuerbach's view of the human situation that occasions a religious response as well as the pattern of interpretation he followed. To account for the gods as a result of the imagination seizing upon certain qualities or abstractions of nature, as the later Feuerbach does, is to give up the notion that the gods are produced by some necessary, involuntary, and unconscious process and to adopt the view that it is an erroneous but not an unintelligible belief in which feeling and desire lead the imagination to misinterpret certain physiognomic features of the natural environment or to reify the most abstract of all abstractions, Being itself.

By arguing in this fashion, Feuerbach, even though he may not have admitted it, was, in effect, offering reasons for the rise and persistence of religious belief; reasons of such a sort that the theorist need not appeal to involuntary causes, inner psychic mechanisms, and the like. If it is protested that he proposed the imagination to be just such a cause, then I would answer that this looks suspiciously like the creation of a mental faculty rather than a cause and, hence, explains nothing at all because everyone, both religious and irreligious, possesses such a faculty. The imagination, as Feuerbach himself conceded, does not inherently or necessarily personify nature. It does so only in what he regarded as "uneducated and subjective" people. In the educated, it leads to poetry and art.

If the above contrast between the two conceptions of projection is valid, then it would be less confusing to call Feuerbach's later theory a suspicious theory of religious belief than a projection theory. He set before his readers an account of why, given what we know about human nature, *Dasein* seems incorrigibly religious, and why religion so frequently takes the form of anthropomorphism. What it shares with projection theories is the claim that religion has to do with anthropomorphic beings and that these beings do not exist. But he did not attempt to explain these beliefs as he did in *Christianity*, in terms of some psychological mechanism which then provides the clue to their interpretation.

Most religious believers, of course, will find this characterization of his later project less prejudicial to religious belief than his earlier view, even if they reject his negative conclusions regarding it. It is less prejudicial because it does not imply from the outset that religion is simply an illusion, and it offers the possibility of a more rational discussion between believers and unbelievers. By assuming that religious believers think they have grounds and reasons for their beliefs Feuerbach, in principle, seems to classify religious beliefs as metaphysical even though they also suspiciously coincide with the deepest desires and wishes of humankind. But as Freud himself acknowledged, it does not follow because theism is an object of human wishes that it is thereby false. An illusion is not necessarily a delusion. The term "projection" applied to religious belief, at least in the most familiar sense of the term, precludes that possibility.

Once this distinction is made one might point out that many contemporary Christian theologians could accept the later Feuerbach's existentialist paradigm of faith even though they do not accept the conclusions he drew from it. Many theologians, for example, could accept Feuerbach's analysis of the I confronted by the not-I and the religious feeling this confrontation awakens. They could also accept the analysis of the role of anxiety, the will to life, and the desire for recognition and meaning. They, too, believe that the decision of faith is whether to believe that the circumambient powers of nature that impinge on the self from within and without are the actions of a benign and unified whole or the outworkings of chance. The difference, of course, is that Feuerbach believes that the religious interpretation of the world leads to intolerable rational contradictions and to a repudiation of the value of this sensuous earthly life, whereas the theologian believes that it leads to a life that can affirm the contingency of life without despair. For Feuerbach, the desire for recognition is just that, an unachieved desire. For the theologian, faith is the "acceptance of acceptance," to use Paul Tillich's formulation.

This structural similarity to some Protestant theology becomes apparent when one places Feuerbach's conception of religious faith alongside that of a Schleiermacher, a Tillich, or even an H. Richard Niebuhr. Consider Schleiermacher. Despite Feuerbach's protestations, Feuerbach's conception of religious feeling has more in common with Schleiermacher's than he was willing to concede. Feuerbach argued that religious feeling arises when the ego stands over against the not-I, which includes those unconscious aspects of its own being upon which it is dependent. The I feels that even its freedom is given to it, that it lives but is powerless to live, that it wills but wills involuntarily. For Schleiermacher also the religious feeling arises when the self feels that even its own freedom, its ability to affect others, is given to it. But for Schleiermacher the feeling of *absolute* dependence only arises when one sees oneself as part of an entire system of mutually determining causes and effects (nature) that itself is contingent. So far as one is a member of the system of secondary causes, one still has some feeling of freedom, however slight. But when one senses that the entire system of causes is contingent upon a "whence," the religious feeling of absolute dependence arises. In fact, the term "God" was for Schleiermacher the name for the whence (*Woher*) of this system of interdependent causes of which we are a part. Indeed, he could write that all the attributes ascribed to God refer not to something special in God but only to "something special in the manner in which the feeling of absolute dependence is to be related to him."[78]

Feuerbach, of course, believed that it was an error to think of the entire system of secondary causes as a whole that was itself dependent

---

[78] Friedrich Schleiermacher, *The Christian Faith*, trans. from the 2nd German edition and ed. H. R. Mackintosh and J. S. Stewart (Edinburgh: T. & T. Clark, 1928), p. 194.

upon a "whence." Or better, he believed that to think of the system as a whole does not require the appeal to some transcendent "*Woher*," nor does it justify giving it a proper name. Nevertheless, the pictures the two thinkers paint of the human situation that gives rise to the religious feeling have much in common, even to the point that both of them see the attributes of God as necessarily interpretations of nature or the causal nexus.

A more contemporary theological example of the way in which religious faith can be understood as an interpretation of the totality of forces impinging upon the self can be found in the writings of H. Richard Niebuhr. For Niebuhr, faith has to do with how one understands

the last shadowy and vague reality, the secret of existence by virtue of which things come into being, are what they are, and pass away. Against it there is no defense. This reality, this nature of things, abides when all else passes . . . It surrounds our life as the great abyss into which all things plunge and as the great source whence they all come.[79]

For Niebuhr faith is the decision to put one's confidence in this "X," this abyss into which all things plunge. The problem is whether one can attach faith, hope, and love to this "slayer of all." It is whether one can have confidence in Being. A similar notion of faith may also be found in the writings of Protestant theologians such as Fritz Buri and Paul Tillich as well as in those of such Catholics as Karl Rahner and David Tracy. One might say that they all regard the problem of religious faith to be whether the great Void into which all things tumble, to use Alfred North Whitehead's phrase, can be seen as the great companion.

Feuerbach, too, regarded religious faith in similar terms, and he probably would not have objected to these parallels drawn between his views and those of liberal Christian theologians, even Schleiermacher. He, too, believed that humans beings desire nothing more than that the Void be transformed into a companion. But he would surely have reminded us that the real question is not whether he and the theologians similarly depict the situation that gives rise to religion but whether there are any rational grounds for unifying the nature system or seeing the forces that impinge on the self as emanating from a personal power of some kind. He would have asked if it is only an

[79] H. Richard Niebuhr, *Radical Monotheism and Western Culture with Supplementary Essays* (New York: Harper & Row, 1970), p. 122.

arbitrary decision whether or not we interpret the not-I as personal, and further, whether there are not sacrifices and costs in so doing.

Indeed, one may argue that the whole design of Feuerbach's strategy in the *Lectures* is to argue that although the difference between faith and unfaith is, to be sure, a matter of the interpretation of the not-I, it is not an arbitrary decision which interpretation is adopted. His aim, as I shall attempt to establish in the next chapter, is to show that the religious interpretation can only arise when, first, the causal nexus appears to be a unified whole, and second, the believer thinks that there are some reasons, albeit not rising to the level of proof, why this whole testifies to a purposeful divine being. The religious believer when confronted with the question of the truth of faith adopts, in short, what might be called a "weak apologetic." This weak apologetic argues that although the pattern of nature does not prove the existence of a purposeful divine being, the existence of a divine being is compatible with the order of nature and no other explanation is as satisfactory as the theistic one. Feuerbach wished to undermine even these reasons. He wanted to offer a counter-interpretation of them.

In a sense, Feuerbach, the suspicious interpreter of religion, can also be said to engage in an interpretation of the not-I. But he thought that it provides no justification for viewing the whole as unified, purposeful, or benign, that it is more realistic to see these religious beliefs as expressions of human desire and the fear of death. Consequently, we might say that the task of Feuerbach's hermeneutics of suspicion is to mount a counter-interpretation, so to speak, a counter-interpretation that provides reasons, first of all, why there are no legitimate reasons to consider the whole or Being as such as anything more than a reified abstraction, and, second, to demonstrate that certain intellectual contradictions as well as deleterious existential consequences follow from religious faith.

This, as we shall see in the next chapter, is the interpretive strategy of the *Lectures*. His aim was to present and defend this counter-interpretation, a task which is quite different in kind than the critique which is found in *The Essence of Christianity* and which logically follows from giving up the Hegelian schema found there.

CHAPTER 6

The new interpretative strategy

CRITIQUE AS COUNTER-INTERPRETATION

In the preceding chapters I have argued that Feuerbach's later interpretation of religion differs sufficiently from his earlier that it deserves to be considered a new theory. Although he claimed that he was only filling a gap in the old theory by adding nature to the formula "theology is anthropology," this amendment seriously alters the pattern of his enterprise in five important respects: First, the idea of god is no longer the objectification of the species concept but is the personification of nature; second, the attributes of deity (omnipresence, omniscience, even benevolence) are not derived from human consciousness but are abstractions from nature; third, the religions are no longer to be regarded as progressions in self-knowledge and, hence (fourth), the spiritual religions are no longer said to be superior to the natural. And finally, all of these changes require a different interpretative strategy from that built on the Hegelian schema of objectification–alienation–reappropriation.

In order to claim that we have a new theory in Feuerbach's later writings, it is not necessary to deny all continuity with the old. Quite the contrary. What we have in the new version is not the complete abandonment of the old but the elevation to the point of dominance of those naturalist-existentialist motifs that had been subordinate in *Christianity* and the minimalization of the previously dominant Hegelian motifs. There still remains the emphasis on self-differentiation and self-consciousness, the emergence of the I over against the not-I, but this process is no longer articulated in Hegelian terms: the objectification of the species concept and its subsequent reappropriation. But since this Hegelian schema had determined the entire strategy of *Christianity* – how the idea of God emerged, how Christian doctrines are to be interpreted, and how they can be appropriated – we have in the later works something new. In this new theory we do not have the self objectifying the concept of the species; we have, rather, *Dasein*, driven by its sense of contingency and its drive for happiness, transforming the powers of nature into a subject concerned with human well-being. Seizing upon and unifying the qualities of nature, *Dasein* transforms the not-I into a Thou, a Thou that can satisfy its deepest wishes, especially the wish not to die. The basic and latent function of religion, then, is no longer to serve the development of self-knowledge; rather, it "has no other task and tendency than to change the unpopular and mysterious being of Nature into a known, unmysterious being."[1]

If this argument is valid, then one should expect the hermeneutical principles dominating the interpretative strategy of *Christianity* to be absent from *Religion* and the *Lectures* and to be replaced by the principles derived from the naturalist-existentialist model. Of the five interpretative principles I isolated in Chapter 2 above, the first two – the overall schema of objectification–alienation–reappropriation, and the objectification of the species concept – should be lacking, and the other three – the emphasis upon the imagination and the feelings together with the predominance of the felicity principle – should come to the fore.

This is, in fact, what the reader will find in these later works. Feuerbach has quietly adopted a new and decidedly un-Hegelian interpretative strategy without calling any attention to it. Monotheism is no longer regarded as consciousness becoming aware of the species but is the result, first, of *Dasein*'s sense of dependency upon nature and, second, of a series of "natural" intellectual errors arising from the tendency to look for causes and to reify abstractions, especially the abstraction "Being." Consequently, the aim of the interpreter is not to bring the believer to full self-consciousness, as it was in *Christianity*; rather, it is to display the grounds for the rise and persistence of religion but to demonstrate why and how these are misinterpreted. Feuerbach provides, in short, a counter-interpretation of religion. This strategy assumes, as the earlier did not, that believers have intellectual grounds, albeit mistaken, for their beliefs. Moreover, it is not as dramatic a procedure as the "transformative method," although it could be argued that it is more intellectually tenable.

There are several reasons why the overall interpretative strategy of

[1] Feuerbach, *Religion*, p. 40.

the later works is not as apparent as it was in the earlier works. First of all, by adopting the view that religion is an overdetermined phenomenon, Feuerbach lost the elegant Hegelian framework that made *The Essence of Christianity* appear to be such a *tour de force*. The multi-causal analysis of the *Lectures*, with its appeals to nature, the *Glückseligkeitstrieb*, the imagination, and feeling, cannot be captured in a neat formula such as "the method of transformation." There are no organizing dialectical "moments" leading to a final appropriation of the truth of religion, but only a prosaic development of various themes in no rationally compelling order. Second, Feuerbach accepted the invitation to give the *Lectures* on the assumption that they would constitute a commentary on the little book *Religion*. But as his argument unfolded, it was necessary for him to devote more time and space to developing his new themes and to undermining the assumptions of theism. In *Christianity*, he had thought it enough to presume that the Christian religion alienated the individual from the species and that Christian dogma was contradictory. In the *Lectures*, the task was more complicated. He must not only provide a convincing hypothesis concerning the formation of the gods but must also attack the tendencies to attribute purpose to nature and to believe that only Mind could produce other minds. In short, he thought that it was important to deal with the reasons for the reification of universals, and this, in turn, led him to lengthy excursions into the philosophy of language. And finally, he felt he had once again to provide reasons why monotheism in general and Christianity in particular were catastrophes for the human spirit. The nature of this catastrophe is not spelled out, as it is in *Christianity*, in the terminology of the alienation from the species, but, rather, in commonsense naturalistic terms. All of this gives the impression of haphazardness and conceals the form of his interpretative strategy. It is to this strategy that I now turn.

CRITICISMS OF THE MISINTERPRETATIONS OF NATURE

One of the most important differences between the strategy of the *Lectures* and that of *Christianity* is that almost a third of the former – lectures 11–20 – is devoted to showing that monotheism is really a mistaken interpretation of nature. There is nothing in these chapters claiming that the idea of God is an objectification of the essential predicates of human nature through which the human race is gaining self-knowledge. The gods, to be sure, are objectifications in a sense, but it would be more accurate to say that they are misinterpretations of nature. They are errors, albeit understandable errors, springing from the imagination's tendency to reify the qualities and abstractions of the not-I under the pressure of desire, feeling, and the fear of death.

In pursuing this strategy, Feuerbach was forced to step onto the playing field of more traditional philosophy of religion rather than employing the more exciting phenomenology of self-consciousness characteristic of his earlier book. Many of the lectures are, in effect, discussions of the so-called "proofs for the existence of God," and they often plod unimaginatively over ground that has been packed down hard by philosophers since David Hume. These lectures must have taxed the patience of the student audience in Heidelberg who had come to hear the scandalous author who had stood Hegel "on his head" in *The Essence of Christianity*. The various arguments he mounts in chapters 11–20 fall roughly into two groups: (a) refutations of certain traditional arguments for the existence of God, refutations that received their classical formulation in David Hume's *Dialogues*, and (b) arguments having to do with the status of class concepts and their relationship to language. The latter are the more original and interesting, and they anticipate the insights of Nietzsche and pragmatism a half a century later.

There are basically three arguments for the existence of God with which Feuerbach was particularly concerned, because he thought that they were the most persuasive to the common person and because he thought they illustrated the principle that the reification of abstractions was the secret of religious belief: (a) the argument for a First Cause; (b) the argument that the coherence and order in nature require intelligent design; and (c) the argument that it is inconceivable that unconscious nature could have given rise to conscious mind or spirit. Because the arguments and counter-arguments that swirl around the first two "proofs" are so familiar, and because Feuerbach added little that was original to them, we need only discuss them briefly.

As for the notion that the world requires a First Cause, Feuerbach argued, as did David Hume before him, that there are no grounds for thinking that the world is a single effect for which a single cause is required.[2] Hume had pointed out that we can only argue that a given

---

[2] Lectures 11 and 12.

effect requires a certain cause if we have already observed many examples of such a relationship in the past. We can infer that a watch requires a watchmaker, for instance, because we have seen many examples of watchmaking. But we have never experienced worlds being made and, consequently, we have no basis for arguing for a world-maker. Feuerbach simply adopted Hume's argument in this case and concluded that it is absurd to regard nature as a single effect. Nature, he argued, has no beginning or end, and everything is so interrelated that it is both cause and effect, acting and reacting on all sides. Furthermore, there is nothing illicit about an infinite series of causes and effects. Although some might claim that reason legitimately rebels at such a thought, "such an endless series is by no means incompatible with a reason informed by observation of the world."[3]

Large parts of Feuerbach's discussion of this traditional argument in lectures 11 and 12 are neither original nor rigorous, especially when compared, say, with David Hume's and Immanuel Kant's treatments of the same issue. What is original is the pragmatic argument that the idea of First Cause is itself merely a convenient abstraction that we employ to "make things easy for ourselves," a fiction or abbreviation that enables the mind to break off the endless series somewhere.[4] The very nature of thought and speech, he argued, "obliges us to make abbreviations on every hand, to substitute concepts for intuitions, signs for objects, the abstract for the concrete, the one for the many, and accordingly one cause for many different causes" because it would be too tedious to name or track down them all.[5]

Just as man attaches the name of one individual to an invention, to the founding of a state, the building of a city, the rise of a nation, although any number of unknown names and individuals have played a part, so he attaches the name of God to the universe . . . Most of the ancient names of historical or mythical men, heroes, and gods were collective names, which subsequently became individual names. Even the word "God," like all names as a matter of fact, was originally not a proper name but a general or generic term.[6]

The same necessity that leads the mind to replace many causes with one cause is what leads it to the "genesis and preservation of the world with One Being, One Name."[7]

The pragmatic need of the human mind to seek closure is

---

[3] *Lectures*, pp. 94f.; *Vorlesungen*, p. 109.   [4] *Lectures*, p. 95; *Vorlesungen*, p. 109.
[5] *Lectures*, p. 97; *Vorlesungen*, p. 112.   [6] *Lectures*, p. 95; *Vorlesungen*, pp. 109f.
[7] *Lectures*, p. 98; *Vorlesungen*, pp. 112f.

particularly evident, Feuerbach argued, in those three metaphysical ideas which Kant called the postulates of the pure reason: the notion of a cosmos, God, and the soul. In our dealings with the multifarious things in the world, the mind is driven to postulate "the complete determination of all things," the notion of everything that is, the class of all things. Feuerbach conceded that the reason feels a need to postulate such a whole and, as Kant did, the associated idea of an omniscient subject, God, that knows the truth about this whole. But it does not follow because the mind is driven to seek intellectual closure that such a postulated reality exists. All one can say is that the reason feels the need for such a concept.

In this sense it is perfectly right to say that reason, at least as long as reason, not yet disciplined by observation of the world, regards itself uncritically as the essence of the world, as the objective absolute essence, leads necessarily to the idea of divinity. But we must not single out this necessity, this idea, we must not isolate it from other phenomena, ideas, and representations which are *equally* necessary but which we nevertheless recognize as subjective, that is, based only on the peculiar nature of representation, thought, and speech, and to which we ascribe no objective validity and existence, no existence outside of ourselves.[8]

So long as the pragmatic need for abbreviations and fictions is seen for what it is, a need of reason, no harm results from these ideas. But as Nietzsche was to do later, Feuerbach argued that human beings are tempted to believe not only that their abstractions mirror the structures of the true world but that these universals are the causes of those individual things from which the abstractions were made. "Thanks to his faculty of abstraction, man finds common factors in nature or reality; these he abstracts from things of like or similar nature and makes them into an independent being, *distinct from things*."[9] *Dasein*, for example, abstracts time and space from physical things because all things are for it subject to change and extended. But no sooner are space and time abstracted than they are then posited as "the first grounds and conditions of these same things." The totality of sensuous things which for pragmatic reasons we call the world is then thought to have originated in space and time. Some philosophers such as Hegel, Feuerbach noted, have even reasoned that matter not only originates in space and time but springs from them. And scientists, such as Newton, have regarded space and time as God's

---

[8] *Lectures*, p. 97; *Vorlesungen*, p. 112.   [9] *Lectures*, p. 117; *Vorlesungen*, p. 133.

sensorium, "the organ whereby God is present to all things and perceives all things."[10]

Feuerbach had already argued at some length in the *Principles* that Hegel's basic error had been the identification of thought and being, that he had assumed that the categories of reason reflect the structures of absolute reality. In the *Lectures*, Feuerbach pushed this criticism further, to the point of concluding that the secret of both metaphysics and theology is the transformation of names and universals into causes. Theists, he argued, have taken "the *totality* of class concepts, which they call God, as the ground and source of real things; they hold not that the universal had its source in individuals but, on the contrary, that individuals sprang from the universal."[11] Consequently, he claimed that the question of the existence of God really hinges on the question of the existence of universals.

Feuerbach was well aware that this issue around which "the whole history of philosophy revolves" is a difficult one and complicated by the fact that we are "hampered and misled by the nature of language and of thought itself, which is inseparable from language, in short, because every word is a universal, so that language in itself, with its inability to express the particular, is often taken as proof that the sensuous particular is nonexistent."[12] But it is just because this issue is so difficult, he reminded us, that it is not surprising that human beings tend to resolve it according to their inclinations and even temperament.

The second traditional argument for the existence of God that Feuerbach was particularly concerned to refute was the so-called teleological argument. Without the concept of God, it is claimed, reason can bring forward no satisfying ground not only for the contingency of the world but "least of all for the design and order which is met with everywhere to such a wonderful degree (in the small because it is near us even more than in the large)," to use the formulation of Immanuel Kant.[13] This argument was especially important for Feuerbach. It is, first of all, the most popular of all such arguments and expresses the sense of wonder that the average person feels concerning the order in nature. Second, he had himself argued in *Religion* that theism originates only when human beings have

[10] *Lectures*, p. 117; *Vorlesungen*, p. 134.
[11] *Lectures*, p. 124; *Vorlesungen*, p. 141.   [12] *Lectures*, pp. 119f.; *Vorlesungen*, p. 136.
[13] Immanuel Kant, "What is Orientation in Thinking?," in *Critique of Practical Reason and Other Moral Writings in Moral Philosophy*, trans. and ed. with an introduction by Lewis White Beck (Chicago: Chicago University Press, 1949), p. 298.

developed sufficiently to be able to conceive of nature as a coherent whole. He believed that theism could arise only when nature is thought to manifest purpose and intention.

Feuerbach's objections to this teleological argument are also familiar and not original. Like Hume's, his strategy was first to demonstrate that the argument only works if nature is regarded as analogous to a human artifact, and second, to claim that there can be no justification for this analogy without begging the question. Nor is it legitimate to see all of the various and mysterious workings of nature as the result of a plan. Feuerbach, of course, lived before Darwin and could not have argued that the marvelous adaptations of beings in nature are themselves the very conditions of their survival. But he does argue that nature is necessarily an interconnected system of causes and effects. Consequently, there are, admittedly, all sorts of marvelously intricate behavioral systems – the flight of birds, for example – but these processes do not represent the result of purpose or plan.

Just as it is meaningless to ask why there is anything at all, so it is meaningless to ask why this particular thing is as it is and not otherwise; why, for example, oxygen is odorless, tasteless, and heavier than the atmospheric air, why it becomes incandescent under pressure, why even under extreme pressure it does not liquify, why its atomic weight is expressed by the number eight, why it combines with hydrogen only in proportions, measured by weight, of eight to one. These properties define the individuality of oxygen, that is, its determinateness, its special nature, its essence.[14]

Nor was Feuerbach impressed by an ancient argument originating with the Stoics; namely, that it is as unintelligible to think of the world as a product of chance as it is to believe that an accidental combination of the letters of the alphabet could produce a literary classic like the *Annales* of Ennius. These are not the only alternatives, Feuerbach responded, because the sensuous beings of nature are not analogous to the letters of the alphabet, which stand in no necessary relationship to each other and so must be put in place by a printer. Rather, it is the very essence of a natural being to stand in a necessary relationship to others. The body, for example, requires the oxygen that is produced by other natural beings, just as they, in turn, have their own natural and necessary conditions for being. Nature is simply the mutually necessary coinherence of things and beings. If we

---

[14] *Lectures*, p. 129; *Vorlesungen*, p. 147.

wonder, as we do, at its marvelous and intricate patterns or at the emergence of minds which can comprehend it, this should imply nothing more than that we are marveling at nature itself and our relationship to it. "If we wish to marvel at something, we should marvel at the very existence of the earth and confine our theological wonderment and proofs to the original characteristics of the earth."[15]

The third argument undergirding belief in monotheism that Feuerbach was anxious to refute also rests on what might be said to be a commonsense intuition: that only spirit can beget spirit, that the human mind could not possibly have emerged from unconscious nature. If only spirit can beget spirit, then a world in which human spirit has emerged could have had its origins only in a divine spirit. Although this argument is closely related to the argument from design, there were powerful cultural and intellectual reasons why Feuerbach thought it especially important to single it out and attack it. Culturally speaking, the presupposition of the uniqueness of the spirit was the basic premise underlying both Christianity and Hegelian idealism and, hence, that which made it possible for Hegelians to make an alliance with the state in order to protect the spiritual and moral claims of the Church. Hegel had claimed that Christianity holds the same truth in figurative form which the true philosopher holds conceptually. Moreover, he claimed, the same spiritual content will be found in the ideal form of the state. Consequently, the morality of the Church and of the state should mutually guarantee one another, so much so that the ideal state should provide aid to the Church to the extent of demanding that citizens participate in it.

What this meant practically, Feuerbach saw, was that all of the hierarchical evaluations contained in both Hegelian philosophy and Christian morality not only found their justification in this doctrine of the superiority of the spirit but were then embodied in state policy. Hegel could rank past civilizations in such a way that German culture stood at the apex, and he could rank the religions of the world in such a way that Christianity, as the religion of pure spirit, was superior to all others. Moreover, the dualism of mind and body, which expresses itself in countless ordinary valuations, found its ultimate final expression in the doctrine of the immortality of the soul. It was all this to which Feuerbach's "new philosophy" was opposed. He had

---

[15] *Lectures*, p. 129; *Vorlesungen*, p. 147.

rejected the identity of thought and being, and refused to accept the dualism of mind and body with all that this implied. The new philosophy affirmed that *Dasein* was a real, sensuous being, that the body in its totality is the human ego.[16] Consequently, it was crucial for Feuerbach to undermine the one argument which in both its Hegelian and its more popular form was at the core of the Christian belief which dominated his culture.

It was also important for him to refute the argument that only spirit could beget spirit because he believed that this intuition was at the heart of all monotheisms. For even though he argued that the concept of God is simply "the totality of all class concepts," he knew that it was because subjectivity was attributed to this abstraction that it had become an object of worship. "Being-as-such" may invoke awe and wonderment, but it is because this Being takes an interest in human affairs that human beings pray to and worship it.

Perhaps none of the lectures is more representative of Feuerbach's naturalism than the seventeenth, in which he (a) proposed arguments against the independence of the mind from the brain, (b) delivered exhortations concerning how children should be educated to see themselves as products of nature, (c) discussed the panentheism of Schelling, Fritz Baader, and Jacob Böhme, all of whom had speculated that God, too, must have a material, corporeal body.

In dealing with the mind–body problem, which is at the crux of the claim that only spirit can beget spirit, Feuerbach employed the results of the considerable reflection he had already given to this issue when writing an essay entitled "The Dualism of Body and Soul, Flesh and Spirit" in 1846.[17] In that essay, he had presented some of the then-current thinking in both psychology and physiology and argued that our sense of two distinct and separate ontological realms of mind and body arises from the two distinct linguistic categories our minds employ when thinking about them. When we use the language of psychology, for example, we refer to sensations, feelings, perceptions, intentions, and not to nerves, the brain, the stomach, or the heart. But in the realm of physiology, we refer to nerves, blood, oxygen, and the brain, and not to intentions, feelings, and thoughts. We have, in effect, two discrete spheres of discourse.

These two distinct spheres of discourse reflect the subjective

---

[16] *Principles*, para. 36.
[17] Feuerbach, *Kleinere Schriften III, GW* x.122–150. Feuerbach had originally intended this essay to be a supplement to the *Principles*.

perspective of consciousness itself. When we think from the standpoint of the subject, we know nothing about the genealogy of our feelings and striving, just as in indulging in the pleasures of eating we are unaware of the workings of our stomachs and digestive systems. But it does not follow from this that because we can think of ourselves as distinct from the body there is, in fact, an incorporeal reality called the mind that exists independently of it. To conclude this would be analogous to arguing that because we cannot feel within ourselves that we have parents we are, therefore, self-created and owe our existence to no one. The distinction has to do with the perspectives we are compelled to adopt, our mode of knowing, and not with reality itself.[18]

Feuerbach made this same point in the *Lectures*, but emphasized still more the bewitchment of language. The illusion that the mind is independent of the body arises because we use a logically different vocabulary to refer to mental activity than we do to refer to bodily activity.

In language we distinguish the activity of the brain as psychic from the other functions which we call physical. We limit the words bodily or sensory to particular kinds of bodily or sensory activity, and, as I have shown in my books, make that activity that differs from these into an activity of an entirely different class, a spiritual, that is, absolutely nonsensuous and disembodied activity. But the spirit and its activity – for what is the spirit but mental activity, hypostatized and personified by the human imagination and language? – are also physical activity, the activity of the brain, which differs from other activities only insofar as it is the activity of a *different* organ, namely, the brain.[19]

Because the activity of the brain that makes thought possible is not itself an object of consciousness, because it is "the most hidden, withdrawn, soundless, and imperceptible activity, man has come to look upon this activity as an absolutely *disembodied*, inorganic, abstract being, to which he has given the name of spirit."[20]

Feuerbach concluded from all this that one of the most important philosophical and cultural tasks of his generation was to revise the way human beings think about the relationship of mind to nature. The traditional dualism enshrined in Christianity and philosophy could only be construed as an indirect way of saying that although the

---

[18] Feuerbach, *Kleinere Schriften III*, *GW* x.122ff.
[19] *Lectures*, p. 154; *Vorlesungen*, p. 174.
[20] *Lectures*, pp. 154f.; *Vorlesungen*, p. 175.

body has natural origins, the mind can only be explained "unnaturally," which is to say supernaturally. This, in turn, reflects an overevaluation of spirit and an underevaluation of nature that is one of the manifestations of the anthropomorphism at work in human reason. Granted that our minds constitute our highest faculty, our "badge of nobility," it does not follow that what has emerged most recently in the development of nature somehow constitutes the origin of that development. It is merely human vanity and self-love that prods us to think that what is qualitatively first must have preceded everything in time. This is analogous to the tendency of the nobility to regard some characteristic of their own as superior to all others and then to claim divine origin for it.[21]

The educational system, he argued, must train its students to understand that the mind develops along with the body, the senses, and, indeed, the whole person. Spirit is rooted in the brain, and it is intolerable to think that the skull and brain originated in nature but that the mind was created supernaturally. Whatever is the source of the skull and brain must also be the source of the mind, and if nature is the source of the former, then it must also be the source of the latter.

At one point in the seventeenth lecture, Feuerbach acknowledged that some philosophers of religion, such as Schelling and Fritz Baader, had been willing to reject the classical mind–body dualism of traditional theism even to the point of ceasing to regard God as pure spirit. Like some Process theologians in our own time, they abandoned the doctrine of creation *ex nihilo* in favor of the view that God as spirit is the subjective pole of the material cosmos. In short, God as spirit stands to the world much as the human mind stands to the body.

Feuerbach conceded that this doctrine is more rational "up to a certain point" than traditional theism because, like atheism, it begins with nature and lets spirit develop from it. Nevertheless, this doctrine is also irrational because "it cloaks the natural process of development in the mystical darkness of theology."[22] It attributes corporeality and sensuousness to the divine nature, and spirit to matter. Moreover, to the extent that the cosmos is viewed as God's body, this belief is committed to the conclusion that God is an object of our bodily senses. Perhaps some of these philosophers would be willing to concede even this, but to the degree that they do, Feuerbach argued, they abandon the gods whom human beings really desire – the gods who intervene

---

[21] *Lectures*, p. 155; *Vorlesungen*, pp. 175f. [22] *Lectures*, p. 156; *Vorlesungen*, p. 177.

in nature and providentially guide it in terms of human welfare. What the doctrine of panentheism really confirms, Feuerbach concluded, is that God is a concept abstracted from nature. To say that God is not only spirit but body as well only demonstrates that "the divinity of matter in God is a mystical, inverted doctrine, and that the true, rational doctrine, in which the mystical doctrine first finds its meaning, is the atheist doctrine which considers mind and matter as such, without God."[23]

There is very little to be gained at this point by my attempting to assess the cogency of these arguments, because any such assessment would itself soon take us into deeper metaphysical and epistemological issues that resist simple adjudication, if, indeed, these issues can be adjudicated at all. In this case, the deeper issues are Feuerbach's naturalism, his philosophy of language, his nominalism, and his philosophy of *Sinnlichkeit*. Those who share his fundamental premises will be kindly disposed towards his arguments and their assumptions; those who do not will find them unconvincing. My purpose is only to emphasize that the argumentative strategy in the *Lectures* is quite different than that found in his earlier work. I have wanted to demonstrate that the Hegelian schema of objectification–alienation–appropriation plays no important role here and, more strongly, that *it could not have* because the dominant assumption is that the idea of God arises out of confrontation with nature and not out of the objectification of the perfections of the human species. God is the totality of class concepts unified by the imagination into the idea of a personal subject. God is "Being itself" reified.

CONTRADICTIONS IN THE IDEA OF PROVIDENCE

Nothing more clearly reveals how much the bipolar model has eclipsed the Hegelian paradigm in the later works than the disappearance of two of the most important ideas guiding Feuerbach's earlier interpretative strategy: (a) the idea that the objectification of the idea of the species alienates the individual from his/her essential human nature and (b) the idea that the aim of a suspicious interpretation of religion is to enable the religious believer to reappropriate the truth of religion in an unalienated form, which is to say atheism. As I have argued in earlier chapters, these two ideas

---

[23] *Lectures*, p. 158; *Vorlesungen*, p. 179.

enabled Feuerbach to claim that he was really a friend and not an enemy of religion because he was only attempting to recover what the religious consciousness itself felt and thought. But by abandoning the Hegelian objectification–alienation–reappropriation schema, Feuerbach could no longer claim to be a charitable and friendly interpreter of religion because he no longer regarded theism as mystified truth but, rather, as a tissue of errors, a misinterpretation of nature based on ignorance and superstition.

Consequently, the later interpretative strategy is less dialectical than the earlier and more straightforwardly negative. Like Marx, Nietzsche, and Freud, Feuerbach no longer wanted to uncover some truth hidden in religion; rather, he wanted to clear the religious rubble away in preparation for a new and completely secular worldview. There are no attempts in these later works, for example, to argue that the concept of God is a mystified expression of some deeper latent truth about human reality; rather, there is only a litany of objections to monotheism in general and Christianity in particular. If there is any truth to be retrieved in this form of religion, Feuerbach concluded, it is only a certain veneration for nature and an affirmation of "the truth and divinity of the senses."[24]

Most monotheisms, in contrast to pagan religions, he charged, have even obliterated this truth because the God they worship and the ideal form of existence they envisage are absolutely separate from nature. The pagan, at least, "did not break away from the world, from nature; he could conceive of himself only as a part of it." But the Christian, by contrast, worships a completely unearthly, spiritual being and longs for an existence in heaven in which everything sensuous and earthly has been stripped away.[25] For this reason, Feuerbach concluded, pagan religions ought to be preferred over the spiritual monotheisms of the world, an assertion that must have shocked both his Hegelian and non-Hegelian readers because it clearly reversed his earlier view that Christianity is the absolute religion.

One major set of objections to monotheism to which Feuerbach gave a great deal of attention has to do with the intellectual problems arising from the belief that God is the one, absolute power working in the realm of secondary causes, that all happenings in nature are reflections of the divine will. This conviction is not only rooted in the wish of the individual for a power that can transcend nature but is

[24] *Lectures*, p. 88; *Vorlesungen*, p. 102.   [25] *Lectures*, p. 232; *Vorlesungen*, p. 259.

inherent in the theist's view that the coherence and unity of nature as well as nature itself require a powerful First Cause. All of the forms of monotheism, Islamic, Jewish, and Christian, Feuerbach argued, implicitly hold this view. It is what binds together the doctrines of creation, the belief in miracles, and the idea of providence. It is this faith that undergirds the believer's confidence that God can do anything. So much is this the case that Islamic and Christian theologians alike have argued that by the mere force of His will, God could produce any effect that He wishes. Turn wherever you will in the theological literature, Feuerbach noted, and you will find claims similar to that of the Islamic theologian al Ghazzali, who wrote that God

is the only effective cause in all nature; thanks to this cause, it is just as possible that fire should touch tinder without burning it as that tinder should burn without contact with fire. There is no such thing as natural process or natural law; the difference between miracles and natural happenings is non-existent.[26]

Luther also expressed the logic of this view when he wrote that "All creatures are masks and mummery of God," just as did Calvin when he argued that "Divine Providence does not come to meet us naked, but often clothes itself in natural instrumentalities."[27]

Such a view, Feuerbach argued, leads to "the most absurd contradictions" and calls forth the most preposterous sophisms and mental gymnastics, not only because it is impossible for human beings to relinquish their "natural human reason" which tells them that nondivine beings act independently, but also because even theists themselves must concede some autonomy to nature if they are to escape the inference that God is responsible for evil. The only way these contradictions can be avoided is by making a concession to the rationalism that attributes some autonomy to the realm of secondary causes, in the form either of some inherent powers in nature or free will in human beings. Both limit divine power. But a rationalistic theism that limits divine power, however rational it may seem to be, fails to do justice to the heart's desire for a deity who can intervene in nature and save the believer from suffering and injustice. A God who acts only in accordance with natural laws is a God in name only and does not differ from nature.

Such a God is contrary to the concept of a God; for only an unlimited,

---

[26] Al Ghazzali quoted by Feuerbach, *Lectures*, p. 160; *Vorlesungen*, p. 181.
[27] Both Luther and Calvin quoted by Feuerbach, *Lectures*, p. 141; *Vorlesungen*, pp. 159f.

wonder-working God, bound by no laws, a God who, at least in man's faith and imagination, can save us from all trouble and affliction, is truly a God. But a God who helps me only through doctors and medicines when I am sick . . . is an utterly superfluous, unnecessary God, whose existence gives me nothing that nature alone would not give me, and whom I can therefore well afford to lose. The choice is between no monarchy and absolute monarchy, between no God and an absolute God like the God of our fathers.[28]

To construe the dilemma in this way – either an absolute deity or none at all – is all too typical of Feuerbach's argumentation and something to which many Christian theologians quite naturally take exception. After all, they argue, there are many ways in which one may conceive of the relationship between God and the nexus of secondary causes. In defense of Feuerbach, however, it should be said that he did not construct this choice arbitrarily but believed that it is implicit in Christian faith itself, as can be seen in the prayers and hymns of ordinary believers as well as in the writings of representative theologians such as Augustine, Aquinas, and, above all, Luther and Calvin. Feuerbach, as we shall see again below, never abandoned the conclusion to which he had been driven by his practice of "listening" to the utterances of the religious consciousness of ordinary people; namely, that what the believer wants above all is a deliverer, a deliverer not only from sin and failure but from sickness, disease, and death. And this religious desire has implicit within it a conception of the divine power in which God is lord of the universe and can do anything in it. It is the believer who has rejected rationalism.

Moreover, it is just such a conception of divine power, Feuerbach claimed, that although expressed naïvely by the ordinary believer also finds expression in the writings of the most sophisticated theologians. It was Luther, not a naïve believer, who taught that to believe that God was omnipotent was also to believe that there was no natural necessity, limitation, or opposition to human wishes that could not and would not be overcome. And it was Calvin who wrote:

Since a Christian is absolutely certain that nothing happens by chance, that everything occurs in accordance with God's decree, he will always direct his gaze upon God as the most eminent or first cause of things, but he will also accord due recognition to the subordinate causes. He will not doubt that a special Providence, encompassing every detail, watches over him, permitting nothing that does not redound to his welfare and salvation. Consequently, he will relate everything that happens for the best, in accordance with his

---

[28] *Lectures*, p. 149; *Vorlesungen*, p. 169.

heart's desires, to God and regard God alone as its cause, even if he has experienced God's benefaction through the service of man or received help from soulless creatures. For in his heart he will think: Surely it is the Lord who has inclined their souls toward me, in order that they might be the instruments of His benevolence toward me.[29]

Feuerbach found this passage from Calvin to be not only intellectually but morally repugnant, a passage in which "the entire wretchedness of this theological view is brought home to us."[30] In it, he believed, one sees the reprehensible consequences of the view of God's grace as "personified chance or personified necessity."[31] Here we see the consequences of the basic understanding that underlies monotheistic faith; namely, that nothing happens by chance, that since God is the eminent cause working in good people, we are not to trust our own natural feeling and common sense and be grateful to those who are beneficent to us. It also enshrines the contradiction that this all-loving God is the source of the evil that is done as well as the good, a contradiction that has led countless theologians to attribute the good to God but evil to men.

But that is the nature of theology. Its personification, the theologian, is an angel in his dealings with God, a devil in his dealings with man; he imputes good to God and evil to man, the creature, and nature.[32]

There is, to be sure, Feuerbach conceded, some latent truth in the view that human beings do not become what they are simply by virtue of their own free wills. We are historical creatures born in certain times and places, in societies that make us what we are. "I have become what I am only in the context of this people, this country, this place, this century, this nature – only in the context of the environment, conditions, circumstance, and events that constitute my biography."[33] But this confession is not the same thing as saying that a single divine cause is at work in all that has made one what he/she is. It does not negate the rational freedom grounded in nature and that manifests itself as independent activity and self-mastery.

One of the interesting points Feuerbach made in his attack on the belief in God's omnipotence is that theists themselves have been unable to live under the rigorous form of it articulated by Luther and Calvin, not only because a rigorous monotheism violates the irrepressible

[29] Calvin quoted by Feuerbach, *Lectures*, pp. 160f.; *Vorlesungen*, pp. 181f.
[30] *Lectures*, p. 161; *Vorlesungen*, p. 182.   [31] *Lectures*, p. 163; *Vorlesungen*, p. 184.
[32] *Lectures*, p. 162; *Vorlesungen*, pp. 183f.   [33] *Lectures*, p. 164; *Vorlesungen*, p. 185.

human intuition about the autonomy of nature but because one must postulate some sort of autonomy of nature in order to avoid attributing evil to an omnipotent and benevolent being. "All theodicies, all justifications of God," he observed, "are therefore, consciously or unconsciously, based on the idea of an autonomous nature; in them God's activity and omnipotence are limited by the existence and action of nature."[34]

By virtue of this practical attribution of autonomy to nature Feuerbach believed that Christians in effect reject the notion of omnipotence. If there is a good and all-powerful being, he asked, why should one ascribe independent power and efficacy to human beings and the world? But happily for the West, Christians have ignored this inconsistency because it is solely because of "this instinctive atheism and egoism that we owe all progress, all the inventions which distinguish Christians from Mohammedans, and Occidentals in general from Orientals."[35]

With that suggestion, Feuerbach, as he often did, came very close to anticipating the provocative thesis proposed by Nietzsche that atheism in the West is, paradoxically, the unfolding of the consequences of Christianity itself, that Christianity, as it were, is its own grave digger.

IS RELIGION, THEN, PRIMITIVE SCIENCE?

Among Feuerbach's litany of objections to religion in general and monotheism in particular there is one that seems dated and crude to even the most sympathetic modern reader: religion, he argued, is simply the attempt to harness nature in the interest of human happiness. It is nothing but primitive science ignorant as to how to achieve its aims.[36] It follows logically from this, Feuerbach claimed, that when humanity wishes to change nature by building bridges or curing diseases it will be opposed by religion, just as it also follows that as science is more successful religion will wither away.

This view of religion is confirmed, he argued in lecture 23, when one analyzes the two primary forms of religious practice, sacrifice and prayer, both of which contain elements of magic. Both of them are attempts to gain the favor of the beings upon whom human beings are dependent. This utilitarian aim is what explains the elements of petition and demand that appear even in the prayers of the so-called

---

[34] *Lectures*, p. 166; *Vorlesungen*, p. 188.
[35] *Lectures*, p. 167; *Vorlesungen*, p. 189.   [36] *Lectures*, p. 207; *Vorlesungen*, p. 232.

"high" monotheistic traditions, as can be seen in Luther's advice to his parishioners in his *Commentary on Genesis* that when in distress they should not be "too respectful of [God's] sublime majesty but blurt out: now help me, God! God, have mercy!"[37] Prayers and sacrifices are simply the means whereby helpless and perplexed human beings try to force the hand of nature. To be sure, Feuerbach noted with scarcely concealed sarcasm, earlier Christians relied more on prayer than do modern Christians, whose faith has been eroded by rationalism. But even modern Christians still pray for deliverance from the ravages of fire, except that they also "prefer to take out fire insurance."[38]

To complicate the matter still further, Feuerbach, like many other contemporaries, tended to identify knowledge and science with culture. And since religion is primitive science, it must also be the first "crude and vulgar form of culture." Consequently, it follows not only that religion will wither away as science and knowledge increase, but that religion is incompatible with culture. It is not just that religion is infantile but that it is an attempt "to perpetuate ideas, customs, inventions that man made in his childhood, and to impose them as the laws of his adult age."[39] What "uncivilized man" tries to achieve by religion, civilized man tries to achieve by science and culture. Consequently, the "paramount task of our time is not to make men religious but to educate them, to disseminate education in all classes and all walks of life."[40]

The upshot of these two equations – religion with primitive science and science with culture – frequently led Feuerbach, as it did Freud after him, to regard religion as an infantile attempt to control nature by humanizing it. And, like Freud, Feuerbach thought this attempt had an infantile prototype.

Unable to satisfy his desires by his own resources, a child turns to his parents, the beings on whom he feels and knows himself to be dependent, in the hope of obtaining what he wishes through them. Religion has its origin, its true position and significance, in the childhood stage of mankind. But the childhood stage is also the stage of ignorance and inexperience, the uneducated, uncivilized stage.[41]

Perhaps nothing better illustrates the degree to which Feuerbach's earlier dialectical attitude towards religion has given way to a negative view than the two chapters, 23 and 24, from which these

---

[37] Luther quoted by Feuerbach, *Lectures*, p. 208; *Vorlesungen*, p. 233.
[38] *Lectures*, p. 208; *Vorlesungen*, pp. 233f.   [39] *Lectures*, p. 213; *Vorlesungen*, p. 239.
[40] *Lectures*, p. 214; *Vorlesungen*, p. 241.   [41] *Lectures*, p. 209; *Vorlesungen*, p. 234.

quotations are taken. Whereas his earlier model had enabled him to operate on the assumption that there is truth in religion even if in a mystified form, the later model permitted him, or so he believed, to argue that religion is superstition, an expression of ignorance of the true causes of nature that flourishes in times of barbarism.

This negative view was not without its ominous political implications, and when Feuerbach permitted himself a few asides in his lectures he suggested that any civil state in which citizens enjoy free political institutions but are not free from religion cannot be said to be a truly human and free state.   ·

I for my part don't care a farthing for a political freedom that leaves me enslaved to my religious prejudices and imaginings. True freedom is present only where man is also free from religion; true culture is present only where man has become master over his religious prejudices and imaginations.[42]

For those who admire Feuerbach, these occasional political asides are both disturbing and disappointing. They are disturbing because they reveal that despite his well-known opposition to authoritarian governments, an opposition that was the basis of his election as a delegate to the Frankfurt Assembly of 1848, he, like Marx, could not rid himself of a residual authoritarianism.[43] Like Marx, he ominously wrote that "Man's task in the state is not only to believe what he wishes, but to believe what is reasonable."[44] Although ostensibly a liberal, he still could not fully embrace the basic assumptions of a liberal, civic society; namely, that opinions and their expressions, however erroneous or irrational, should not be censored by the state.

A charitable interpreter of the later Feuerbach is tempted to explain such comments away as vestiges of the prejudices of the nineteenth-century German radical thought he was unable to transcend. Thus, one might say that just as the old model of religion in *The Essence of Christianity* was compounded with the arcane remnants of Hegelianism, so, too, the new model retains the vestiges of the "outdated nonsense" that religion is primitive science and should be abolished. ˙

Nevertheless, the comment is disappointing, particularly because

---

[42] *Lectures*, p. 218; *Vorlesungen*, p. 244.
[43] In his essay "On the Jewish Question," Marx had written that even though a constitutional state that guarantees the rights of conscience, property, and freedom of religion is more progressive than a state that does not, such a state still only preserves "egoistic man," separated from the community. See Livingstone and Benton (trans.), *Karl Marx Early Writings*, p. 220.   [44] *Lectures*, p. 219; *Vorlesungen*, p. 245.

Feuerbach's identification of religion with the prediction and control of nature is fundamentally inconsistent with the naturalist-existentialist thread basic to his own new model. We can see this most clearly by turning once again to that remarkable passage appended to the fifth lecture where, it will be recalled, he had returned to his basic theme that self-differentiation is the key to understanding religion. The "ultimate secret of religion," he had written, lies in the fact that *Dasein*

stands at the brink of a bottomless abyss; that abyss is his own unconscious being, which seems alien to him and inspires him with a feeling which expresses itself in words of wonderment such as: What am I? Where have I come from? To what end? And this feeling that I am nothing without a *not-I* which is distinct from me yet intimately related to me, something *other*, which is at the same time my *own* being, is the religious feeling.[45]

It is this relationship of the conscious to the unconscious, the voluntary and the involuntary in one and the same individual, Feuerbach claimed, that sets religious feeling in motion. It is not the desire to control nature from which religious feeling springs, but the sense of living and yet being powerless to live, of being conscious unconsciously, and of willing involuntarily. Schleiermacher saw this more consistently than did Feuerbach. No amount of control over nature could supplant or diminish that sense. It is a concomitant of the structure of self-consciousness itself, as Feuerbach himself confessed when he wrote:

If man were a mere I, he would have no religion, for he himself would be God; but he would also have no religion if he were a not-I, or an I undifferentiated from his not-I, for then he would be a plant or an animal.[46]

Feuerbach's claim that religion will vanish as science progresses seems incompatible with another of the important threads of his naturalist-existential theme; namely, the anxiety associated with the awareness of finitude and death. This theme, also, runs like a silver thread throughout all of his works from beginning to end, so much so that one is particularly disappointed in Karl Barth's otherwise sympathetic essay when he endorses Hans Ehrenberg's criticism that Feuerbach was a "true child of his century, a 'non-knower (*Nichtkenner*) of death' and a 'misknower (*Verkenner*) of evil.'"[47] Far from being a *Nichtkenner*, Feuerbach believed that the acceptance of death was one of the great reluctances of humankind and the source of most religions. He argued this in his first book, *Thoughts on Death and*

---

[45] *Lectures*, p. 311; *Vorlesungen*, pp. 349f.   [46] *Lectures*, p. 312; *Vorlesungen*, p. 350.
[47] Karl Barth, "An Introductory Essay," in *The Essence of Christianity*, p. xxviii.

Immortality, and it appears again in the *Lectures*: the "tomb is the birthplace of the gods."[48]

In his early works, Feuerbach's thoughts about death were closely allied with his theory of the species, because the notion of the species is necessarily linked to the death of the individual. In the *Lectures*, however, the idea of death is related to the individual's encounter with nature. "The thought of death is a religious thought," he wrote,

because in it I confront my finiteness. But if it is clear that without death there can be no religion, it must be equally clear that the feeling of dependency is the most characteristic expression of the ground of religion; for what can impress on me more forcefully, more incisively than death the feeling that I do not depend on myself alone, that the length of my life does not depend on my will?[49]

It is in religion that humanity erects its defenses against death, and this is why in most of them the doctrine of immortality is so central. It is not successful science that will cause this fear to disappear, but an acceptance of the conditions of finitude on which human existence is given.

There is still another observation to be made about Feuerbach's remarks about the relation of religion to science. To the extent that Feuerbach never abandoned the view that the I comes to self-consciousness over against a Thou, he also never abandoned the view that the I craves and needs recognition by another. It is "pleasanter to see oneself imaged in the love-beaming eyes of another personal being, than to look into the concave mirror of self or into the cold depths of the ocean of nature."[50] It was this insight, I argued in Chapter 2, that enabled Feuerbach to be so sympathetic to religious anthropomorphism. It is not just that religious believers want a superhuman helper in times of need and distress, but that they crave acknowledgment and acceptance by another. We saw in the discussion of *The Essence of Christianity* how this view enabled Feuerbach to provide an extraordinarily sympathetic and perceptive view of prayer. It was superficial, he argued, to treat prayer merely as a matter of dependence; rather, it is the desire for affection, the sense of being an end for someone, "the guarantee of one's existence." The same theme is found in the *Lectures*. "I cannot love, revere, and worship a natural force," he wrote. God is essentially a "creature of the heart" and, therefore, a being who fulfills human desires.

[48] *Lectures*, p. 33; *Vorlesungen*, p. 41.
[49] *Lectures*, p. 34; *Vorlesungen*, p. 42.   [50] *Christianity*, p. 140; *Christentums*, p. 247.

And the most heartfelt desire, at least of those men whose desires are not curtailed by natural necessity, is the desire not to die, to live forever; this is indeed man's highest and ultimate desire, the desire of all desires, just as life is the epitome of all blessings.[51]

One might have thought that this insight – that desire for recognition and communion by another is one of the prime motivations of religion – might have caused Feuerbach to doubt, if not reject, the view that religion was basically primitive science. At least it should have foreclosed the crudest of his remarks seen in the preceding paragraphs. Had he thought through more consistently the implications of his own views, he might even have seen how his anthropomorphic view of religion illuminates the fact that religion exists on a continuum from magic to communion.

We might ask what it was beside thoughtlessness that led Feuerbach to ignore his own insight into the nature of religious desire and to equate religion with primitive science. One possible answer is that the view that religion arises out of the feeling of dependency upon nature tempts one to say that whatever reduces this dependency will diminish religion. But in my opinion, there is a more fundamental reason. It is that Feuerbach did not sufficiently explore in the *Lectures* the dialectical relationship between the I's differentiation from the Thou and the I's differentiation from the not-I. In *Christianity*, at least, he had suggested that the otherness of nature is mediated through the encounter with other persons, although, as I have suggested in Chapter 1, he unfortunately left this unexplored and concentrated on the notion of the species idea. But in the *Lectures*, the link between the I–Thou relation and the I–not-I relation is left almost completely unanalyzed. In this respect, ironically, *Christianity* is superior to the *Lectures*. From the *Principles*, we may infer that Feuerbach still retained in the *Lectures* the importance of I–Thou relationships, but it seems that in his desire to emphasize the dependency upon nature, he tended to ignore this essential feature of his earlier thought and so left himself more vulnerable to the prejudice of his time.

CHRISTIANITY AS DISEASED EROS

So far in this chapter, I have been exploring what Feuerbach believed to be the intellectual contradictions that follow when the religious

---

[51] *Lectures*, p. 269; *Vorlesungen*, p. 302.

imagination seizes upon the various abstractions taken from nature, unifies, and then attributes subjectivity to them; that is, when the class of all classes, Being, has been transformed into a divine subject apart from nature. Since Feuerbach regarded this as a misinterpretation of nature, one of his primary aims was to expose this error, first, by providing an alternative account of how the concept of God mistakenly arises, and second, by proposing a series of counterarguments aimed at exposing not only the fallaciousness of theological reasoning but the intellectual contradictions into which religious faith falls.

From the time Feuerbach had first begun to think about religion, he had concluded that religion does not have its roots only in the intellect, although he believed that ignorance of nature was its "negative theoretical cause," but also in the feelings. Religion is rooted in affect, in those feelings and desires that arise out of the structure of consciousness itself. Consequently, he thought that it was a mistake to treat religion primarily as a species of intellectual error, although, as we have seen in the last section, he was not fully consistent in this. Religion, he argued, is an ordering of the desires; and since *Dasein* is basically a sensuous, feeling creature, how it orders its desires constitutes how it exists. Its ordered constellation of desires is its life orientation, its "outlook," and this determines its interpretation of the world. If this interpretation is false in important respects, as he believed the outlook of religion is, then the desires are also ordered falsely. It followed, he thought, that religion may be seen as a "diseased eros," a disorder in the affective life.

This assumption Feuerbach shared with the other more famous "masters of suspicion": Marx, Nietzsche, and Freud. Each of them was convinced that religion is not merely the anachronistic persistence into the present of a more naïve way of relating to nature but an expression of a more fundamental spiritual catastrophe of some kind: an alienating power (Marx), a sickness (Nietzsche), a collective neurosis (Freud). In our own time, the critics of religion tend to view it as a benign and private illusion and, hence, see no need to take it seriously. The "masters of suspicion," by contrast, believed Christianity to be a spiritual disaster and, consequently, felt compelled both to explain and attack it.

In *The Essence of Christianity*, as we have seen, Feuerbach chose to characterize religion as alienation, and in this respect his original position was closer to Marx's than it was to Nietzsche's or Freud's. This concept was especially useful because it enabled him, like Hegel, to take a very dialectical view of Christianity. On the one hand, religion was a form of life through which humankind must necessarily pass, an early and indirect form of self-knowledge. On the other hand, it was alienating because it assigned to God those attributes that properly belonged to humanity. But with his relinquishment of the Hegelian schema and its correlative notion of alienation, Feuerbach's view of Christianity became less dialectical and more unambiguously negative. Like Nietzsche, he came to believe that Christianity was a misinterpretation which, in turn, expressed a disorder of the instincts, a disease, a sickness.

Although this negative theme came to dominate the *Lectures*, it had not been altogether absent from *The Essence of Christianity*. Alongside the theme of alienation, it will be remembered, Feuerbach had also argued that Christian faith not only embodies intellectual contradictions but also corrupts the inner life. A similar type of argument comes to the fore in the last chapters of the *Lectures* as well. But where the earlier book had focused on the inner contradiction between faith and love, the latter focused on the Promethean wish to transcend nature and death, to become immortal. Christian belief, it becomes clear in this book, is, to be sure, an intellectual mistake, a misinterpretation of nature, but it is also a disordering of the desires and, hence, a grotesque form of self-understanding. The Christian's desires, unlike the pagan's, "exceed the nature of man, the limits of this life, of this real sensuous world."[52] Christians do not accept and affirm themselves as parts of nature but live only for another life that transcends nature. Their desires are unearthly, supersensuous, supernatural desires. Earthly glory is nothing compared with heavenly glory. Consequently, the Christian can only regard this world not merely as provisional but as sick.

What is health in the eyes of the Christian? Why, this whole life is nothing but a sickness; only in eternal life, as St. Augustine says, is there true health.[53]

These passages naturally remind the reader of Nietzsche's attacks on Christianity almost three decades later, the core of which was the charge that for two thousand years Western culture – its science, art, philosophy, religion, and political institutions – had been founded on the Platonic–Christian world-view in which the apparent world only mirrored in some distorted way a "true world" lying behind it. Moreover, this apparent world is not only derived from the true world

---

[52] *Lectures*, p. 231; *Vorlesungen*, p. 259.   [53] *Lectures*, p. 232; *Vorlesungen*, p. 260.

but finds its justification in it. It is only because of the true world that the apparent world has any significance or worth. Unable to affirm the apparent world with its uncertainties, "semblances," and injustice, the Christian accepts the burden of this world only because of the promise of salvation in the next one. Unable to accept the world as an aesthetic phenomenon, the Christian demands that it must be justified in moral terms. Consequently, Nietzsche charged, Christianity from the beginning represents "life's nausea and disgust with life, merely concealed behind, masked by, dressed up as, faith in 'another' life."[54]

Feuerbach also argued that Christians live only for the hope of life in another world and, hence, have turned their backs on the existing world. But unlike Nietzsche, he argued that this faith was rooted not so much in the desire for a moral justification of life as in the wish to be free from the limitations of nature.

For the only real barrier to human desires is nature. The barrier to the desire to fly like an angel . . . is gravity; the barrier to the desire for a life devoted exclusively to religious meditations and emotions is my bodily needs; the barrier to the desire for a life of beatitude, free from sin, is my carnal, sensuous nature; the barrier to my desire to live forever is death, the necessity of finiteness and mortality.[55]

The Promethean eros of the Christian manifests itself in two closely related forms: (a) the wish for a free "lord of nature" who is not bound by the causal nexus, and, hence, who can fulfill the wishes of the Christian, who does not want to be so bound; and (b) the desire for immortality, a personal existence free from necessity. The desire for the latter, of course, can only be guaranteed by the existence of the former. "For a Christian's only guarantee that his supernatural desires will be fulfilled lies in his conviction that nature itself is dependent on a supernatural being and owes its existence solely to the arbitrary exercise of this being's will."[56]

It is this two-fold desire that places belief in miracles at the center of the Christian faith despite the efforts of rationalist and liberal theologians to minimize its importance. For Feuerbach, it is essential that miracles be seen not merely as wonderful occurrences but as demonstrations of the power of God to fulfill human hopes and desires. This is why they inevitably occur in times of stress and are

[54] Friedrich Nietzsche, *The Birth of Tragedy and The Case of Wagner*, trans. with commentary by Walter Kaufmann (New York: Random House, 1967), p. 23.
[55] *Lectures*, p. 233; *Vorlesungen*, p. 261.   [56] *Lectures*, p. 234; *Vorlesungen*, p. 262.

deliverances from those things considered evil. The healing miracles of Christ, for example, not only satisfy human needs but are demonstrations of His power over the forces of nature.

Feuerbach was contemptuous of modernist attempts to minimize the miraculous element in Christian faith. However naïve orthodox believers may appear to liberal theologians, they are only following the logic of their faith when they insist that a God who is unable to perform miracles is a God to whom they cannot pray, a "useless God" who cannot fulfill our desires. For a miracle says the same thing as a doctrine "except that the doctrine says in universal terms, in words, what the miracle expresses in tangible examples."[57]

The belief in miracles is closely related to the fear of death and the desire for immortality, as can be seen by their close association in many religions, including Christianity. And, as we have seen, Feuerbach believed that the fear of death was the fundamental fear giving rise to religion. This fear is so pervasive that he concluded that belief in the gods is primarily a function of the more basic wish not to die. Although in theory immortality is a consequence of belief in God, in practice belief in immortality is the motive for belief in God.[58]

It is one of the interesting features of the *Lectures* in contrast to *Christianity* that Feuerbach interpreted the Christian doctrine of the Incarnation in the light of the desire for immortality. The Christian doctrine of the God-man, he argued, brings together and synthesizes the most fundamental motifs of religion but also synthesizes and unifies distinctively Christian wishes and desires. This doctrine illustrates not only the general principle that the gods exist for the welfare of humanity but also the specifically Christian wish to be raised from the dead and, above all, to become a god.

Liberal Christian theologians and rationalists, Feuerbach argued, do not sufficiently understand the emotional power inherent in the Christian notion of the God-man. The figure of Jesus is not merely a model of ethics and an assurance of God's love but the guarantee that God has indissolubly joined His divine nature with human nature. The Christian finds in this doctrine the veritable identity of the divine and the human, the human elevated to the divine and the divine embodied in the human. Moreover, Jesus Christ as model is the pledge not just of the divinity and immortality of the reason but of the embodied person. The God-man Christ makes abundantly manifest

---

[57] *Lectures*, p. 238; *Vorlesungen*, p. 267.
[58] *Lectures*, p. 267; *Vorlesungen*, p. 299.

"that the divine being is not a being distinct from man."[59] It is not simply that Jesus is the promise of life after death but that "As true as God is man, man is God, and consequently God's attribute of deathlessness, of exemption from the necessity of an end, is also an attribute of man."[60] Without this identity of the divine and the human, there would be no real basis for inferring human immortality from the existence of God because it is theoretically possible that there could be life after death but no divinity. Rather, it is the kinship between the divine and the human, the kinship which is exemplified in Jesus Christ, that secures this connection, that enables Christians to assure themselves of their divine origins and thereby their immortality.

In short, the unity, the identity of divinity and immortality, hence of God and man, is the solution to the riddle of religion, especially of the Christian religion. Just as nature – but nature as an object and product of human desire and imagination – is the core of nature religion, so man – but man as an object and product of man's desires, imagination, and faculty of abstraction – is the core of spiritual religion, the Christian religion.[61]

It is this desire to live forever and to become gods that constitutes the diseased eros of Christian faith. If Feuerbach's criticism of this desire in *The Essence of Christianity* had been that it subordinated the species to the individual, here his complaint was that Christians are no longer able to affirm the earth. Their wishes are fantastic, unearthly wishes, wishes that involve a rejection of embodied, sensuous existence. Although it is true that *Dasein* is largely desire because without desire there would be no humanity, there is a difference between those wishes that conform to nature and those that exceed it. The difference between those wishes that require a deity and those that do not is simply this:

that religion has wishes that can be fulfilled only in the imagination, in faith, whereas man as man, the man who replaces religion with culture, reason, science and replaces heaven by earth, has desires that do not exceed the limits of nature and reason and whose realization lies within the realm of natural possibility.[62]

It is clear that this objection to human wishes exceeding the limits of nature and reason presupposes some normative conception of natural wishes, and it is when Feuerbach fills out this conception of the natural that we can see how much his philosophy of *Sinnlichkeit* has

---

[59] *Lectures*, p. 270; *Vorlesungen*, p. 303.   [60] *Lectures*, p. 271; *Vorlesungen*, p. 304.
[61] *Lectures*, p. 275; *Vorlesungen*, p. 309.   [62] *Lectures*, p. 249; *Vorlesungen*, pp. 278f.

come to dominate his critique of religion since *Christianity*. In that earlier work, his criticism of Christianity had been that it elevated the individual above the species. In the *Lectures* his complaint is that the Christian's desire for a spiritual life after death is, in effect, a rejection of an embodied, sensuous existence. Since it is only those wishes rooted in our "innermost being" that persons transform into gods, it tells volumes about the self-understanding of Christians that their deity is a wholly spiritual being without sensuous needs, a being who embodies their own desire for an existence without such needs, an existence in which there will be no need for food, drink, or sexuality. Although it can be said that Christians have projected their own being onto God, it is also true that this deity is not a whole person in the way that we understand persons. The deity, rather, is only a part of the human, a being "torn out of the whole, an aphorism of human nature."[63] "How," Feuerbach asked rhetorically, "can an abstracted, nonsensuous, disembodied being, a being without sensuous needs, impulses, passions, expect me, a bodily, sensuous, real being, to emulate Him?"[64] And what sort of an ideal human future can it be in which there are only pure spirits?

Once again, there are striking similarities between Feuerbach and Nietzsche, even to the point of their use of metaphors. Both castigate Christianity for elevating the spirit over the body and a future over a present life, for worshiping a "castrated, disembodied" being in contrast to a real being with sensuous needs. So similar are they that it would be an interesting experiment to place before the reader the following passage and ask from whose hand it has come.

The Christian sets aside his sensuous nature; he wants to hear nothing of the common, "bestial" urge to eat and drink, the common, "bestial" instincts of sexuality and love of young; he regards the body as a congenital taint on his nobility, a blemish on his spiritual pride, a temporarily necessary degradation and denial of his true essence, a soiled traveling garment, a vulgar incognito concealing his heavenly status.[65]

Like Nietzsche, Feuerbach also saw the solution to the diseased eros of the Christian to be the affirmation of the earth. He, too, could have endorsed that part of Zarathustra's sermon in which the prophet spoke to the circus crowd and said, "I beseech you, my brothers,

---

[63] *Lectures*, p. 256; *Vorlesungen*, p. 287.
[64] *Lectures*, p. 257; *Vorlesungen*, p. 287. [65] *Lectures*, p. 260; *Vorlesungen*, p. 291.

remain faithful to the earth."[66] But whereas Zarathustra's entreaty to "remain faithful to the earth" was part of a teaching concerning a mysterious and future Overman who is not bound by morality and for whom present humanity is but an overture, Feuerbach's hopes for humanity are not only more limited but more traditionally ethical. His argument is that *Dasein* should not only learn to accept its historicity and the limiting condition of death but the I–Thou structure of life, the fact that we are social creatures bound to one another. The limitations of time, space, and the body which religion seeks to annul are, in fact, the conditions that make authentic human life possible and cannot be disassociated from it. We are, in fact, creatures of the earth, and the attempt to abolish these conditions of our existence is, in effect, to reject what makes any recognizable human life possible. Immortality is an "absurd, extravagant desire."[67] Consequently, despite our fantasies, it cannot be a wish that we would really want to see fulfilled. Were we to live forever, we would soon yearn for death because death is what makes distinctive human life what it is. It is only against premature and unnatural deaths – the death of a child or a person in the prime of life – that we should inwardly rebel.[68]

So, also, the desires for omniscience and absolute perfection are imaginary desires. No one who thought carefully about the matter would want to know everything, but only those things to which he/she is drawn by interest. Nor is it intelligible to speak about an "unlimited, insatiable lust for happiness, which the good things of this earth cannot assuage."[69] Human desires are rooted in one's historicity and social location, in one's family, city, country, which, in turn, constitute the horizon of one's responsibilities.

We must therefore modify our goals and exchange divinity, in which only man's groundless and gratuitous desires are fulfilled, for the human race or human nature, religion for education, the hereafter in heaven for the hereafter on earth, that is, the *historical future*, the future of mankind.[70]

Because Christians had for so long ignored these attainable desires

---

[66] Friedrich Nietzsche, *Thus Spake Zarathustra, A Book for All and None*, trans. with preface by Walter Kaufmann (New York: Penguin, 1966), p. 13.

[67] Feuerbach, *Lectures*, p. 277; *Vorlesungen*, p. 313.

[68] Feuerbach was himself no stranger to such premature deaths. In October of 1844, he was shattered by the death of his beloved child, Mathilde, who suffered an excruciatingly painful death which he could only observe and do nothing about. See *Briefwechsel II, GW* xviii.400–412.

[69] *Lectures*, p. 279; *Vorlesungen*, p. 313.   [70] *Lectures*, p. 281; *Vorlesungen*, p. 315.

in favor of those that were unattainable Feuerbach thought that Christianity had eroded any widespread confidence in a better life on earth. He was confident that atheism would give back to nature and humankind the dignity that had been taken from it, that the negation of the next world would have as its consequence the affirmation of this one.[71]

Looking back from the perspective of the end of the twentieth century, this confidence now seems naïve, another touch of outdated nonsense that Feuerbach shared with some of his late nineteenth-century revolutionaries. It may be that the Christian ideal is unreal and fantastic, but it does not follow, as we have painfully learned from recent history, that the "negation of the next world has as its consequence the affirmation of this world." But even if this consequence does not automatically follow, the injunction to affirm the earth still has its own validity, and Feuerbach stated his position at least once in a less Utopian and more straightforward form – as an expression of his own hope for humankind. In the concluding sentence of his book he wrote,

My only wish is . . . to transform friends of God into friends of man, believers into thinkers, devotees of prayer into devotees of work, candidates for the hereafter into students of this world, Christians who, by their own profession and admission, are "*half animal, half angel*," into *persons*, into *whole persons*.[72]

---

[71] *Lectures*, p. 283; *Vorlesungen*, p. 318.
[72] *Lectures*, p. 285; *Vorlesungen*, p. 320. I have taken the liberty of rendering the German term *Mensch* as "person" rather than as "man," which is, I think, appropriate in this case.

CHAPTER 7

Feuerbach and contemporary projection theories

RECAPITULATION AND A GLANCE FORWARD

From the previous chapters there emerges a different picture of Feuerbach than the one familiar to the English-speaking world. This Feuerbach has progressed beyond the inversion of Hegel's philosophy of Spirit to develop an original and still interesting critique of religion. Religion is no longer regarded as an involuntary projection inherent in and necessary for complete self-consciousness as it was in *The Essence of Christianity*; rather, it is an erroneous, belief-like interpretation of the all-encompassing and mysterious nature upon which the self knows itself to be dependent, an interpretation that springs out of the confrontation of the I with the not-I and the desire for recognition by this other.

This new theory of religion, I have argued, is not only different than but superior to that with which Feuerbach's name is usually identified. It is superior, first of all, because it does not rest on a highly speculative and problematical theory of consciousness in which the self, in differentiating itself from others, seizes upon the predicates of its own essential nature, and then objectifies and transforms these predicates into an individual being, a god. Consequently, the new theory is not committed to the view that "religion is man's earliest and indirect form of self-knowledge," and, hence, a necessary stage in the development of human consciousness.[1] Nor does this new theory of religion commit the theorist to the view that belief in God is necessarily a form of alienation because it invests God with those perfections which rightly belong to the human species as a whole.

However imaginative the theory of religion in *Christianity*, the idea of the divine is primarily generated from within and is only indirectly a response to anything external. Therefore, it remains a mystery how

[1] Feuerbach, *Christianity*, p. 13; *Christentums*, p. 47.

with this conception of religion Feuerbach could account for the religious believer's sense of being in touch with a transcendent reality outside of the self. The deity is simply the idea of the species invested with objectivity. In this respect, it still resembles Hegel's philosophy of Spirit in which Spirit produces externality out of its own inner being and then reappropriates it.

In Feuerbach's later thought, by contrast, the gods arise out of the confrontation with nature upon which the self is absolutely dependent for its well-being. This "nature" includes not only all the external forces that impinge on the self but also the inner unconscious forces that strike the conscious ego as also external to it, as "other." Polytheisms personify these powers but monotheism arises when everything external to the conscious ego, including the unconscious, is unified and transformed by the imagination into an individual personal being. Consequently, God is necessarily experienced as "other," as "real" because it is the name for all those powers that impinge upon the self. It is the all-powerful, everywhere present, encompassing, eternal, infinite, mysterious, and awesome reality who sustains and confronts all beings and from whom there is no escape.

This new theory of religion in the nature of the case is less systematic and elegant than the earlier. There are no successive and necessary Hegelian "moments" in the spirit's objectification of itself, no necessary dialectical moves that lead, finally, to self-realization. Rather, religion is, as it were, an overdetermined phenomenon, and it varies from culture to culture, depending upon how this "not-I" is symbolized. It is grounded in both subjective and objective factors. It springs from the self's differentiation from others and nature, but it has as its object the powers of nature that can harm, bless, or kill it. This is no less clear in the so-called religions of nature than it is in the monotheisms of the so-called high religions in which the nexus of secondary causes is regarded as the action of God. With Schleiermacher, Feuerbach argued that *Dasein* desperately wants to believe that "in, with, under" all that impinges on us, there is a Subject who acknowledges, loves, and affirms the individual.

Among the theoretical advantages this theory has over the earlier one is that it does not attempt to explain the origins but the persistence of religion. Although Feuerbach, to be sure, sometimes seemed to think he was explaining the origins of religion, the primary concern of this new theory is not to explain the beginnings of religion but why it continues to have such a grip on the human soul. In *The*

Essence of Christianity, Feuerbach proposed that religion is a stage in the development of self-consciousness and must, therefore, evolve into philosophy. Consequently, it remains inexplicable why religion continues to persist among intelligent human beings, including philosophers. In Feuerbach's later thought, however, this is not a problem because religious faith is not an involuntary reflex of the self but an interpretation, albeit mistaken, of the all-encompassing "not-I," the sea of Being, in which the human is immersed. The emergence of spirit from matter, the mind's need for causal explanations, the orderliness of nature, the tendency to reify universals, all these become mysteries that the self attempts to explain by the concept of God, and this idea, in turn, meets the human longing for recognition and acceptance by a being who can save the self from suffering and death. Religion is grounded in the experience of self-transcendence and wonderment which asks:

What am I? Where have I come from? To what end? And this feeling that I am nothing without a not-I which is distinct from me yet intimately related to me, something *other*, which is at the same time my own being, is the religious feeling.[2]

The elegance of *The Essence of Christianity* was, of course, largely a function of the dominating idea of the book, the notion of projection. The model informing the later works is, in the nature of the case, less elegant. One might in some unspecific sense argue that the attribution of personhood to the beings of nature is a "projection," but this attribution is not the result of some psychic mechanism or an involuntary and necessary reflex of consciousness itself as it is in *Christianity*. Rather, religion is an interpretative response to the constellation of forces that impinge upon the self. Consequently, Feuerbach's later strategy was to provide, as it were, a "counter" or suspicious interpretation. He wanted to show why the religious interpretation offers such powerful solace and comfort but also why it is both intellectually and existentially untenable.

In the remainder of this chapter and in the next I should like to bring to the fore more explicitly than I have those questions that have influenced and guided the preceding "rational reconstruction" of the later Feuerbach. One of the features of a "rational reconstruction," it will be remembered, is that it is confined to a relatively brief section of the past philosopher's work and is dominated by issues that have

---

[2] *Lectures*, p. 311; *Vorlesungen*, pp. 349f.

come to prominence in some recent work. One way to accomplish this reconstruction, then, is to bring our ideal Feuerbach into what is fashionably called "the modern conversation." But the difficulty is that there is no single conversation regarding the things about which he wrote, not even in the discipline called religious studies. This academic discipline, like most, is divided into countless sub-groups with different interests, methods of research, and styles of inquiry.

Given this diversity, it seems wise, then, to select certain contemporary scholars with quite different approaches to the phenomenon of religion who have wrestled with those issues with which Feuerbach himself was concerned and about which we might imagine him having something important to say. My purpose in so doing is not to engage in the intellectual game Professor Wartofsky calls "precursoritus" but to bring out more clearly by comparison some of the most distinctive and interesting as well as problematic features of Feuerbach's later position.

There are three important overlapping and interrelated issues upon which I shall focus. The first has to do with the problems at the heart of Feuerbach's early work but which seem to have vanished in the later; namely, the concept of projection itself, and its meaning and utility as regards religion. The second issue surfaces from time to time among those who are engaged in the social-scientific study of religion and has to do with the problem of defining and explaining the persistence of religion. There are those scholars who believe that any progress in the study of religion requires some definition of religion and that the only definition that can facilitate explanation is a substantive one; namely, that religion is basically culturally patterned interaction with anthropomorphic beings. Since Feuerbach's project seems to be similar to this, it is not surprising that his name is frequently invoked by these scholars, albeit often only ceremoniously. Finally, there is a third issue that is not easy to describe simply. Here the issue is not so much the concept of projection or even the definition of religion but has to do with the philosophical anthropology that underlies social-scientific work generally and, hence, the study of religion. In this respect, it is Feuerbach's existentialist paradigm that is most relevant and intriguing.

RELIGIOUS PROJECTION: THE BEAM METAPHOR

When we attempt to bring the later Feuerbach's views into relationship with contemporary theories of projection, we are immediately confronted with two problems. The first is the sheer diversity of such theories. Although the term "projection" tends to be associated in the minds of lay readers with psychoanalysis, most obviously with Freud and Jung, the term appears also in the writings of anthropologists, sociologists, and philosophers. Moreover, since a technical term acquires its meaning from the theoretical context in which it is employed, and since many of these contemporary theories are incommensurable in fundamental respects – Emil Durkheim's theory of projection, for example, claims not to make any appeal to individual psychology at all, while those of Freud and Jung are rooted in theories of the individual psyche – we must decide to which of these various projection theories it would prove most useful to compare the later Feuerbach's view.

The second problem is related to the first. Many of these contemporary theories of projection are parts of more comprehensive theories of human behavior in which religion plays only a subordinate role. Freud's theories, for example, were not developed to explain religion but human behavior generally and, moreover, found their employment and whatever justification they received in therapeutic practice. To complicate matters, these theories have, in the twentieth century, become the intellectual side of specialized academic disciplines within the university, each of which has acquired its own terminology, style of discourse, and methods of procedure for the adjudication of differences and arguments. They have spawned their own research traditions. Consequently, most nineteenth-century thinkers who lived before this specialization of knowledge, such as Feuerbach, will inevitably appear to be gifted armchair theorists, thinkers whose non-specialized reasoning often transgresses the self-imposed boundaries of a professionalized academic discipline. It will not always be easy to relate Feuerbach's wide-ranging reasoning to that of the twentieth-century disciplinary "expert."

These behavioral theories have become a part of the culture of the university and have had an enormous influence on intellectuals in the humanities: on historians, literary critics, and students of religion. One might even say that the sociological theories of Marx, Weber, and Durkheim, as well as the psychological theories of Freud and Jung, have become a part of the common discourse of a larger intellectual culture. These theories have been especially attractive to scholars in religious studies because they have opened up new and illuminating avenues of inquiry. They have enabled the scholar to relate hitherto unrelated phenomena and to pose new and interesting possibilities of interpretation. Just as the literary critic has been able to look at texts through Freudian or Marxist eyes, so, too, the religious scholar often looks at religious belief and behavior though the eyes of a Weber or Foucault. It is not an exaggeration to say that the modern intellectual is more or less characterized by a commitment to some type of methodologically disciplined inquiry, and to the degree that these modes of inquiry stand in stark contrast to the traditional modes of thought in the past, these theories, as Peter Berger has argued, constitute a transformation of consciousness.[3]

Given these two problems, it seems that a fruitful way to proceed is not to attempt to discuss as many projection theories as possible, which would require another book, but, first, to attempt to impose some classificatory scheme on the diversity of these theories with the aim of (a) showing their logical or formal features, (b) establishing what features the types have in common, and (c) reflecting on those types and features for which the later Feuerbach's position has something interesting to say.

When one attempts to do this, one notices that projection theories of religion tend to fall roughly into two opposite types. At the one end of the spectrum, there are those theories in which the term "projection" refers to the externalization of some aspect of the self – its feelings, wishes, instincts, faculties, or subjectivity itself – and the reification of this externalization. Consequently, this type of theory tends to equate the religious projection with anthropomorphisms of various sorts, and it tends to employ metaphors taken from the technology of the cinema or the magic lantern, as it did in the nineteenth century. The self "throws," "casts," or "beams" its images onto a blank wall or curtain and then, like Plato's prisoners in the cave, takes the images to be real.

A typical use of this imagery occurs in Erwin Goodenough's *The Psychology of Religious Experiences*, in which human beings everywhere are described as confronted with the inchoate terrors that arise from forces from within and without the self and which he calls the "tremendum." Persons are ignorant for the most part of these forces, and they are unable to endure the helplessness they feel when confronted with them. Consequently, they fight off reabsorption into the tremendum and act as if it were under their control.

---

[3] Peter Berger, *Invitation to Sociology*, chap. 2.

Man throws curtains between himself and the tremendum, and on them he projects accounts of how the world came into existence, pictures of divine or superhuman forces or beings that control the universe and us, as well as codes of ethics, behavior, and ritual which will bring him favor instead of catastrophe. So has man everywhere protected himself by religion.[4]

At the other end of the spectrum, there are those types of projection theory in which "projection" refers not to the externalization of some aspect of the self but to the symbolic or categorical schemes by means of which human beings organize their experience. If the first type tends to use metaphors taken from the cinema, the second employs those grounded in cartography. Projections are likened to the "grids" (conceptual frameworks or categorical schemes) by means of which human beings orient themselves in the world. Unlike individual psychological projections, these conceptual schemes or grids are decisive for any given culture because they mold the consciousness of all individuals within it and provide the basis of identity for persons in those cultures. As a kind of terminological shorthand, we may pin the label "Beam theory" on the first type and "Grid" on the second. In this section, I shall bring the later Feuerbach into relation with the first model; in the next, with the second.

Most of us tend to identify the term "projection" with the Beam type, primarily because it has received so much attention in psychoanalysis. As I indicated in Chapter 5, this type contains four closely related ideas. First, because projection is defined as the externalization of the self or its attributes, this type of projection theory tends to view anthropomorphism as the paradigmatic type of religious belief. The gods are most commonly persons or agents. Second, because the religious projection does not appear to be a cognitive response to the object, Beam theories tend to postulate some sort of inner psychic mechanism that causes and, hence, explains the religious projection. As a result of this postulation, these theories are generally associated with some theoretical account of a deep-seated psychic process believed to explain the inevitability and universality of projection. Sometimes these accounts are highly theoretical, as in the case of Freud's conjectures about the instincts, or Carl Jung's view of the archetypes in the Collective Unconscious, but sometimes they are quite general, as in the case of Goodenough.

A third feature of Beam theories, as we have seen earlier, is the close

---

[4] Erwin R. Goodenough, *The Psychology of Religious Experiences* (New York: Basic Books, 1965), p. 8.

conceptual relationships among (a) the view of human nature, (b) the postulated inner mechanism, and (c) the hermeneutical principles that guide the interpretation of the religious projection. Since in most such theories, the projecting "mechanism" lies below the level of consciousness, the Beam theorist will naturally assume that the symbols cast up by the inner mechanism have to be decoded. It is assumed that the symbols have a latent and hidden meaning of which the projectors themselves are not even aware. In Freud's projection theory, for example, the religious projection is decoded with the aid of a theory of human nature, a theory which contains not only a hypothesis about the various functions of the self – id, superego, and ego – but also a hypothesis concerning how the self develops through time, a development in which one particular stage, the Oedipal, is crucial. In *Moses and Monotheism*, for example, Freud not only makes use of his two hypotheses concerning the self but links the developmental schema to his speculations concerning the origins of religion in the murder of the father of a primal horde, the repression of its memory, subsequent guilt, and, finally, the "return of the repressed." So, too, Jung's interpretation of the image of God involves a theory of the Collective Unconscious, a theory concerning how certain archetypes rather than others come to expression as the self strives towards wholeness and individuation.

Finally, a fourth feature of Beam theories is that the theory of human nature which explains the workings of the projecting mechanism and yields the principles of interpretation also provides the criteria for judging whether the religious projection is true or false (an illusion) and, further, whether this illusion should be regarded as healthy or pathological. I write "further" because it cannot be taken for granted that an "illusion," even though false, is necessarily unhealthy or pathological. Some Object Relations psychologists, for example, while placing God in the same category of "transitional objects" as teddy bears and dolls, nevertheless argue that these imaginary objects, including God, can be healthy illusions.[5]

In Freud's view, convinced as he was that science was the only valid form of knowledge, the two issues of truth and health overlap. Because the projection rises entirely from the instincts and has no correlation to the features of the object upon which the image is projected, Freud regarded the religious projection as both untrue and unhealthy

---

[5] See Ana-Maria Rizzuto, *The Birth of the Living God: A Psychoanalytic Study* (Chicago: Chicago University Press, 1979).

(neurotic) because it is essentially infantile. Religions are "mass delusions" and restrict the play of choice and adaption by distorting the real world.[6] Jung, by contrast, argued that the psychologist qua psychologist has no competence to judge the truth of the religious projection, but, nevertheless, the healthiness or lack of it is judged by the degree to which the projection serves to integrate rejected instincts into the overall synthesis of the self. Thus Jung claims that certain projections are unhealthy and others healthy. The resurgence of the Teutonic God Wotan in Nazi Germany and the patriarchal deity of the Old Testament are examples of the former, and the quaternity of God – the Father, the divine Son, the Holy Spirit, and the Virgin Mary – is an example of the latter.[7]

Psychoanalytic theories generally, as these brief allusions to Freud and Jung would suggest, are typical instances of the Beam type of theory, although there is a certain feature of Jung's projection theory – the notion of archetypes as templates that determine how we categorize and think about others – that has affinities with the Grid model. And it would also seem that the projection theory proposed in *The Essence of Christianity* is an exemplar of this same type, although we also find there some elements that suggest affinities with the Grid type; for example, Feuerbach's view that every species sees the world through its species-specific cognitive apparatus.

In psychoanalytic theory, the concept of projection is also often connected with the concept of transference, which plays such an important role in psychoanalytic practice. Transference refers to the process that occurs in therapy when the patient displaces (projects) onto the therapist those feelings, qualities, and attributes once felt towards an important figure in the patient's earlier life. The patient, Freud wrote, "sees in his analyst the return – the reincarnation – of some important figure out of his childhood or past, and consequently transfers on to him feelings and reactions that undoubtedly applied to this model."[8] Moreover, this logical kinship between transference and projection imparts a certain structure to the beliefs of the

---

[6] Sigmund Freud, *Civilization and its Discontents*, trans. and ed. James Strachey (New York: Norton, 1962), pp. 28–32.

[7] See C. G. Jung, "Answer to Job," in *The Portable Jung*, ed. with intro., chronology, notes, and biblio. by Joseph Campbell, trans. R. F. C. Hull (New York: The Viking Press, 1971). See also *Psychology and Western Religion*, trans. R. F. C. Hull, Bollingen Series xx (Princeton: Princeton University Press, 1984), chap. 1.

[8] Sigmund Freud, *An Outline of Psychoanalysis*, trans. James Strachey (New York: Norton, 1949, p. 66.

psychotherapist about projection: it is assumed that because transference is a fact, so also is projection. The only question is how to account for this fact. Thus almost all of the schools of psychoanalysis affirm the fact of projection but differ, as I have noted above, as to its explanation, which is to say, the "mechanism" that generates the projection.

This close relationship between transference and projection in psychotherapy, it should be noted, can tend to obscure some very important differences between the two phenomena. In the case of transference, the patient transfers previous feelings and attitudes onto an objectively experienced psychotherapist with whom the patient interacts. In the case of the religious projection, by contrast, the term "projection" refers to the act of creating an illusory being. Consequently, in discussions with psychoanalytic theories it is important to establish whether the concept of "projection" is being used to refer to the postulation of the *existence* of a divine being or whether it is being used to refer to the transference of feelings and attributes onto something already believed to exist, such as nature.

This distinction, which is often overlooked in psychoanalytic treatments of religion, has been made in a recent book on religious projection by an Object Relations psychologist, Ana-Maria Rizzuto. In her book *The Birth of the Living God*, Rizzuto makes a distinction between the God concept and the God image, the private representation of this figure in the mind of the believer. She argues that the belief in the existence of God is culturally mediated but that the believer tends to project onto this culturally mediated concept the qualities and attributes derived, for the most part, from the believer's parents.[9] Although she includes the figure of God in the category of all those imaginary figures (such as teddy bears) known as transitional objects, her argument is that projection (like transference) is grafted onto an already existing belief. This distinction then enables Rizzuto to argue that it is no part of her program to question the existence of God (the culturally transmitted concept); she is only concerned with the way in which patients transfer their own private images onto this already culturally mediated idea. In Jung's psychology, by contrast, it is

---

[9] Rizzuto, *The Birth of the Living God*, pp. 208–211. Although Rizzuto makes this distinction between the idea of God and the image or representation of God, she frequently blurs it, as when she argues that Freud was correct in suggesting that "God has his origins in parental imagos and that God comes to the child at the time of resolution of the Oedipal crisis" (p. 208). Or again, "God, psychologically speaking, is an illusory transitional object" (p. 177).

unclear whether the Collective Unconscious produces the existence of deity or only provides the image that is projected onto the existing reality. Despite Jung's own claim that the psychologist has no business pronouncing on the existence or non-existence of deity, it seems clear that when some archetypal energy erupts from the Collective Unconscious it must appear to the conscious ego as external and objective. In Freud, in contrast to both Rizzuto and Jung, the notions of transference and projection coalesce in the case of God. The existence of God is the projection of a wish, and transference then paints this wished-for reality as a father.

Because the traditional views of both Feuerbach and Freud attribute some version of the Beam theory to them, it seems natural to compare them. Indeed, more than one scholar has echoed the suspicion voiced by Saul Rawidowicz that had Freud been more gracious than he was in acknowledging those to whom he was intellectually indebted, he would have placed Feuerbach in the first rank. His dependence on Feuerbach's basic conception of religion (*Religionsauffassung*) is obvious not only in the early works, such as *Totem and Taboo*, but also in the famous and late *The Future of an Illusion*.[10] In this late work, Rawidowicz claims, we find almost all of the distinctive Feuerbachian themes: the helplessness of human beings before the implacable forces of nature, the natural tendency of human beings to regard every event as the manifestation of a being like themselves, the deep human wish that life serve some higher purpose, the view that everything that happens must somehow be the expression of the intention of a higher, intelligent being, the role of religion in compensating for the defects of culture, and, finally, the necessary retreat of religion before science.

There is something to be said for Rawidowicz's charge, but the issue is far more complicated than he suggests. It is complicated, first, because, as I have argued, there is not just one Feuerbachian theory but two, and furthermore, the later theory cannot be considered an example of the Beam type. Although the later Feuerbach regarded religion as personification, he did not explain it as caused by some inner psychic mechanism but as the result of many factors: the sense of wonderment that the I experiences over against all the internal and

---

[10] Rawidowicz, *Ludwig Feuerbach*, pp. 348f. Philip Rieff notes that Freud privately admitted to his indebtedness to Feuerbach but that in his major works he "kept his humanist literacy under wraps." See his *Freud: The Mind of the Moralist*, 3rd ed. (Chicago: Chicago University Press, 1979), p. 24.

external forces that impinge upon it (nature or the not-I); the sense of being "given" to oneself and, hence, the sense of gratitude; the *Glückseligkeitstrieb* that expresses itself in desire, on the one hand, and anxiety before death, on the other; the longing for recognition; and, finally, the ceaseless activity of the imagination in the service of the wishes and the feelings. But the issue is complicated also because there does not even seem to be only one consistent Freudian theory, as I shall argue below. Consequently it is not at all clear how we can simply characterize Freud's dependence on Feuerbach.

If it were simply a matter of establishing with greater sophistication the degree of Freud's indebtedness to Feuerbach, this would be a relatively uninteresting issue. But in this case, a brief discussion may prove rewarding because (a) it reveals why it is mistaken to claim as is commonly done that whatever was viable in Feuerbach has been assimilated by Freud, and (b) it throws into relief certain important differences between Freud's theory and Feuerbach's more mature formulation.

It is important to observe, first, that although the concept of projection played a central role in Freud's thought about religion, myth, dreams, and even paranoia, and although he employed the concept throughout his career – his first reflections date from the early 1890s and his last from 1929 – he never systematically formulated his views in relation to it. In his analysis of the Schreber case in 1911, an analysis in which the concept of projection is central, he acknowledged that although he had become aware that more general psychological problems were involved in the question of the nature of projection, he had decided "to postpone the investigation of it (and with it that of the mechanism of paranoic symptom-formation in general) until some other occasion."[11] Unfortunately, he never found that occasion.

This lack of any systematic discussion of the concept of projection is regrettable because, as many commentators have noted, even though Freud regarded it as an important notion, he tended to use the term "projection" in various ways: sometimes to describe the general tendency of primitives and infants to attribute responsibility for their thoughts to the external world, sometimes as a name for the externalization of some aspect of the self, and sometimes to designate a defensive reaction of an unconscious wish or drive. On the whole, he used the word to refer to the phenomenon whereby a person

---

[11] Sigmund Freud, *Three Case Histories*, ed. with intro. by Philip Rieff (New York: Macmillan, 1963), p. 169.

experiences his/her own feelings, impulses, and perceptions as true of someone else, but this, it should be noted, is primarily a descriptive rather than an explanatory statement; indeed, as a description it is compatible with many different types of explanations. It is not surprising, then, that some commentators have claimed that it is the most inadequately defined term in the whole of psychoanalytic theory.[12]

In his major works on religion, Freud uses the concept of projection in two ways. One of them is virtually devoid of any distinctively Freudian concepts, and the other is heavily dependent upon them. The first is best illustrated by *The Future of an Illusion*, in which the concept of religious projection is proposed so generally – as an expression of human helplessness and dependence and the longing for a father – that it does not require or depend upon psychoanalytic theory, as Freud himself conceded.[13] One might even say that we have here "a theory-free theory," by which I mean that it is remarkably silent about the role of some inner psychic mechanism generating the religious projection. All that seems to be presupposed is a tendency of the human mind that Freud had previously claimed in *Totem and Taboo* is observable in primitives and infants; namely, the tendency to "impose the laws governing mental life upon real things," a tendency that is reinforced when it satisfies some psychic need or brings mental relief by bolstering our sense of control over nature.[14] In *Illusion*, Freud simply appealed to the helplessness of the self over against nature, the recurrence of the infantile prototype of dependence upon the parents, and the power of the wish for a cosmic helper.

There is a second type of theory of projection, however, that is heavily dependent upon Freudian theory, not only on the theory of the instincts but on the theory of childhood development and the notion that ontogeny recapitulates phylogeny. And here there are two sub-types of theory: one in which the dominating concepts are taken from Freud's theorizing about "the family romance"; the other in which the theory is linked to the "vicissitudes of the instincts." The first sub-type occurs in *Moses and Monotheism*, in which the idea of God is linked not only with development of the individual self in the

---

[12] See L. Banks, "Religion as Projection: A Re-appraisal of Freud's Theory," *Religious Studies*, 9 (1973), 401–426.

[13] Sigmund Freud, *The Future of an Illusion*, p. 60.

[14] Sigmund Freud, *Totem and Taboo: Some Points of Agreement between the Mental Lives of Savages and Neurotics*, trans. James Strachey (New York: Norton), p. 91.

context of the "family romance" – sexual jealousy of the father, the desire to replace (kill) him, the repression of this desire and the resultant guilt – but with what Evans-Pritchard has called Freud's "just-so story" about the primeval events surrounding the constitution of the earliest human society. In this story, human beings first lived in small hordes dominated by the oldest and strongest male, who prevented sexual promiscuity among the members. Once upon a time, the "brothers" of the horde were overcome with jealousy and envy and they murdered and devoured the patriarchal father. Later, overcome with remorse and guilt, they instituted a sacrificial feast, a totem meal, and, in an act of deferred obedience, reconstituted the incest taboo. "They thus created out of their filial sense of guilt the two fundamental taboos of totemism, which for that very reason inevitably corresponded to the two repressed wishes of the Oedipus complex."[15]

The second sub-type of theory Freud proposed is less known and occurs in those texts of 1911 in which he theorized about the paranoid Dr. Schreber. To understand the significance of what he wrote there, it is important to recall that by 1911 Freud had become especially interested in the early development of the self and the role that the pleasure principle played in self-differentiation and the appropriation of reality. By 1919, he was writing about the process by which the ego, in the interests of self-preservation, comes to replace the pleasure principle by the reality principle. The ego does not abandon the aim of pleasure altogether, but postpones satisfaction and temporarily tolerates displeasure "on the long indirect road to pleasure."[16] But since this cannot account for a great deal of displeasure, Freud felt obliged to give an account of such displeasure and of how the ego dealt with it. In a chapter of *Beyond the Pleasure Principle*, in which he indulged in what he conceded to be a "far-fetched speculation," he hypothesized how the organism must have been forced to develop a shield against strong and unwanted stimuli from without. But what about all those unpleasurable stimuli from within? Freud suggested, with his characteristic display of theoretical imagination, that this state of things produces two results: first, the feelings of pleasure and displeasure predominate over external stimuli; and second,

a particular way is adopted of dealing with any internal excitations which produce too great an increase of unpleasure: there is a tendency to treat them

[15] Freud, *Totem and Taboo*, p. 143.
[16] Sigmund Freud, *Beyond the Pleasure Principle*, trans. James Strachey, intro. by Gregory Zilboorg (New York: Norton, 1961), p. 4.

as though they were acting, not from the inside, but from the outside, so that it may be possible to bring the shield against stimuli into operation as a means of defence against them. This is the origin of *projection*, which is destined to play such a large part in the causation of pathological processes.[17]

The view that projection is a defense mechanism which plays a crucial role in pathological processes, especially paranoia, became for Freud the clue to the solution in 1911 to the strange case of Dr. Schreber. Schreber had been a relatively prominent jurist who, after developing a severe hypochondriac condition in which he thought he was dead and decomposing, suffered a bizarre paranoia accompanied by a complex religious delusional pattern in which he believed that he had a mission to redeem the world. This redemption could only be accomplished if he were transformed into a woman. The details of the delusion itself need not concern us. What is important for our purposes is Freud's delineation of the mechanism of projection. Building on his previous reasoning that projection must be a defense against unacceptable and unpleasurable "endopsychic" perceptions, he argued that Schreber's projection was the result of the repression of an unacceptable homosexual wish. Thus the mechanism of symptom formation in his case, a mechanism that he thought "deserves the name of *projection*," is that

An internal perception is suppressed, and, instead, its content, after undergoing a certain degree of distortion, enters consciousness in the form of an external perception. In delusions of persecution the distortion consists in a transformation of affect; what should have been felt internally as love is perceived externally as hate.[18]

In other words, the "logic" of paranoidal projection is that the feeling "I hate him" becomes transformed by projection into "He hates and persecutes me and this justifies me hating him."[19]

Freud then went on to note that projection does not always play the same role in all forms of paranoia and, moreover, makes its appearance under other psychological conditions. "In fact," he wrote,

it has a regular share assigned to it in our attitude towards the external world. For when we refer the causes of certain sensations to the external world, instead of looking for them (as we do in the case of the others) inside ourselves, this normal proceeding also deserves to be called projection.[20]

---

[17] Freud, *Beyond the Pleasure Principle*, p. 23.
[18] Freud, *Three Case Histories*, p. 169.   [19] Freud, *Three Case Histories*, p. 166.
[20] Freud, *Three Case Histories*, p. 169.

Freud's suggestion that there is a "normal proceeding" alongside of paranoia that deserves the name of projection while at the same time he postponed any attempt to reconcile the two concepts has naturally occasioned scores of articles by Freudian interpreters. Some have concluded that there is no coherent concept of projection at all in his writings despite its fundamental importance for his concept of religion as well as his theory of paranoia. Others have argued that he vacillated among pre-analytic and genuinely explanatory concepts of projection and that only the latter are useful for psychoanalysis. Still others have argued that although he did slide imperceptibly between the pre-analytic and causal, he primarily used the more neutral word when discussing animism and primitive mentality but became more interested in the causal mechanism when he turned to paranoia. It just happens that in the course of his career he placed less and less emphasis upon the nondefensive uses of "projection" and more on its defensive uses.[21]

In my view, this last charitable interpretation is not fully convincing, although an attempt to justify my opinion to the reader would require a more thorough analysis of Freud's work than is feasible here. But among the points I would make are these. First of all, *The Future of an Illusion* is one of Freud's late works and represents in many respects a return to the "pre-analytic" views found in *Totem and Taboo*, and so it cannot be the case that in the course of his career he placed less and less emphasis upon the nondefensive views of projection. But more important, I believe that it can be shown that there is a fundamental tension if not incompatibility between the view that projection is the result of the repression of an unacceptable wish or desire, as is dictated by the distinction between introjection and projection and as is argued in the Schreber case, and projection as a manifestation of the deep human longing for a cosmic protector, as in *The Future of an Illusion*. In the former case, projection is preceded by denial, and is a result of the repressed energies finding an acceptable form in a distorted belief. In the latter case, projection is the expression of a deep human wish springing out of helplessness. The former concept requires an interpretative strategy aimed at uncovering some unconscious and unacceptable desire hidden from the subject, an interpretation that the subject resists. The latter concept requires no

[21] Darius Ornston, "On Projection: A Study of Freud's Usage," *Psychoanalytic Study of the Child*, 33 (1978), 117–166.

decoding at all because the content of the belief is conscious and manifest both to the believer and to the interpreter. If Freud had recognized this contradiction and reformulated his concept of projection, he would surely have had to reconceive the distinction between introjection and projection in which the former is correlated with pleasure and the latter with unpleasure.

But whether Freud's theory of projection is coherent or not is less important to me than the comparisons and judgments made possible by looking at it in terms of the formal features of the Beam model. For we are now able to see, first of all, that the correlations to be made between Feuerbach and Freud are far more complex than appear on the surface. If we were to talk about their formal similarities and affinities at all, they would have to be between the early Feuerbach and the Freud who postulated a psychic mechanism, on the one hand, and between the Feuerbach of *Religion* and the *Lectures* and the Freud of *Illusion*, on the other. The formal similarities between these pairs, of course, do not dictate that the substance of their views is the same. For even if the early Feuerbach and the Freud of the Schreber case are both exemplars of the Beam model, the interpretative strategy of Feuerbach does not require the reduction of the meaning of religion to an unconscious wish in the sense that Freud's does. Nor does the fact that both the Freud of *Illusion* and the later Feuerbach appeal to human longing rather than a projecting psychic mechanism necessarily mean that their analyses of this longing are similar.

Indeed, it is precisely when we compare the later Feuerbach's analysis with Freud's *Illusion* that we can see how superficial and even false is the claim that whatever was suggestive in Feuerbach has been assimilated by Freud. On the contrary, it is difficult to imagine how any fair-minded contemporary reader could compare the two works and not conclude that Feuerbach's work is by far the more suggestive and persuasive. Freud's argument in *Illusion* is at best a thin summary of the Enlightenment claim that religion is the result of human helplessness augmented by the longing for a father. For Feuerbach, by contrast, there are a host of reasons, both subjective and objective, that give rise to the personification of reality. Religion is an overdetermined phenomenon because it is rooted in *Dasein*'s differentiation from the not-I, all those forces that impinge on it from within and without and in confrontation with which it has the sense of being both thrown and "gifted." Being absolutely dependent upon these forces that fill it with wonder and terror, and being in the grip of the desire to live, to flourish, and, above all, to be recognized, *Dasein* seizes upon those qualities in the Encompassing that impress the imagination and transforms them into personal beings. In the West, this has culminated in the personification of Being as such.

By concentrating as we have on the formal characteristics of the Beam model, we are also able to see how determinative the conception of human nature is for it. It bears on how the religious projection is conceived as well as on how it is interpreted and evaluated. Here, too, we can see how fundamental are the differences between the later Feuerbach and psychoanalytic theories such as Freud's and Jung's. Despite the superficial similarities between them as regards human helplessness and the longing for an "other," the two psychoanalytic theories tend to interpret religion in terms of the structure of instincts and drives, whereas in Feuerbach's thought the self is relational. Although Feuerbach, too, talks about a *Glückseligkeitstrieb* driving the individual, the I is constituted basically in relationship to the Thou and finds its fulfillment in human relationships. *Dasein* is basically a relational or social self, and because this is so, its own fundamental drive is inherently a drive for recognition by an other. Anthropomorphism is not just a "tendency" but springs out of *Dasein*'s quest for significance and meaning.

RELIGIOUS PROJECTION: THE GRID METAPHOR

There is another type of projection theory in which the term "projection" is used to refer not to the externalization of some aspect of the self – its feelings, attributes, or subjectivity itself – but to the symbolic or conceptual forms that human beings superimpose on their experience in order to make it intelligible. Projection refers to the framework by means of which humans organize, coordinate, and orient their lives. Just as the metaphor "beam" suggests the casting of an image onto a blank screen, the metaphor "grid" suggests coordinates on a map or a template for guiding the flow of an electrical current.

The most crucial difference between this and the Beam type of theory is that here the religious projection does not denote a discrete experience which is an exception to what we normally call knowledge; rather, it refers to the very structure of concepts, categories, and rules that makes what is called "knowledge" possible.

The use of the term "projection" in this extended fashion exploits certain linguistic associations inherent in the classical verb "to project," which also has the connotations of "to cast" and "to throw." We can see a contemporary example of this exploitation in the reasoning of the English translators of Martin Heidegger's *Sein und Zeit*, one of the more influential books of modern times. Heidegger used the German verb *entwerfen* (to throw or cast) to convey his view that the distinctive feature of *Dasein* is that it interprets and categorizes its experience in terms of its projects. The mind, he argued, does not apprehend essences of objects, as classical philosophy has traditionally claimed, but conceives of the world with which it is engaged in terms of its instrumental purposes. The English translators argue that these connotations of *entwerfen* are best conveyed by the English verb "to project," because this word has been linked not only with "throwing" but with the more abstract mental process of designing and sketching, as when we say that a geometer projects a curve upon a plane.[22] Thus, the conceptual scheme with which *Dasein* organizes or interprets its experience becomes a "projection."

The extension of the term "projection" to include religion itself has seemed to many philosophers of religion like a natural move once a religion is regarded as a conceptual scheme or worldview by means of which people orient themselves to life. And this natural move has in fact been made in some of the most influential literature in religious studies, as both demonstrated and criticized in a recent book by Terry F. Godlove.[23] The basic assumption underlying this literature is that any view of the world is "scheme bound," that is, is a way of organizing, classifying, and "carving up" the world. Religion is one such mode of organization. Indeed, in a particularly important essay, Clifford Geertz proposed that the very definition of religion is

(1) a system of symbols which acts to (2) establish powerful, pervasive, and long-lasting moods and motivations in men by (3) formulating conceptions of a general order of existence and (4) clothing these conceptions with such an aura of factuality that (5) the moods and motivations seem uniquely realistic.[24]

This definition is thought to be particularly applicable to the so-called "high religions." Thus, Gordon Kaufman has written that

---

[22] Martin Heidegger, *Being and Time*, trans. John Macquarrie and Edward Robinson (New York: Harper, 1962), p. 185, n. 1.

[23] Terry F. Godlove, Jr., *Religion, Interpretation, and Diversity of Belief: The Framework Model from Kant to Durkheim to Davidson* (Cambridge: Cambridge University Press, 1989).

[24] Clifford Geertz, *The Interpretation of Cultures* (New York: Basic Books, 1973), p. 90.

the indispensable feature of the "great religious frameworks" is that they are able to interpret "every feature of experience."[25]

Once the term "projection" is extended in this fashion, we can observe some striking formal differences between the Beam and the Grid models. In the first place, we can understand why Beam theorists tend to define religion in terms of anthropomorphism and personification whereas Grid theorists do not. If religions are believed to be externalizations of human attributes, then this would naturally explain why religions are anthropomorphic. Grid theorists, by contrast, tend to view religions as sacred worldviews, and, hence, the religious projection may include sacred classifications and symbolic structures of many sorts. In so far as any given religion anthropomorphizes reality, this may be considered as merely one sub-type of the Grid theory. All religions are grids, but not all religions are anthropomorphic grids.

Another characteristic that differentiates Grid from Beam theories is this. Because Beam theories tend to derive their basic hermeneutical principles from the theory of human nature in which a psychic mechanism generates the projection, they rarely appeal to social structures or cultural influences in their interpretation of religious symbols. The dynamism of the instincts themselves is regarded as the prime cause of both the form and the content of the symbols. We have already seen this in the case of Freud and Jung. Grid theorists, on the other hand, tend to be distrustful of appeals to individual psychology because they believe that the specific social and cultural processes in which a religion originated or functions determines its symbolism. Consequently, in Grid theories, the idea of projection itself does not play as large a material role in the actual exegesis of religion as it does in Beam theories. That religion is projection is simply a formal presupposition of the interpretation of religion. The interpretation of any specific religion proceeds by inquiring into the specific social and cultural institutions that the society has "projected" and taken to be normative for its consciousness. At its most extreme, as in the case of Marx, religious sensibility itself is taken to be a cultural product.

The third and perhaps most important difference between the two models of projection is not easily stated, because it has to do with the range and complexity of the epistemological possibilities open to Grid theories. Once the term "projection" is used to refer to the conceptual

---

[25] Gordon D. Kaufman, *The Theological Imagination: Constructing the Concept of God* (Philadelphia: Westminster Press, 1981), pp. 32f.

scheme by means of which experience is organized, this grid may be conceived of in many different ways. And how it is conceived, as we shall see below, determines, first, how the relation of religion to culture is construed, and second, whether one can talk about the truth of religion.

One possibility, for example, is to argue, as some interpreters of Immanuel Kant have, that there are certain inherent and deep categories such as causality, substance, and quality that are inherent in human reason itself and that make knowledge itself possible. These categories, when employed, enable us to make judgments, acquire knowledge, and orient ourselves in experience. In Kant's view, the employment of these categories also requires certain basic transcendental and regulative ideals: the notion that there is a determinate order of things that we can call reality (the Whole); an organizing and synthetic activity of the reasoner who receives impressions, organizes them, and makes judgments (the transcendental ego); and God, the ground and source of the existence and order of the world. Human reason, Kant argued, needs these transcendental assumptions in order to unify its experience even if, in the nature of the case, one cannot prove that these ideals actually refer to anything in reality. The categories and the ideals are the presupposition of any possible knowledge and not themselves objects of experience. Thus, in Kant's view, belief in God does not spring out of some discrete wish or instinctual longing, as in the Beam view, but is an implicate of the structure of reason itself.[26]

There is a variant on this Kantian view that leads, ironically, to a quite different conclusion regarding religion. Friedrich Nietzsche, for example, argued that there are, indeed, certain fundamental categories like "cause," "self," and "thing" that human reason invariably uses to organize experience, but, unlike Kant, he did not regard them as

---

[26] See Immanuel Kant, "What is Orientation in Thinking?," in Beck (ed.), *Critique of Practical Reason and Other Moral Writings.* I am aware that Prof. Godlove thinks it a mistake to regard Kant as a proponent of the framework model because his position does not rest on the distinction between a neutral and undifferentiated experience (content) and an organizing framework (scheme), a distinction Godlove thinks is crucial to the framework model and which he believes that Donald Davidson has demolished. By identifying Kant as a proponent of the Grid model I am not claiming that Godlove is wrong in this. My point is that Kant may be interpreted as holding roughly the view I describe and that this is one possible variant of the Grid model. My assumption is that the Grid model does not necessarily commit one to the scheme–content distinction, but to argue this here would take me beyond the permissible limits of this book.

inherent in reason itself but as "fictions" and "projections."[27] As a post-Darwinian, he thought of the human intellect in biological and pragmatic terms, and he concluded that the fundamental categories that we employ like "cause" and "ego" are the result of a long evolutionary process of adaptation and survival. These categories emerge out of our need to simplify and quantify our experience and are not inherent in reason itself. Our intellects are not designed for "knowledge" but only for the practical purpose of survival. They impose only as much regularity and form upon the flux of life as our practical needs require. Indeed, Nietzsche suggested, the human intellect may have cast up innumerable categorical schemes before it hit upon the categories (grid) that we now employ and which Kant regarded as constitutive of "pure reason." The Kantian categories are merely "fictions" and habits of thought. They are merely the "conditions of life" for us. And even if it could be shown that "God" and "ego" are among these conditions of life for us, they could for all that be "false." A belief, however necessary it may be for the preservation of the species, has nothing to do with the truth. "Truth," Nietzsche wrote, "does not necessarily denote the antithesis of error, but in the most fundamental cases only the posture of various errors in relation to one another . . . An assumption that is irrefutable – why should it for that reason be 'true'?"[28]

The most prevalent and influential form of the Grid theory in contemporary religious studies, however, is neither Kantian nor Nietzschean. It is, rather, the view that the conceptual schemes by means of which any conceivable human experience is organized are "social constructions." The "world" that any human being inhabits and takes for granted, it is claimed, is seen and experienced through a complex ideational lattice composed of language, categories, repre-sentations, rules, and typifications provided by culture. Religions are normally a part of this socially constructed lattice. Sometimes they are the sacralization of the cultural grid itself, and sometimes they are relatively autonomous symbolic forms, like science, that exist alongside of others within the culture.

A final contrast between Beam and Grid theories is worth noting. As I observed in the previous section of this chapter, one of the

[27] Friedrich Nietzsche, *The Will to Power*, trans. Walter Kaufmann and R. J. Hollingdale, ed. with commentary by Walter Kaufmann (New York: Random House, 1968), paras. 470–593. Sometimes Nietzsche uses *projiziert* and sometimes *interpretiert*.
[28] Nietzsche, *The Will to Power*, para. 535.

characteristic features of Beam theories is that the underlying conception of human nature yields the criteria by means of which the theorist decides that a given projection is true or false, healthy or pathological. Since Beam theories, generally, believe that the religious projection is generated entirely from within, it is at best regarded as an illusion, a wish, and at worse as a delusion. The issue of truth in Grid theories, by contrast, is far more complicated because the conceptual grid is what makes it possible to make judgments of truth or falsity at all. Since a judgment, normally considered, is the attribution of a predicate (which is itself dependent on some classificatory scheme) to a subject (which can only be picked out by means of the rules of the scheme), it borders on unintelligibility to ask whether the grid as a whole is true or false. Conceptual schemes may be applied or utilized, be successful or unsuccessful for given purposes, but they cannot themselves be said to be true or false. They constitute the framework within which "true" and "false" can be meaningfully employed.

Given this view, it is not accidental that Grid theories are especially attractive to religious apologists, because they make possible two defensive strategies. First of all, if religions are regarded as totalizing conceptual schemes, the apologist may concede that they are projections but deprive this term of the pejorative meaning it has traditionally carried. Furthermore, the apologist can argue, as we have seen, that it is illegitimate to invoke the categories of truth and falsity with respect to religion. A religion is a worldview, and one can only adopt or "dwell in" a worldview and the form of life that it makes possible. The test of a worldview is not whether it corresponds with reality, a phrase that has no meaning, but whether it makes possible certain kinds of experiences, whether it enables one to orient oneself to the world in certain ways. Moreover, it follows that one cannot compare the truth of one religion with that of another; one can only embrace a way of life.

A second apologetic strategy the grid analogy makes possible is the claim that religion is one type of conceptual scheme among others, its distinctiveness lying only in the fact that it originates in an experience of the sacred. Just as Heidegger, for example, could argue that our taken-for-granted utilitarian attitude towards the world ultimately finds its most logical expression in the objectifying mode of thought called science, so the religionist can argue that the religious projection finds its logical expression in religious symbolism. For those who have not encountered the sacred or do not have the religious interest, the symbolic structure or grid will naturally be meaningless. But this is also the case with the scientific grid.

Both of these apologetic strategies raise important epistemological and philosophical questions: Are conceptual frameworks the sort of things that can be adopted at will? Can two conceptual frameworks, such as religion and science, be held by one and the same person? But even if, for the moment, we accept the characterization of religion as a projective grid about which it is meaningless to ask whether it is true or false, it is important to note that so far as the critics of religion are concerned there is still the question whether religion is damaging to human beings in some way, whether it is healthy or not. And this, in turn, is related to one's view of human nature and what is believed to be needed for its flourishing. Nietzsche's objection to Christianity, for example, was not so much that it is false, since Nietzsche's own view of the "fictional" nature of the grid makes this criticism unintelligible, but that it inculcates and expresses the belief in an absolute truth. It is, he wrote, "Platonism for the 'the people.' "[29] Moreover, he argued, Christianity assumes, as Platonism does, that the world must be justified as a moral phenomenon. But given the cruelties and wastefulness of the evolutionary process, the indifference of the cosmic process to individual persons, the world can be justified only as an aesthetic phenomenon, as the incredible and awe-inspiring outpouring of myriad forms of life indifferent to moral values. This opinion, of course, is itself an aesthetic judgment, as Nietzsche realized, and given the notoriously difficult task of justifying aesthetic judgments, the quarrel between Christianity and atheism is virtually a non-adjudicable dispute. Whether one accepts the moral or the aesthetic point of view, a Christian might then say, is a matter of "faith," if "faith" is the proper category to employ for the adoption of a grid.

PROJECTION AS PERCEPTUAL GRID

Because of the diversity and complexity of grid theories of projection, it is less useful to relate Feuerbach's views to the type in general than to some concrete and specific variants of it. Consequently, I have selected two. The first analyzes religion in terms of perception; the second in terms of culture. The first theory was proposed by Fokke

---

[29] Friedrich Nietzsche, *Beyond Good and Evil: Prelude to a Philosophy of the Future*, trans. with commentary by Walter Kaufmann (New York: Random House, 1966), p. 2.

Sierksma, a Dutch psychologist of religion, in a work that was hotly debated in Europe when it first appeared in 1956 but remained virtually unknown in the United States until it was recently praised in *Religious Studies Review* as having "opened fresh horizons for the theory of religious projection."[30] The second theory was advanced by Peter Berger in his sociology of religion, *The Sacred Canopy*, which, in turn, is built on the arguments of his collaborative work, *The Social Construction of Reality*, a very influential popularization of the "social construction of reality" thesis.[31]

Sierksma's book *De Religieuze Projectie* created a sensation in the Netherlands when it was first published.[32] It had been intended as a response to an earlier controversial book on religious projection by Simon Vestdijk, *The Future of Religion*, in which Vestdijk had distinguished between those religious traditions in the West, in which the gods must be regarded as projections in Freud's sense of the word, and those in the East, like Buddhism, in which religious projections were "seen through" and withdrawn in favor of deeper mystical insight. Although a member of the theological faculty of the University of Leiden, Sierksma surprisingly came to Vestdijk's defense. He agreed that Western deities should be seen as projections, but he argued that one could properly understand what this meant only if one placed the discussion in the context of the problem of perception generally. Drawing upon the philosophical anthropology of Helmuth Plessner and Jakob von Uexküll as well as upon contemporary theories of perception, Sierksma argued that projection need not be seen as an illusory phenomenon and, hence, regarded negatively. Rather, it should be seen as a normal and necessary part of the perceptual process by means of which animals and human beings create and stabilize their worlds. Religious projection is a special type of projection that occurs in humans by virtue of the possession of self-consciousness.

Sierksma's theory rests on two broad pillars: a general theory of perception in both animals and humans such that perception itself is

---

[30] Lee W. Bailey, "Religious Projection: A New European Tour," *Religious Studies Review*, 14, 3 (1988), 207–211.

[31] Peter L. Berger, *The Sacred Canopy: Elements of a Sociological Theory of Religion* (Garden City, N.Y.: Doubleday, 1967). Peter L. Berger and Thomas Luckmann, *The Social Construction of Reality: A Treatise in the Sociology of Knowledge* (Garden City, N.Y.: Doubleday, 1967).

[32] Fokke Sierksma, *Projection and Religion: An Anthropological and Psychological Study of the Phenomena of Projection in the Various Religions*, trans. Jacob Faber, foreword by Lee W. Bailey (Ann Arbor, Mich.: UMI Books on Demand, University Microfilms International, 1990).

considered to be a type of projection; and a theory of human nature in which the possession of self-consciousness generates the religious projection.

One of the initial advantages of seeing the problem of projection within the context of perception, Sierksma argued, is that we are able to resist the seduction of those semi-conscious associations of projection with the technology of the cinema in which projection refers to an image cast by a beam of light upon a blank screen. These cinematic metaphors, Sierksma claimed, contain a grain of truth, but they also block any sophisticated and precise analysis of the process because they rest on the assumption that perceptions are true but projections are purely subjective additions to them. Of course, Sierksma conceded, human beings do attribute their own subjectivity to others – in this sense "project" – but a deeper, more sophisticated problem arises when we understand that perception itself is a subjective modification of the world. In perception we do not just passively copy the real world, but make it different from what it really is. Since this is the case, then the religious projection may best be seen as a special type of perception-projection that occurs in the human species.

What does it mean to say that perception itself is a subjective modification of the world? Sierksma's argument, drawing upon modern theories of perception, goes something like this. Every species, including the human, relates to the world through its own unique perceptual–somatic–noetic apparatus; that is, through the number and type of its sensory organs. This apparatus is necessarily selective because any given organism is able to perceive only some features of the world and not others. Those features the organism is able to perceive are contingent upon its own idiosyncratic "world of signs" to which its sense organs are attuned. From the infinite number of stimuli that emanate from the world as such, the finite organism responds to very few. For example, the dog's world is based on smell and differs from the world of the spider, the ant, the bird, the fish, and the amoeba. Since each species perceives only a fragment of the entire possible range of signs, those aspects of the world to which a species is not sensorially tuned simply do not exist for it. And like Nietzsche before him, Sierksma claimed that those features of the world to which an organism is attuned are those that have proved crucial in its struggle for survival. Perception is the means by which it "goes at the world" spontaneously; that is, seeks to control and assimilate it. In this sense, every species necessarily subjectively modifies or falsifies the world in the very process of perception. In this sense, perception is projection.

The second pillar upon which Sierksma's position rests is the uniqueness of human nature. The human's world, no less than the animal's, is constituted by its somatic–perceptual apparatus, its perceptual grid, and we must also assume that perception is the way in which the human species stabilizes and controls its world. The problem, then, is to understand the distinctive perceptual structure of the human organism and how this structure creates a different "world" from that which the animals encounter. Sierksma, like Plessner, argued, first of all, that the difference between them lies in the fact that the animal species is instinctually programmed whereas the human is not. Although human beings, like animals, are tied to their sensory apparatus – a fact that will, as we shall see, have implications for religious projection – they also possess self-consciousness. The I can objectify both the external and the internal world. It can make the "me" an object. Many animals possess consciousness but not self-consciousness, and it is the latter that enables human beings to evaluate their perceptions and to objectify both the external and the internal world. They can, as it were, distance themselves from their projections. Because they are able to do this, they are also able to realize that there is much that escapes their perceptual grids. They can become aware that there are dimensions of reality that remain hidden and opaque to their senses. They can become aware that they project.

The possession of self-consciousness does not just mean that human beings can become aware that they project but that they project differently than do animals. They are not only able to stand back, as it were, from their projections, but they project more broadly and deeply.

As the being who nonetheless remains fixed to himself and his world he projects, like other "fixed" living beings; but man not only projects his sensory limitations but *he also projects himself.* The animal lives itself but is not given to itself, and therefore cannot project a relation to itself. Man is given to himself in a mysterious excentric relation to himself, and therefore projects this relation, that is, himself. Only if he could be absolutely objective would man not project. Being a mixture of subjectivity and objectivity, he projects that subjectivity and at the same time criticizes his subjective projections by virtue of his objective capacities.[33]

---

[33] Sierksma, *Projection and Religion*, p. 21.

Because human beings have an excentric relationship to themselves, they experience a type of disequilibrium that animals do not. Determined by their instinctual nature, animals live in a kind of natural equilibrium. Human beings must complete themselves. This means, among other things, that they are oriented towards the future in a fashion unlike other organisms. They can contemplate possibilities and experience anxiety about their ability to actualize these possibilities. These anxieties, in turn, arise out of an awareness of a certain "irreducible givenness," not only the givenness of external nature but the givenness imposed by one's body and character structure. Thus a human being becomes aware that his/her internal as well as his/her external world is separate to some degree, that it, too, has its own patterns and laws that limit possibility. The I comes to feel that it stands between an internal and an external world and must achieve some balance between them. These facts, Sierksma wrote, "can only lead to the conclusion that man lives between his inner and outer worlds, between 'the world' and the 'reality of the soul.' "[34]

Having to achieve a delicate balance between the inner and the outer world, the human being struggles on two fronts. Just as perception is the way in which the animal stabilizes its world, so, too, projection is the way in which the human being stabilizes his/her world. When it is threatened from without, it seeks to restore its balance by subjectivizing the external world. When it is threatened from within, it falls into some psychic state similar to sleep or unconsciousness. Without the defensive reaction of projection, the human being would simply be overcome by the powers of the inner and outer world, although in general no sharp distinction can be made between projection resulting from disruption of the equilibrium between the self and its inner and outer worlds. What happens is that upon disruption of this equilibrium subjective elements are added to those that are already inherent in all perception. The aim of projection is to maximize stability.

Man must live in the oscillating equilibrium between his inner and outer worlds, between subjectivity and objectivity. Projection is the perceptual tool he uses to create this unbalanced balance, and to restore it if necessary.[35]

There are a vast array of possibilities by means of which the human being can stabilize his/her world, and it is a mistake, Sierksma argued, to restrict the phenomena of projection to religious imagery.

[34] Sierksma, *Projection and Religion*, p. 33.　　[35] Sierksma, *Projection and Religion*, p. 45.

Religious projection is simply one class of projective phenomena that is not fundamentally different from other such phenomena. The human being can project anything that is part of his/her nature – body parts, feelings, thoughts, even his/her own excentric nature, as Aristotle did when he made "thinking about thought" the distinctive nature of the divine. Very generally, however, the distinction between inner and outer threats is important because there are religious projection phenomena that seem to function primarily as a defense against external threats, as in the case of so-called primitive religions, and others, like spiritual pietism and mysticism, in which guilt is predominant. These seem to be aimed at human deficiency in the face of an inner world. What is important in both cases, however, is to bring an equilibrium to the psyche.

We have in Sierksma's work, then, the distinction between projection in general, the subjective modification of the world that takes place in perception generally, and the religious projection, a further modification aimed at reducing perceived threats from either the external or the internal world. How are these two forms of projection related? What is distinctive about the religious projection? Sierksma's answer seems to be that the religious projection springs primarily from the awareness that there is "something more" that escapes our normal projective grids, that there is, so to speak, a reverse side of things that hides behind what we perceive. Indeed, the only minimal definition of religion that is scientifically tenable, he claims, is that religion is characterized by the awareness that there is a "hidden surplus of the world," a hidden power of some kind that hides but sometimes reveals itself. "It is this hidden 'something' behind the things and the world, as well as behind man himself, which ignites the religious experience – that is the ultimate meaning of the term *deus absconditus* (the hidden or absent god), of whom not only the Christian speaks, but also for instance the Maori, with reference to his own God."[36]

It is not necessary that everyone subjectivize this unknown "surplus." It is possible that some people put it aside or devote themselves to the investigation of it. The irreligious are those who have acquired a "counterpoise" without being conscious of their fundamental instability. They do not lack the capacity for religious experience; it remains latent. But whether religiously or irreligiously

---

[36] Sierksma, *Projection and Religion*, p. 100.

interpreted, this "surplus" normally becomes a part of the heritage of every culture and is interpreted by it. In some cultures, the hidden something is a father-god behind all things; in another, the spirit of an ancestor. But in any given culture some one predominant image usually determines the structure of religion. Normally, human beings confine themselves to the reality of everyday life, but there are moments when the "surplus" looms on the horizon of life, and then human beings embrace the familiar images with which they have been conditioned and behave accordingly. Suddenly confronted by his/her own insufficiency – a dream, a nagging feeling of guilt – the individual

becomes aware of "something" in himself that judges him, unseen and not objectifiable; when he shudders before the mystery of the groundless ground of his own soul. It is precisely that which is unknowable, ungraspable, overpowering, mysterious that gives man the feeling that he is no longer at home in his trusted, stabilized perceptual world, that he is *unheim-lich* (home-less) . . . He experiences bodily that man stands in nothingness; that, although with his perception and his hands he has conquered a part of the world, of which he thought it was *the* world, this turns out to be only a small part of the world, a *Merkwelt* . . . Beyond it is the reverse side of the world, is mystery.[37]

Sierksma's book concludes with a discussion of Buddhism. It, too, is a religion because it is based on the experience that there is something more, a surplus. It, too, takes human excentricity and insufficiency with the greatest seriousness. But it differs from the other religions because it relates projection to perception and has developed a religious practice devoted to revoking projection and perception. It attempts to "guard the senses," and it criticizes all forms of objectification, even the notion of a self. It cannot even be called a mysticism because it does not project some sort of transcendental unity in which all beings participate. Nirvana, Sierksma claimed, is a boundary concept. Consequently Buddhism is the only religion in which

man draws the consequences from his excentric structure. The being who feels he lives in a germinal split, fully realizes the split. The being who in perception must always seek a compromise between appearance and reality, thrusts through to the ultimate reality of the Nothing on which his existence, and therefore his world, is founded.[38]

Sierksma's theory of projection has been hailed by a recent

[37] Sierksma, *Projection and Religion*, p. 102.   [38] Sierksma, *Projection and Religion*, p. 138.

reviewer as having opened up new horizons in our thinking about projection, of having placed it in the context of "post-modern thought in fields such as archetypal psychology, the sociology of knowledge, philosophical worldmaking, literary deconstruction, and theological hermeneutics."[39] Indeed, the reviewer claims that Sierksma has established that

religious projections cannot be dismissed as illusory wish fulfillments. On the contrary, religion's function is to create, destroy, and then recreate entire systems of perceived natural and social worlds, shifting the balance between subjective and objective elements.[40]

This reviewer's praise reveals how easily Grid theories lend themselves to religious apologetics. Because all perception is seen as projection, the subjective modification of reality in the interests of stabilizing reality, and the religious projection is viewed as merely one type of stabilization, it is claimed that religious projections "cannot be dismissed as illusory wish fulfillments."

To be sure, Sierksma has advanced an imaginative and suggestive hypothesis concerning the function of religion, but this hypothesis is also consistent with a different conclusion; namely, that religion is a defense mechanism whose content varies with the culture. In this sense it is an illusion. We can see more clearly how this conclusion is also possible when we reflect briefly on the similarities and the dissimilarities between Sierksma's and Feuerbach's positions. The similarities are striking and have to do with the anthropology that underlies both views. The dissimilarities have to do with the degree to which the religious projection can be assimilated to perception.

To deal with the similarities first, anyone familiar with Feuerbach cannot help but observe that he shares two of Sierksma's assumptions: (a) the species-specific nature of perception and, hence, thought, and (b) the distinctive nature of self-consciousness. Feuerbach's later views, especially, are predicated upon what Sierksma has called the "excentric" nature of the human, the disequilibrium introduced into the human psyche by self-consciousness. Feuerbach, too, thought that the source of religion was to be found in the self-differentiation of the I from the not-I, a not-I that included the powers of both the outer and the inner world. As regards the former, the source of religion, he wrote, is our dependency on all the external forces that impinge on us and give us the feeling that we are not the cause of our own being. As

[39] Bailey, "Religious Projection," p. 209.   [40] Bailey, "Religious Projection," p. 209.

regards the inner world, the ego stands at the "brink of a bottomless abyss" that is its own unconscious being and that seems alien to it and that inspires it. Feuerbach, too, thought that the function of religion was to reduce the *unheimlich* nature of the world.

The dissimilarity between Sierksma and Feuerbach has to do with the former's desire to assimilate the religious projection to projection as such and this, in turn, to perception. One way to characterize the difference between the two authors, then, might be to say that Feuerbach lived before the alleged insights of "postmodernism," that he was an old-fashioned realist as regards perception and, therefore, could not accept that it was a subjective modification of the real world and, hence, a projection. For Feuerbach, one might say, our perceptions are valid, but our subjective modifications of them are false. Feuerbach, in short, was a premodern positivist.

There is an element of truth in this view, but it is also profoundly misleading. As we have seen in Chapter 4, it is not at all clear that Feuerbach thought that only sense perception was veridical and that all subjective modifications were false. But even if we could get no agreement on this issue here, one could, from Feuerbach's point of view, pose an important objection to Sierksma's formulation of the relationship between perception and projection. The problem arises, first, by virtue of defining perception itself as a subjective modification or falsification of the world, because it cannot tell us "the way the world really is." "Truth" is then correlated with "the way the world really is," which, in the nature of the case, can never be achieved because of the finitude of our sense organs; and "falsity" is correlated with the way we actually perceive it.

But this way of posing the issue is fruitless and perhaps even meaningless. In our ordinary usage, the words "truth" and "falsity" pertain to the range of judgments that we make *within* our limited perspectives. They are evaluative terms by means of which we discriminate among the claims we make within the limits of our sensory apparatus. They do not refer to the range of judgments that are only possible for a creature with a "God's-eye" view, who can see the world "the way it really is." If we were to define all perception as false in the nature of the case, then it would soon become pragmatically necessary to introduce some distinction between "true" and "false" perceptions within the entire sphere of (false) perceptions. Some "false" perceptions would prove to be truer than others. And once this distinction had been made, we would once again be faced with something like the traditional issue of truth and falsity. In short, to call all perception false is possible only if one invokes an unreal and inaccessible sphere of truth. Our words "true" and "false" can only function within the framework of our species-specific perceptual apparatus.

If we call religion a projection in the same sense that we call perception a projection, a subjective modification of the world in the interests of stabilizing reality, the problem is complicated still further. We can see this by observing that in perception, the world is presumably "subjectively modified" by all members of the species in the same way because they all have the same sensory apparatus. Or, if that way of putting the issue seems to be too universalistic, we can say that in perception, members of the same species rely on the same type of sensory organs and, hence, are attuned to the same range of signals or signs – smells, heat, light waves, sounds. In the case of the human species, any given culture will agree on the categories, names and significance that will be attributed to these signs.

In the case of the religious projection, however, there does not seem to be some shared sensory apparatus, some organ for perceiving the sacred comparable to the species-specific organs that are attuned to perceptual "signs." Moreover, sacredness is not a perceived quality in the way color is. This explains why if there were disputes within a given culture over the color of a specific object, it would make sense to ask one of the disputants to look again. But if there were disputes about sacrality within a culture, it would make no sense to ask the disputants to adjust their organ for perceiving the sacred.

What I am suggesting is that the logic of religious attribution and, hence, projection is of a different sort than the logic of attribution arising from perception. Consequently, it is not conducive to clarity to attempt to assimilate projection to perception on the grounds that both are subjective modifications of reality.

The relation between projection and perception is further complicated by virtue of Sierksma's argument that the religious projection arises only at the limits of perception, that it has to do with the "surplus" or hidden side of things which cannot be perceived. It is from this hidden something, Sierksma claims, that the religious imagination takes fire. But if this is the case, then it weakens even more the attempt to assimilate religious projection to perception generally. In the case of sense perception, we are all necessarily restricted to certain inputs or signs capable of being received by our sensory mechanism. It is just because we can appeal to these shared inputs and the shared vocabularies for describing and identifying them that we can get agreements with others. In the case of religion, however, we are dealing with something that is hidden from us and which escapes our perceptual net and, hence, by definition, does not activate our common apparatus. Why, then, should both perception and religion be called projection and the latter seen as a sub-type of the former?

There are other contrasts to be made between Feuerbach and Sierksma. Sierksma's view is that religion has to do with the "surplus" or hidden nature of things, that which is mysterious because it lies behind appearances. Feuerbach, too, seemed to argue on occasion that the function of religion was to change the uncanny being of nature into a known and comfortable being.[41] And in the *Lectures*, he had written that the imagination "unchecked by reason or sense perception" was the principal organ of religion.[42] But there is an important difference between these two views. In Feuerbach's view, the imagination does not focus on what eludes the human perceptual net but precisely on those sensuous features of the world that strike *Dasein* most vividly – on objects and qualities in nature that benefit or harm the self. In the case of monotheism, as we have seen, Feuerbach thought that the attributes of God are abstracted from nature as a whole – its omnipresence, power, order, eternity, and the like. The not-I, to be sure, is mysterious and the source of wonderment, but basically religion has to do with the sensuous and not with what eludes the senses.

In short, the truth of nature religion is based on the truth of the senses. Thus *The Principles of Philosophy* confirms *The Essence of Religion*. But though I defend nature religion because and insofar as it is based on the truth of the senses, I by no means defend the way in which it makes use of the senses, the way in which it looks at and worships nature. Nature religion has no other foundation than sensory impressions, or rather, the impression which sensations make on man's mind and imagination.[43]

Feuerbach, I suspect, would not have wished us to consider these theoretical differences with Sierksma to be trivial, because they

---

[41] *Religion*, para. 34.
[42] *Lectures*, lecture 21.
[43] *Lectures*, p. 88; *Vorlesungen*, p. 102.

concern the more fundamental issue of how the excentricity of human nature is to be conceived and interpreted. It has to do with the theoretical anthropology informing the theory. Once again, we find here a superficial agreement that conceals important differences. Both thinkers, as I have noted, stress the importance of self-consciousness and the excentricity of the self. But having agreed with Sierksma about the excentric nature of *Dasein*, Feuerbach would have argued that Sierksma has not properly formulated the relationship between the I and the Not-I. In Sierksma's model, it seems as though perception determines the normal relationship to the world and that religion arises as a defense against whatever escapes the perceptual net. Religion is primarily seen, then, as a defense reaction, and its aim is to restore the delicate balance which the self maintains between the inner and the outer world.

Feuerbach would not have denied that religion sometimes serves as a defensive reaction – for example, against the fear of death – but he would have argued that it is a much more complicated phenomenon. Religion, as we have seen, springs out of the intense rage-to-live and to flourish. But because of the social nature of human existence, a human being's deepest wish and happiness lie in recognition and acceptance by an other.

Finally, from Feuerbach's point of view, Sierksma's conception of the religious projection as a defensive reaction, together with his Darwinian assumption that all distinctively human modes of behavior must serve an adaptive function, too easily lends itself to what he would have regarded as an apologetic for the necessity of religion in general and, hence, the justification of any given religion. Thus the reviewer quoted above concludes his review of Sierksma's work with the claim that Sierksma has shown that the religious projection "is no longer 'nothing but' a delusory, merely subjective, internal pathology. Projection is a necessary, though changeable, aspect of perception in the 'marked world.' "[44] Feuerbach would have considered this conclusion to be both tendentious and disputable: tendentious because Sierksma himself had suggested that at least one religion is not projective, Buddhism; and disputable because what Sierksma has shown is not that religious projection is necessary to survive but that human beings have a profound and deep need to humanize the hidden world.

[44] Bailey, "Religious Projection," p. 209.

PROJECTION AS SOCIALLY CONSTRUCTED GRID

The second Grid theorist with whom it is easy to imagine our reconstructed Feuerbach seeking a conversation is Peter Berger. Indeed, in many respects Berger's work would probably be more interesting to Feuerbach than Sierksma's. Not only is the concept of projection at the heart of his theory of religion, but this, in turn, is part of a larger behavioral theory that attempts to synthesize the insights of a wide spectrum of American and Continental thinkers including George Herbert Mead, W. I. Thomas, Irving Goffman, Emil Durkheim, Max Weber, Alfred Schutz, Martin Heidegger, and Karl Barth. But although this larger behavioral theory claims to be empirical and immune to philosophical and theological critique, it makes use of ideas that Feuerbach would immediately recognize as neo-Hegelian: the human subject pours out (externalizes) his/her activity and thoughts into culture, objectifies and reifies them, and by doing so becomes estranged or alienated. And, of course, Feuerbach could hardly fail to notice that Berger, more than any other sociologist of religion, has been especially laudatory of Feuerbach's work, even though, like so many others, he equates that work with the inverted Hegelianism of *The Essence of Christianity*. It was Feuerbach, Berger claimed, who has profoundly changed the modern understanding of the phenomenon of religion. If Hegel had in a metaphysical context developed the idea that reality can be construed as the conversation between consciousness and what lies outside of it, then Feuerbach, by arguing that God was a product of human consciousness, could be seen as claiming that reality may be understood as the conversation between humankind and its productions. Berger concluded:

A good case could be made that not only Marx's and Freud's treatment of religion, but the entire historical-psychological-sociological analysis of religious phenomena since Feuerbach has been primarily a vast elaboration of the same conception and the same procedure. A sociological theory of religion, particularly if it is undertaken in the framework of the sociology of knowledge, pushes to its final consequences the Feuerbachian notion of religion as a human projection, that is, as a scientifically graspable producer of human history.[45]

Berger's theory of religion is really a part of a larger theory of culture which, in turn, is viewed from the perspective of the sociology of

[45] Peter L. Berger, *A Rumor of Angels: Modern Society and the Rediscovery of the Supernatural* (Garden City, N.Y.: Doubleday, 1969), p. 46.

knowledge. And at the core of this theory is an anthropology that, like Sierksma's, rests on the claim that the human species is unique because of its relatively unspecialized instinctual structure. If the animal is determined by its programmed drives and instincts and, consequently, lives in a species-specific environment, the human being is "unfinished" at birth and has an "open" world. Because of this instinctual instability and plasticity, the human species must provide a stable environment for itself by constructing its own ordered world. Society and culture provide those structures and controls that are lacking biologically. In this process of world construction – Berger calls it "externalization" – human drives become molded, formed, and specialized.

Once society, the institutional infrastructure of culture, and culture are created, they acquire stability ("facticity") and objectivity. They are collectively maintained by constant collective recognition, by forms of social control, and also by those processes by means of which all societies force the individual to internalize those categories, norms, rules, and recipes for action which constitute the cultural grid. The members of a culture must adopt their thinking and behavior in conformity with it. Indeed, "The final test of its objective reality is its capacity to impose itself upon the reluctance of individuals."[46] This is as true of the immaterial aspects of culture as the material. Human beings create language, for example, and then find that their thinking is dominated by its grammar.

Society provides not only the coordinates (name, legal descent, civil status, occupation) within which individuals comprehend their autobiographies but the institutions, roles, and associated self-images that become the paradigms for human conduct and self-identification. Thus, what was regarded as an external facticity, a world of social objectifications "out there," becomes an internal facticity. What was objective and external is absorbed into the consciousness so that the structures of the objectivated world determine the structures of consciousness. Thus, "the individual's own life appears as objectively real, to himself as well as to others, only as it is located within a social world that itself has the character of objective reality."[47]

Culture and society, then, may be regarded as an expression of the world-constructing or ordering ("nomizing") activity of the human species, an activity rooted in its biological nature. They provide the structure for human experience and shield it from the terror of chaos

[46] Berger, *The Sacred Canopy*, p. 11.   [47] Berger, *The Sacred Canopy*, p. 13.

and anomy. Despite the apparent objective character of the socially constructed world, it is inherently fragile and precarious. It can, for example, be threatened and challenged by other societies with other constructed "worlds" as well as by those marginal experiences on the fringes of consciousness such as dreams, fantasies, and death. Death, above all, threatens society because of its threat to the continuity of human relationships and to the basic assumption of order upon which society rests.[48] Socially constructed worlds are like patches of light in an abysmal darkness where there lurk monsters of irrationality and chaos.

To keep this chaos at bay, every society requires procedures and rationalizations to insure the "reality orientation" of its members, a continuing consensus regarding what can be taken for granted as real. One of the most important of these procedures of legitimation is the socially objectivated "knowledge" that serves to explain and justify the social order. But classically, the most powerful of all forms of legitimation has been religion. For two reasons. First of all, religion bestows upon the cultural grid an "ultimately valid ontological status" by locating it within a sacred and cosmic frame of reference.[49] Nomos and cosmos converge.[50] Second, religion deals directly with those marginal situations such as death by integrating them into a comprehensive nomos. These anomic and horrific events are given a certain plausibility or sense.

Because religion performs this function of legitimation, it may be regarded as a theodicy because the classical function of a theodicy is to provide a cosmic "why" sufficiently convincing to enable the self to withstand the chaos created by the marginal situations that disrupt ordinary human life. Berger has many interesting things to say about theodicies and their relationships to social structures; but his claim that an irrational and masochistic attitude underlies all theodicies would surely have captured Feuerbach's attention.[51] In Berger's view, every society necessarily demands a certain denial of the individual self and its needs and problems. Indeed, one of the important functions of cultural grids is to facilitate this surrender, because such a surrender renders the terrors of existence less intolerable to the individual. The intensification of this self-denial is of special interest so far as religion is concerned, because the ecstasy of complete surrender, which Berger does not hesitate to call the "attitude of masochism" (the "attitude in which the individual reduces himself to an inert and thinglike object

[48] Berger, *The Sacred Canopy*, pp. 23f.   [49] Berger, *The Sacred Canopy*, p. 33.
[50] Berger, *The Sacred Canopy*, p. 25.   [51] Berger, *The Sacred Canopy*, p. 54.

vis-à-vis his fellowmen"), cuts through the ambiguities of individual subjectivity and is experienced as profoundly liberating.[52] It provides the means by which individual suffering and death can be radically transcended.

It is against this theoretical background regarding the relation of religion to culture that one can understand three closely related and important terms in Berger's theory: "estrangement," "false consciousness," and "alienation." These terms refer to the process through which the self necessarily passes as it emerges into society. As we have seen, Berger had argued that society in the nature of the case forces the individual to internalize the objective meanings (language, categories, role definitions, etc.) of the society. This internalization is the process whereby the cultural grid comes to mold large parts of the consciousness of the individual. The individual then comes to order the world in the same fashion as the culture does. Nevertheless, this socialization is never completely successful, and there always remains a nonsocialized remainder. The socialized self then stands over against the nonsocialized remainder in "uneasy accommodation."[53] It confronts the unsocialized part of the self as a hard fact, and an internal confrontation within the consciousness occurs that recapitulates the external confrontation between the individual and the society. The individual then becomes strange to himself and to certain aspects of his socialized self.

Berger argues that this estrangement is simply given with the sociality of humankind. There is no escape from it. It is an anthropological necessity.[54] There are, however, two ways a person can deal with it: one can reappropriate the strangeness of the world and the self by "recollecting" that both the world and the social self are products of human activity; or one can forget this fact and permit the social world and the social self to "confront the individual as inexorable facticities analogous to the facticities of nature."[55] The latter alternative is called alienation, and it occurs when individuals forget that they are the co-producers of the socially constructed world, or, at least, that they voluntarily consent to it and maintain it. Alienated consciousness is undialectical or false consciousness because it assumes that the structures of the world are absolute and sacred. A

---

[52] Berger, *The Sacred Canopy*, pp. 55f.   [53] Berger, *The Sacred Canopy*, p. 83.
[54] Berger, *The Sacred Canopy*, p. 85. It is interesting that in Berger's view alienation is not a late development of the self but a condition of the emergent social self. Consequently, the phylo- and ontogenetic development of the self is from alienation to de-alienation and not from innocence to alienation.   [55] Berger, *The Sacred Canopy*, p. 85.

result of this false assumption is that the world ceases to be an open arena for human freedom and becomes instead a world of fate and necessity. Both archaic religion and infantile consciousness are of this alienated sort because both experience the world as facticity.[56]

Since religions have classically been the vehicles for the sacralization and absolutization of cultural grids, it follows that religions have classically been the most powerful instruments of false consciousness and human alienation. They mask the empirical contingency of the grid and impose a fictitious inexorability and absoluteness upon the humanly constructed world. The fundamental recipe of religion is to throw a sacred canopy over the socially constructed grids and to transform human products into suprahuman facticities. The result is the mystification of human institutions and roles because human norms have been transformed into sacred norms.

Moreover, it should be noted, this tendency is inherent in religious consciousness itself because the religious experience of the sacred is, from the standpoint of consciousness, a genuine encounter with otherness, with "something *totaliter aliter* as compared to ordinary, profane human life."[57] It is just this otherness that accounts for the religious feelings of awe and dread. But

whatever else the constellations of the sacred may be "ultimately," empirically they are products of human activity and human signification – that is, they are human projections. Human beings, in the course of their externalization, project their meanings into the universe around them. These projections are objectivated in the common worlds of human societies. The "objectivity" of religious meanings is *produced* objectivity, that is, religious meanings are objectivated projections. It follows that, insofar as these meanings imply an overwhelming sense of otherness, they may be described as *alienated projections.*[58]

Given this argument and its importance for the overall theory, the reader is somewhat unprepared for Berger's sudden and surprising claim that although "the fundamental recipe of religion" is to create false consciousness, religion is not intrinsically alienating. The reason he gives is that religions can "legitimate de-alienation" by radically relativizing social fictions and by withdrawing sanctity from human institutions.[59] And as an example of this de-alienating function Berger,

---

[56] Berger, *The Sacred Canopy*, p. 86. It is an interesting aspect of Berger's view, in contrast to Eliade's, that archaic consciousness is alienated consciousness.
[57] Berger, *The Sacred Canopy*, p. 87.   [58] Berger, *The Sacred Canopy*, p. 89.
[59] Berger, *The Sacred Canopy*, p. 96.

like Sierksma, appeals to those Indian religions that regard the social order as *maya* or illusion. Unlike Sierksma, however, Berger also claims that there are elements in the Jewish and Christian traditions that also de-alienate because they shatter the micro–macro cosmic pattern characteristic of so many of the world's religions. In short, the paradox of religion is that it appears in history as both a world-maintaining and a world-shaking force.

If we look back at the above sketch of Berger's sociology of religion, it might seem anachronistic to imagine a conversation between this contemporary American sociologist and our nineteenth-century German philosopher, especially in the light of Berger's claim that his own argument moves "strictly within the frame of reference of sociological theory" and, hence, is "not susceptible" to arguments coming from non-empirical and non-normative disciplines.[60] Nevertheless, there are good reasons why such an imagined conversation is not implausible. On the positive side, Berger himself has noted that he regards his own project as an extension of Feuerbach's. On the negative side, there is no need to be intimidated by Berger's claim that his own theory moves completely within the empirical framework of contemporary sociology. It can be shown that the most important operative categories in his theory can hardly be claimed to be empirical.[61] The concept of consciousness, which is at the core of it, for example, cannot be empirical. Nor can the argument underlying the theory of alienation; namely, that when consciousness is socialized the effect is to congeal or estrange one part of consciousness from the rest so that internalization entails an anthropologically necessary alienation.[62]

Furthermore, it seems clear that despite Berger's disclaimer, his own anthropology does in fact generate a number of normative categories, such as "false consciousness," "estrangement," and "alienation," all of which presuppose human freedom. His basic assumption is that human beings can and should take responsibility for being co-producers of the socially constructed world. The non-empirical nature of these claims, it is important to note, does not necessarily mean that they are illegitimate or false, but it does mean that our reconstructed Feuerbach need not feel like an outdated amateur, someone who lived before the disciplinary rigors of empirical social science. Finally, there

---

[60] Berger, *The Sacred Canopy*, p. 179.
[61] I have attempted to establish this in "Some Problematical Aspects of Peter Berger's Theory of Religion," *Journal of the American Academy of Religion*, 41, 1 (1973), 75–93.
[62] Berger, *The Sacred Canopy*, p. 85.

are many important ideas that the two figures have in common: the excentric nature of the human self, that religions are theodicies, and that they classically serve to estrange the human consciousness.

There is, however, one important contrast between the two figures which, in turn, leads to others. It has to do with the way in which each conceives of the relation of religion to culture. Berger links the excentricity of the human consciousness to its world-building activities. Like Hegel, he argues that human nature cannot rest within itself but must continually objectify itself in culture.[63] But unlike Hegel, he does not regard religion in the first instance as one of these forms of objectification; rather, religion is said to arise as a response to those marginal situations that threaten the fragile socially constructed grid. In Feuerbach's view, by contrast, the religious feeling arises directly out of the I's self-differentiation from the not-I. Religion is not a response to marginal situations but accompanies the differentiation of the self from all-encompassing nature.

It could be argued that Berger's placement of religion within the context of culture is more suggestive than Feuerbach's proposal because it enables Berger to account for one of the central functions of religion: its absolutization of cultural values and norms. Feuerbach, by contrast, never really formulated a clear and convincing view of the relation of religion to culture. As we have seen, he tended to waver between the view that religion is the wish to be free from the necessities of nature and the view that religion is the attempt to control nature for the sake of human needs and happiness. The first view permitted him to argue that the ultimate aim of religion is to be free from the laws of nature, to become as gods; the second allowed him to claim that every scientific and technological advance means the diminution of religion. He could even claim, as we have seen, that religion was the first "crude and vulgar form of culture."[64] The first view is more consistent with his main line of argument that the religious sentiment is innate, that the "ultimate secret of religion is the *relationship* between the *conscious* and *unconscious*, the *voluntary* and *involuntary in one and the same individual*."[65] The second view commits him to the thesis that religion will wither away before science and technology. Berger's position clearly avoids that unwarranted claim. Religion arises because culture itself is fragile and in constant need of legitimation.

[63] Berger, *The Sacred Canopy*, p. 4.
[64] Feuerbach, *Lectures*, p. 209; *Vorlesungen*, p. 235.
[65] *Lectures*, pp. 310f.; *Vorlesungen*, p. 349.

But by linking religion so closely to the legitimization and rationalization of culture, Berger tends to regard religion primarily as one of the legitimating strategies society employs to defend itself against any disorder and chaos. The sacred stands in irrevocable opposition to chaos and disorder so that "To be in a 'right' relationship with the sacred cosmos is to be protected against the nightmare threats of chaos."[66] Whereas Sierksma argued that religion finds its occasion in the "something more" that eludes the conceptual net of consciousness, Berger claims that religion finds its foothold in the marginal situations that threaten the cultural grid itself. This is the reason he can claim that all religions are theodicies, not in the sense that they explain evil but in the sense that they enable "the individual to integrate the anomic experiences of his biography into the socially established nomos and its subjective correlate in his own consciousness."[67] Religions are just a special case of the "implicit theodicy of all social order" that "antecedes any legitimations, religious or otherwise."[68]

It is because Berger so stresses this legitimating function of religion that we can imagine our ideal Feuerbach taking issue with his formulation of the relation of religion to culture, even though both of them believe that the roots of religion lie in the excentric human consciousness. And the argument Feuerbach would surely propose is similar to the one he would have advanced against Sierksma; namely, that it is a mistake to regard religion solely as a response to threat, whether to the psyche (Sierksma) or to the social grid with which one is identified (Berger). To be sure, threats play an important role in the religious consciousness because desire and anxiety are omnipresent realities; but it is too simplistic to regard them as the sole occasions for religion. Religion, Feuerbach would have argued, is an overdetermined phenomenon. It is naturally concerned with anything that threatens the self, but it also springs out of the multiform needs and desires of human existence. Among these, to be sure, is the need to explain anomalous phenomena, but there are also those needs which Melford Spiro has labeled "substantive needs" – for food, victory in war, favorable weather, recovery from illness, the health of a loved one, and the like.[69] There are also expressive needs which spring from feelings of inadequacy and guilt, shame, and moral anxiety, just as there is the

---

[66] Berger, *The Sacred Canopy*, p. 27.
[67] Berger, *The Sacred Canopy*, p. 58.   [68] Berger, *The Sacred Canopy*, p. 55.
[69] See Melford E. Spiro, *Culture and Human Nature: Theoretical Papers*, ed. Benjamin Kilborne and L. L. Langness (Chicago: Chicago University Press, 1987), pp. 211–213.

need for acceptance and recognition. "We must not account for . . . [religion] . . . by any single cause," Feuerbach wrote, "or rather, we must assign each cause its proper place."[70] And we only discover what these "causes" are, Feuerbach would have argued, by listening carefully to the utterances and expressions of religious believers themselves.

A related but more complicated issue over which we can imagine a spirited dialogue between the nineteenth-century philosopher and the modern sociologist of religion has to do with what Feuerbach would surely regard as Berger's confused normative judgment concerning the alienating role of religion in human affairs. For despite Berger's claim that his treatment of religion is strictly empirical, it in fact yields a devastating criticism of religion as well as the positive claim that some religions have been the most powerful liberating forces in history. On the one hand, we are told that the "fundamental recipe" of religion is to breed "false consciousness," and on the other, we are told that religion has served to create a demystifying and hence liberating consciousness.

A Feuerbachian would argue that this paradoxical conclusion results from a confusion in Berger's thought. In order to see the grounds of this Feuerbachian complaint, it is necessary to distinguish two distinct but related reasons for Berger's apparently negative evaluation of religion. First of all, he argues, as we have seen, that there is a pretheoretical masochism at work in any individual's socialization into society because any society rests on and requires the denial of the individual self and its needs, anxieties, and problems.[71] In fact, one of the key functions of the cultural grid is to facilitate this desire to surrender itself to the collectivity in the individual consciousness. Religion simply intensifies this self-denying surrender of the individual to society. If such self-denial causes pain, this may even serve to ratify the denial because the self-denial removes all the ambiguities and anguish of separate individual existence and the anxiety of freedom. Human beings, Berger argues, cannot abide loneliness, and the masochistic surrender to the power of the collective is therefore liberating. The religious attitude rests on this pretheoretical masochism.

A second reason leading to a negative evaluation of religion follows from Berger's conception of humankind as a free co-producer

[70] *Lectures*, p. 199; *Vorlesungen*, p. 224.   [71] Berger, *The Sacred Canopy*, p. 55.

of the world together with his view that the central function of religion is to legitimate the cultural grid. His argument is that the sacralization of the cultural grid necessarily mystifies the institutions, roles, mores, and values of the culture and, hence, conceals the fact that cultural grids are co-produced and maintained by individual choice and consent. It would be bad enough to absolutize the cultural grid without the benefit of religion, but religion compounds the problem because "One of the essential qualities of the sacred, as encountered in 'religious experience,' is otherness, its manifestation as something *totaliter aliter* as compared to ordinary, profane human life."[72] It is this otherness that is at the heart of religious awe and dread. Since the sacred is regarded as alien to the human world, the sacralization of human meanings and constructions is disastrous to authentic, free human existence.

It might initially seem that the issue here between Feuerbach and Berger is simply that the former would have agreed with the latter's negative claims about religion but not with the positive. But the issue is more complicated than this and, moreover, instructive. First of all, even if the later Feuerbach had retained his earlier concept of "alienation," this term has a different meaning for him than it has for Berger. For Berger, the concept of alienation has to do with the absolutization of the socially constructed grid. Any human construction that has become absolutized is alienating because it conceals the contingency of these constructions. This is the reason why Berger argues that the very act of socializing the child involves taking the socially constructed world for granted and, hence, is alienating. Thus he is committed to the view that human beings necessarily emerge as alienated selves and only later become de-alienated.[73]

For the early Feuerbach, by contrast, alienation occurs when the human bestows its own essential attributes on the divine and thus relinquishes them for itself. Alienation does not mean that human constructions are taken as absolute. Consequently, Feuerbach's early concept of alienation leads to a quite different critique of religion than the one Berger offers.

Furthermore, Feuerbach, unlike Berger, does not define religion in terms of the sacred or equate the sacred with the encounter with otherness. Indeed, Feuerbach would not find it unintelligible or

---

[72] Berger, *The Sacred Canopy*, p. 87.   [73] Berger, *The Sacred Canopy*, pp. 86f.

alienating that human beings attribute both sacredness and otherness to nature. What he objects to is the personification of this not-I and the intellectual, moral, and existential contradictions to which this anthropomorphism leads.

Having made these distinctions and reservations, however, it is virtually certain that Feuerbach would have agreed with Berger's judgment that religion has classically mystified human institutions. Like Berger, he believed that human beings are free, conscious beings who are co-producers of the cultures in which they live and for which they are responsible. Feuerbach also believed that religion fosters self-surrender to the collective; and he, too, thought that religion – and he would have added "metaphysics" – invariably conceals the contingency of all human aspirations and products. Indeed, this criticism lay at the heart of the Young Hegelians' objections to religion from the beginning. "My primary concern is and always has been," he wrote, "to illumine the obscure essence of religion with the torch of reason, in order that man may at least cease to be the victim, the plaything, of all those hostile powers which from time immemorial have employed and are still employing the darkness of religion for the oppression of mankind."[74]

But just because Feuerbach would have agreed with Berger on this point, he would have looked with suspicion on the latter's claim that religion has also played a liberating role in history. He would surely have asked, "What is it that enables Berger, after having laid the theoretical basis for a devastating critique of religion, to recoil suddenly from the obvious conclusion and claim that religion can sometimes legitimate de-alienation?"

The answer, of course, lies in Berger's view that religions are to be assessed primarily in terms of their legitimating function. He argues that if we observe the history of religion we discover that there are some religions that have radically relativized the socially constructed world. Like Sierksma, he appeals to those soteriologies in the East in which the world and its norms are regarded as *maya* or illusion and which propose meditative techniques enabling the devotee to "see through" all human constructions. So, too, Berger appeals to those mystical traditions that withdraw sanctity from all earthly institutions. But Berger, unlike Sierksma, argues that there are demystifying religious traditions in the West. The Hebrew Prophets, for example,

---

[74] Feuerbach, *Lectures*, p. 22; *Vorlesungen*, p. 30.

proclaimed an utterly transcendent God in the face of whom all institutions were seen as merely human. Indeed, it was this proclamation that set off Israel sharply from its surrounding cultures. This debunking motif was then resurrected in the Protestant Reformation with Luther's doctrine of the Two Kingdoms, and it shattered the sacred hierarchical cosmos of Roman Catholicism and laid the foundation for the secularization of society in the Western world. Secularization, by implication, is a good thing in so far as it reflects a human consciousness "come of age," which is to say, a consciousness that recognizes that we live in a socially constructed world for which we are responsible.

Feuerbach would surely have found this to be a very unconvincing argument, an argument that trades on those ambiguities made possible by concentrating on the legitimating function of religion rather than on its defining characteristic: the projection of human meanings onto the cosmos that are then taken to be sacred.

Consider the concentration on the legitimating function of religion. Berger, as we have seen, writes that although "religion has an intrinsic (and theoretically very understandable) tendency to legitimate alienation, there is also the possibility that de-alienation may be religiously legitimated in specific historical cases."[75] So formulated, this sentence permits the reader to assume that as regards function, religion is really neutral; that is, able to legitimate either alienation or de-alienation. But by assuming that religion is neutral, Berger passes over his earlier claim not only that religion, quite apart from function, is an expression of human masochism but, more fundamentally, that it *is to be defined* as "objectivated projections" and that, "insofar as these meanings imply an overwhelming sense of otherness . . . [they] may be described as *alienated projections*."[76] But if religion *by definition* is an alienated projection, how can it be assumed to be neutral as regards function?

What enables Berger to formulate the issue in this ambiguous way is, of course, that he sometimes defines religion substantively (as the experience of the sacred or as the projection of human meanings onto the cosmos), and sometimes functionally, as a legitimating device. If he had defined religion purely as the experience of the sacred, then he need not necessarily have regarded it as intrinsically alienating because there is nothing in the experience of otherness as such that

---

[75] Berger, *The Sacred Canopy*, p. 96.
[76] Berger, *The Sacred Canopy*, p. 89.

requires that one absolutize it.[77] But if religion is the projection of human meanings onto the world that are then regarded as sacred, then it must by definition be alienating. And since this is the way in which Berger has defined it, there is no way that a religion can both be the projection of human meanings taken as sacred and function to "legitimate de-alienation."

Berger's historical examples reflect this same confusion of substance and function. It hardly makes any historical sense, for example, to claim that the Hebrew Prophets and the Protestant Reformers did not project human meanings onto the universe, or that they did not regard these meanings as absolute. The Prophets made their moral and political pronouncements in the name of God just as the Protestant Reformers did. These Reformers held that the Bible was the inspired Word of God and that the moral and spiritual truths contained therein were authoritative and absolute. They may have regarded the ways of the world as sinful, as Luther did, but they also believed that the inherent structures of the world (natural law) were God-given and, hence, that certain human constructions such as monogamy were absolute. Buddhism, of course, is a different type of case, but even it does not support Berger's analysis. In so far as Buddhism does demystify the world it is just because, as Sierksma argued, it advocates the withdrawal of all human projections considered to be sacred; in short, just in so far as it does not meet Berger's stipulation of religion as the projection of human meanings which are then taken to be sacred.

There are still other factors at work in Berger's view that enable him to block the obvious negative conclusion regarding religion to which his analysis leads. Consider, for example, what transpires when he combines his views on the methodological limits of the sociologist with the notion of projection. The sociologist, he claims, is strictly limited by the empirical framework within which he/she works, and within these limits religion must be seen as a projection. Moreover, because of these same methodological limits, even the terms "false consciousness," "bad faith," and "alienation" must be seen as value-free.[78] Thus we need not assume, he concludes, that because sociological theory must view religion as a projection we need

---

[77] Berger's identification of otherness with alienation would be subject to the same criticism that the young Marx made of Hegel; namely, that he had identified objectivity with alienation. See Livingstone and Benton (trans.), *Karl Marx Early Writings*, pp. 384–400.

[78] Berger, *The Sacred Canopy*, p. 180.

conclude that religion does not actually refer to something outside of the projecting consciousness. In other words, to say that religion is a human projection "does not logically preclude the possibility that the projected meanings may have an ultimate status independent of man."[79] It is possible that "the anthropological ground of these projections may itself be the reflection of a reality that *includes* both world and man so that man's ejaculations of meaning into the universe ultimately point to an all-embracing meaning in which he himself is grounded."[80] In short, the theologian, who is not bound by the empirical limitations of the sociologist, may believe that the religious projection is true.

By drawing this sharp line of demarcation between the work of the empirical, value-free sociologist and that of the theologian, Berger is able as a sociologist to regard religion as an alienating projection but as a theologian to believe both that the adjective "alienating" is harmless (because value-free) and that a given religious projection is true. Indeed, by conceiving the issue in this way, Berger can even suggest a Feuerbachian program for theology. Feuerbach, he argues, regarded religion as a gigantic projection of man's own being and in so doing took over Hegel's notion of dialectic, although changing its significance. Hegel's dialectic refers to the "conversation" between consciousness and the products of consciousness that lie outside it. Hegel, of course, grounded this dialectic in his metaphysics and his theology. The absolute consciousness has a "conversation" with its production, human creation. Feuerbach simply turned Hegel on his head and argued that religion is the conversation between human consciousness and its products.

Berger's sociology of religion claims only to push Feuerbach's own conception to its logical limits. But this inversion of Hegel, Berger observes, obviously depends on one's "ultimate assumption about reality," and since the theologian has different ultimate assumptions, he/she may legitimately simply turn Feuerbach "on his head" again as he once did to Hegel and conclude that

man projects ultimate meanings into reality because that reality is, indeed, ultimately meaningful, and because his own being (the empirical ground of these projections) contains and intends these same ultimate meanings. Such a theological procedure, if feasible, would be an interesting ploy on

---

[79] Berger, *The Sacred Canopy*, p. 181.
[80] Berger, *The Sacred Canopy*, p. 181.

Feuerbach – the reduction of theology to anthropology would end in the reconstruction of anthropology in a theological mode.[81]

In *The Sacred Canopy*, Berger only suggests what he calls this "man-bites-dog feat" to the theologian; in his *A Rumor of Angels*, he takes a stab at the enterprise. He argues that just as mathematics is "a pure projection of human consciousness" but, nevertheless, somehow corresponds to a "mathematical reality external to . . . [the mathematician]," so, too, the religious projection may correspond with reality. "In any case, it would seem that any theological method worthy of the name should be based on this possibility."

The theological decision will have to be that, "in, with, and under" the immense array of human projections, there are indicators of a reality that is truly "other" and that the religious imagination of man ultimately reflects.[82]

If this theological decision has any validity, Berger continues, then it seems reasonable to look for traces of this "other reality" in the projector himself. Such traces, Berger proposes, occur in what he calls certain prototypical human gestures, such as the propensity for order, play, humor, and justice. Given these universal propensities or "signals of transcendence," we have the basis for a new theological program that would be firmly anchored in fundamental human experience and, therefore, not subject to the "constantly changing winds of cultural moods."[83]

One can see in Berger's "man-bites-dog feat" how the Grid model of projection tends to lead its proponents immediately into complex epistemological issues and how these, in turn, easily provide openings for the most diverse, even contradictory, implications for religion. Sierksma, as we have seen, drew the conclusion that since all conception is projection, the Buddhist is correct in asking us to withdraw all projections and recognize that we cannot know reality as it is. Berger, on the other hand, advises the theologian to assume that religious projections, like mathematics, reflect a reality that has a "fundamental affinity" with our consciousness.

Because of these complexities it is impossible to imagine a conversation about the possibility of theology between Berger and the later Feuerbach that would not spill over the confines of this chapter and even the whole book. There would be debates over such issues as

---

[81] Berger, *The Sacred Canopy*, p. 181.
[82] Berger, *A Rumor of Angels*, p. 47.   [83] Berger, *A Rumor of Angels*, p. 52.

these: (a) whether it is intelligible for Berger to claim that the sociology he has sketched is both empirical and value-free, so that "false consciousness," "masochism," "bad faith," and "alienation" are to be regarded simply as technical terms with no pejorative implications;[84] (b) whether the theologian must not agree that religion inculcates "bad faith" just to the extent that he/she also believes that human beings are co-producers of the world;[85] (c) whether the two frameworks, sociology and theology, can logically coexist or whether, if the sociologist is correct, the theologian must take account of his/her views; (d) whether mathematics can be said to be a legitimate analogy to religious projections; and, finally, (e) whether Berger's solution requires, as he himself concedes, a return to something like the metaphysics of Hegel; namely, that all the projections of the human mind reflect a correspondence of some kind to an underlying reality that includes both the world and man, a correspondence which, in his earlier work, was regarded as a false consciousness.

Berger's comparison of mathematics with religious projection is a good example of how complicated any such discussion would be. There is the initial question whether the religious projection performs like a grid or whether, as Berger seems to say, it is primarily a response to marginal situations that threaten the cultural grid. If belief in a personal devil, for example, is an attempt to deal with an anomalous situation that threatens the cultural grid, how can this same belief be regarded as of the same logical type as the grid itself? Or how can Buddhism or mysticism be understood as an ordering projection like mathematics? And, finally, what happens to the analogy of religion to mathematics if it is the case that there are several possible mathematical systems just as there are several religious projections? The existence of more than one mathematics would seem to lead to the pragmatic

---

[84] Berger, *The Sacred Canopy*, p. 180.

[85] I have argued in another context that Berger, in his earlier incarnation as a Barthian theologian, held the view that religion did, in fact, induce "bad faith" and, hence, that the Christian faith, as he defined it, was not a religion. He had written that "religion is needed in society because men need bad faith" (see his *The Precarious Vision: A Sociologist Looks at Social Fictions and Christian Faith* (Garden City, N.Y.: Doubleday, 1961)). This theological view, I claimed, was then consistent with his sociology of religion, but he increasingly came to see that this view of Christianity was untenable sociologically speaking and abandoned it. He then sought to form a modus vivendi with sociology by claiming that the former was strictly within the realm of the empirical and, hence, could not say anything about the truth of religion. See my "Religious Faith and the Sociology of Knowledge: The Unburdening of Peter Berger," *Religious Studies Review*, 5, 1 (January 1979), 1–10.

judgment that we use one type of mathematics for some purposes and another type for others. None of them give us the truth about the world. Are we then to assume that Buddhism is true for some purposes while Hinduism and Christianity are true for others? But this conclusion would not fit the underlying Hegelian assumption that our minds reflect a reality that includes both the world and man.

At the end of the day, however, there is a sense in which this debate over the issue of projection would finally be irrelevant for our ideal Feuerbach because having put the debate "in play" with *The Essence of Christianity* he subsequently abandoned the Hegelian version of it and had no continuing investment in it. I believe that he would have viewed the attempts to resurrect the concept of projection, whether as Beam or Grid, as a mistake. So far as the Beam theories are concerned, one might as well call the religious projection a belief and lose nothing of any importance. And although it seems clear that there are important epistemological issues raised by the Grid theorists, there is the unavoidable issue whether some of the religious grids can be correlated to some metaphysical reality "out there." A theologian who accepts Berger's "man-bites-dog" project has, in the final analysis, the same intellectual task theologians have always faced; namely, to give convincing reasons why some "prototypical human gestures," such as the mother's assurance that "everything is all right," justify belief in a benign and loving metaphysical being.

The later Feuerbach knew that such reasons have been and will continue to be given for believing in such a reality. His project was to argue that these beliefs persist not because they are rational but because human beings desire above all things that a being exists who fulfills their deepest wishes and who knows and affirms them.

CHAPTER 8

Feuerbach, anthropomorphism, and the need for religious illusion

RELIGION AS ANTHROPOMORPHISM

Because the concept of projection has acquired such diverse and even contradictory meanings in the theoretical literature, it was inevitable, perhaps, that someone should attempt to salvage the substance of Feuerbach's view – that religions are anthropomorphic interpretations of the world – but abandon the term "projection" because it suggests that this anthropomorphic interpretation is caused in some way, whether by repressed instincts, archetypal energies, emotions, or even wishes. And this is precisely the proposal recently advanced by a contemporary cultural anthropologist, Stewart Guthrie.[1] Following a prestigious line of predecessors from E. B. Tylor to Robin Horton, Guthrie argues that religion is best understood as the attribution of humanlike qualities to the nonhuman world. But unlike many of them, he claims that this attribution is not irrational but an inevitable and natural mode of cognition, an attempt to bring coherence and significance to human experience. Religion is simply the most generalized and systematic form of it. It is systematized anthropomorphism.

Guthrie's proposal is interesting to us for several reasons. First, it springs from the conviction, which he shares with Evans-Pritchard, Clifford Geertz, and others, that humanistic theories of religion are in disarray and that the anthropology of religion is in "a general state of stagnation" and lacks any theoretical framework within which an analysis of religion can take place. Second, Guthrie, like Sierksma, holds that the discussion of anthropomorphism needs to be set within

---

[1] Stewart Guthrie, *Faces in the Clouds: A New Theory of Religion* (New York: Oxford University Press, 1993). Cf. his "A Cognitive Theory of Religion," *Current Anthropology*, 21, 2 (1980), 181–203. Guthrie has applied the theory to one of the new Japanese religions in *A Japanese New Religion: Rissho Kosei-kai in a Mountain Hamlet* (Ann Arbor: Center for Japanese Studies, 1988).

the context of an adequate theory of perception. It is a way of cognizing the world. And finally, his view that religion is an uncaused anthropomorphic interpretation of the world seems, on the surface at least, to have striking affinities with the later Feuerbach's views.

Guthrie is quite aware that there are several obstacles to a reconsideration of what he calls his "neo-Tylorean, cognitive theory" of religion: the still widespread use of functionalist social theory; the association of anthropomorphism with irrationalistic motivations of various sorts; and, above all, the distinctions among religion, science, and magic that have dominated so much theorizing about religion. Consequently, his latest book is an attempt to sweep these obstacles aside and to construct a new theory of religion on more adequate epistemological principles, the chief of which is that all of our cognitive dealings with the world are theory-laden and, hence, a type of interpretation. Religion is simply the systematization and generalization of one of the most basic and natural forms of human interpretation: perceiving the nonhuman world as humanlike.

It is impossible to discuss these obstacles to neo-Tylorean theory, Guthrie argues, without first dealing with the work of Emile Durkheim, on the one hand, and Bronislaw Malinowski, on the other. Durkheim, who was "The most influential theorist of religion as social glue,"[2] not only argued that religion basically serves the function of strengthening the commonly held beliefs and values of the group, its "collective representations," but polemicized against any attempt to define religion as anthropomorphism. Anthropomorphism cannot be the defining characteristic of religion, he claimed, because one of the great religious traditions of the world, Theravada Buddhism, lacks personal deities. The only substantive generalization that can be made about religion, Durkheim held, is that it deals with the sacred in contrast to the profane.

Guthrie attempts to show that these Durkheimian claims are false. Against Durkheim's functionalism he reiterates those now familiar criticisms made against functionalism in general: social systems are not completely integrated and cannot be treated as organisms; there are societies in which religion plays a divisive, not an integrating role and, hence, may become dysfunctional; and finally, morality and religion are not always connected with one another. But it was Durkheim's claim that anthropomorphism cannot be the defining

---

[2] Guthrie, *Faces*, p. 17.

characteristic of religion because there are no personal deities found in Theravada Buddhism that Guthrie believes is the greatest barrier to reconsidering Tylor's hypothesis.[3] But this claim, he argues, rests on a typical Western misunderstanding of these traditions. What Durkheim did not see is that these traditions combine philosophy and psychology in such a way as to tempt Western scholars into emphasizing their philosophical articulations and minimizing or ignoring their popular and mainstream expressions. Popular Buddhism is "well supplied with gods; indeed, they have pantheons."[4] Citing the works of Evans-Pritchard, Melford Spiro, and others, Guthrie claims that although there are atheistic Buddhist philosophies just as there are also atheistic Hindu and even Christian philosophies, it is a mistake to confuse these philosophies with popular religious belief and practice. Although in Theravada Buddhism the Buddha is not believed to be a creator, nevertheless, he is believed to possess superhuman powers such as omniscience. Although this status of the Buddha may seem ambiguous to Westerners, there is abundant evidence that popular Buddhism is replete with superhuman beings to whom prayers and petitions are directed.[5]

If Durkheim's functionalism made it difficult to entertain the thesis that religion was anthropomorphism in the service of interpreting the world, then it was Malinowski's famous distinctions among magic, science, and religion that seemed to thoroughly discredit it. Malinowski had argued that among the Melanesian islanders, who had been the object of his field work, there was a clear-cut division between the knowledge (science) needed to engage in agriculture and fishing, on the one hand, and magic, on the other. Although the islanders used magic in both agriculture and fishing, to be sure, it was only used to ward off those contingent events that they knew could thwart their best knowledge, such as bad weather, danger in the outer lagoons, noxious insects, and the like. But the islander, Malinowski claimed, would never assume that magic could be used as a substitute for knowledge. The two activities served two quite different functions, and there was a clear-cut distinction between them.[6]

---

[3] Guthrie's is only one of several recent attacks on Durkheim's hypothesis concerning Eastern religion. See Marco Orru and Amy Wang, "Durkheim, Religion, and Buddhism," *Journal for the Scientific Study of Religion*, 31, 1 (1992), 47–61.

[4] Guthrie, *Faces*, p. 19.

[5] Guthrie, *Faces*, pp. 191f.

[6] Bronislaw Malinowski, *Magic, Science and Religion and Other Essays*, with an intro. by Robert Redfield (Garden City, N.Y.: Doubleday, 1954), pp. 28ff.

Just as there is a distinction between knowledge and magic, there is also a sharp division between both of them and religion. Whereas magic has a definite and clear aim, the performances of religion, by contrast, have none. Initiation ceremonies, for example,

are a ritual and dramatic expression of the supreme power and value of tradition in primitive societies; they also serve to impress this power and value upon the minds of each generation, and they are at the same time an extremely efficient means of transmitting tribal lore, of insuring continuity in tradition and of maintaining tribal cohesion.[7]

This integrating function of religion, Malinowski claimed, can best be seen in mortuary rituals, where the power and fear of death threaten to disintegrate the group. Religion, by sacralizing and standardizing the instincts and impulses, "counteracts the centrifugal forces of fear, dismay, demoralization, and provides the most powerful means of reintegration of the group's shaken solidarity and of the reestablishment of its morale."[8]

Guthrie believes that Malinowski was correct in seeing that religion enables people to face uncertainty and risk but wrong in concluding that this differentiates it from science or common sense. In fact, magic, science, and religion are all attempts to make human experience coherent, and none of the reasons that are usually given for distinguishing among them can sustain critical analysis; particularly the reason that science has to do with empirical realities while religion deals with the supernatural. The difficulty with that and similar claims is, first of all, that the empirical–supernatural opposition, as Thomas Luckmann has noted, is a "vestige of 19th century scientism,"[9] but more fundamentally, this distinction rests on a faulty theory of knowledge in which it is assumed that the mind has immediate access to the structures of reality. We now know this naïve realism to be false, Guthrie claims, because all of our perceptions and cognitions are theory-laden, mediated by language, and informed by a "moveable host of metaphors, metonymies, and anthropomorphisms," to use Nietzsche's colorful language.[10] Our thoughts about the world, including our scientific thoughts, are laboriously realized constructions,

[7] Malinowski, *Magic, Science and Religion*, p. 40.
[8] Malinowski, *Magic, Science and Religion*, p. 53.
[9] Quoted by Guthrie in "A Cognitive Theory," p. 185.
[10] Friedrich Nietzsche, "On Truth and Lies in a Nonmoral Sense," in *Philosophy and Truth: Selections from Nietzsche's Notebooks of the Early 1870s*, trans. and ed. by Daniel Breazeale with a foreword by Walter Kaufmann (Atlantic Highlands, N.J.: Humanities Press, 1979), p. 84.

which is to say, interpretations. If, then, the distinction between science and religion rested on the assumption of a naïve realism, and if religious epistemologies tried to justify knowledge of the supernatural, then both

are refuted by the now apparent facts that religion, science, common sense, and indeed most "simple" sensory perception . . . *all* are forms of model-use, that models are analogical and metaphoric . . . and that anthropomorphic analogy is, a priori, neither more nor less rational than any other analogy.[11]

Guthrie's book is an attempt to justify the view that anthropomorphism is a natural and inevitable element in perception and cognition, and that religion is only the most systematized case of it. I cannot hope to do justice here to the complexity or the richness of the argument, but it is important to identify the main elements of it if one wishes to understand his position. Basically, they look something like this: All of the phenomena that human organisms perceive through the senses are initially ambiguous and must be interpreted in some fashion. Unlike many animals and insects, the human organism is instinctually underdetermined and is forced, therefore, to organize its experience by bringing it under some sort of conceptual and linguistic framework. These linguistic frameworks must not only be able to categorize phenomena but enable us to recognize them on subsequent occasions. If we are to be able to act, we cannot allow the world to remain ambiguous. Consequently, we resolve the ambiguity by means of a set of models based on experience of analogous phenomena. And we select these models on the basis of certain implicit criteria: whether the model and the phenomena are analogous in some respect; whether occurrences of phenomena can be anticipated from features of the model; and whether the model has subjective importance so far as the practical utility is concerned.

It should not be surprising, then, that human beings naturally select humanlike models in order to understand experience, or, to put the matter more abstractly, that they measure ambiguous phenomena against a human template. These humanlike models bring a high degree of unity to the diversity of human experience; they generate a wide variety of phenomena because they are multi-faceted and complex; and they are subjectively important to other humans. Moreover, since there are continuities of morphology and phylogeny between human and other forms of life so that it is not possible to draw

[11] Guthrie, "A Cognitive Theory," p. 186.

a sharp line between them, it is quite natural to interpret nonhuman behavior in anthropomorphic terms.

So compactly stated, Guthrie's theory may not seem very convincing, so let us briefly consider his discussion of animism, the attribution of life to the inanimate, which Tylor had argued was the origin of religion. Rather than being a primitive mode of thinking, animism should be seen, Guthrie argues, as an act of interpretation arising out of the important need to distinguish what is alive from what is not. This task is far more difficult than we moderns realize because animals in their natural environment are difficult to see and because the criteria of life are not at all evident and certain. Therefore, because we are frequently in doubt as to whether something is alive or not, and because this distinction is crucial in most circumstances, persons adopt the strategy "when in doubt assume that it is alive."[12]

From this example, we can see that the notion of "adopting a conceptual strategy" is fundamental to Guthrie's thesis. He holds the view that human beings do not simply see objects but always see them as something. Perception is "seeing as"; that is, seeing something as exemplifying a pattern of some sort.[13] The brain has a bias for seeing something rather than nothing, and it naturally jumps to whatever pattern makes the most sense out of an ambivalent situation. Since the perceptual world is underdetermined, and since multiple interpretations of it are always possible, the organism tends to bet, so to speak, on one interpretation rather than another. These unconscious choices naturally reflect implicit criteria such as coherence, the generation of the most information, relevance, and the like. If, then, perception may be considered as a kind of wager, and if the pay-off is significance, "the first bets to cover – those with the biggest payoff – are bets as high on the scale of organization as possible. The discoveries of order they yield are those we most need."[14]

For archaic persons – indeed, for all persons – the stakes are very high in the decision whether something is alive or not. And since uncertainty is also great, we are programmed to act on the best perceptual wagers or bets. And since animism is the best bet to make when confronting something we cannot see to be inanimate, perception usually produces it.[15] This is why animism is so natural to children, as Piaget has documented.

[12] Guthrie, *Faces*, p. 41.　　[13] Guthrie, *Faces*, chap. 2.
[14] Guthrie, *Faces*, p. 45.　　[15] Guthrie, *Faces*, p. 47.

Tylor was correct, then, in viewing animism as a mode of interpretation, Guthrie argues, but he erred in two respects: in defining it as the postulation of invisible spiritual beings, and in thinking that it had its origins in the attempt to explain death and dreams. Guthrie believes that his wager theory explains more, especially when combined with another hypothesis as to why spirits are so often believed to be invisible. Invisibility, he contends, is quite naturally attributed to beings once we recognize how widely it is found in nature – the invisibility of animals in their natural settings, their protective coloration, their ability to deceive in countless ways, and the like. These natural deceptions create great uncertainty about what is and what is not alive, which is, in any case, a difficult distinction to make, as biologists attest. Consequently, adults as well as children tend to see objects as either animate or inanimate, and it is not surprising, then, that animism is so pervasive throughout culture. Guthrie concludes:

Animism, then, seems intrinsic to perception. It is grounded in a sound perceptual strategy: to discover as much significance as possible by interpreting things and events with the most significant model. Significance in turn depends upon organization, and an organism typically is more significant than is inorganic matter. An account of animism thus needs no speculation about death and dreams, no inability to tell self from other, no wish fulfillment, and no peculiar irrationality. Instead, animism is a thread of interpretation that necessarily runs throughout perception. The mistake embodied in animism – a mistake we can discover only after the fact – is the price of our need to discover living organisms. It is a cost occasionally incurred by any animal that perceives.[16]

Given that nothing is more important to us than other human beings and that we are, therefore, especially sensitive to any possible human presence, it should not be surprising that we unconsciously "fit the world first with diverse humanlike templates."[17] Thus, anthropomorphism has many forms, ranging from the most literal to the metaphoric. Religion may be understood simply as the most integrated, generalized, and systematized form of it.[18] And since one of the most distinctive aspects of the human species is language, it also should not be surprising that religions tend to treat the world as a system of signs, as communication from "others." This would account, Guthrie suggests, for the very close relationship between magic and religion, because both direct messages to the nonhuman

[16] Guthrie, *Faces*, p. 61. [17] Guthrie, *Faces*, p. 91. [18] Guthrie, *Faces*, p. 200.

world and both "share an overestimation of its organization."[19] "Religion credits the nonhuman world with speaking a language, and magic credits it with sending and receiving calls."[20] If we ask why this overestimation of the world occurs, the answer lies in the human tendency to economize thought and action by ordering, generalizing, and building systems. Religious system building is merely an instance of the natural tendency to totalize experience.

Guthrie believes that his cognitive theory of religion has many virtues. First, it delineates anthropomorphism as a recognizable and universal phenomenon. Second, it has an internal coherence and simplicity other theories lack. Third, it does not claim that religion springs from special and irrational emotions or social causes, and, consequently, does not lead to unprofitable debates over the rationality of religion. Religion is simply one instance of model use, differing from others by virtue of its high degree of generalization and systematization. And finally, it is a general theory that links religion to other diverse phenomena. Indeed, it can even suggest how we consider the question whether animals have religion. If chimpanzees, for example, react with emotion and threats to rainstorms and waterfalls, as they seem to do, we might hypothesize that the animal's analogue to anthropomorphism is the "application of animal-like models to inanimate phenomena. If human religion is a kind of anthropomorphism, the animal analogue is a kind of zoomorphism."[21]

Among those who have previously regarded religion as anthropomorphism, Guthrie recognizes two philosophers and one anthropologist who have carried out the project most consistently: Hume, Feuerbach, and Horton. He naturally agrees with much that they have written, but his disagreements are especially illuminating, especially those with Horton and Feuerbach. Of the three, he finds Horton's position most congenial because it, too, is intellectualistic. His criticism is that Horton has nothing to say about anthropomorphism elsewhere in human culture and that he thinks the power of the anthropomorphic model in religion is due to its lack of alternative models. Consequently, when in industrial societies science offers a competitive model, Guthrie takes Horton to mean that anthropomorphism

---

[19] Guthrie, "A Cognitive Theory," p. 190.
[20] Guthrie, "A Cognitive Theory," p. 190.
[21] Guthrie, "A Cognitive Theory," p. 193.

necessarily withers.[22] Religion, in short, will inevitably be succeeded by science. But Guthrie holds that "Gods are uniquely intelligible," if, that is,

we define intelligibility as the ratio of information yielded to assumptions required. They give much explanatory return for little investment. Hypothesizing a humanlike being at work behind appearances accounts for effects of unparalleled diversity. This principle, that efficiency in explanations is the ratio of effects predicted to hypotheses made, underlies Occam's razor: do not multiply hypotheses unnecessarily . . .

As theories, then, humanlike models are parsimonious by virtue of the organization, diversity, and power of their originals . . . Humanlike models thus account for a vast array of things and events. They explain much with little.[23]

As regards Feuerbach, Guthrie, like so many others, identifies his position with that in *The Essence of Christianity* and seems unaware of the degree to which he later abandoned a causal view of projection. Hence, at least one of Guthrie's two major criticisms reflects this identification. The first is that Feuerbach did not realize that anthropomorphism need not be interpreted as a projection of the self once we realize that it is not unique and that there are occasional failures in its application.[24] The second criticism is more on the mark because it would apply to some degree to the later as well as the early Feuerbach: Feuerbach, like Hume, Marx, and Freud, overstresses the element of wish-fulfillment. Wish-fulfillment cannot be the basis of religion, Guthrie argues, because so many gods are wrathful, capricious, and terrifying.[25] Religion, Guthrie insists, springs not from wishes, fear, or any other emotion, but from our natural cognitive need to make sense of the world.

Among the many comments and criticisms in response to Guthrie's first published version of his cognitive theory of religion there were a few that articulated what, in general at least, would surely have been Feuerbach's own response to any primarily intellectualistic interpretation of religion: It does not follow, he would have argued, that because religion has a cognitive component it primarily serves cognitive needs. There is no reason, as some have argued, to see

---

[22] This is not the position that Horton took in his 1960 article "A Definition of Religion, and its Uses," to which I referred in Chapter 1, n. 82. There, it will be remembered, one of the functions of anthropomorphism in religion was that it served the purposes of communion.

[23] Guthrie, *Faces*, p. 189.

[24] Guthrie, *Faces*, p. 188.

[25] Guthrie, *Faces*, p. 13.

cognitive and emotional desires as disjunctive.[26] Furthermore, religion is an overdetermined phenomenon, as Feuerbach himself saw. It serves many functions and satisfies many needs. The issue is not whether religion serves cognitive needs but whether the same sort of explanatory interests we find in science and common sense can itself account for the persistence of religion or for religious behavior.

This is a point that the anthropologist Melford Spiro has consistently made. Like Guthrie, he also believes that the defining characteristic of religion is anthropomorphism, but he argues that religion persists because it satisfies powerful emotive and expressive as well as cognitive desires. Indeed, he thinks it important in discussing religion to distinguish three types of human desires: cognitive, substantive, and expressive.[27] So far as cognitive desires are concerned, no one need doubt that religious belief systems serve to "provide the members of society with meaning and explanation for otherwise meaningless and inexplicable phenomena."[28] But it should also be observed that "meaning" in this case not only has the narrow cognitive sense of "explaining" but also a "semantic-affective use," as when one asks about the meaning of a fortuitous accident, suffering, or death. It is this "semantic-affective" use of the term, Spiro notes, that we find in Max Weber's writings on religion, where he insists that the main function of the so-called high religions is to provide meaning for suffering as well as some prescription for escaping from or transcending it. In this sense, religions serve a cognitive need, but what they provide are not merely explanations in the scientific sense but "theodicies," a function that is difficult to ascribe to scientific explanations.

There is also an obvious set of desires, Spiro continues, that may be called "substantive" – for rain, the flourishing of crops, the abundance of animals, for food, nirvana, immortality, victory in war, recovery from illness, the health of a loved one, and numerous others. These substantive desires, Spiro has concluded, are probably the most important basis of religious behavior, and he argues that

---

[26] See J. H. M. Beattie, "On Understanding Ritual," in Bryan R. Wilson (ed.), *Rationality* (Evanston and New York: Harper & Row, 1970), pp. 240–268.

[27] Spiro is much more precise in his attempts to distinguish among "needs," "wants," "desires," "wishes," and "functions" than most anthropologists, including Guthrie. "Wants," he argues, do not have causal powers, nor do functional requirements unless they are recognized and satisfaction of them becomes the object of desire. Consequently, he prefers to use the term "desire." See his *Culture and Human Nature*, chap. 8.

[28] Spiro, *Culture and Human Nature*, p. 209.

this conclusion was not reached on the basis of some theory but from listening to what believers themselves say. "The most obvious basis for religious behavior is the one which any religious actor tells us about when we ask him – and, unlike some anthropologists, I believe him."[29] Spiro, in short, employs the same hermeneutical principle that guided Feuerbach: If one wishes to understand the religious consciousness, then one must pay attention to its most immediate and naïve utterances. And what the religious consciousness seems to desire is not a retrospective explanation but that some concrete wish be met.

Normally, Spiro notes, substantive human desires that can be met by naturalistic goals must be satisfied, and in the absence of competing technologies, religious techniques are believed to satisfy them. But, of course, there are everywhere those human needs and desires that arise from the unsatisfactory nature of existence, from suffering, or from death itself, and "*in the absence of competing goals for the reduction of anxiety*, belief that one is successfully pursuing these religious goals (heaven-like or nirvana-like states) serves to reduce this anxiety."[30] "Religions, as Weber points out, not only provides an explanation for, but it also promises redemption from, suffering. Religious techniques – performance of ritual, compliance with morality, faith, meditation, etc. – are the means by which this promise is felt to be fulfilled."[31]

Finally, there are what Spiro calls "expressive desires" that constitute a motivational source of religious behavior and belief, desires that emanate from those painful drives that seek reduction and about which "psychoanalysis has taught us so much."[32] In this respect, religion has to do with feelings of inadequacy, of guilt and shame, of moral anxiety, and the like. These drives and motives, unlike substantive desires, are largely unconscious because they are too painful to remain in consciousness. Nevertheless, in the absence of other cultural means of dealing with them, the vehicle by means of which they can be symbolically handled is in some, perhaps most, societies religion.[33]

It would, of course, be anachronistic to attribute Spiro's three sets of desires motivating religion to Feuerbach, especially the third set, about which "psychoanalysis has taught us so much." I have

[29] Spiro, *Culture and Human Nature*, p. 211.
[30] Spiro, *Culture and Human Nature*, p. 211.   [31] Spiro, *Culture and Human Nature*, p. 211.
[32] Spiro, *Culture and Human Nature*, p. 213.   [33] Spiro, *Culture and Human Nature*, pp. 213ff.

appealed to Spiro's writings only as an illustration of how it is possible to argue that cognitive and other types of needs are not disjunctive as Guthrie seems to suggest. Nevertheless, since there is an elective affinity, as I have suggested, between Feuerbach's views and some of Freud's, this affinity links him more closely to Spiro, who is a psychoanalyst as well as anthropologist, than to Guthrie. The basis of this affinity lies, of course, in Feuerbach's anthropology, his emphasis on the unique combination in the human organism of self-consciousness, embodiment, and the *Glückseligkeitstrieb*, a combination that creates anxiety when humans are confronted with the necessities of nature and death, and, above all, the desire for unconditional recognition from others. This view of the human situation also led him to acknowledge "cognitive," "substantial,'and "expressive" desires at work in religion, to use Spiro's terminology. Indeed, he so emphasized the desire for explanation and control that he sometimes argued, as I have shown, that religion would wither away as science and technology progressed.[34] Nevertheless, this motif, although undeniably present, is also incompatible with the dominant motif in his work, a motif that came so clearly to expression in that passage to which I have frequently appealed throughout this book:

Man with his ego or consciousness stands at the brink of a bottomless abyss; that abyss is his own unconscious being, which seems alien to him and inspires him with a feeling which expresses itself in words of wonderment such as: What am I? Where have I come from? To what end? And this feeling that I am nothing without a *not-I* which is distinct from me yet intimately related to me, something *other*, which is at the same time my *own* being, is the religious feeling.[35]

RELIGION AND THE NEED FOR TRANSFERENCE

It is extraordinary how well Feuerbach's later views stand up when compared with those of contemporary theorists; so much so that one can, by adopting his position, mount important criticisms of these theories. As I have shown, one of the principal reasons for this is that despite all of the methodological sophistication exemplified in these contemporary theories, they, too, are grounded in some conception of human nature, some philosophical anthropology. And it is on this topic that Feuerbach had the most interesting things to say.

[34] Feuerbach, *Lectures*, lecture 23.   [35] Feuerbach, *Lectures*, p. 311; *Vorlesungen*, pp. 349f.

Nevertheless, it also seems clear from these comparisons that Feuerbach's model, however suggestive, lacks certain elements that have made these contemporary theories interesting and suggestive. For example, even though Feuerbach might have criticized Berger's claim that religion is a response to marginal situations that threaten the cultural grid, Berger's theory of religion has one important feature Feuerbach's lacks, a theory of the relationship between religion and culture. This defect is, in turn, related to a second. Feuerbach concentrated his analysis of religion almost entirely on anthropomorphic religions and ignored those in which personal deities play a less central role, as in the case of Buddhism and those archaic religions so beloved by Mircea Eliade in which micro–macro symbolic patterns play a crucial role.

From the standpoint of modern social-scientific studies of religion, however, the main limitation of Feuerbach's view of religion, however suggestive its philosophical anthropology, is that his insights led to no positive research program. Social-scientific theories are distinguished from philosophical theories just because they generate new questions that can be answered only by empirical investigations of various sorts. Even though one can use Feuerbachian insights to criticize certain arguments in Freud, Sierksma, and Berger, his theory of religion cannot really be considered a viable one until it leads to further empirical inquiry. In Sierksma's case, for example, it follows from his theory of projection that, among other things, religions will fall into two broad classes: those primarily aimed at threats from external reality, such as primitive religions, and those intended to deal with internal threats, such as mysticisms and pietisms. This inferential hypothesis then lends itself to further investigation. Or in the case of Berger's theory, one can explore whether or not religions can best be seen as dealing with marginal situations that threaten to undermine the cultural grid. Is it the case, for example, that mysticisms lead to the relativizing of the secular world and, hence, prove to be a "worldshaking force"? How is it, then, that some mystical traditions have proved to be socially conservative? Or again, is it historically true that Protestantism provided the theological foundation for the secularization of the modern Western world? These questions all arise from Berger's theory. But what, one might ask, are the profitable questions that arise from the later Feuerbach's naturalist-existentialist approach? Is it not the case that we have here a philosophy of religion rather than a theory that might lead to a research program?

Perhaps these issues can best be addressed by engaging in one final "conversation," this time with the late cultural anthropologist Ernest Becker. Becker's work is especially relevant for three reasons. First of all, he was, like Feuerbach, primarily interested in the conceptions of human nature that underlie behavioral theories. Convinced that modern cultural theory "is in a state of useless overproduction" and that its "insignificant fragments" have been magnified all out of proportion to its major insights, Becker believed that it was time for a harmonization and synthesis of "the Babel views on man and on the human condition."[36] Second, his own unique intellectual synthesis led him to explore the relevance of it for both culture and religion. Third, although Becker was not himself interested in the implications of his view for an empirical research program, it has, in fact, spawned a very interesting one.[37]

But the most striking feature of Becker's work is that, although there is no evidence of his having ever read either the earlier or the later Feuerbach, the arguments of his last two books, as we shall see below, eerily echo just those themes that constitute what I have called the existentialist paradigm informing Feuerbach's *Religion* and *Lectures*. The human being differs from other organisms by virtue of being an embodied consciousness. As embodied, he/she has in common with all other organisms the "absolute dedication to Eros"; as conscious, he/she is able to transcend the body and to envisage his/her own death. This dual nature of the human constitutes the human dilemma: on the one hand, the person is driven to enjoy continued existence; on the other, he/she is "cursed with a burden no animal has to bear" – the awareness that he/she will die.[38] As a conscious and free creature, he/she is continually confronted with possibility; as finite and limited, these possibilities are themselves hemmed about by necessity, the main one of which is death. The roots of religion lie in this ontological structure of human being: the Promethean urge of the human organism to flourish and expand, and the anxiety of the psyche in the face of necessity and death. Confronted by loneliness

[36] Ernest Becker, *The Denial of Death* (New York: The Free Press, 1973), p. x.
[37] See Sheldon Solomon, Jeff Greenberg, and Tom Pyszczynski, "A Terror Management Theory of Social Behavior: The Psychological Functions of Self-Esteem and Cultural Worldviews," *Advances in Experimental Social Psychology*, 24 (1991), 93–185. See also Tom Pyszczynski, Jeff Greenberg, Sheldon Solomon, and James Hamilton, "A Terror Management Analysis of Self-Awareness and Anxiety: The Hierarchy of Terror," *Anxiety Research*, 2 (1990), 177–195.
[38] Ernest Becker, *Escape from Evil* (New York: The Free Press, 1975), p. 3.

and insignificance in the face of nature, it desires recognition and seeks self-esteem.

Perhaps the similarity of Becker's to Feuerbach's viewpoint is not so surprising when we consider that Becker's views were hammered out in dialogue with three important thinkers, two of whom were directly influenced by Feuerbach, Marx and Freud, and a third, Kierkegaard, who came out of the same post-Hegelian milieu as Feuerbach did. Although the perspectives of these three thinkers may seem irreconcilable, especially those of Freud and Kierkegaard, Becker himself believed that they were intimately related at many points and reinforced one another. As regards Freud and Kierkegaard, for example, he argued that "it was not until the epoch of the scientific atheist Freud that we could see the scientific stature of the theologian Kierkegaard's work."[39] It was Kierkegaard who taught us to see that human character is formed in the process of moving through the anxiety given with human freedom, on the one hand, and the awareness of limitation and death, on the other. Kierkegaard's view, Becker claimed, now enables us to see that Freud's preoccupation with sexuality was really a screen for his deeper preoccupation with the body and death. Psychoanalysis, in short, is really a doctrine about creatureliness, not sexuality. It is the human body that is the "curse of fate," and it is culture that is built upon the repression not of sexuality but of death; "not because man was a seeker only of sexuality, of pleasure, of life and expansiveness, as Freud thought, but because man was also primarily an avoider of death. *Consciousness of death* is the primary repression, not sexuality."[40]

The conception of human nature that Kierkegaard proposed and which Becker has adopted and modified is very familiar to any reader of the Christian theology that flourished in the period immediately after the Second World War: the theology of Rudolf Bultmann, Fritz Buri, Emil Brunner, the Niebuhr brothers, Paul Tillich, and Karl Rahner, to mention only the most prominent. But what makes Becker's appropriation of this anthropology both unique and yet similar to Feuerbach's view is that Becker does not simply emphasize the existential dilemma of consciousness and embodiedness but, like Freud, stresses the importance of Eros and desire. In fact, it is not an exaggeration to claim that we find here a contemporary restatement of Feuerbach's *Glückseligkeitstrieb* or metaphysical egoism, an egoism

[39] Becker, *Denial*, p. 67.   [40] Becker, *Denial*, p. 96.

characterized by Feuerbach in a statement that could as easily have been written by Becker:

By egoism I mean the necessary, indispensable egoism – not moral but metaphysical, i.e., grounded in man's essence without his knowledge or will – *the* egoism without which man cannot live, for in order to live I must continuously acquire what is useful to me and avoid what is harmful; *the* egoism that is inherent in the very organism, which appropriates those substances that are assimilable and excretes those that are not.[41]

For Becker this natural narcissism or drive to expand and flourish makes it imperative for humans to avoid evil and, as we shall see, to achieve self-esteem. This drive, he argues at some length in his book *Escape from Evil*, is, as the anthropologist Hocart also argued, the basis for ritual in archaic societies because ritual is a technique for giving and acquiring more life. By means of it, human beings have imagined that they took control of nature "and at the same time transcended that world by fashioning their own invisible projects which made them supernatural, raised them over and above material decay and death."[42]

Although Becker's emphasis on "the absolute dedication to Eros" may be regarded as almost a direct philosophical corollary to Feuerbach's *Glückseligkeitstrieb*, Becker linked this motif to a stark post-Darwinian vision of the struggle for existence that it would, of course, be anachronistic to attribute to Feuerbach. For Becker, the human consciousness is not merely faced with an indifferent nature upon which it is absolutely dependent, as was the case with Feuerbach, but with this "bone crushing, blood-drinking drama in all its elementality and necessity."[43] The human organism is not merely confronted with a mysterious not-I but with

a gory spectacle, a science-fiction nightmare in which digestive tracts fitted with teeth at one end are tearing away at whatever flesh they can reach, and at the other end are piling up the fuming waste excrement as they move along in search of more flesh.[44]

For Becker, as for Elias Canetti, "each organism raises its head over a field of corpses, smiles into the sun, and declares life good."[45]

This dual nature of the individual – conscious, on the one hand, and linked to the earth by the body, on the other – is the foundation upon

[41] Feuerbach, *Lectures*, p. 50; *Vorlesungen*, p. 61.
[42] Becker, *Escape from Evil*, p. 7.   [43] Becker, *Escape from Evil*, p. 2.
[44] Becker, *Escape from Evil*, p. 1.   [45] Becker, *Escape from Evil*, p. 2.

which Becker constructed several interesting and related intellectual themes, three of which are worth pausing over here. The first of these can hardly be called Feuerbachian and is, in fact, the source of a number of intellectual problems in Becker's thought that I am unable to pursue here. Becker argued that given the awe and terror the universe evokes in the human breast, the human person is driven to restrict his/her possibilities by developing a character, a character that he describes as a "vital lie."[46] The animal is prepared by virtue of its programmed instincts to close out certain perceptions and so to achieve a kind of equanimity. But the human self is continually confronted with horror and anxiety. It lives "in fear and trembling" at least some of the waking day.[47] Unable to face this absurdity, the average person blocks it out and over time constructs a character for the precise purpose of placing it between the lived terror of existence and himself/herself. Character is the way by which human beings make "routine, automatic, secure, self-confident activity possible."[48]

The value and importance of Freud, Kierkegaard, and, above all, Otto Rank, Becker believes, consists in their having come to grips with this central human problem. They saw that anxiety is endemic to self-consciousness and that to avoid anxiety human beings must impose limitations on their own characters and engage in self-deception. The individual learns to repress the entire spectrum of experience globally because it wants warmth and security. Kierkegaard gave us a picture of the ways in which one escapes this anxiety and avoids "becoming spirit," and Freud discovered how much human illness is caused by this repression. But "In the science of man it was Otto Rank, above all, who brought these fears into prominence, based his whole system of thought on them, and showed how central they were to any understanding of man."[49]

A second Beckerian theme is more distinctively Feuerbachian, and by now the reader will be familiar with it: the anxiety of the human self in the face of death. This anxiety of the self, Becker argued, as did Feuerbach, is a function of the rage-to-live together with the awareness of the dependence of the organism. But once again, Becker gave this theme a contemporary restatement. The vulnerability of the organism and, hence, the omnipresence of death are mediated to the conscious self through its own body and its physical processes; through sexuality, eating, and defecation. Becker believed that it was

[46] Becker, *Escape from Evil*, chap. 4.
[47] Becker, *Denial*, p. 59.   [48] Becker, *Denial*, p. 60.   [49] Becker, *Denial*, p. 53.

Freud who, more than any other thinker, saw how this human vulnerability found expression in certain neurotic patterns that have come to be identified with his theory: the Oedipus and Electra complexes, sexual anxieties of various sorts, anality, fear of castration, fetishism, and the like. But whereas Freud, especially in his early work, argued that these neurotic patterns are to be explained in terms of sexual repression, Becker argued that they may be better understood as ways in which the self deals with the vulnerability of the body. It is the fear of death rather than sexuality that is continually being repressed. Or, more precisely, sexuality is at the heart of repression because sexuality is that bodily activity most intimately and symbolically compounded both with the urge to live and the fear of dying.

A third theme is also Feuerbachian – the human need for self-esteem. And it is in the development of this theme that Becker made an intellectual move that Feuerbach, unfortunately, failed to make. I write "unfortunately" because it might have provided the link between culture and religion his theory so badly needs. Feuerbach, it will be remembered, had argued – inconsistently, I claimed – that religion has the practical purpose of harnessing nature to the human striving for happiness and, hence, that it is the first crude form of culture and will wither away as scientific knowledge and control increase.[50] Becker, like Berger, argued that it is one of the functions of culture to provide a structure for the instincts that is lacking biologically and to imbue the world with meaning and significance. But Becker differs from Berger in stressing that the primary function of culture is to provide the vehicle by means of which the human being can transcend death and gain self-esteem. Cultures erect the symbolic systems that enable the human

to transcend death not only by continuing to feed his appetites, but especially by finding a meaning for his life, some kind of larger scheme into which he fits; he may believe he has fulfilled God's purpose, or done his duty to his ancestors or family, or achieved something which has enriched mankind. This is how man assures the expansive meaning of his life in the face of the real limitations of his body; the "immortal self" can take very spiritual forms, and spirituality is not a simple reflex of hunger and fear. It is an expression of the will to live, the burning desire of the creature to count, to make a difference on the planet because he has lived, has emerged on it, and has worked, suffered, and died.[51]

[50] Feuerbach, *Lectures*, lecture 23.   [51] Becker, *Escape from Evil*, p. 3.

Cultures, then, are systems of heroism in the broad sense that to be a hero means to leave something behind that witnesses to the worthwhileness of existence. It involves the feeling that one has lived for a transcendent purpose. Since this is also the function of religion, culture is sometimes also considered to be sacred. When it is, "Culture is in this sense 'supernatural'" because it has "in the end the same goal: to raise men above nature, to assure them that in some ways their lives count in the universe more than merely physical things count."[52]

It is this postulated relationship between culture and self-esteem, which, in turn, is rooted in his conception of human nature, that has attracted the attention of a group of empirically minded social psychologists in the United States, because they believe that it provides the basis for a sophisticated, empirical research program in their academic discipline, social psychology.[53] Contemporary social psychology, they argue, does not at present contain a general theoretical conception of human social behavior that can both adequately account for the behavior of human beings in historical and cultural contexts and organize and integrate existing empirical work or guide future research. Social psychology, rather, is dominated by a number of "mini-theories" each of which is directed at some narrowly circumscribed form of behavior. But progress in most scientific disciplines has been made possible by the existence of broad theoretical paradigms, such as evolution in biology and quantum mechanics in physics. Ernest Becker's work, they maintain, presents just such a broad and powerful framework because it explains a wide range of existing data on human social behavior and it raises important questions and issues not currently addressed by other theoretical frameworks. And although psycho-dynamically based theories of personality have often been dismissed as nonfalsifiable by social psychologists, the proponents of this "Terror Management Theory" argue that a large array of important and empirically testable hypotheses are generated by it.

This theory assumes that one of the most important functions of culture is to assuage the anxiety engendered by the human awareness of vulnerability and death. Culture does this by creating a sense of order and a meaningful conception of reality that enable persons to acquire self-esteem when they have met the standards inherent in the

---

[52] Becker, *Escape from Evil*, p. 4.   [53] See n. 37 above.

social roles and "recipes for behavior" that constitute culture. Self-esteem consists in the perception that one has been recognized as a valuable member of a culture. To the degree that one of the basic impulses of life is to avoid anxiety and terror, it should follow that individual lives are focused on maintaining self-esteem. Thus by maintaining the "cultural-anxiety buffer" and by meeting the standards set by the culture, the individual is able to keep the terror associated with the awareness of mortality out of consciousness. "In essence, the cultural-anxiety buffer facilitates the repression of anxiety concerning one's vulnerability and mortality."[54]

Although Becker's theory of religion and culture is based on an anthropology that is remarkably similar to Feuerbach's, one of the important but interesting ironies is that he came to a conclusion about the value of religion directly opposite to Feuerbach's. If Feuerbach argued that religion is basically an illusion born out of the confrontation of the self with an indifferent nature, Becker argued that the religious illusion is justified because it enables the self to live with the "lived terror of creation." Under the influence of Otto Rank, Becker concluded that given the anxiety which the existential dilemma precipitates, human beings have an inherent need for religion and "should cultivate the passivity of renunciation to the highest powers no matter how difficult it is."[55]

This argument is particularly interesting because it suggests the possibility that Berger once proposed when he suggested that it might be possible to turn Feuerbach on his head as he had once done to Hegel. It might be possible to argue on Feuerbachian grounds that religious faith not only is an expression of the deepest human desire but serves genuine human needs and, hence, is legitimate. Human beings need to deal with the indifference of nature by acquiring some sense of significance, and religion provides it.

To understand how Becker arrived at this conclusion, it is first necessary to rehearse briefly the basic elements of his discussion of transference, the term he uses to denote religious belief. This term, as I have already noted in Chapter 7, emerged out of the discourse of psychoanalysis and normally has close associations with the word "projection." Technically construed, the term refers to the process by which patients displace onto their psychotherapist feelings and ideas

---

[54] Solomon, Greenberg, and Pyszczynski, "A Terror Management Theory of Social Behavior," pp. 101f.

[55] Becker, *Denial*, p. 174.

derived from previous figures in their lives.[56] But just as the term "projection" has been broadly construed, so also has "transference." Becker used the term to refer to the way in which the human self focuses on and places its hopes and aspirations in heroes, group leaders, magic helpers of all kinds, and, even, the universe. And he also believed that Freud and others had shown that this is a universal tendency in human nature because the human is a "trembling animal." But Becker concluded that just because transference is a universal human tendency, this phenomenon must be seen in terms of the basic structure of the human organism itself; that is, in terms of the basic existential dilemma faced by a conscious organism in the grip of the will to live, on the one hand, and confronted with the awe and terror of creation and death, on the other.

This existential dilemma leads, as we have seen, to a paradoxical situation in which the fear of death leads to a fear of life, that is, of fully experiencing one's own unique individuality and its possibilities. From this standpoint, transference is rooted in the desire to tame the terror of creation, to overcome one's sense of helplessness and impotence by endowing the transference object with transcendent powers. This transference object then becomes the focus of one's freedom because everything is dependent upon it. It is, in fact, a form of fetishism, and since the fetish sums up all of the other natural forms of dependence and emotions, the loss of this transference object strikes fear into the human heart.[57] If the fear of life is one aspect of transference, the companion fear of death is another, and it also leads to taking comfort from the power of the transference object. Indeed, it is this fear that explains the urge to deify these objects, to place certain persons on pedestals and to attribute to them extra powers. By identifying with these objects the self hopes to achieve a type of immortality.

It might be useful to note in passing that by using the term "transference" in contrast to "projection" and then linking it to what he has called the "twin ontological motives" – the urge to stand out as an individual, and the urge to lose oneself in a larger whole – Becker was able to deal with one of the criticisms frequently made of Feuerbach; namely, that he tended to identify religion with anthropomorphism. For Becker, transference may take two forms: the first, in which a premium is put on uniqueness and individuality;

[56] Charles Rycroft, *A Critical Dictionary of Psychoanalysis* (New York: Penguin, 1968), p. 168.
[57] Becker, *Denial*, p. 146.

and the second, in which the self merges with the rhythms and vitalities of nature and so overcomes the isolation of the individual ego. Both types of transference find a religious form of expression: the first in anthropomorphic religions in which the symbol system is such that the self is made to stand out; the second in participatory religions, in which the organism surrenders itself to the rhythms and vitalities of nature in order to overcome the "terror of history." From Becker's point of view, then, we might say that Feuerbach explored only one of the basic modes of transference, anthropomorphism, although there was nothing in his model that logically precluded him from investigating the other.

Because transference seems to spring out of either helplessness (Freud) or inner emptiness (Fromm), it might seem that it should be regarded negatively. But Becker argues that just because transference is so connected to the very foundations of organismic life, it would be wrong to do so. And to defend this claim, he appeals to something like Feuerbach's *Glückseligkeitstrieb*. Human beings long to "feel right" and good about themselves, and they push themselves to maximize this feeling. They need to infuse their lives with value so that they can pronounce them good. Indeed, "The transference-object is then a natural fetishization for man's highest yearnings and strivings."[58] Rank saw that the human being is a theological and not only a biological being, and by making the universe itself the subject of awe, religion deprives the finite idols and fetishes of their power. "Transference heroics gives man precisely what he needs: a certain degree of sharply defined individuality, a definite point of reference for his practice of goodness, and all within a certain secure level of safety and control."[59] "Projection is necessary and desirable for self-fulfillment. Otherwise man is overwhelmed by his loneliness and separation and negated by the very burden of his own life."[60]

But given the "twin ontological motives" it is impossible to maximize this longing in any straightforward way. On the one hand, the individual self wants to be recognized as unique, to stand out from the rest of creation; on the other, it is fearful of standing out and wants to merge its identity with some larger whole. The individual feels small and impotent in the face of transcendent nature and wants to have a "feeling of kinship with the All."[61] The dilemma, then, is that if the self gives in to the longing to submerge its identity in the whole, it

[58] Becker, *Denial*, p. 155.   [59] Becker, *Denial*, p. 158.
[60] Becker, *Denial*, p. 158.   [61] Becker, *Denial*, p. 152.

fails to become a concrete individual. If, on the other hand, the individual "expands Eros" by cutting itself off from its natural dependency and "from duty to a larger creation . . . [it] . . . pulls away from the healing powers of gratitude and humility that . . . [it] . . . must naturally feel for having been created, for having been given the opportunity of life experience."[62] The issue for Becker, then, is not whether there will be a religious transference but "What is *creative projection*? What is *life-enhancing* illusion?"[63]

In the last chapter of *The Denial of Death* entitled "Psychology and Religion: What is the Heroic Individual?" Becker attempted to answer this question, to state the basic conditions for a life-enhancing illusion, an illusion that will strike the delicate balance between the urge to stand out, on the one hand, and the longing to merge with the Whole, on the other, an illusion that will combine the most intrinsic Eros with the most complete Agape. From a Feuerbachian perspective, this is an edifying chapter, not because it is successful but because Becker's attempt to build a case for religion on this anthropological foundation so clearly collapses. Although seeming to endorse the power and insight of the traditional religions regarding the true condition of humankind – he believes that Judaism, Christianity, and Buddhism all hold that "man is doomed to his present form"[64] – it ends with a solution that is clearly incompatible in some important respect with all of them. Arguing that neither science nor religion should obscure the truth that "creation is a nightmare spectacular taking place on a planet that has been soaked for hundreds of millions of years in the blood of all its creatures," Becker concludes his book with a Stoical observation worthy of Freud, of whom he was so critical: "The most that any one of us can seem to do is to fashion something – an object or ourselves – and drop it into the confusion, make an offering of it, so to speak, to the life force."[65]

Becker's failure, I will argue, is not due to the limits of his own ability to imagine a religious illusion but to the inability of any religion to meet the three criteria he has stipulated for a healthy religious transference: (1) The transference must strike a balance between the two "ontological motives"; (2) it must acknowledge the limits of human nature; and (3) it must not obscure in any way the "lived truth of creation," a truth Becker has summed up forcefully in this fashion:

[62] Becker, *Denial*, p. 153.   [63] Becker, *Denial*, p. 158.
[64] Becker, *Denial*, p. 281.   [65] Becker, *Denial*, p. 285.

The soberest conclusion that we could make about what has actually been taking place on the planet for about three billion years is that it is being turned into a vast pit of fertilizer. But the sun distracts our attention, always baking the blood dry, making things grow over it, and with its warmth giving the hope that comes with the organism's comfort and expansiveness.[66]

It is, for example, because the Utopian visions of Norman O. Brown, Herbert Marcuse, and Alan Harrington fail to meet this second criterion, the limits of human nature, that Becker rejects them as well as the contemporary therapeutic blends of psychotherapy and religion that are so fashionable. Becker found Brown's and Marcuse's call for a completely liberated and unrepressed life to be quite naïve psychologically, just as he thought that Harrington's vision of a society without death was utterly unrealistic. Why, he asked, "do brilliant thinkers become so flaccid, dissipate so carelessly their own careful arguments?"[67] The same appeal to the limits of human nature is also made against all of the recent attempts to blend psychotherapy with religion, attempts that Becker believed inevitably wind up with an untenable mixture of psychology and speculative metaphysics of various sorts. Although psychotherapy can achieve many good things, the notion that it can give self-knowledge is a deception. And as for its pretense to religion, it simply cannot give human beings what they want most, immortality, an argument Feuerbach might also have made.

It is Becker's treatment of the more traditional religions, however, that is most revealing, because despite his apparent endorsement of them, they seem as incompatible with his criteria for life-enhancing illusions as do the humanistic Utopias of Brown and Marcuse. Ironically, we can see this most clearly in his treatment of those two philosopher-theologians, Kierkegaard and Tillich, with whose anthropology Becker has most in common. The example of Kierkegaard is particularly interesting if only because throughout his book Becker has appealed to him as a corrective to Freud. It was Kierkegaard, we were told, who "understood the problem of human character and growth with an acuity that showed the uncanny mark of genius, coming as it did so long before clinical psychology."[68]

Given Becker's dependence upon Kierkegaard, we might reasonably have expected him to endorse also Kierkegaard's concept of religious faith because faith is precisely the human movement of the spirit that

---

[66] Becker, *Denial*, p. 283.　　[67] Becker, *Denial*, p. 264.　　[68] Becker, *Denial*, p. 93.

enhances individuality, on the one hand, while emphasizing creaturely necessity, on the other. Becker did, in fact, regard Kierkegaard's "knight of faith" as one of the most beautiful and challenging creative illusions ever put forth by an author, an illusion, he added, that "is contained in most religions in one form or another."[69] But no sooner had he lauded Kierkegaard's leap of faith as a human ideal than Becker suddenly drew back from it because Kierkegaard, as a good Christian, believed that this leap of faith does not depend upon human effort at all but is a gift of grace. Apparently, one cannot be a knight of faith, Becker observed, without first having been dubbed by some higher majesty.[70]

Even more surprising, Becker concluded his discussion of the "knight of faith" with the observation that if one compares Kierkegaard's own life as a Christian with Freud's as an agnostic, "there is no balance sheet to draw." For every shortcoming in Freud, there is a corresponding one in Kierkegaard. Consequently, there is nothing to choose, we are told, between "religious creatureliness and scientific creatureliness."[71] In fact, the very ideal of a redeemed hero itself appears fantastic and unreal because "The most one can achieve is a certain relaxedness, an openness to experience that makes him less of a driven burden on others."[72]

But, we may ask, if there is nothing to choose between Kierkegaard and Freud, between religious and scientific creatureliness, what is the possible justification for the claim that "Projection is necessary and desirable for self-fulfillment"?

Becker's treatment of Paul Tillich is even more instructive. Tillich's *Systematic Theology* was an attempt to provide a modern restatement of the Christian faith, and it revolves around a reformulation of the Christian doctrine of redemption in Jesus Christ. The traditional doctrine of the Incarnation, Tillich had argued, can better be stated in terms of the concept of the New Being. By this, Tillich meant to say that in Jesus of Nazareth, the Christian believes that a New Being has occurred under the conditions of estranged existence. This being is new because it has conquered the gap between essence and existence and because it has overcome the estranged character of existential being.[73]

Becker seemed almost as dubious about this gospel of the New Being as he did about Kierkegaard's more traditional formulation of

---

[69] Becker, *Denial*, p. 258.   [70] Becker, *Denial*, p. 258.
[71] Becker, *Denial*, p. 259.   [72] Becker, *Denial*, p. 259.
[73] Tillich, *Systematic Theology*, II.118.

faith. "What can it mean," he skeptically and rhetorically asked, "for something new to emerge from such an animal and to triumph over his nature?"[74] Granted that Tillich conceded that the New Being is a myth and that "The only argument for the truth of this Gospel of the New Being is that the message *makes* itself true,"[75] nevertheless, this does "not let us off the hook so easily about the nature of the real world."[76] Consequently, Becker turned away from the Christian theologian of the *Systematic Theology* to the philosopher of *The Courage to Be*. In the latter book, Tillich argued for a faith that transcends theism, and he defended a type of courage in which persons absorb into their being the maximum amount of nonbeing; or, in other words, they turn away from any hope for redemption in the world and embrace the anxiety of meaninglessness. The meaninglessness of existence, Becker argued, is what humans must face. Consequently, any truly life-enhancing illusion must forsake the ideal of "a creature who is transformed and who transforms the world in turn in some miraculous ways" in favor of a creature who "takes more of the world into himself and develops new forms of courage and endurance."[77]

Feuerbach could easily have agreed with the previous sentence. The human problem is to develop new forms of courage and endurance in the face of meaninglessness, if by meaninglessness it is meant that the universe is utterly indifferent to individual human welfare and that no creature can be miraculously redeemed or redeem the world. But Feuerbach would also have observed that it is just this ideal that makes it impossible for Becker to salvage anything significant from traditional religions or to distinguish his own position from agnosticism, because it is the essence of religion to believe that the universe is not utterly indifferent and that human beings can be miraculously redeemed. It was for this reason that he argued that miracles are so important for religious faith, far more important than rationalists concede. Miracles are crucial not because the believer is indolently attracted by the wondrous and inexplicable or is inherently superstitious but because a miracle is held to be "proof positive that the being who performed it is all-powerful, supernatural, and divine."[78] Miracles represent the triumph of possibility over necessity, of grace over nature. It is the very nature of faith, as both Luther and Kierkegaard saw, to believe that with God everything is possible and

[74] Becker, *Denial*, p. 277.
[75] Quoted by Becker, *Denial*, pp. 278f.   [76] Becker, *Denial*, p. 278.
[77] Becker, *Denial*, p. 279.   [78] Feuerbach, *Lectures*, p. 238; *Vorlesungen*, p. 267.

that everything is done "for us." This is why the event of redemption in Christ is as central to the Christian as the Exodus is to the Jew. They confirm, prove, and attest that life is not meaningless because there is a Lord of nature and history who is able to redeem and to save.

Becker further compounds his difficulties in reconciling his life-enhancing vision with religion by reason of his post-Darwinian view of nature. It is not a benign context for human life but a science-fiction nightmare, the outpouring of a blind force that "seeks to expand in an unknown direction for unknown reasons."[79] Like Schopenhauer's blind Will or Nietzsche's will-to-power, it has no aim or purpose. Its creator, if it has a creator, can only be what Sylvia Plath named "King Panic," the King of the Grotesque. And Becker not only accepts this but makes its acceptance the criterion of any religious illusion worthy of the name.

What are we to make of a creation in which the routine activity is for organisms to be tearing others apart with teeth of all types – biting, grinding flesh, plant stalks, bones between molars, pushing the pulp greedily down the gullet with delight, incorporating its essence into one's own organization, and then excreting with foul stench and gasses the residue. Everyone reaching out to incorporate others who are edible to him . . . Not to mention the daily dismemberment and slaughter in "natural" accidents of all types: an earthquake buries alive 70 thousand bodies in Peru, automobiles make a pyramid heap of over 50 thousand a year in the U.S. alone, a tidal wave washes over a quarter of a million in the Indian Ocean. Creation is a nightmare spectacular taking place on a planet that has been soaked for hundreds of millions of years in the blood of all its creatures.[80]

The reason this vision of the world compounds Becker's difficulty is obvious. It is psychologically impossible for a Jewish, Christian, or Muslim monotheist first to accept the "lived truth" that creation is a nightmare spectacular and then to embrace the faith that creation is "good." The first vision excludes the second, if by "good" is meant what these religious traditions mean; namely, that God loves and is concerned for the creatures. The "eyes of faith," we have been told by generations of Jewish and Christian theologians, tell us that we see the discord and evil in the world as the result of human sin and not God's will. The eyes of faith see that "in, with, and under" what may appear to be an indifferent world order there are the "everlasting arms" of a being who is loving beyond imagination. To be sure, this beneficence may not be present to the eyes of unfaith, but for those who believe in

<hr />

[79] Becker, *Denial*, p. 284.   [80] Becker, *Denial*, pp. 282f.

revelation, reality is transformed. Indeed, one of the functions of revelation is to enable the believer to believe that an apparently indifferent world order is actually a manifestation of infinite wisdom.

But if this is the nature of faith, one cannot both praise the insights of Judaism and Christianity because they teach that human beings should "wait in a condition of openness toward miracle and mystery, in the lived truth of creation" and equate this lived truth with a "science-fiction nightmare."

It is ironical that in this respect Feuerbach, who was more hostile to religion than Becker, actually provided the religious believer with a less radical alternative than did Becker, who argued that religion is necessary for human fulfillment. In Feuerbach's pre-Darwinian view, *Dasein* views the all-encompassing nature upon which it is absolutely dependent in more complex terms than as a nightmare spectacular. Nature can be seen as eternal, infinite, omnipresent, wise, just, even good.[81] Indeed, it is just because nature has these qualities that the religious imagination can fasten on them and abstract, unify, and personify them. It can then explain the evils that occur as punishments or as the work of an evil being. It is this logic that "accounts for the Christian belief that nature was once a paradise, in which there was nothing hostile to man, but that this paradise was lost through sin, which aroused God's anger."[82] And it is for the same reason that Feuerbach claimed that he was sympathetic to nature worship because he felt the same motives in his own heart, "motives which, if they were not countered by culture, science, and philosophy, would still make me a nature worshiper today."[83] For him, then, the problem that nature presents is not that it is a nightmare spectacular but that it does not present itself to the individual as a feeling being, a *Gemütswesen*, moved by human wishes and desires. *Dasein* is an affective being and it cannot, finally, worship an affectless being, a being who does not recognize and act on behalf of the believer.[84] The individual wants a living, feeling being, a God with both power and a heart.

Feuerbach would surely have concluded that Becker could not possibly have thought his own life-enhancing illusion to be compatible with monotheism had he observed the basic hermeneutical rule of listening to what believers themselves say. Any hermeneutics of

[81] Feuerbach, *Lectures*, pp. 111f.; *Vorlesungen*, p. 126.
[82] *Lectures*, p. 112; *Vorlesungen*, p. 128.
[83] *Lectures*, p. 90; *Vorlesungen*, p. 104.   [84] Feuerbach, *Religion*, para. 32.

suspicion must begin with this initial and basic act of charity. And what believers wish and desire comes to expression in their hymns, prayers, and expressions of devotion. In this sense, Feuerbach might have criticized Becker for the same reason he chastised Hegel.

Speculation makes religion say only what it *itself* thought and expressed far better than religion; it assigns a meaning to religion without any reference to the *actual* meaning of religion; it does not look beyond itself. I, on the contrary, let religion itself speak; I constitute myself only its listener and interpreter, not its prompter.[85]

When investigators listen to what believers themselves say, they will discover that these believers' hopes and beliefs are not bounded by the limits of nature. Nor do these believers find it to be good news that creation is a science-fiction nightmare. What they hope for and desire can be seen in their hymns and prayers; and what these hymns and prayers reveal, Feuerbach argued, is the faith that each one of them is the object of a personal, divine subject who transcends nature and who will, in the end, enable them to transcend it also. That is the religious illusion; and although Feuerbach could understand why it has such a hold on human existence, he finally rejected it for all of the reasons given in this book.

[85] Feuerbach, *Christianity*, pp. xxxvf.; *Christentums*, pp. 16f.

Select bibliography

PRIMARY WORKS

There are two complete editions of Feuerbach's work in German, but none in English. The first is the Bolin–Jodl edition (*Sämtliche Werke*) published in ten volumes between 1903 and 1911 by Frommann Verlag in Stuttgart. These ten plus two additional volumes were then reprinted in facsimile between 1960 and 1964 under the editorship of Hans-Martin Sass. The eleventh volume contains Feuerbach's inaugural dissertation (in Latin), his *Thoughts on Death and Immortality*, and an extensive bibliography of Feuerbach scholarship. The twelfth is a double volume containing Sass's expanded version of Bolin's *Selected Correspondence from and to Ludwig Feuerbach* together with some of Bolin's memoirs.

The second edition of Feuerbach's work is a new critical edition prepared under the editorship of Werner Schuffenhauer (*Gesammelte Werke*) and published by Akademie-Verlag in Berlin (1981–1993). As of this date, it comprises nineteen volumes and includes everything from his earliest writings to his correspondence. It is indispensable for serious scholarly work because it presents the textual variations of the various editions of Feuerbach's major works, a particularly valuable feature in the case of *The Essence of Christianity*, and it restores the original text of the *Theogonie*, which the Bolin–Jodl edition had sought to make more comprehensible by radical cuts and editing.

I have used Schuffenhauer's critical edition, but for the convenience of the English reader I have first cited an English translation when it exists and then noted the corresponding passages in the *Gesammelte Werke*. I have occasionally altered the English translation where I thought accuracy was served and have restored Feuerbach's characteristic practice of italicizing words for emphasis. A key to the abbreviations of works most often cited is to be found at the beginning of the book.

PRIMARY WORKS IN ENGLISH TRANSLATION

The Essence of Christianity, translated by George Eliot, with an introductory essay by Karl Barth and foreword by H. Richard Niebuhr (New York:

Harper & Row, 1957). This is the translation of the second edition by the famous English novelist; it was first published in 1854.

The Essence of Faith According to Luther, translated and with an introduction by Melvin Cherno (New York: Harper & Row, 1967). This is a translation of the slightly worked over edition that Feuerbach himself prepared for the first volume of his collected works in 1846.

The Fiery Brook: Selected Writings of Ludwig Feuerbach, translated with an introduction by Zawar Hanfi (Garden City, N.Y.: Doubleday, 1972). In addition to other selections this paperback volume contains translations of the important *Towards a Critique of Hegel's Philosophy* (1839) as well as *Preliminary Theses on the Reform of Philosophy* and *Principles of the Philosophy of the Future*.

Lectures on the Essence of Religion, translated by Ralph Manheim (New York: Harper & Row, 1967).

Principles of the Philosophy of the Future, translated with an introduction by Manfred H. Vogel, Library of Liberal Arts (Indianapolis: Bobbs-Merrill, 1966). This is a translation of the text that appeared in the Bolin–Jodl edition, and the paragraph numbers vary slightly from those in the critical edition.

Thoughts on Death and Immortality from the Papers of a Thinker, along with an Appendix of Theological-Satirical Epigrams, Edited by One of his Friends, translated with introduction and notes by James A. Massey (Berkeley: University of California Press, 1980). Massey's introduction is especially interesting.

BIBLIOGRAPHIES OF LITERATURE ON FEUERBACH

There are four bibliographies in addition to the then definitive one compiled by Hans-Martin Sass in volume XI of the *Sämtliche Werke* listed above. The first is an enlargement of his earlier bibliography by Sass himself and appears as an appendix to Hermann Lübbe and Hans-Martin Sass (eds.), *Atheismus in der Diskussion, Kontroversen um Ludwig Feuerbach* (Grunewald: Chr. Kaiser Verlag, 1975). The second has been complied by Uwe Schott in *Die Jugendentwicklung Ludwig Feuerbachs bis zum Fakultätwechsel 1825* (Göttingen: Vandenhoeck & Ruprecht, 1973), which, although it is less extensive than Sass's enlargement, has a few items that Sass seems to have missed. The third is by Erich Schneider in *Die Theologie und Feuerbachs Religionskritik: Die Reaktion der Theologies des 19. Jahrhunderts auf Ludwig Feuerbachs Religionskritik mit Ausblicken auf das 20. Jahrhundert und einem Anhang über Feuerbach* (Göttingen: Vandenhoeck & Ruprecht, 1972), which, as the title indicates, primarily has to do with the reaction of nineteenth-century theologians to Feuerbach's work. The fourth is a bibliography compiled by Scott Stebelman covering English-language material about Feuerbach published from 1873 to 1991 in Walter Jaeschke (ed.), *Sinnlichkeit und Rationalität: Der Umbruch in der Philosophie des 19. Jahrhunderts: Ludwig Feuerbach*, Internationale Gesellschaft der Feuerbach-Forscher (Berlin: Akademie-Verlag, 1992). There is also a useful annotated bibliography in Michael von Gagern, *Ludwig Feuerbach: Philosophie-und-Religionskritik Die "Neue" Philosophie* (Munich: Anton Pustet, 1970).

SELECTED WORKS ON FEUERBACH AND USEFUL BACKGROUND READING

Barth, Karl, "Feuerbach," in *Protestant Thought: From Rousseau to Ritschl: Being the Translation of Eleven Chapters of Die Protestantische Theologie im 19. Jahrhundert*. Translated by Brian Cozzens (New York: Harper, 1959).

Braun, Hans-Jürg, *Die Religionsphilosophie Ludwig Feuerbachs: Kritik und Annahme des Religiösen* (Stuttgart-Bad Cannstatt: Friedrich Frommann Verlag, 1972).

Ludwig Feuerbachs Lehre vom Menschen (Stuttgart-Bad Cannstatt: Friedrich Frommann Verlag, 1971).

Brazill, William J., *The Young Hegelians* (New Haven: Yale University Press, 1970).

Cherno, Melvin, "Ludwig Feuerbach and the Intellectual Basis of Nineteenth Century Radicalism." Ph.D. dissertation, Stanford University, 1955.

Fiorenza, Francis Schüssler, "Feuerbach's Interpretation of Religion and Christianity," *The Philosophical Forum*, 11, 2 (1979–1980), 161–181.

von Gagern, Michael, *Ludwig Feuerbach: Philosophie- und Religionskritik "Die Neue" Philosophie* (Munich: Anton Pustet, 1970).

Glasse, John, "Why did Feuerbach Concern himself with Luther?" *Revue internationale de philosophie*, 26, 101 (1972), 364–385.

Harvey, Van A. "Feuerbach on Religion as Construction," in *Theology at the End of Modernity: Essays in Honor of Gordon D. Kaufman*, ed. Sheila Greeve Davaney (Philadelphia: Trinity Press International, 1991), pp. 249–268.

Hook, Sidney, *From Hegel to Marx: Studies in the Intellectual Development of Karl Marx* (New York: The Humanities Press, 1950).

Janowski, J. Christine, *Der Mensch als Mass: Untersuchungen zum Grundgedanken und zur Struktur von Ludwig Feuerbachs Werk*, Ökumenische Theology (Cologne: Benziger Verlag Zurich; Gütersloh: Gütersloher Verlagshaus Gerd Mohn, 1980), vol. VII.

Kamenka, Eugene, *The Philosophy of Ludwig Feuerbach* (London: Routledge & Kegan Paul, 1970).

Löwith, Karl, *From Hegel to Nietzsche: The Revolution in Nineteenth-Century Thought*, translated by David E. Green (Garden City, N.Y.: Doubleday, 1967).

Lübbe, Hermann and Hans-Martin Sass (eds.), *Atheismus in der Diskussion: Kontroversen um Ludwig Feuerbach, Systematische Beiträge*, No. 17 (Munich: Chr. Kaiser Verlag, 1975).

McLellan, David, *The Young Hegelians and Karl Marx* (New York: Praeger, 1969).

Massey, Marilyn Chapin, "Censorship and the Language of Feuerbach's *Essence of Christianity* (1841)," *The Journal of Religion*, 65 (1985), 173–195.

Rawidowicz, S., *Ludwig Feuerbachs Philosophie: Ursprung und Schicksal*, 2nd ed. (Berlin: Walter de Gruyter, 1964).

Rotenstreich, Nathan, *Basic Problems of Marx's Philosophy* (Indianapolis: Bobbs-Merrill, 1965).

Sass, Hans-Martin, *Ludwig Feuerbach in Selbstzeugnissen und Bilddokumenten dargestellt* (Hamburg: Rowohlt Taschenbuch Verlag, 1978).

Schmidt, Alfred, *Emanzipatorische Sinnlichkeit: Ludwig Feuerbachs anthropologischer Materialismus*, Reihe Hanser 109 (Munich: Carl Hanser Verlag, 1973).

Smart, Ninian, John Clayton, Patrick Sherry, and Steven T. Katz (eds.), *Nineteenth Century Religious Thought in the West*, 3 vols. (Cambridge: Cambridge University Press, 1985).

Toews, John Edward, *Hegelianism: The Path Toward Dialectical Humanism, 1805–1841* (Cambridge: Cambridge University Press, 1980).

Tomasoni, Francesco, *Ludwig Feuerbach und die nicht-menschliche Natur. Das Wesen der Religion: Die Entstehungsgeschichte des Werks, rekonstruiert auf der Grundlage unveröffentlichter Manuskripte*, Spekulation und Erfahrung, Texte und Untersuchungen zum Deutschen Idealismus, part II, vol. XX (Stuttgart-Bad Cannstatt: Frommann-Holzboog, 1990).

Wartofsky, Marx, *Feuerbach* (Cambridge: Cambridge University Press, 1977).

Wilson, Charles A., *Feuerbach and the Search for Otherness*, American University Studies, Series V, Philosophy, vol. 76 (New York: Peter Lang, 1989).

SOME RELEVANT LITERATURE ON THE THEORY OF RELIGION WITH SPECIAL EMPHASIS ON PROJECTION

Banks, L., "Religion as Projection: A Re-appraisal of Freud's Theory," *Religious Studies*, 9 (1973), 401–426.

Becker, Ernest, *The Denial of Death* (New York: The Free Press, 1973).

Berger, Peter L., *A Rumor of Angels: Modern Society and the Rediscovery of the Supernatural* (Garden City, N.Y.: Doubleday, 1969).

The Sacred Canopy: Elements of a Sociological Theory of Religion (Garden City, N.Y.: Doubleday, 1967).

Godlove, Terry F., Jr., *Religion, Interpretation, and Diversity of Belief: The Framework Model from Kant to Durkheim to Davidson* (Cambridge: Cambridge University Press, 1989).

Guthrie, Stewart Elliott, *Faces in the Clouds: A New Theory of Religion* (New York: Oxford University Press, 1993).

Hochheimer, Wolfgang, "*Über Projektion*," *Psyche*, 9 (1955), 279–305.

Hurry, Anne, Jack Novick, and Kerry Kelly Novick, "Freud's Concept of Projection," *Journal of Child Psychotherapy*, 4, 2 (1976), 75–88.

Israel, Joachim, *Der Begriff Entfremdung: Makrosoziologische Untersuchung von Marx bis zur Soziologie der Gegenwart*, Rowohlts Deutsche Enzyklopädie (Reinbeck bei Hamburg: Rowohlt Taschenbuch Verlag, 1972).

Jones, James W., *Contemporary Psychoanalysis and Religion: Transference and Transcendence* (New Haven: Yale University Press, 1991).

Jung, C. G., *The Archetypes and the Collective Unconscious*, translated by R. F. C. Hull, Bollingen Series xx (Princeton: Princeton University Press, 1959).

La Barre, Weston, *The Ghost Dance: Origins of Religion* (New York: Dell, 1970).

Murstein, Bernard I., and Ronald S. Pryer, "The Concept of Projection: A Review," *Psychological Bulletin*, 56 (1959), 353–374.

Novick, Jack and Kerry Kelly, "Projection and Externalization," *Psychoanalytic Study of Children*, 25 (1970), 69–95.

Ornston, Darius, "On Projection: A Study of Freud's Usage," *Psychoanalytic Study of the Child*, 33 (1978), 117–166.

Proudfoot, Wayne, *Religious Experience* (Berkeley: University of California Press, 1985).

Richter, Horst Eberhard, *Der Gotteskomplex: Die Geburt und die Krise des Glaubens an die Allmacht des Menschen* (Reinbeck bei Hamburg: Rowohlt Verlag, 1979).

Ricoeur, Paul, *Freud and Philosophy: An Essay on Interpretation*, translated by Denis Savage (New Haven: Yale University Press, 1970).

Rizzuto, Ana-Marie, *The Birth of the Living God: A Psychoanalytic Study* (Chicago: Chicago University Press, 1979).

Schacht, Richard, *Alienation*, with an introductory essay by Walter Kaufmann (Garden City, N.Y.: Doubleday, 1971).

Sierksma, Fokke, *Projection and Religion: An Anthropological and Psychological Study of the Phenomena of Projection in the Various Religions*, translated by Jacob Faber, foreword by Lee W. Bailey (Ann Arbor, Mich.: UMI Books on Demand, 1990).

Smythies, J. R., "Analysis of Projection," *British Journal of Philosophy of Science*, 5 (1954), 120–133.

Spiro, Melford E., *Culture and Human Nature: Theoretical Papers*, edited by Benjamin Kilborne and L. L. Langness (Chicago: Chicago University Press, 1987).

Watts, Alan, *Psychotherapy East & West* (New York: Random House, 1975).

Index